STEAMBOATING
on the Upper Mississippi

William J. Petersen

DOVER PUBLICATIONS, INC.
NEW YORK

*To the memory of Charles L. Petersen
who spent thirty-eight years of adventure with the Diamond Jo Line Steamers*

and to

*Bessie Rasmus Petersen who for thirty-
eight years has encouraged the writer
in pursuit of his favorite subject.*

Copyright

Published in Canada by General Publishing Company, Ltd., 30 Lesmill Road, Don Mills, Toronto, Ontario.
Published in the United Kingdom by Constable and Company, Ltd., 3 The Lanchesters, 162–164 Fulham Palace Road, London W6 9ER.

Bibliographical Note

This Dover edition, first published in 1995, is a slightly altered republication of the work first published by The State Historical Society of Iowa, Iowa City, in 1937 and expanded to include the Author's Introduction and illustrations in 1968, under the title, *Steamboating on the Upper Mississippi: On the Water Way to Iowa.* For the Dover edition the maps, which originally appeared in two colors on the endpapers, have been moved and are printed in black and white. Also, the section titled "From the Editor," which appeared in the 1937 edition, has been omitted.

Library of Congress Cataloging-in-Publication Data

Petersen, William John, 1901–
    Steamboating on the upper Mississippi / William J. Petersen.
      p.   cm.
    Originally published: Iowa City : State Historical Society of Iowa, 1968.
    Includes bibliographical references and index.
    ISBN 0-486-28844-7 (pbk.)
    1. Mississippi River—History. 2. Mississippi River—Commerce. 3. River steamboats—Mississippi River. I. Title.
F353.P47 1995
977—dc20
                                         95-33669
                                              CIP

Manufactured in the United States of America
Dover Publications, Inc., 31 East 2nd Street, Mineola, N.Y. 11501

Author's Introduction

The subject of this book, *Steamboating on the Upper Mississippi,* was a natural for the author since I was born on the Mississippi at Dubuque. Furthermore, my father was associated with the Diamond Jo Line Steamers from 1873 to 1911 as Agent for that "old and reliable" Company at Dubuque. From boyhood days I had collected steamboat pictures, had listened to yarns of old time rivermen, and had spent many happy hours playing on the levee in front of my father's office while waiting the arrival of the *Dubuque,* the *Sidney,* the *Quincy,* or the *St. Paul,* the last four steam packets of the Diamond Jo Line. To me the Mississippi had become a very important, a very intimate part of my life. I was pleased when my topic, "Steamboating on the Upper Mississippi," was approved for my doctoral dissertation in history at the University of Iowa in 1927.

Three years later, in 1930, having received my Ph. D. degree, I was invited by Dr. Benj. F. Shambaugh to join the staff of the State Historical Society of Iowa as Research Associate. Although engaged in many other tasks, I continued my research on steamboating. In 1935, Dr. Shambaugh asked me to expand and prepare my dissertation for publication by the Society. In 1937, after ten years of intensive research and writing, during which time I traveled 20,000 miles in quest of material, read the newspaper files in rivertowns from St. Louis to St. Paul, combed through the United States Steamboat Inspectors and Collector of Customs records between Dubuque and Pittsburgh, and consulted scores of books of travel and thousands of manuscripts, *Steamboating on the Upper Mississippi* was ready for the press.

The book described the story of steamboating from the voyage of the *Virginia* in 1823 to the close of the immigration period around 1870. It received such warm reviews from both professional scholars and river authorities that the edition of 2,000 copies (about 1,500 of which went out to members, depositories, and exchanges) was exhausted in less than nine months. Then, in 1938, it won the Iowa Library Association's Johnson Brigham Award for the best contribu-

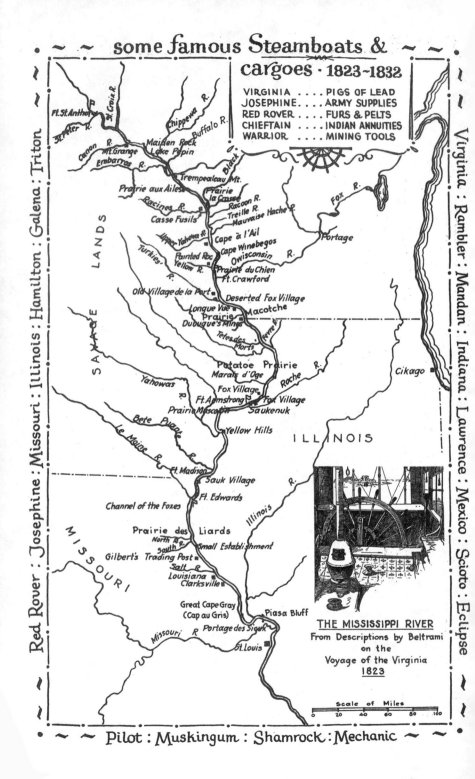

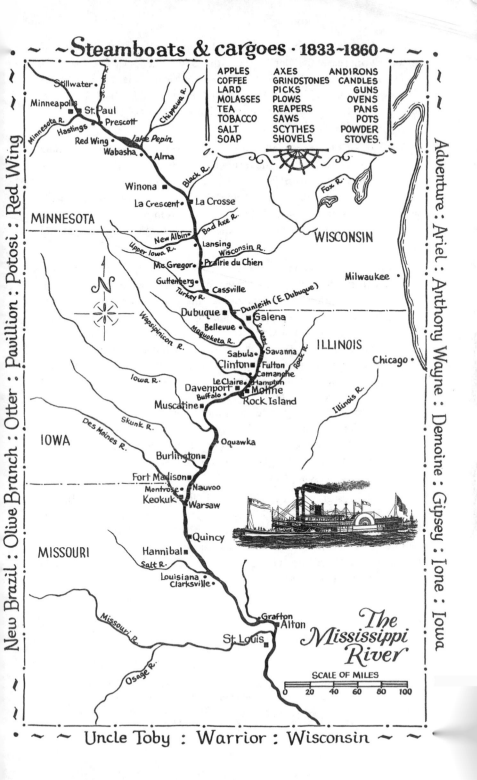

~ ~ Steamboats & cargoes · 1833~1860~ ~ ~

APPLES	AXES	ANDIRONS
COFFEE	GRINDSTONES	CANDLES
LARD	PICKS	GUNS
MOLASSES	PLOWS	OVENS
TEA	REAPERS	PANS
TOBACCO	SAWS	POTS
SALT	SCYTHES	POWDER
SOAP	SHOVELS	STOVES

Stillwater

Minneapolis
St. Paul
Prescott
Hastings
Red Wing
Lake Pepin
Wabasha
Alma

Minnesota R.
Chippewa R.

Winona
La Crescent
La Crosse
Black R.
Fox R.

MINNESOTA

New Albin
Bad Axe R.
Lansing
Wisconsin R.
Upper Iowa R.
Mc Gregor
Prairie du Chien

WISCONSIN

N

Guttenberg
Turkey R.
Cassville

Milwaukee

Dubuque
Bellevue
Maquoketa R.
Dunleith (E. Dubuque)
Galena

Wapsipinicon R.

ILLINOIS

Sabula
Savanna
Clinton
Fulton
Camanche
Iowa R.
Le Claire
Hampton
Davenport
Buffalo
Moline
Muscatine
Rock Island

Chicago

Skunk R.
Des Moines R.

Oquawka

IOWA

Burlington

Illinois R.

Fort Madison
Montrose
Nauvoo
Keokuk
Warsaw

Quincy

MISSOURI

Hannibal
Salt R.

Louisiana
Clarksville

Missouri R.

Grafton
Alton
St. Louis

The Mississippi River

Osage R.

SCALE OF MILES
0   20   40   60   80   100

Red Wing : Potosi : Pavillion : Otter : Olive Branch : New Brazil

Adventure : Ariel : Anthony Wayne : Demoine : Gipsey : Ione : Iowa

~ ~ ~ Uncle Toby : Warrior : Wisconsin ~ ~ ~

tion to American Literature by an Iowan. This signal recognition helped to increase the demand for the book and prices for it soon ranged from $25 to $60 on the Rare Americana market. In 1962, *Steamboating on the Upper Mississippi* was rated at from $25 to $100 among the 11,620 "uncommon and significant" books listed in *U.S. I A N A (1650-1950).*

This reprint of *Steamboating on the Upper Mississippi* has two new features not contained in the original volume. The first feature is the addition of four 16-page pictorial inserts of photos of steamboats, bills of lading, old woodcuts, and steel engravings. About three-fourths of these are from the author's personal collection and no credit line is given them. The second feature is the four decorative maps appearing in the end covers. *

It is hoped, in a second volume, to cover the century of river transportation from 1870 to 1970. This second volume would contain such chapters as the grain trade, the rise of the packet companies, steamboating on Upper Mississippi tributaries, the advent of the railroad, the bridging of the Mississippi, the decline of the packet boats, and the emergence of the excursion boats. In addition, there would be chapters on steamboat personalities and steamboat nomenclature, steamboat boatyards, and the Mississippi in music and song. Several of these chapters have already been printed, such as "Steamboats Dubuque" and "Diamond Jo Reynolds" in *The Palimpsest;* "The Keokuk Packet Company" in the *Iowa Journal of History;* "Floating Namesakes of the Sucker State" in *Papers in Illinois History* (1939), and "Steamboating on the Minnesota River" in *Minnesota History.* A number of other chapters are already in manuscript form.

The author is grateful to William Talbot of the Lee County Historical Society, to Floyd Risvold of Minneapolis, Henry A. Meyer of Evansville, and Paul C. Rohloff of Chicago for items relating to steamboat postal history. Special thanks goes to S. Durward Hoag of Marietta, Ohio, and to George Brooks of the Missouri Historical Society for valuable help.

WILLIAM J. PETERSEN

Office of the Superintendent
State Historical Society of Iowa
Iowa City, Iowa

*NOTE: in this edition two of the maps ("Some famous Steamboats & Cargoes, 1823–1832" and "Steamboats & cargoes, 1833–1860") appear on pages 4 and 5, while "Railroads reach the Mississippi" and "Locks & Dams in the Towboat Era" remain on the inside covers.

Contents

Contents

ILLUSTRATIONS
Section One: Between 80-81
Bills of Lading — 1844-1866

Section Two: Between 176-177
Historic Steamboats; Scenic Mississippi; Cabin & Deck Passengers

Section Three: Between 320-321
Major Packet Companies — 1842-1875
ST. LOUIS AND KEOKUK PACKET COMPANY

35. *J. McKee; War Eagle* and *Golden Eagle;* Keokuk Northern Line card.
36. Front cover of sheet music — *Tom Jasper Schottisch.*

MINNESOTA PACKET TO NORTH WESTERN UNION PACKET

37. Galena levee scenes — *General Brooke; Saint Paul, West Newton, Minnesota, Ben Campbell; War Eagle, City Belle.*
38. *Grey Eagle;* Captain D. S. Harris; *Itasca.*
39. Captain Harris's application for inspection of the *Grey Eagle.*
40. Postal covers and steamboat stamp cancellations.

THE NORTHERN LINE

41. *Burlington; Davenport; Muscatine.*
42. *Keokuk; Clinton; Dubuque.*
43. *Henry Clay; Sucker State; Red Wing.*
44. Postal covers of the *Minneapolis* and the *Burlington.*

DIAMOND JO LINE STEAMERS

45. Joseph Reynolds; *Lansing* (blown up); Guttenberg warehouse.
46. Cabin of the *Quincy; Diamond Jo* with tow of grain barges.
47. Diamond Jo advertisement showing rail and city connections.
48. Diamond Jo map showing steamboat landings, distances, population.

Section Four: Between 400-401
Lead, Furs, Indians, Soldiers, Grain, Immigrants, Civil War

49. Steamboat *Nominee* at Galena; Port of Dubuque in 1848.
50. Captain Joseph Throckmorton; Furs to St. Louis by steamboat.
51. Steamboats at St. Louis levee — 1840; 1850's; 1860.
52. Steamboat warehouses at Bellevue; East Dubuque warehouses in high water.
53. Main cabin *Grand Republic;* Typical Upper Mississippi main cabin.
54. Wm. F. Davidson; Appletime on the St. Louis levee.
55. Steamboat races; *Robert E. Lee* vs. *Natchez; Phil Sheridan* vs. *Hawkeye State.*
56. Excursions: Leaving Clinton; *Josephine* and barge; *Musser.*
57. *Walk-in-the-Water;* Fort Benton; Red River Oxcart.
58. *Eagle* (1841); *Robert Harris* (1888); *Phil Sheridan; Canada; Hawkeye State.*
59. Emigration to Minnesota; *Minnesota; Alex. Mitchell.*
60. *Hawkeye State; Bill Henderson;* Dubuque Governor Greys.
61. Troops leaving Cairo, Illinois; Explosion of *Sultana* above Memphis.
62. Bombardment and capture of Island No. Ten; Hospital steamboat *Imperial;* Estes House at Keokuk.
63. Capture of Vicksburg July 4, 1863; Opening of Mississippi to New Orleans.
64. Museums: Jefferson Memorial in St. Louis and Keokuk and Clinton in Iowa. Other museums are at Clarksville, Missouri, Quincy and Galena, Illinois, Prairie du Chien, Wisconsin, and Winona, Minnesota.

1

Mississippi : The Great River

From the Land of the Ojibway

FAR FLUNG and powerful was the Algonquian nation, ranging all the way from the Passamaquoddy Indians of Maine to the Arapaho of Montana, and from the Cree around Hudson Bay to the Pamlico in North Carolina. Of the many tribes that composed this great woodland stock of North American Indians none was more powerful than the Ojibway.

Fierce warriors of the lake and forest, the Ojibway became the scourge of surrounding tribes once they secured firearms from the French traders late in the seventeenth century. They drove the Fox Indians from northern Wisconsin. They sent the Sioux scurrying across the Mississippi and on to the Minnesota River. They were likewise successful in battle against the dreaded Iroquois. Finally, the Ojibway occupied the vast range of territory between Lake Superior and the Red River of the North.[1]

Knowing that the lakes and streams which they traversed in birch canoes paid tribute to a mighty river, the Ojibway called this waterway the Mississippi, which means Great River.[2] This name, at first used only in reference to the headwaters of the Great River, was passed on by the various Algonquian tribes to the French fur traders and missionaries, who in turn applied it to the river as it coursed southward. In time the name Mississippi displaced the various Indian names in use along the lower river, such as Chucagua, Tamaliseu, Tapatu, and Mico. At least thirty or more names had been applied to the Mississippi, such as Rio Grande, Palisado, and Escondido by the Spanish; and St. Louis, Conception, Buade, and Colbert by the French. Adopting a spelling based on the Indian sound, Hennepin called it Meschasipi on his map of 1697; while William Delisle, the brilliant cartographer to the French king, spelled it uniformly Mississipi on his maps of 1703, 1718, and 1750. Jonathan Carver used the present spelling, and later writers and map-makers have followed his example.[3]

For many years the boundary between war-like tribes and mighty nations, the Mississippi served as the main highway in the discovery and exploration of an inland empire. Over its waters passed wave upon wave of pioneers eager to build enduring Commonwealths west of the Great River. Upon its placid bosom floated rich argosies of grain and merchandise. To this day the Mississippi remains for the white man what it was to the dusky Ojibway — the Great River.

2
Veritas Caput : Itasca
What's in a Name

MANY NOTABLE men ventured into the wilderness to discover the true source of the Mississippi. Their exploits have been recorded in history; and the names of many of them may still be found on the map of the Upper Mississippi Valley. The achievements of Zebulon M. Pike, Lewis Cass, Giacomo C. Beltrami, and Henry R. Schoolcraft form part of this dramatic story of exploration: faced by starvation and the danger of Indian attack, each modestly inscribed his name in the story of the discovery of the headwaters of the Mississippi.

First to carry the flag of discovery to the sources of the Mississippi was Lieutenant Zebulon M. Pike. Braving the frozen northland in the dead of winter, Pike managed to reach Leech Lake on January 31, 1806. Fourteen years later, Lewis Cass, with a party of thirty-eight men, among whom was Henry Rowe Schoolcraft, entered Cass Lake but failed to reach the headwaters of the Mississippi. Cass learned, however, from the "best information" obtainable, that the Mississippi had its origin in a lake called "La Biche" or Elk Lake. In 1823 Beltrami, a man of courage and endurance (even though he may have been a "hero-worshipper, with but one hero, and that himself"), placed the sources of the Mississippi in Lake Julia, a tributary of Turtle Lake. It was not until 1832 that the true source of the Great River was discovered by Henry Rowe Schoolcraft.

Schoolcraft was born in Albany County, New York, on March 28, 1793. Trained in languages and the natural sciences, he began his career as an explorer in the mineral region of Missouri and Arkansas in 1817-1818. His published account of this expedition won instant recognition; and in 1820 the government requested him to join Governor Lewis Cass of Michigan on what turned out to be an unsuccessful exploration of the Upper Mississippi.

Ten years later (in 1830) Henry Rowe Schoolcraft, then serving as Indian Agent, was ordered to "proceed into the Chippewa country, to endeavor to put an end to the hostilities between the Chippewas and Sioux." Schoolcraft set out in June of 1831 with twenty-six men, but low water caused him to change his plans. After holding Indian conferences on the St. Croix and Chippewa rivers, he paddled down the Mississippi and up the Fever River to Galena. Here the party divided, some returning by the Wisconsin River, others by way of the Pecatonica and its branches to Fort Winnebago, the Fox River, and Green Bay.[4]

In the following spring the War Department again ordered Schoolcraft to "proceed to the country upon the heads of the Mississippi, and visit as many of the Indians in that, and the intermediate region, as circumstances will permit." Accordingly, on June 7, 1832, Schoolcraft set out with a force of thirty men, including Lieutenant James Allen and ten soldiers detached for topographical duty, Dr. Douglas Houghton, a surgeon and geologist, and George Johnston, a half-breed interpreter. Reverend William T. Boutwell, a missionary to the northwestern Indians, was invited to accompany the exploring party: he was destined to play a unique rôle in the expedition.

The Schoolcraft expedition reached the Mississippi from Lake Superior by ascending the St. Louis River and portaging into and descending the Sandy Lake River. Beginning the ascent of the Mississippi on July 4, 1832, the party passed through Thundering [Grand] Rapids, Pokegama Falls, Lake Winnebagoshish, and on to Cass Lake.

It was at Cass Lake that Schoolcraft chose a "select party" to explore the source of the Mississippi. A Chippewa Indian named Ozawindib (The Yellowhead) acted as guide. The party of sixteen included Schoolcraft, Allen, Houghton, Boutwell, George Johnston, three Indians, seven engagés, and a cook. "These, with their travelling beds", Schoolcraft relates, "were distributed among five canoes, with provisions for ten days, a tent and poles, oil cloth, mess basket, tea-kettle, flag and staff, a medicine chest, some instruments, an herbarium, fowling pieces, and a few Indian presents."

Ozawindib guided Schoolcraft and his men up the hitherto unknown east fork of the Mississippi to its source. Thence the party made a six-mile portage which required thirteen stops (called by the voyageurs a "posè" or "place of putting down the burthen"). Despite heavy loads, the expedition pressed on eagerly. Suddenly, on turning out of a thicket into a small weedy opening, Schoolcraft came upon the "cheering sight of a transparent body of water . . . It was Itasca Lake — the source of the Mississippi."

Everyone was delighted with the picturesque surroundings. Schoolcraft noted that "Itasca Lake, the *Lac la Biche* [Elk] of the French, is, in every respect, a beautiful sheet of water, seven or eight miles in extent, lying among hills of diluvial formation, surmounted with pines, which fringe the distant horizon . . . The waters are transparent and bright, and reflect a foliage produced by the elm, lynn, maple, and cherry". The lake had a "single island" upon which the exploring party landed and raised the American emblem on a flagstaff. The island is known to this day as Schoolcraft Island.

After a scant three hours the expedition departed down the Mississippi through the outlet of Lake Itasca, which Schoolcraft described as "perhaps ten to twelve feet broad, with an apparent depth of twelve to eighteen inches. The discharge of water appears to be copious, compared to its inlet. Springs may, however, produce accessions which are not visible, and this is probable both from the geological character of the country, and the transparency and coolness of the water."

Jubilant over the success of his expedition, Schoolcraft paddled swiftly down the Mississippi from Lake Itasca, holding occasional conferences with Indians on the way. Upon his return to Sault Ste. Marie he prepared his "Nar-

Veritas Caput : Itasca

rative of an Expedition Through the Upper Mississippi to Itasca Lake, the Actual Source of this River" in 1832.[5] Four years later (in 1836) the distinguished French scholar, J. N. Nicollet, found other "inconsiderable affluents" of Lake Itasca, but contended that this lake was the "principal reservoir". Nicollet generously declared that "the honor of having first explored the sources of the Mississippi, and introduced a knowledge of them in physical geography, belongs to Mr. Schoolcraft and Lieutenant Allen. I come only after these gentlemen; but I may be permitted to claim some merit for having completed what was wanting for a full geographical account of these sources".[6]

Whence came the beautiful name Itasca? That is a question which has kept historians in a quandary for several generations. At the time neither Schoolcraft, nor Allen, nor Houghton, nor Boutwell, seem to have given a satisfactory explanation of the origin and use of this name. In 1853 Mrs. Mary H. Eastman published the *American Aboriginal Portfolio* in which she recounts that Itasca was the daughter of Nanabozho, the Spirit God of the Chippewa, whose falling tears formed the lake. Mrs. Eastman declared that Schoolcraft had received the story from his Chippewa guide and had told it to her. Schoolcraft a little later confirmed this theory when he himself wrote a poem on the lovely Itasca which was included in his *Summary Narrative* of the expeditions of 1820 and 1832 published in 1855. In the same book, however, he states that Ozawindib had given the Indian name for the lake as Omushkös, which was the Chippewa name for elk. In 1872 new light was shed on the origin of the name by Reverend William T. Boutwell. Replying to an inquiry as to the origin of the word Itasca, Boutwell declared that while paddling slowly westward across Lake Superior, Schoolcraft had turned to him and said : "I would like to give a name to Elk Lake that will be significant or expressive, as the *head* or *true source* of the Mississi[ppi]. Can you give me any word in Latin or Greek that will convey the idea. I replied no one word will express the idea — the nearest I can come to it is Veritus Caput — or if you prefer the noun Veritas — you may coin something that will meet your wishes. In less than five minutes he replied I have got the thing — handing me a slip of paper on which was the word *Itasca* . . . It was then & there & in just this manner the word, the name *Itasca* was coined. The Ojibwas invariably called the lake Omushkos Sagaeigun [Elk Lake]."

Thus, at the suggestion of Boutwell, the name Itasca was coined by Schoolcraft by taking from the expression *veritas caput* the last four letters (*itas*) of the word *veritas* and combining them with the first two letters (*ca*) of the word *caput* — which gives the new word Itasca. It may be added that the fanciful creation of new words or names by dividing two familiar words and combining the parts as in the case of Itasca was not uncommon in the period of the Schoolcraft explorations.

Although the Boutwell explanation of the name Itasca was generally accepted in the years that followed, some writers still clung to the Chippewa legend. And there were others who believed that the word might have been derived from the Ojibway words *ia* (to be), *totosh* (the female breast, implying origin), and *ka* (terminal subinflection), the whole *ia-totosh-ka* signifying *a fount*. This explanation was actually accepted in the 1882 edition of Webster's Dictionary. Students of the Dakota Indians also pointed to a possible origin from the language of that nation.

Meanwhile, Boutwell's explanation received further corroboration from Reverend Jeremiah Porter in a letter to Jacob V. Brower in the early nineties. Porter declared that upon the return of Schoolcraft, Houghton, and Allen in 1832 "they told me how they had named so beautifully the lake from two Latin words." [7]

After a period of sixty years the question still remained unsolved in 1932 when the Minnesota Historical Society and other organizations celebrated at Itasca State Park the centennial of the discovery of the source of the Mississippi.[8] Hundreds of pages had been written about the park and its name, but the matter still lay open to debate. After a careful evaluation of the problem, Dr. Theodore C. Blegen, superintendent of the Minnesota Historical Society, concluded : "In the light of Porter's corroboration, the case at present seems to lean toward the Boutwell explanation, though the episode of the Latin words may possibly have occurred on the return journey rather than on the trip west. It is obvious that something is lacking in the evidence, however. It is an intriguing little problem and it is to be hoped that from some source will come the key that will unlock the mystery." [9]

That key — a contemporary verification of Boutwell's *Veritas Caput* by a member of the expedition — may now be presented. It comes from Schoolcraft himself! Leaving Lake Itasca on July 13, 1832, the day of the discovery, Schoolcraft hastened down the Mississippi, arriving at Fort Snelling eleven days later. On the following day (July 25, 1832) he wrote a letter to Dr. Addison Philleo, editor of a Galena newspaper, describing the expedition to the true source of the Mississippi River. The concluding paragraphs of Schoolcraft's letter furnish all the evidence needed to substantiate the Boutwell explanation. [10]

"The Mississippi [above Cass Lake], expands into several lakes, the largest of which is called lac Traverse. A few miles above this it forms into a south west and north west branch. We ascended the latter [sic], through a number of lakes to its source in a small creek. From thence we made a portage of 6 miles, with our canoes, into La Biche or Itasca Lake (from a derivation of the expression *veritas caput*) which is the true source of this celebrated stream, being at the same time, its most western and northern head. This lake is about 7 miles long, having somewhat the shape of the letter Y. It has clear water and pleasant woody shores. It has a single island, upon which I landed, caused some trees to be felled, and hoisted the national flag. I left this flag flying, and proceeded down the N. W. or main fork. A descent of about 180 miles brought us back to our party at Red Cedar, a Cape [or Cass] lake."

Veritas Caput : Itasca

Ver *itas ca* put! The letter signed by Schoolcraft him -
self solves the riddle of the naming of Lake Itasca. No
longer need there be even a shadow of doubt cast upon the
origin of the name of the lovely Lake Itasca — the headwaters of the Mississippi.

The Schoolcraft letter of July 25, 1832, as first published in the August 22, 1832,
issue of *The Galenian* and later copied in the December 1, 1832, issue of *Niles'
Register*, was discovered in November, 1936, by Dr. William J. Petersen, Research
Associate in the State Historical Society of Iowa and author of the pages of this
book. — The Editor.

3

The Journey of the Waters

ONE MAY think of the Great River of the Ojibway as comprising the Upper Mississippi, which includes the journey of the waters all the way from Lake Itasca to the mouth of the Missouri, and the Lower Mississippi as Old Man River rolls along from the mouth of the Missouri to the Gulf of Mexico. The Falls of St. Anthony abruptly breaks this journey of the waters, separating the Upper Mississippi in its flow through the "land of the sky blue waters" from its course southward into the heart of the Great Valley which shares the glory of its name.

Rising almost imperceptibly in north central Minnesota out of the multitude of lakes and streams that empty into Lake Itasca (the most remote of which is Lake Hernando de Soto with an elevation of 1571 feet above sea level), and flowing swiftly through pine forests interspersed with birch, balsam, and tamarack, the Upper Mississippi glides peacefully through Cass Lake and Winnebagoshish Lake and then swiftly passes Grand Rapids, Little Falls, and St. Cloud. Its precipitate flight through the land of ten thousand lakes once reached a thundering climax at the Falls of St. Anthony. But now the hand of man has robbed the Great River of much of its pristine grandeur by restraining its wild course with walls of concrete.

By the time St. Paul is reached the Mississippi has

The Journey of the Waters

dropped almost 900 feet in the 600 mile journey from its source. Already it has flowed a hundred miles farther than the renowned Seine, and three times as far as the historic Jordan in its entire course. And yet at St. Paul this Great River has barely reached adolescence : its journey has just begun.[11]

After leaving the land of sky blue waters (a region renowned in fable and history) the Mississippi flows southward for 660 miles from the Falls of St. Anthony to the mouth of the Missouri : six hundred miles of water and a thousand reminders of history and romance. For this is the Mississippi of Joliet and Marquette; the Mississippi of Julien Dubuque and the mines of Spain; the Mississippi that played a rôle in the Revolutionary War and the War of 1812; the Mississippi that resounded with the war call of Black Hawk and swallowed the blood of his fellow tribesmen. On its banks at Hannibal, Mark Twain grew to man's estate; and at Le Claire, Buffalo Bill went to school and developed his "love for skiff riding on the Mississippi". This is the river which the pioneers of Iowa had to cross. Here is the true "Upper Mississippi" on which the steamboats *War Eagle, Grey Eagle, Itasca,* and *Hawkeye State* and many others carried the rich argosies which nurtured to maturity the newly-born Commonwealths of Illinois, Missouri, Iowa, Wisconsin, and Minnesota.

It is here that the Mississippi winds through a valley that bears mute evidence of millions of years of scouring and polishing. Towering ramparts, such as Maiden Rock and Trempealeau in Wisconsin, Barn Bluff and Dresbach in Minnesota, Capoli Bluff and Pike's Peak in Iowa, stand like sentinels on guard. Below Dubuque the river flows past the historic towns of Clinton, Davenport, Muscatine, Burlington, Fort Madison, Nauvoo, Keokuk, Quincy, Hannibal, and on to St. Louis. During the course of the 660 mile journey from St. Paul to St. Louis the Great River drops from 680 to 384 feet above sea level. With the exception of occasional outcroppings (like Cap au Gris, Elsah, and Piasa Rock) the river below Keokuk runs through wide valleys hemmed in by low-lying bluffs.

Between the Falls of St. Anthony and the mouth of the Missouri, the Mississippi presents a wonderland of natural and rugged beauty. In the early days visitors from foreign lands stood spellbound on the decks of steamboats as the grandeurs of an ever-changing panorama unfolded before them. Europeans invariably compared the river between Dubuque and Lake Pepin with the historic Rhine; while Americans likened its fantastic bluffs to the palisades of the lordly Hudson.

In width, but not in depth, this middle section of the Father of Waters actually surpasses the Lower Mississippi. And small wonder, for on its way it has been nourished by the St. Croix, the Chippewa, the Black, the Wapsipinicon, the Rock, the Iowa, the Skunk, and scores of smaller streams; and it has been fed by the Illinois, the Wisconsin, the Minnesota, and the Des Moines, streams which in length surpass the Delaware and the Hudson.

Just above St. Louis the Mississippi receives the muddy

The Journey of the Waters

waters of the Missouri whose yellow silt has been pilfered from the soil during the course of its almost three thousand mile journey from the Rocky Mountains. Between the mouth of the Missouri and the Gulf of Mexico the Mississippi enters the final lap of its journey to the sea. For over twelve hundred miles it flows past cotton plantations and squalid homes of negroes and poor white folk. This is the Mississippi of De Soto and La Salle, of Antoine Crozat, of John Law and the Mississippi Bubble. This is the river over which Napoleon and Jefferson haggled after years of French and Spanish intrigue. Here courses the Mississippi that tempted Aaron Burr, led Fulton and Livingston to dream of monopoly, and inspired Andrew Jackson in his heroic defense of New Orleans. Down this mighty waterway went the youthful Lincoln to get his first glimpse of the slave block. Around towering Vicksburg the remorseless Ulysses S. Grant forged a ring of steel that split the Confederacy in twain and doomed the cause of the South. Along this great highway floated keelboats and flatboats, steamboats and showboats. Up its swift current raced the *Natchez* and the *Robert E. Lee* while a nation cheered them on.

The Great River below St. Louis has reached strong maturity; but an interesting journey is still before it. Fifty-five miles downstream from the metropolis of the Mississippi lies Ste. Genevieve, the oldest white settlement in Missouri : it was settled in 1735, almost a century before the Black Hawk War opened the Iowa prairies to the white pioneers. Farther downstream at the confluence of the

Steamboating on Upper Mississippi

Ohio with the Mississippi lies Cairo, where Charles Dickens learned to his sorrow the hazards of American land speculation. For over one thousand miles below Cairo, the Mississippi winds through a level flood plain from fifty to one hundred miles wide. Behind high-banked levees cowers many a hapless river town : none more fearful than New Madrid when Old Man River goes on a rampage. Mighty tributaries like the Arkansas and the Red rivers join the swirling waters — to whose volume the Ohio has contributed thirty-one per cent, the Upper Mississippi nineteen per cent, and the Missouri only fourteen per cent. Flood losses along the Lower Mississippi are immense : in 1922 they were set at $17,087,790; in 1927 at about $285,000,000; and in 1937 floods along the Ohio-Lower Mississippi reached a staggering total which will run far in excess of these sums. During low water the Lower Mississippi discharges into the Gulf of Mexico about 70,000 cubic feet of water per second, compared with 2,300,000 cubic feet during flood stage. Measured by the volume of water carried, the renowned St. Lawrence pales before the Father of Waters.[12]

Ancient is this river : geologists place its beginnings some sixty million years ago. But those who dwell upon its banks are prone to think of it in terms of modern commerce, industry, and power. Thus the mighty Mississippi and its more than fifty navigable tributaries furnish about 14,000 miles of waterways which border or traverse twenty-seven States, seventeen of which are entirely or very largely within the Mississippi drainage system. If one includes the Great Lakes cities, which are economically and politically a part of it, the Mississippi Valley now produces almost half the manufactured goods of the nation. The gigantic dam at Keokuk ranks as one of the great power plants of the world.

This fertile basin of the Mississippi, which has been aptly called the "body of the nation", surpasses in area the historic valley of the Nile. It is twice as large as the valley of the Volga, and fourteen times greater than the Rhine basin. In extent it is exceeded only by the Amazon and the Kongo. Here, in this breadbasket of the nation, is found sixty-five per cent of the improved land and over half of the population of the United States. No other section of this vast inland empire can compare in wealth and fertility with the five States of the Upper Mississippi Valley.[13]

4
Under Four Flags

THE DISCOVERY and exploration of the Mississippi River is a story of epic proportions. The colorful pageant opens with the swash-buckling De Soto hacking his way through the wilderness in 1541 : it concludes with the discovery of Lake Itasca by Schoolcraft in 1832. Throughout the drama intrepid soldiers, hardy fur traders and miners, and black-robed Catholic priests stalk across the stage. Of the many actors who played a part none showed greater courage than did Hernando de Soto under the flag of Spain.

De Soto is said to have begun his career with nothing but his sword and shield. Possessing rare qualities of leadership, this courageous Spaniard so distinguished himself with Pizarro that he returned from Peru with over one hundred thousand pesos of gold. He was appointed governor of Cuba and commissioned to conquer and settle at his own expense what is now the southern part of the United States.

In May, 1539, De Soto left Havana with 620 men and 223 horses. Landing at Tampa Bay he moved slowly in a northwesterly direction, fighting Indians, enduring sickness and disease, "determined to send no newes of himself until hee had found some rich country." From the Chickasaw Bluffs below present-day Memphis, De Soto and his ragged army first viewed the Mississippi River on May 8, 1541. As a member of this expedition a Portuguese gentleman from Elvas has left what is perhaps the earliest recorded description of the Mississippi:

"The River was almost halfe a league broad. If a man stood still on the other side, it could not be discerned whether he were a man or no. The River was of great depth, and of a strong current; the water was alwaies muddie; there came downe the River continually many trees and timber."

De Soto spent a month building barges with which the expedition crossed the Mississippi. Traveling for almost a year in what is now Arkansas De Soto finally returned to the banks of the Great River, broken in health and depressed in spirit. There he died on May 21, 1542. His body was wrapped in blankets weighted with sand, "wherein he was carried in a canoe, and thrown into the middest of the River." [14]

More than a century passed before the curtain rises on the next act. The scene is shifted to the St. Lawrence Valley and the Great Lakes, where the French were searching for the Western Sea. By 1634 Jean Nicolet had reached the Winnebago Indians in the Green Bay region. Upon his return to Quebec, Nicolet observed that "if he had sailed three days' journey farther upon a great river which issues from this lake [Michigan] he would have found the sea" which led to distant China. [15]

A generation later Radisson and Groseilliers, two obscure French coureurs de bois, plunged into the wilderness beyond Lake Superior and Green Bay. Of his third journey, made about 1660, Radisson wrote : "We weare 4 moneths in our voyage without doeing any thing but goe from river to river. We mett severall sorts of people . . . we went into ye great river that . . . has 2 branches, the one towards the west, the other towards the South, whi^{ch} we believe runns toward Mexico, by the tokens they gave us." This description led some scholars to believe Radisson and Groseilliers actually entered the Mississippi. If so, their accomplishment was unknown to the French officials and the Jesuits. Indeed, the first reference to the Mississippi by its present name was not made until 1666 when Father Allouez referred to the "great river named Messipi" in a letter to his Jesuit superiors.[16]

It remained for Joliet and Marquette to give the first definite account of the Upper Mississippi. Setting out from the Jesuit Mission of St. Ignace on May 17, 1673, with five French companions, Joliet and Marquette paddled steadily westward through Lake Michigan, Green Bay, and the Fox River. On June 7th they reached a village of Miami, Mascoutens, and Kickapoo Indians. According to their journal no Frenchman had "yet gone any farther" than this "Maskoutens" village of the "fire Nation" (after whom Muscatine County takes its name). Pressing onward, Joliet and Marquette portaged from the Fox to the "Meskousing" or Wisconsin River and "safely entered Missisipi" on June 17, 1673.

As they glided down this "renowned River", Marquette observed that the Mississippi took its "rise in various lakes

Under Four Flags

in the country of the Northern nations." They saw deer,
wild cattle or buffalo, swans, turkeys, bustards, and many
other wild birds and animals. Huge catfish struck their
frail craft with such violence as "about to break the Canoe
to pieces". For eight days they saw no trace of Indians.
Finally, on June 25, 1673, they "perceived on the water's
edge some tracks of men" and followed them to a village
of the "Peouarea" or Illinois Indians. This first meeting of
the white man and the red man on the Upper Mississippi
is believed to have occurred near the mouth of the Iowa
River. After a few days Joliet and Marquette continued
downstream as far as the mouth of the Arkansas whence,
learning of the presence of Spaniards and fearing capture,
they returned up the Mississippi to Lake Michigan by way
of the Illinois River.[17]

Between 1673 and 1762 France extended and strength-
ened her grip on the Mississippi Valley. La Salle dispatched
the prudent and courageous Michel Aco to reconnoiter
the Upper Mississippi in 1680. Aco was the first white
man to explore the Mississippi up to the Falls of St. Anthony (so named by the mendacious Louis Hennepin in
honor of his patron Saint).[18]

In 1685 Nicolas Perrot was appointed "Commander of
the West": he immediately commenced building Fort St.
Nicolas at the mouth of the Wisconsin River. Thus
Prairie du Chien traces its history back to the period that
witnessed the beginnings of Philadelphia. Perrot also built
forts farther up the Mississippi at Lake Pepin. On May 8,
1689, seven years after La Salle stood at the mouth of the

Mississippi and took possession of the land drained by the Father of Waters, Nicolas Perrot went through the same colorful ceremony on the shore of Lake Pepin, amid the chanting of Latin hymns, shouts of "vive le roi", and salvos of musketry. Hastening to the mineral region in 1690 at the urgent request of the Miami Indians, this energetic Frenchman is the first white man known to have mined lead in the Galena-Dubuque region.[19]

France secretly ceded her land west of the Mississippi to Spain in 1762 and relinquished her claim to Canada and the country east of the Mississippi to England the following year. Thereupon two new flags were planted on the banks of the Great River.

The English flag on the Upper Mississippi was most ably carried by two Connecticut Yankees, Jonathan Carver and Peter Pond. Both were veterans of the French and Indian Wars and loyal subjects of George III : both visited the Upper Mississippi on the eve of the American Revolution.

Carver was the first to reach the Mississippi, setting out from Boston in June, 1766, to explore the wilderness beyond the Great Lakes and acquire a "knowledge that promised to be so useful" to both his King and his country. On October 15, 1766, he "entered that extensive river the Mississippi" with a party of fur traders. Paddling up the Mississippi, Carver wintered among the Sioux Indians on the Minnesota River. The following spring he returned to the Falls of St. Anthony to secure supplies to enable him to continue to Oregon. When these failed to arrive, he returned to Prairie du Chien in May, 1767, and spent the remainder of the summer exploring the "Chipeway" River country. In 1768 he returned to Boston and set out for England where he died a pauper. His book, *Travels Through the Interior Parts of North America,* published in London in 1778, went through many editions.

On May 1, 1767, at Carver's Cave in the lower part of Dayton Bluff (now included in modern St. Paul), two Sioux chiefs granted Carver and his heirs a large tract of land in the present States of Minnesota and Wisconsin. The litigation which ensued highly publicized Carver's Cave, which later became a show place for steamboat passengers bound for St. Paul.[20]

Peter Pond visited the Mississippi as a fur trader in 1773. Pond was brave in heart, if poor in spelling. He traded with the Sioux on the Minnesota River, returning to Prairie du Chien in the spring of 1774. There he saw a "Large Colection [of Indians and traders] from Eavery Part of the Misseppey who had arived Before us — Even from Orleans Eight Hundred Leages Belowe us."[21]

The Spanish flag flew over the west bank of the Mississippi from 1762 until that region was transferred to France following the Louisiana Purchase in 1803. Spain endeavored to tighten her grip on the Upper Mississippi through a system of land grants. Thus Julien Dubuque was granted the right to work a princely tract in the lead district in 1796; and subsequently grants were made to Basil Giard on the present site of McGregor, and to Louis Honoré Tesson in what is now Lee County, Iowa.[22]

Steamboating on Upper Mississippi

Meanwhile England did not fare so well on the east bank of the Mississippi. It was during the American Revolution that George Rogers Clark wrested Post Vincennes and the French settlements in southern Illinois from the English. At the close of the struggle England recognized the claim of the Americans to the east bank of the Mississippi. With the consummation of the Louisiana Purchase in 1803 the American flag was planted on both banks of the Mississippi.

The United States lost no time in securing a firm hold on these new possessions. In 1803 Jefferson ordered Lewis and Clark to explore the Missouri and the streams leading from its headwaters into the Pacific Ocean. Two years later Lieutenant Zebulon M. Pike was sent to discover the source of the Mississippi. Both expeditions resorted to much the same means of transportation that had been in use during the Spanish and French periods of exploration. Lewis and Clark had a large boat and two pirogues, all complete with sails, oars, poles, and rope. Pike had a seventy-foot keelboat, with which he could make some twenty miles a day upstream in a favorable wind.[28]

After a winter in the wilds of Minnesota, Pike returned to St. Louis on April 30, 1806, having gotten no farther than Leech Lake. He had failed in his quest. On the very day Pike was being welcomed at St. Louis, Lewis and Clark were leaving their camp at the mouth of the Walla Walla River on their journey home. Battling their way back over the Rockies and down the Missouri, Lewis and Clark did not reach St. Louis until September 23, 1806. By that time even Jefferson had given them up for lost. Their return was hailed with delight and their exploits were still ringing in the ears of Americans when Robert Fulton inaugurated an entirely new mode of transportation.[24]

5
Fulton's Folly : A Mississippi Dream

A CLOUDLESS blue sky hung over lower Manhattan on August 17, 1807. Early risers did not suspect that the day was destined to be particularly eventful. At breakfast, however, many smug New Yorkers sat up in amazement upon reading the following notice in the *American Citizen* :

"Mr. Fulton's ingenious steamboat, invented with a view to the navigation of the Mississippi from New Orleans upward, sails to-day from the North River, near State's Prison, to Albany. The velocity is calculated at four miles an hour. It is said it will make a progress of two against the current of the Mississippi and if so it will certainly be a very valuable acquisition to the commerce of Western states." [25]

News of the departure of Lindbergh in the *Spirit of St. Louis* on his trans-Atlantic flight in 1927 could scarcely have created greater excitement than this steamboat announcement. A large crowd hastily assembled on the dock at Greenwich Village where the *Clermont* lay steaming up. The most sanguine spectator might readily be forgiven for not waxing enthusiastic over the rude craft which had been dubbed "Fulton's Folly". Compared with the palatial vessels of the halcyon days of steamboating, the *Clermont* was aptly described as a "Long Island skiff".

Fulton's Folly : A Mississippi Dream

The *Clermont* was 133 feet long, had an 18-foot beam, a 7-foot hold, and measured about 160 tons. The diameter of her cylinder was two feet and she had a four-foot stroke of the piston. She was decked for a short distance at stem and stern; but her Boulton & Watt engine, which was placed in the hold in the center of the boat, lay open to view. From the engine aft a rude cabin covered the boiler and the apartment for the officers. Her side wheels were equipped with twelve huge paddles. There were no paddle-boxes, and the wheels, when in motion, sent water splashing on deck with every revolution. The *Clermont's* rudder was shaped like that of a sailing vessel, and was moved by a tiller. Her boiler was set in masonry, and the condenser stood in a large cold-water cistern — the two greatly diminishing the buoyancy of the vessel. The thirty-foot smokestack rose almost as high as her two masts. Should her engine fail, Fulton could hoist sails on the two masts.[26]

Skeptics were not slow to point out the weaknesses of the *Clermont*. There were doubting Thomases even among Fulton's guests, whose anxiety increased as the hour for departure approached. The inventor alone remained calm and serene. Tall, slender, and very handsome, Fulton moved about the boat with an air of confidence, making last minute adjustments. "The morning I left New York", he wrote afterwards, "there were not perhaps thirty persons in the city who believed that the boat would ever move one mile an hour, or be of the least utility, and while we were putting off from the wharf, which was crowded

with spectators, I heard a number of sarcastic remarks."
But the sneers were changed to tumultuous cheers as the
Clermont swung out into the current at one o'clock in the
afternoon and churned proudly upstream. A new era had
dawned in American transportation.[27]

The progress of the *Clermont* up the Hudson was viewed
with mingled fear and astonishment. Sailors gazed in
amazement at the novel craft driven by a "tea-kettle"
which, without the use of sails, rapidly overhauled their
river sloops. Some of the more timid actually ran their
boats ashore and fled to the woods in terror. On a high
bluff opposite Poughkeepsie a group of villagers stood as
though transfixed. Some thought the *Clermont* a sea
monster, while others believed her to be a sign of the approaching judgment. One eye-witness considered her a
"backwoods saw-mill mounted on a scow and set on fire."
Coughing and wheezing as she plowed along, the *Clermont*
reached Albany in thirty-two hours.[28]

Fulton was pleased with the performance. To his friend
Joel Barlow,[29] poet-statesman, he wrote exultantly upon
his return : "The distance from New-York to Albany is
one hundred and fifty miles : I ran it up in thirty-two
hours, and down in thirty. I had a light breeze against me
the whole way, both going and coming, and the voyage
has been performed wholly by the power of the steam-
engine. I overtook many sloops and schooners beating to
windward, and parted with them as if they had been at
anchor . . . The power of propelling boats by steam is
now fully proved." [30]

Fulton's Folly : A Mississippi Dream

A guest aboard the *Clermont* was equally delighted with her performance : "As we passed the farms on the borders of the river, every eye was intent, and from village to village, the heights and conspicuous places were occupied by the sentinels of curiosity, not viewing a thing they could possibly anticipate any idea of, but conjecturing about the possibility of the motion. As we passed and repassed the towns of Athens and Hudson, we were politely saluted by the inhabitants and several vessels, and at Albany we were visited by his excellency, the governor, and many citizens . . . She is unquestionably the most pleasant boat I ever went in. In her the mind is free from suspense. Perpetual motion authorizes you to calculate on a certain time to land; her works move with all the facility of a clock; and the noise when on board is not greater than that of a vessel sailing with a good breeze." [31]

An unforeseen incident occurred at Albany. The chief engineer, a Scotchman, went ashore and imbibed too freely in celebration of the successful voyage. He was promptly discharged. Fortunately the assistant engineer was familiar with the engine, and so the return trip was made without mishap.

The voyage of the *Clermont* marked an epoch in more than Hudson River navigation. Robert Fulton and his financial supporter, Chancellor Robert R. Livingston, had broader visions : both had turned their eyes westward toward the Mississippi Valley where American pioneers were hewing out a mighty empire in the wilderness. "Whatever may be the fate of steamboats for the Hudson", Fulton reminded Livingston after a successful trial run, "every thing is completely proved for the Mississippi, and the object is immense." To Barlow he declared that steamboats would "give a cheap and quick conveyance to the merchandise on the Mississippi, Missouri and other great rivers, which are now laying open their treasures to the enterprise of our countrymen; and although the prospect of personal emolument has been some inducement to me, yet I feel infinitely more pleasure in reflecting on the immense advantage my country will derive from the invention." [32]

But it would take more than Fulton's enthusiasm and inventive genius to establish a line of steamboats on the western waters : a little hard cash would also be needed. Fortunately Fulton had won the support of Robert Livingston, a statesman and diplomat as well as an experimenter in his own name. Livingston himself had been intrigued for a number of years by the possibilities of steam navigation. He had been associated with the attempts of such men as John Fitch, Samuel Morey, John Stevens, and Nicholas J. Roosevelt. The construction of the *Clermont* had been made possible by the liberal donations of Livingston, and in gratitude Fulton had named the boat after the Chancellor's estate on the Hudson.[33]

6

Monopoly on the Mississippi

As THE *Clermont* was steaming merrily up the Hudson on her maiden voyage, Chancellor Robert R. Livingston made a strange prophecy. Before the end of the century, he assured his listeners, vessels propelled by steam alone might make the voyage to Europe! His guests were too polite to laugh outright, but John R. Livingston is said to have whispered to a cousin : "Bob has had many a bee in his bonnet before now, but this steam folly will prove the worst yet!" But history records that the American steamship *Savannah* crossed the Atlantic as early as 1819.[34]

If Thomas Jefferson did not provide the bee for Livingston's steam folly, he at least may have focused the Chancellor's attention on our western waters. In 1801 Jefferson had sent Livingston as minister to France with instructions to forestall the rumored retrocession of Louisiana to France. The following year, the retrocession having been confirmed, Jefferson wrote Livingston that "There is on the globe one single spot, the possessor of which is our natural and habitual enemy. It is New Orleans, through which the produce of three-eighths of our territory must pass to market, and from its fertility it will ere long yield more than half of our whole produce and contain more than half of our inhabitants." Jefferson concluded his letter by threatening to marry the United States to the

Steamboating on Upper Mississippi

British fleet and nation the day France took possession of New Orleans.[35]

But Napoleon Bonaparte did not relish the idea of fair Columbia embarking on the holy sea of matrimony with John Bull. War with England was impending. And Napoleon, suddenly changing his tack, offered to sell all of Louisiana to the United States. The Louisiana Purchase was officially consummated on April 30, 1803. As Livingston was affixing his signature to the treaty he observed to James Monroe : "We have lived long, but this is the noblest work of our whole lives." He went on to prophesy that the Louisiana Purchase would "change vast solitudes into flourishing districts" which would cause the United States to take its place "among the powers of the first rank".[36]

There was little in the previous development of the Mississippi Valley to support this rosy vision. At the time of the Louisiana Purchase only three States — Kentucky, Tennessee, and Ohio — had been admitted into the Union. Less than four hundred thousand settlers occupied the territory between the Alleghenies and the Mississippi, with Kentucky alone boasting over half the total. In 1800 New Orleans with a population of 9650 inhabitants dominated the entire valley. Pittsburgh contained only 1565 souls; Cincinnati had but 750; and a scant 600 had settled at Louisville. In 1799 Governor Carlos Dehault de Lassus found only 6028 people in Upper or Spanish Louisiana. St. Louis could count only 925 inhabitants, one-third of whom were colored.[37]

Monopoly on the Mississippi

Following the Louisiana Purchase, Thomas Jefferson divided his new acquisition into two territories. He appointed William C. C. Claiborne as governor of Orleans Territory, which included nearly the same boundaries as present-day Louisiana. All the remaining wilderness northward to the Canadian line between the Mississippi River and the Rocky Mountains was designated Louisiana Territory. Out of this vast domain four States were destined to be carved along the Mississippi. But in 1807 Arkansas, Missouri, Iowa, and Minnesota were not even geographical expressions.

When Governor Claiborne visited New York City in the autumn of 1810 he discussed with Fulton and Livingston the possibilities of introducing steamboats on the Mississippi. Both men demanded a complete monopoly for steam transportation before embarking on such an enterprise. Claiborne apparently was sympathetic. Whereupon Fulton and Livingston opened a correspondence with the various governments along the Ohio and Mississippi to secure similar monopolies. At that time Kentucky and Tennessee were the only States bordering on the Mississippi, and their western borders were far beyond the fringe of settlement. Mississippi Territory, which comprised what is now Mississippi and Alabama, lay directly below Tennessee. North of the mouth of the Ohio lay Illinois Territory, which embraced present-day Illinois, Wisconsin, and Minnesota east of the Mississippi.[38]

Because of his great influence Livingston experienced little difficulty in pushing the desired monopoly through the New York legislature. But consummate skill would be needed to secure similar grants from western States and Territories. Livingston's technique was brought to light a quarter of a century ago when two small boys stumbled upon a box of papers yellowed with age in an unused loft in Galena, Illinois. The signatures on one of the letters quickly caught their attention.[39]

Clermont, State of New York, August 20th, 1810.
To his Excellency, The Governor of Upper Mississippi;
Sirs;

Wishing to extend the benefit of steamboat navigation to the Mississippi River, a capital approaching to two hundred thousand dollars will be required, which capital must be raised by subscription; but subscribers cannot be obtained until an effectual law presents a fair prospect of securing to them such exclusive right as will return emolument equal to the risk and trouble. In this point the patent law of the United States is at present imperfect, hence after the example of encouragement granted by the State of New York we have applied to the different governments bordering on the Mississippi for their protection and patronage and thus take the liberty to transmit to you our petition. To improve the navigation of the Mississippi by transporting goods for three fourths of the sum which is now paid and in three fourths of the time; to render such an establishment periodical, uniform and secure is an object of such immense importance to the states bordering on the Mississippi, a work of so much labor and hazard to the undertakers as we hope will excite the most lively feelings of patronage and protection both in your Excellency and the Honourable, the Legislature of Upper Louisiana. On the receipt of these papers we shall esteem it a particular favor to be honored with an answer from your Excellency, expressing your opinion on this subject.

We have the honor to be respectfully,
Your Excellencies most obedient,
ROBT. R. LIVINGSTON.
ROBT. FULTON.

Monopoly on the Mississippi

Only one government hearkened to Fulton and Livingston, despite their adroit plea. On April 19, 1811, the legislature of Orleans Territory passed an act granting Livingston and Fulton "the sole and exclusive right and privilege to build, construct, make use, employ and navigate boats, vessels and water crafts, urged or propelled through the water by fire or steam, in all the creeks, rivers, bays and waters whatsoever, within the jurisdiction of the territory, during eighteen years from the first of January, 1812."

All might have gone well for the monopolists had not Congress in April, 1812, declared that as a condition for the admission of Louisiana "the river Mississippi, and the navigable waters leading into it, and into the gulf of Mexico, should be common highways, and forever free, as well to the inhabitants of that state as to those of the other states and territories of the United States, without any tax, duty, impost or toll". Fortunately for Livingston and Fulton, however, the new State apparently saw fit to continue the monopoly.[10]

It would be a mistake to think that Livingston and Fulton were blind to the many hazards of their undertaking. They were fully aware of the great distances and the archaic means of traveling in the West. Louisville was ten times as far from New Orleans as Albany was from New York. And Pittsburgh was some six hundred miles farther up the Ohio from Louisville.

The commerce of this inland empire was largely dependent on crude river craft capable of floating downstream but unable to stem the swift currents of the Mississippi and Ohio rivers. Only a few models — such as keelboats and barges — could return upstream. Freight barges required a year for the round trip between one of the Ohio towns and New Orleans. It took three months of back-breaking labor to shove and pull a barge from Louisville to Pittsburgh. Keelboats were much faster. These sleek crafts could run from Louisville to New Orleans in six weeks; but they consumed four and one-half months on the return trip. It required unusual effort to pole a keelboat from Louisville to Pittsburgh in less than a month.[41]

The voyage of the *Clermont* meant little to most of the people of that day. Even the most sanguine could scarcely conceive of a time when (in 1844) the steamboat *J. M. White* would make the round trip between St. Louis and New Orleans in nine days. On this same trip the *J. M. White* made the upstream voyage between New Orleans and St. Louis in three days, twenty-three hours and nine minutes — a record which stood until 1870 when the *Robert E. Lee* and the *Natchez* battled for supremacy. Nor could they envision in that very same year (1844) the *Sultana* running from New Orleans to Louisville in five and one-half days. This record was destined to be gradually lowered until 1853 when the *Eclipse* came snorting up to Louisville in four days, nine hours, and thirty minutes, averaging fourteen miles an hour upstream.[42]

But to talk of such feats in 1809 would have elicited derisive guffaws. In their wildest dreams Fulton and Livingston could only conceive of a steamboat traveling distances in three-fourths of the time required by cruder river craft. Even then they felt the western waterways ought to be studied from the standpoint of the commerce offered as well as from the practicability of navigation itself. What they needed was a competent, courageous partner to study these western waters and report to them. They found such a man in Nicholas J. Roosevelt.

7

A Flatboat Odyssey

NICHOLAS J. ROOSEVELT was molded upon the genuine Roosevelt pattern. Of sturdy Dutch stock, members of the Roosevelt clan have usually manifested an adventurous, bold, courageous, and self-reliant spirit. Many social and political reformers have come from their ranks. Some displayed inventive genius; many harbored a deep and abiding love for the sea and ships. Nicholas Roosevelt was an inventor and an engineer in his own right. His courage and enthusiasm and his vision and enterprising spirit were well known to Fulton and Livingston.

Nicholas Roosevelt was no novice in steam transportation. In 1782, at the age of fifteen, he had built a model boat, propelled by paddle wheels over the sides which were revolved by hickory and whalebone springs unwinding a cord wrapped around the axles. At the age of thirty he entered into an agreement with Chancellor Livingston and John Stevens to build a steamboat. On October 21, 1798, this boat, which was named the *Polacca*, made a successful trial trip, attaining a speed equivalent to three miles an hour in still water. Just before the trip Roosevelt had proposed to Livingston (an ardent proponent of stern-wheelers) that they "throw two wheels of wood over the sides", but the Chancellor sharply replied that such a plan was "out of the question!"

[48]

A Flatboat Odyssey

When Livingston became minister to France in 1801 their experiments ceased. Meanwhile Roosevelt found his business on the verge of collapse. He had erected a rolling mill to supply the government with rolled and drawn copper for six 74-gun ships only to be suddenly "cut off" by a change of administration. By 1809 he seems to have recouped some of his losses, for when Livingston and Fulton outlined their scheme to him he was eager to join in the venture. It was agreed that Roosevelt should set out for the West at once. His pretty bride of six months, Lydia Latrobe of Baltimore, determined to accompany him.[43]

Transportation was just emerging from a pristine state when Roosevelt arrived at Pittsburgh in May, 1809. The creation of the Northwest Territory in 1787 had been followed by a flood of immigrants into the Ohio Valley. As the years rolled on, thousands of land-hungry settlers were floated down the Ohio on a flotilla of fantastic craft. Boat yards and outfitting establishments did a thriving business in the embryonic towns on the Ohio, Monongahela, and Allegheny rivers. Some boats were strongly constructed, but any of them might fall a victim to snags, sandbars, or hidden boulders. Pittsburgh, Wheeling, and Brownsville were the principal points of embarkation and many famous Upper Mississippi steamboats were destined to be launched from their boat yards. When Nicholas Roosevelt arrived these cities were still in the flatboat era, although keelboats and barges were in general use.[44]

The first problem confronting Roosevelt was the type of craft best suited for his work. The most simple boat was the log canoe which could be bought for three dollars or less. Then there was the pirogue, which was a large canoe often forty or fifty feet long, from six to eight feet wide, and capable of carrying a family and several tons of household goods. Both the canoe and pirogue were unpopular for long trips on western streams not only because they were unwieldy and heavy on portages but also because of the danger of Indian attack. They were much too small for Roosevelt.

Another type was the flat-bottomed skiff in which two or three might venture on a long trip; Roosevelt did not overlook this possibility. Then there was the bateau, a big skiff capable of carrying an entire family. Several pairs of long oars or sweeps propelled the bateau downstream, while poles were used for ascending the river. Since Roosevelt did not intend to return upstream he quickly discarded the bateau as a possible means of transportation.[45]

The resourceful Dutchman found that the flatboat, a creation of the Ohio Valley, was the most popular craft for pioneer families. Flatboats varied greatly in size, measuring from twenty to sixty feet in length and from ten to twenty feet in width. The smaller flatboats were usually called "Kentucky boats", after their destination in Kentucky or the lower Ohio. The big "flats" bound for the Lower Mississippi were generally called "New Orleans" boats. Some flatboats had two large sweeps projecting like horns from each side; these were called "broadhorns". Emigrants sometimes compared the Kentucky "broadhorn" to a "New England pig-sty set afloat". Flatboats

A Flatboat Odyssey

cost from a dollar to a dollar and a half for each foot of length.

The hull of the flatboat was constructed of large squared pine or hardwood timbers hewn from the forests of western Pennsylvania. The average craft rose from three to six feet above the water's surface and drew from one to two and one-half feet of water when fully laden. As they floated down the Ohio loaded with men, women, and children, horses and cows, cats, chickens, and dogs, grindstones, powder, household furniture, and farm implements, the flatboats resembled a "mixture of log cabin, fort, floating barnyard and country grocery." Their rugged construction made them bullet-proof, while withering volleys could be poured through loopholes on marauding bands of Indians or the murderous white riffraff of the Ohio-Mississippi country. Such a boat presented the qualities most needed by Roosevelt.[46]

There were, however, two other types of craft (the keelboat and the barge) which could not be overlooked. These resembled each other closely and were capable of upstream navigation. Keelboats were sharp at bow and stern, and although of light draft they could carry from twenty to forty tons of freight. They were called keelboats because of the heavy four-inch square timber that extended from the bow to the stern along the bottom of the boat. This timber was placed so as to take the shock of a collision with a submerged snag or other obstruction.

Keelboats were constructed of heavy planks and had planked ribs like a ship. They were usually from forty-five to seventy-five feet long and from seven to nine feet wide. Sometimes they carried a mast and sails to take advantage of any favoring breeze. A captain or steersman and two men at the sweeps could propel a keelboat downstream, but upstream navigation required a steersman and from six to ten men provided with poles. The work of these men was hard and fatiguing : it developed a hardy and robust type of riverman who bore a striking resemblance to the Upper Mississippi log raftsmen.

Although keelboat transportation was tedious and expensive it was as superior to horse-packing as the steamboat was destined to be to the keelboat. A man with five horses could transport one-half a ton of freight about twenty miles in one day. A keelboatman could pole two or three tons the same distance upstream in the same time. In truth keelboats were the rapid transit express boats until the advent of the steamboat.[47]

Barges cost about five dollars for each foot of length and were modeled somewhat after a ship's longboat. They were usually from thirty to seventy feet long, from seven to twelve feet in width, and carried a mast, sails, and rudder. Four long oars accelerated progress downstream which ordinarily ranged from four to five miles an hour. Poles were used for upstream navigation but barge captains availed themselves of every favorable breeze to aid the sweating crew. Even then two miles an hour against the current was considered good time. Because of their comparative celerity both barges and keels were often used by business men, land speculators, and government officials.

A Flatboat Odyssey

After surveying the types of craft in use, Roosevelt determined to use a flatboat. Since accuracy rather than speed was important, and since he would be obliged to live in his craft for six months, Roosevelt built a flatboat that contained all the "necessary comforts for himself and wife". The young bride described her new home as "a huge box containing a comfortable bed room, dining room, pantry, and a room in front for the crew, with a fire-place where the cooking was done. The top of the boat was flat, with seats and an awning."

Securing a pilot, three hands, and a male cook, Roosevelt and his young bride left Pittsburgh with its more than four thousand inhabitants and started down the Ohio. Cincinnati, Louisville, and Natchez were the only points of importance in the entire distance between Pittsburgh and New Orleans. Cincinnati had a population of twenty-five hundred in 1810, while Louisville was about one-half the size of Cincinnati.

As they drifted down the Ohio, Roosevelt constantly studied the rapidity of the current. He carried letters of introduction to the leading citizens, and he was received kindly and hospitably entertained. At Louisville he remained on shore some three weeks. The westerners listened respectfully to his explanation of the purpose of the voyage and the benefits of steam navigation. But no one, merchant or boatman, gave him a single word of encouragement. In answer to his stories of the experiments on the Hudson and other eastern rivers, the rough river pilots would simply point to the turbid, whirling Ohio as a conclusive answer to all his reasoning. Undaunted, Roosevelt continued his studies of the Ohio and Mississippi. "He gauged them: he measured their velocity at different seasons; he obtained all the statistical information within his reach, and formed a judgment with respect to the future development of the country".[48]

Fortunately Roosevelt did find a few sources of information. Thus, below Louisville lay the Falls of the Ohio — a particularly dangerous spot which required the services of special pilots during low water. These pilots kept an account of the number of boats and the amount of products they piloted over the Falls. During the seven-month period beginning October 5, 1810, regular pilots took 743 boats over the Falls. They estimated that fully one-third as many more passed over the Falls during high water. Among the commodities listed were flour, bacon, pork, lard, corn, oats, butter, and $355,624 worth of merchandise. Over nine thousand barrels of whiskey and almost four thousand barrels of cider were also included in the estimate. Lumber, hemp, yarn, cordage, shoe thread, country linen, apples and dried fruit, beans, onions, and tobacco, horses, hogs, and a miscellaneous assortment of articles complete the merchandise which Fulton, Livingston, and Roosevelt sought to offer a cheap, speedy, and safe transport to New Orleans.[49]

Leaving Louisville and the Falls of the Ohio behind, the flatboat continued down *La Belle Rivière*. Gliding silently along they passed "many a scene of revelry and bloodshed". One night, as their boat lay tied to the bank of the

A Flatboat Odyssey

Mississippi, Roosevelt was aroused by two Indians in his bedroom, calling for whiskey. Nor would the dusky red men leave until Roosevelt gave them firewater.[50] As they floated lazily downstream with the current they encountered many drinking, cursing, fighting rivermen. Bitter rivalry existed among the crews on the flats, keels, and barges. Each had its own bully or champion who usually stood ready to challenge a rival — particularly if the chances of winning were good.

Typical of the keelboatmen was that justly famous character, Mike Fink. What Daniel Boone was to Kentucky or Sam Houston to Texas, Mike Fink was in legend and fact to the story of keelboating on the Ohio and Mississippi.

As king of the keelboatmen, this is how Mike was wont to modestly describe himself to a foe who dared question his supremacy. "I'm a Salt River roarer! I'm a ring-tailed squealer! I'm a reg'lar screamer from the ol' Massassip'! Whoop! I'm the very infant that refused his milk before its eyes were open, and called out for a bottle of old Rye! I love the women an' I'm chockful o' fight! I'm half wild horse and half cock-eyed alligator and the rest o' me is crooked snags an' red-hot snappin' turkle. I can hit like fourth-proof lightnin' an' every lick I make in the woods lets in an acre o' sunshine. I can out-run, out-jump, out-shoot, out-brag, out-drink, an' out-fight, rought-an'-tumble, no holts barred, ary man on both sides the river from Pittsburgh to New Orleans an' back ag'in to St. Louiee. Come on, you flatters, you bargers, you milk-white mechanics, an' see how tough I am to chaw! I ain't had a fight for two days an' I'm spilein' for exercise. Cock-a-doodle-doo!" [51]

Such were the characters encountered by Roosevelt on the Mississippi and in the unkempt western settlements. A few days were spent at Natchez, where Roosevelt conferred with leading citizens and disposed of the flatboat. Nor was Natchez the most genteel place in which to sojourn. According to one account, "Natchez is a land of fevers, alligators, niggers, and cotton bales . . . where to refuse grog before breakfast would degrade you below the brute creation . . . where bears, the size of young jackasses, are fondled in lieu of pet dogs; and knives, the length of a barber's pole, usurp the place of toothpicks . . . where nigger women are knocked down by the auctioneer". [52]

From Natchez-under-the-hill the Roosevelts set out in their skiff down the Mississippi to New Orleans, which they reached in early December after a nine day trip. At New Orleans they took passage on the first vessel ready to sail for New York. It was a hard voyage, for the captain took sick and yellow fever broke out aboard the vessel. They were allowed to leave the ship at Old Point Comfort; and they completed their journey by stagecoach, arriving in New York about the middle of January. [53]

8

The Voyage of the *New Orleans*

BOTH LIVINGSTON and Fulton were delighted when the heavy stagecoach that carried Roosevelt and his young wife rumbled into New York City. Did Roosevelt bring good news or bad news? Were their hopes and dreams to be shattered by a gloomy report? The grave anxieties which they must have entertained during Roosevelt's long absence were quickly dispelled as that enthusiastic gentleman painted a rosy picture of the prospects for steam navigation in the Mississippi Valley. Then, while Roosevelt hurried back to Pittsburgh, his partners lost no time incorporating the Ohio Steamboat Navigation Company to operate a fleet of vessels on the western waters under the Fulton-Livingston patents.[54]

Roosevelt arrived in Pittsburgh in the spring of 1810 and commenced building a steamboat according to plans furnished by Fulton. He established a boat yard under a lofty bluff on the Monongahela about a mile from the "Point". The hull was constructed of native white pine. The copper boiler was made in New York and transported across the Alleghenies, but skilled eastern mechanics were required to install the engine. Named the *New Orleans* after the port of her destination, the boat was launched in March, 1811. The pioneer steamboat of the Mississippi Valley was ready to start on her maiden voyage the following October.

Steamboating on Upper Mississippi

The *New Orleans* was a side-wheeler, measuring between 300 and 400 tons burden. The bow of the boat was reserved for freight; the engine and smokestack stood exposed in the center; and the cabin was built in the rear. This cabin was divided, one aft for the ladies and a larger one forward for gentlemen. The ladies' cabin contained only four berths, but was comfortably furnished. The *New Orleans* also carried two masts equipped with sails. It has been said that she was "a large and heavy boat combining incongruous features of marine and river craft". The cost of the *New Orleans* was said to be $38,000, but it seems unlikely that anywhere near this sum was expended.[55]

The construction of the *New Orleans* produced considerable speculation and wonder. "It will be a novel sight, and as pleasing as novel", Zadok Cramer observed in *The Navigator*, "to see a huge boat working her way up the windings of the Ohio, without the appearance of sail, oar, pole, or any manual labour about her — moving within the secrets of her own wonderful mechanism, and propelled by power undiscoverable! This plan if it succeeds, must open to view flattering prospects to an immense country, an interior of not less than two thousand miles of as fine a soil and climate, as the world can produce, and to a people worthy of all the advantages that nature and art can give them".[56]

A large crowd gathered at Pittsburgh to witness the departure of the *New Orleans* on Sunday, October 20, 1811. Skeptics shook their heads gravely, and experienced

The Voyage of the *New Orleans*

rivermen expressed concern for the safety of those on board. But neither Roosevelt nor his young wife could be dissuaded from the rash adventure; and handkerchiefs and hats waved "God speed" as the boat swung out in the current. Puffing bravely upstream a short distance, the *New Orleans* triumphantly arched around in the current and sped past the cheering throng. A moment later she disappeared behind the first headlands on the right bank of the Ohio.

It was a small crew that served under Captain Nicholas Roosevelt on this epoch-making voyage of the *New Orleans*. Nicholas Baker acted as engineer, and his faithful performance of this important duty led to his promotion to the captaincy by the time the boat reached New Orleans. Andrew Jack served as pilot. There were also "six hands, two female servants, a man waiter, a cook, and an immense Newfoundland dog, named Tiger." [57]

The progress of the *New Orleans* down the Ohio was viewed with amazement. Backwoodsmen flocked to the banks of the Ohio to catch a glimpse of the strange craft. At Point Pleasant at the mouth of the Great Kanawha, Roosevelt cajoled the keeper of the "Traveller's Rest" to part with some cordwood. "While the wood was being toted aboard the singular craft," a local historian relates, "nearly all the one hundred inhabitants examined, commented, criticized. Some claimed it was an attempt to chain nature's forces and would end in disaster to crew and owners, a mere invention of the Devil's. Others watched every movement, took notes of all machinery, and resolved to 'make a like machine or spoil a home'." [58]

Steaming downstream at a speed of eight to ten miles an hour, the *New Orleans* cast anchor at Cincinnati two days later amid the plaudits of the townsmen who had assembled on the bank. "Well, you are as good as your word; you have visited us in a steamboat, but we see you for the last time", said many of those who had met Roosevelt on his former visit. "Your boat may go *down* the river; but, as to coming up it, the very idea is an absurd one." Rugged keelboatmen, their shoulders toughened by poling many weary miles against the current,shook their heads disparagingly. All agreed that the steamboat would never return.

After taking on a supply of wood the *New Orleans* proceeded to Louisville which was reached at midnight on the fourth day in "sixty-four hours sailing from Pittsburg." A brilliant moon flooded the shimmering surface of the Ohio as the boat dropped anchor opposite the quiet town. The roar of escaping steam caused the sleeping inhabitants to spring from their beds and rush down to the river to discover the cause of this weird sound. Some insisted that the comet of 1811 had fallen into the Ohio and produced the hubbub. [59]

The next morning many citizens came aboard to express their congratulations "accompanied by regrets that it was the first and last time a steamboat would be seen above the falls of the Ohio." A local newspaper declared that the boat could "accommodate from sixty to eighty cabin and steerage passengers, in a style not inferior to any packet in the union." A public dinner was tendered Roosevelt a few days later. Then Roosevelt invited his hosts to dine aboard the *New Orleans*. While the feast was at its height the guests suddenly heard rumbling accompanied by a very perceptible motion in the boat. Panic-stricken at the thought that the boat had slipped her anchor and was drifting toward the Falls and almost certain destruction, all rushed to the deck only to find the *New Orleans* churning bravely upstream leaving Louisville far behind. Thus did Roosevelt convince his "incredulous guests" to their own "surprise and delight".

Low water prevented the *New Orleans* from crossing the Falls of the Ohio, so Roosevelt ran an excursion to Cincinnati where he was hailed with wild enthusiasm. On one occasion the *New Orleans* ran thirteen miles in two and one-half hours in the presence of a number of "respectable gentlemen". These trial runs upstream did much to promote confidence in steam navigation.[60]

Rain in the upper Ohio Valley finally allowed Roosevelt to risk the perilous descent of the Falls. Just before the start Mrs. Roosevelt gave birth to a child but this could not deter her from joining her husband. Soon all hands were on deck; an experienced "rapids pilot" took his place beside the regular pilot in the bow; and the *New Orleans* weighed anchor. Steam had been crowded into the boiler in order that the speed of the boat would permit easier guidance through the swift current. With her safety valve shrieking and her wheels lashing the Ohio into a foam, the *New Orleans* made a wide circuit for the Indiana channel and then headed downstream. "Instinctively, each one on board now grasped the nearest object, and with bated breath awaited the result. Black ledges of rock appeared only to disappear as the *New Orleans* flashed by them. The waters whirled and eddied, and threw their spray upon the deck, as a more rapid descent caused the vessel to pitch forward to what at times seemed inevitable destruction. Not a word was spoken. The pilots directed the men at the helm by motions of their hands. Even the great Newfoundland dog seemed affected by the apprehension of danger, and came and crouched at Mrs. Roosevelt's feet." But the crucial passage was finally made; and, with feelings of "profound gratitude to the Almighty", Roosevelt ordered the *New Orleans* to round to below the Falls. There the rapids pilot bade them adieu, while preparations were made to continue the journey downstream.

As the *New Orleans* churned on down the Ohio the consternation of the scattered settlements increased. Opposite William Henry Harrison's farm at North Bend a family was "much alarmed" when a neighbor came dashing up shouting, "The British are coming down the river." All rushed to the bank only to see something resembling a "saw mill" making its "slow but solemn progress with the current." The frightened family breathed a sigh of relief upon learning it was one of those new "contraptions" called a steamboat.[61]

Nicholas Roosevelt had looked forward to "plain sailing" after passing the Falls of the Ohio. Instead he was subjected to "days of horror" as the first tremors of the

The Voyage of the *New Orleans*

New Madrid earthquake shook the cable and boat as the *New Orleans* lay at anchor, causing those aboard to experience a "nausea resembling sea sickness." The shocks continued throughout the night; and it was some time before the true character of the "dread visitor" was realized. When the *New Orleans* resumed her journey the next morning the machinery prevented those aboard from noting any disturbance — that is, all save Tiger, who "prowled about, moaning and growling" whenever he seemed to become aware of the shocks.[62]

The passengers aboard the *New Orleans* found the Mississippi a raging flood with the bottom lands submerged. Once a large canoe of Chickasaw Indians darted from the forest and set out in pursuit of the boat. Greatly outnumbered by the redskins, Roosevelt crowded on steam. A close race ensued from which the *New Orleans* finally emerged victorious. Screaming their disappointment, the enraged Chickasaw gave up the chase and turned back into the forest whence they had come.

Shortly after this incident Roosevelt was aroused one night by loud shouts and the scuffling of many feet. Springing from his bed, he seized the nearest weapon (which proved to be a sword) and dashed out of the cabin to do battle with the Chickasaw. Instead he met a more dangerous enemy — the forward cabin of the *New Orleans* was on fire! After great exertion the fire was extinguished, but the incident did little to soothe the jaded nerves of the crew already worn by the terrors of the earthquake.

Steamboating on Upper Mississippi

Each afternoon Roosevelt allowed the crew to go ashore
and cut enough wood for the next day. Squatters often
came aboard to tell their harrowing experiences as the
ground trembled beneath their feet. At New Madrid
many panic-stricken settlers begged to be taken aboard,
but Roosevelt was forced to turn "a deaf ear to the cries
of the terrified inhabitants of the doomed town." One
night an island to which the *New Orleans* had been anchored was swallowed by an earthquake : it was necessary
to cut the hawser to free the boat. The ravages of flood
and earthquake so changed the normal features of the
river that the pilot was often at a loss as to which way to
steer. During this period of "anxiety and terror" Mrs.
Roosevelt records that she "lived in a constant fright,
unable to sleep or sew, or read." [63]

At last the terrors of the New Madrid earthquake were
left behind and the *New Orleans* soon hove in sight of
Natchez. "Expecting to remain here for a day or two,
the engineer had allowed his fires to go down, so that
when the boat turned its head upstream, it lost headway
altogether, and was being carried down by the current far
below the intended landing. Thousands were assembled on
the bluff and at the foot of it; and for a moment it would
have seemed that the *New Orleans* had achieved what she
had done, so far, only that she might be overcome at last.
Fresh fuel however was added, — the engine was stopped
that steam might accumulate, presently the safety valve
lifted — a few turns of the wheels steadied the boat, — a
few more gave her headway; and, overcoming even the

Mississippi, she gained the shore amid shouts of exultation and applause."

The remainder of the journey was made without incident. Once the *New Orleans* was "detained by the breaking of one of her wheels"; but on the evening of January 10, 1812, she arrived at the port for which she was named.[64] Although the *New Orleans* was eighty-two days out of Pittsburgh the captain stated that the boat had actually consumed only ten days and nineteen hours running time. His work as the pioneer steamboat captain on western waters completed, Roosevelt left the *New Orleans* in charge of Captain Baker to run in the New Orleans-Natchez trade. She continued in this trade for two years, until snagged on July 14, 1814, two miles above Baton Rouge. Her boiler and part of her machinery were salvaged and placed in the second *New Orleans*.[65]

A grateful nation did not forget the work of this trailblazer on the American steamboat frontier. A century later, on October 31, 1911, a colorful flotilla of steamboats lay marshaled along the Monongahela at Pittsburgh. Gaily festooned in flags and bunting an armada of some fifty vessels had assembled to celebrate the centennial of western steamboat navigation. President William Howard Taft and a group of other dignitaries were aboard the *Virginia* which served as flagship of the squadron. The nearest lineal descendants of the Livingston, Fulton, and Fitch families, together with some sixty thousand people, were present to witness the christening of the "quaint" little

Steamboating on Upper Mississippi

New Orleans by Alice Roosevelt Longworth, daughter of Theodore Roosevelt whose grand uncle Nicholas J. Roosevelt had launched the first steamboat on western waters exactly a century before. Built by the city of Pittsburgh at a cost of $10,500, the diminutive craft was as close a replica of the *New Orleans* of 1811 as steamboat inspection laws and fragmentary information would permit. Following the christening of the new boat, President Taft spoke briefly. At the conclusion of his address the whistles of the entire fleet saluted the little side-wheeler with wild acclaim. The *New Orleans* then led the flotilla in a spectacular review before the President.[66] In 1811 the first *New Orleans* had ushered in an era in river transportation whose halcyon days could still be remembered in 1911 by many a hoary-headed riverman as he watched with tear-dimmed eyes this colorful pageant of the packets. As the replica of the *New Orleans* churned proudly by with her sister ships in the line, the scene doubtless brought back phantom memories of such sleek floating palaces as the *Eclipse*, the *Baltic*, and the *J. M. White*; the *Sultana*, the *Princess*, and the *Southern Belle*; the *Peytona*, the *Natchez*, and the *Robert E. Lee*.

A century had witnessed many changes in the Mississippi Valley. The centennial celebration of 1911 attracted a throng that doubled the combined population of Pittsburgh, Cincinnati, Louisville, St. Louis, and New Orleans in 1810. Pittsburgh in 1911 could boast three times the population living in what is now the States of Indiana, Illinois, Missouri, Arkansas, Louisiana, and Mississippi in

1811. Illinois and Indiana contained a million more inhabitants than did the entire United States in 1810. There
were more people munching corn pone in Arkansas than
there were inhabitants west of the Alleghenies a century
before. The steamboat had played a significant and dramatic rôle in the settlement and development of the Mississippi Valley.[67]

9

Henry Miller Shreve

FOR THE Mississippi Valley the voyage of the *New Orleans* was as distinct a triumph as the Fulton-Livingston monopoly was a severe blow. Were the builders of the other steamboats already under construction destined to lose all? The answer of at least one man, Henry Miller Shreve, was an emphatic No! In the bitter struggle against the Fulton-Livingston monopoly no name ranks higher than Shreve's. No man contributed more than he to the popularization of steamboating during the first decade of steam navigation on western waters.

Henry M. Shreve (after whom Shreveport, Louisiana, is named) was born in New Jersey in 1785. He settled with his parents at Perryopolis in western Pennsylvania in 1788, the same year that Julien Dubuque commenced mining lead in Iowa. In 1807 Captain Shreve took a 35-ton barge to St. Louis, returning to Pittsburgh with one of the first cargoes of furs destined for Philadelphia by that route. In 1810, the year Julien Dubuque died, Shreve took his barge to Fever River and returned with a cargo of lead. This venture, which marks the beginnings of the American lead traffic on the Upper Mississippi, netted Shreve about $11,000. With these profits he was able to inaugurate a thriving barge service between Pittsburgh and New Orleans.[68]

Henry Miller Shreve

Between 1811 and 1815, while Shreve was engaged in the New Orleans trade, the Ohio Steamboat Navigation Company launched four steamboats — the first *New Orleans*, the *Vesuvius*, the *Etna*, and the second *New Orleans*. Before the *Vesuvius* left the ways, another enterprising American, Daniel French, launched the 25-ton *Comet*, a stern-wheel steamboat featuring the vibrating cylinder. Shreve was an impelling force in French's venture, contributing one-fifth of the capital to the company. The *Comet* steamed to Louisville in the summer of 1813, and the following spring descended to New Orleans. After making two trips to Natchez, she was sold, taken apart, and her engine installed in a cotton factory.

The fate of the *Comet*, together with the threat of confiscation on the part of the monopoly, only stiffened Shreve's resistance to the Fulton-Livingston corporation. While at New Orleans with a barge in 1814, he secured the legal services of A. L. Duncan, a prominent member of the Louisiana bar. The Livingston interests already had the service of every other lawyer in New Orleans, but failed in their effort to entice Duncan away from Shreve.

Meanwhile French launched the *Enterprise* on the Monongahela at Brownsville. The new boat made two trips to Louisville during the summer of 1814. On December first Shreve assumed command and steamed to New Orleans in fourteen days. Upon his arrival he procured bail in case of seizure — which actually took place the following day. But martial law had been proclaimed; and Andrew Jackson, who was delighted with Shreve's celerity, promptly pressed the *Enterprise* into government service. General Jackson knew that some keelboats were making their way slowly down the Mississippi with additional supplies; and he sent Shreve upstream to meet them. Shreve performed this service with great dispatch. The *Enterprise* returned with the military stores in six and one-half days, having traveled 654 miles.

Jackson then ordered Shreve to run the British blockade of the Mississippi under cover of darkness in order to carry supplies to destitute Fort St. Philip. He executed this dangerous mission without being discovered. The next night, however, while endeavoring to return past the bristling batteries, the *Enterprise* was sighted and the British opened fire. Fortunately only a few cannon balls struck the boat and these bounced harmlessly off the cotton bales with which the *Enterprise* had been protected. This daring feat was loudly acclaimed by Jackson and his troops; and Shreve was the hero of the hour. On January 8, 1815, the *Enterprise* did effective work in repulsing the British at the battle of New Orleans.[69]

In the following spring the *Enterprise* advertised her departure from New Orleans for Pittsburgh on May 6th. The Fulton-Livingston monopoly again had her seized, but Attorney Duncan was ready with bail and Shreve went on his way rejoicing. The *Enterprise* was the first steamboat to ascend the Mississippi and Ohio, reaching Louisville in twenty-five days. Continuing upstream she steamed into Brownsville fifty-four days out of New Orleans, twenty days having been spent in taking on and discharging freight at the various ports along the way.[70] Soon after his return Shreve determined to superintend the construction of a steamboat upon a design radically different from any thus far used. His vivid imagination and rare inventive genius had discovered many flaws in the *Enterprise*, as well as in the half dozen other craft that had appeared on western waters. Every steamboat that had been built thus far was simply a keelboat with engine and boilers dumped in the hold. The freight and passengers also found their way into the holds of these crudely fashioned craft. Such sharply modelled vessels usually drew from six to ten feet of water, far more than the floating palaces of the sixties measuring a thousand tons. Furthermore, Shreve found that low-pressure engines did not develop sufficient power : the *Enterprise* had made slow time upstream even when the Mississippi was overflowing its banks. Finally, passenger accommodations were inadequate and even hazardous, particularly if a boat was suddenly snagged or if she exploded.

In August of 1815 the timbers of the *Washington* were "growing in the woods". When some New York gentlemen inspected her the following summer they declared that her accommodations exceeded anything on the Hudson. The *Washington* measured 403 tons — the largest steamboat afloat on western waters. She was the first "two decker" to be built in the West — a design that was distinctly Shreve's. Her cabin was placed between the decks, the main cabin being sixty feet long. She also had three "handsome private rooms" and a commodious barroom.

Her boilers were placed on the main deck instead of in the hold — a plan speedily adopted by other boat builders. In place of Fulton's vertical stationary cylinders or the vibrating cylinders invented by French, Shreve substituted horizontal cylinders with the vibrations to the pitmans. Both Fulton and French had used single low-pressure engines. Shreve employed a double high-pressure engine, the first of its kind on western waters.

When the *Washington* arrived at New Orleans, Edward Livingston is said to have remarked to Shreve after a critical examination : "You deserve well of your country, young man; but we shall be compelled to beat you if we can."

But Livingston reckoned without his competitor. An angry mob formed when Shreve was arrested at New Orleans for trespassing upon Fulton-Livingston waters. Shreve, however, expressed the wish that no demonstration take place. Upon reaching Livingston's office the popular skipper was immediately released. His attorney applied for an order to give bail for damages caused by the *Washington's* detention and the court granted it. Livingston was panic-stricken. He offered to admit Shreve on an equal share in the monopoly with his company if only he would "instruct his counsel so to arrange the business that a verdict might be found against him." Shreve rejected this bait "with scorn and indignation", for he realized that "the West looked to him for the free navigation of its waters".[71]

The originality of his improvements over those of both

Henry Miller Shreve

Fulton and French was demonstrated throughout the legal struggle; and it was "further shown that western commerce could never have benefited under either the Fulton or French patent." But Judge Dominick A. Hall of the United States District Court for the Louisiana District dismissed the case in 1817 on the ground that neither the plaintiff nor the defendant was a resident of Louisiana. Thanks to Shreve the monopoly claims of Fulton and Livingston with relation to the Mississippi were finally withdrawn in 1819. Five years later Chief Justice Marshall put an end to the Fulton-Livingston monopoly in New York in the celebrated case of Gibbons *vs.* Ogden. From that time on no further attempt was made to parcel out American waters to private individuals.[72]

In addition to introducing an almost entirely new steamboat and breaking the Fulton-Livingston monopoly, Shreve deserves to be remembered for one more important thing. Prior to 1817 no steamboat had conclusively demonstrated the practicability of upstream navigation. Western settlers had never considered the trip of the *Enterprise* as convincing because it had been made when the Mississippi overflowed its banks and the boat had made many short cuts, often in still water. But the arrival of the *Washington* at Louisville in twenty-one days from New Orleans in the spring of 1817 marked an era in steam transportation : it removed all doubt as to the future of upstream navigation. At a public dinner tendered Shreve by the citizens of Louisville the ingenious captain predicted that the time would come when the trip would be made in ten days : in 1853 the *Eclipse* steamed from New Orleans to Louisville in four days and nine hours.

When Henry Miller Shreve died in 1851 the St. Louis *Republican* declared that his name had been "for nearly forty years closely identified with the commerce of the West, either in flatboat or steam navigation." To his *Post Boy* went the honor of first attempting (in 1819) to carry mail by steamboat on western waters. A decade later Shreve built the *Heliopolis*, the first successful snag-boat in the Mississippi Valley. During the thirties he was busy removing the great Red River raft, and it was while thus engaged that his name became associated with the city of Shreveport.

To Shreve of St. Louis went the honor of sending (in 1848) the first message eastward to the President of the United States over the newly erected telegraph line. But the defeat of the Fulton-Livingston monopoly and the trip upstream with the *Washington* are Shreve's greatest achievements. "To him", declared the St. Louis *Republican*, "belongs the honor of demonstrating the practicability of navigating the Mississippi with steamboats." [73]

10

St. Louis : A Port of Call

TWELVE YEARS before the signing of the Declaration of Independence, a French fur trader, Pierre Laclede Liguest, established a trading post on the present site of St. Louis. For two generations following 1764 the history of St. Louis was as colorful as her growth was slow. During the American Revolution it was St. Louis that beat off a superior force of British and their Indian allies. On April 9, 1804, her citizens witnessed the transfer of Upper Louisiana from Spain to France; and on the following day they saw France turn it over to the United States. In 1806 they welcomed Zebulon M. Pike upon his return from the Upper Mississippi; and they cheered Lewis and Clark when those two trail-blazers returned from their conquest of the Missouri. From St. Louis the intrepid Manuel Lisa sallied forth up the Missouri in quest of furs and pelts for the Missouri Fur Company. From this same frontier community Wilson Price Hunt, at the behest of John Jacob Astor, set out in a keelboat in 1811 to establish Astoria. Lead from the Herculaneum shot tower below St. Louis helped Andrew Jackson to victory over the British at New Orleans.

Out of such dramatic episodes is the warp and woof of the early history of St. Louis patterned. But this romantic record stands in sharp contrast with her economic growth.

Steamboating on Upper Mississippi

It was not until July 12, 1808, that the first newspaper west of the Mississippi was printed at St. Louis. The publication of the *Missouri Gazette* was a hazardous economic venture, for St. Louis had scarcely a thousand souls at that time. A post office was established the same year, but mail service was costly and irregular : in 1809 St. Louis received no mail from the East for two months.

By 1816, however, the *Missouri Gazette* could describe the place as an "opulent city" with lead, soap, and candle factories, and one million dollars in capital. But the city needed factories, steam mills, seminaries, churches, banks, and steamboats. She lacked a courthouse and a city hall. The *Gazette* believed a distillery ought also to be counted among her liquid assets, for St. Louis bought annually more than five thousand barrels of whiskey.

The dreams of the *Missouri Gazette* began to be realized in 1817 when the first Presbyterian Church was organized, a public school system inaugurated, the Bank of Missouri incorporated, and a courthouse erected. One vitally important thing was still lacking : not a single steamboat had ventured north of the mouth of the Ohio. The reasons for their non-appearance are not hard to find.[74]

Between 1811 and 1816 the evolution and growth of steamboating was slow. Not more than ten steamboats had been built on the Ohio and Lower Mississippi, and the mortality rate was very high. The great cost, the danger from snags and sandbars, the difficulty of passing the Falls of the Ohio, the War of 1812, and the Fulton-Livingston monopoly all served to hinder construction and navigation on these streams. The danger of explosions during these experimental years also made navigators wary. Finally the westward movement, as evidenced by the admission of States, had not yet reached its high tide. Indiana was admitted as a State in 1816, Illinois in 1818, and Missouri in 1821. The influence of the Ohio and the Mississippi rivers on Indiana and Illinois is indicated by the manner in which the pioneers clung to the banks of these waterways, leaving the northern two-thirds of each State virtually unpopulated.[75]

It is not strange, therefore, that steamboats did not venture above the mouth of the Ohio before 1817. The small number of boats and the increasing volume of trade seem to have kept them on the Ohio and Lower Mississippi. When eight steamboats were launched on western waters in 1817, news trickled west to St. Louis that a steamboat would soon visit that port. The announcement was hailed with delight.

Weeks passed and no steamboat came. Finally, on August 2, 1817, just as the people of St. Louis had given up hope of seeing a steamboat that year, Captain James Read docked the *Zebulon M. Pike* at the foot of Market Street amid the enthusiastic cheers of the citizens who had assembled on the bank. The red man alone did not welcome her : indeed, the glare of her furnace fire, coupled with the black smoke rolling from her lone smokestack, so alarmed the Indians that they fled to the rear of the village and could not be induced to approach the evil monster.[76]

The advent of the *Zebulon M. Pike* was a landmark in

Steamboating on Upper Mississippi

St. Louis and Upper Mississippi Valley history. The boat was scarcely a paragon of beauty; nor did she represent any advance in construction. On the contrary, she was a dingy little scow built on the model of a barge at Henderson, Kentucky, in 1815 : she measured only 31.76 tons. Next to the *Comet*, she was the smallest steamboat documented in the Mississippi Valley. Her cabin was situated on the lower deck; her paddles had no wheelhouses. Since her low-pressure engine was scarcely able to stem the current of the Mississippi, the crew frequently resorted to poles and the running boards as in keelboating. Six weeks had been required to make the trip from Louisville to St. Louis.[77]

During the years 1818 and 1819 over sixty steamboats were built for western commerce. That was four times the number constructed in the previous seven years. It was quite natural, therefore, that there should be a gradual increase and expansion in their use, but even with this added number it is not likely that more than a third of the total trade on western waters was carried by steamboats. Earlier, however, in 1817, nine-tenths of the trade had been carried by other types of boats.[78]

The port of St. Louis kept pace with this rapid expansion of steam commerce. The *Pike* was not the only steamboat to arrive in 1817. In October of the same year the *Constitution* appeared. During 1818 there were several arrivals; and from that time on the number gradually increased. Few cities have been more advantageously located to command the inland commerce of an empire. St. Louis served as the hub of a system of waterways which included the Upper and Lower Mississippi, the Ohio, the Missouri, and the Illinois. Over these rivers and their tributaries there was destined to pass a steam tonnage greater than that of the entire British Empire in 1843.

In 1817 St. Louis had clamored for a steamboat. By 1819 the arrival of a steamboat had become commonplace. But it was not only steamboats that made St. Louis a port of call. Ocean steamers also docked at her wharves!

Early in 1819 the *Maid of Orleans* steamed from Philadelphia to New Orleans. The steamer *Sea-Horse* arrived from New York about the same time. These were probably the first steam craft to make an ocean voyage of any length, since the *Savannah* (the first steamer to cross the Atlantic) did not set out for Liverpool until May 26, 1819. Several weeks before the departure of the *Savannah* the captain of the *Maid of Orleans*, not content with his deep-sea honors, brought his trim craft snorting up the Mississippi to St. Louis, arriving there about the first of May.[79]

It was only human that St. Louis should become enthusiastic over her commercial prospects. "In 1817, less than two years ago", crowed the *Missouri Gazette*, "the first steamboat arrived at St. Louis. We hailed it as the day of small things, but the glorious consummation of all our wishes is daily arriving. Already during the present season we have seen on our shores five steamboats and several more daily expected. Who would or could have dared to conjecture that in 1819 we would have witnessed the arrival of a steamboat from Philadelphia or New York?"

Steamboating on Upper Mississippi

But St. Louis was destined to even greater things in 1819 as this "great American invention" opened up a "new arena" for her merchants. With pardonable pride the *Missouri Gazette* declared that "A steamboat . . . has started from St. Louis for Franklin, two hundred miles up the Missouri, and two others are now here destined for the Yellowstone. The time is fast approaching when a journey to the Pacific will become as familiar, and indeed more so, than it was fifteen or twenty years ago to Kentucky or Ohio." [80]

The Yellowstone expedition was more than a landmark in Misouri River history. It was the steamboat *Western Engineer* which first ascended the Big Muddy as far as present-day Omaha and Council Bluffs. It was this same diminutive craft which, in 1820, ascended the Upper Mississippi to what is now Keokuk, blazing a trail and pointing the way for the steamboat *Virginia* and her epoch-making voyage to Fort Snelling three years later. The story of the *Western Engineer* is a unique chapter in Upper Mississippi steamboating.

THOMAS WEBSTER & Co.,
FORWARDING AND COMMISSION MERCHANTS,
St. Louis, Mo.

Shipped, In good order and well conditioned, by THOMAS WEBSTER & CO., For account and risk of whom it may concern, on board the good Steamboat called the *White Cloud* whereof _____ is Master for the present voyage, now lying in the Port of Saint Louis, and bound for *New Orleans* Being marked and numbered as below, and are to be delivered, without delay, in like good order and condition, at the said Port of *New Orleans* (unavoidable dangers of the river and fire, only, excepted,) unto *Mess James McGregor* or to *their* assigns; he or they having freight at the rate of (10) *Ten Cents for one Hundred Pounds* ⟨⟩

In witness whereof, the Owner, Master or Clerk of said Steamboat hath affirmed to _____ Bills of Lading; all of this tenor and date, one of which being accomplished, the others to stand void.

Dated at St. Louis, this *ninth* day of *Septbr* 184 4

MARKS.	ARTICLES.	WEIGHT.
J C	400 Pigs Lead	28,400 lbs

Four Hundred Pigs of Lead weighing Twenty eight Thousand Four Hundred Pounds

W R Clayton

J A 28.40

Entd

WHITE CLOUD

The *White Cloud* was built at Pittsburgh in 1843. She was 166 feet long, 26 feet beam, 6 feet 4 inches depth of hold, and measured 261 tons. On September 9, 1844, while lying at the St. Louis levee, she took aboard 400 pigs of lead weighing 28,400 pounds which were destined for New Orleans, at ten cents per 100 pounds—or $28.40 for the 1,200-mile trip. The lead probably came from the Galena-Dubuque area.

Five years later, on May 17, 1849, the *White Cloud* caught fire at the St. Louis levee. One contemporary version was that an attempt was made to set her adrift but an offshore breeze jostled her against twenty-two other boats, setting them all on fire. Another version was that the fire spread to the *Edward Bates* which was lying next to the *White Cloud* and spread from her to the other boats when she broke loose and set the others on fire. Whatever version is correct, in the holocaust that followed 15 city blocks of St. Louis were consumed by flames

THE GREAT FIRE OF 1849 AT ST. LOUIS.

and property damage was estimated at $5,500,000. The *White Cloud* had no cargo aboard but the fully insured boat was a total loss. The following Upper Mississippi steamboats were lost:

Boat	Master	Value	Cargo	Loss	Insurance
American Eagle	Cossen	$14,000	None	Total	$ 3,500
Edward Bates	Randolph	22,000	None	Total	15,000
Montauk	Legrand Morehouse	16,000	$8,000	Total	10,000
Red Wing	Barger	6,000	3,000	Total	None
St. Peters	Ward	12,000	None	Total	9,000

In addition to the above, the *General Brooke* and two steamboats listed in the Missouri trade in 1849—the *Alexander Hamilton* and the *Eliza Stewart*—had plied the Upper Mississippi in previous years. The following eye-witness account is from a letter in the *Risvold Collection*:

Dear Brother

You have heard of the Great Fire that occured [sic] here last night I expect.
I can not give you many of the particulars. It was about 10 Oclock last night when the steamer White Cloud was seen to be on fire I had just gone to Bed and heard the Boat Bells ringing so I thought I would go down When I got there Ed Bates was on fire to[o] and when she got to Burning pretty well she Broke Loose and floating down the warf she fired all the Boats about 36 [21] in number the Levy caught fire above Locust Street and swept evry thing down to the Old market . . . and as far Back as 2nd all the offices of the papers are destroyed except the Union. . . . There is no telling how many lives are lost some Burnt some drounde and some Blown to pieces with Powder there has been seven Bodyes dug out of the ruins some with their heads and legs and arms all Blown off. . . . Evry Body as far Back as 4th Street were moveing out we did not move out but was all ready bundled up. So I did not go to bed attall

Shipped, In Good Order and Well Conditioned, by N. STILLMAN & CO.,

For account and risk of whom it may concern, on board the good Steam Boat called the *Cecilia* whereof Throckmorton is Master for the present voyage, now lying in the port of Galena, and bound for Saint Peters, Being marked and numbered as below, and are to be delivered without delay, in like good order, at the port of Saint Peter (unavoidable damages of the river and fire only, excepted,) unto F. Steele first Mellio, or to his assigns, he or they paying freight at the rate of One Dollar

In Witness Whereof, the Master or Clerk of said Steam Boat, hath affirmed to three bills of lading, all of this tenor and date, one of which being accomplished, the others to stand void.

Dated at Galena, this 25 day of Oct 1845

MARKS	ARTICLES.	WEIGHT.
E × E	Six Kegs Powder	
S P	One Half Bbl Lard	

CHARGES.

Freight advanced, ...
Charges do. . . . .
Storage, ...
Labor, ...
Drayage, ...
Advancing, ...
Receiving and forwarding,
Bills Lading, ...

CECILIA

The *Cecilia* was a 111-ton craft that was built at Pittsburgh in 1841. She was later enlarged to 128 tons. Joseph Throckmorton was sole owner and captained the *Cecilia* in 1845 and 1846. When the Mexican War broke out, Captain Throckmorton brought the United States Dragoons stationed at Fort Crawford and Fort Atkinson down to St. Louis on the *Cecilia*. During the remainder of the season many volunteers crowded her decks. The *Cecilia* plied the Upper Mississippi until 1847 when she was abandoned and disappeared from the records.

The six kegs of powder and one-half barrel of lard were directed to the attention of Franklin Steele for G. W. and W. G. Ewing. Steele was born in Pennsylvania in 1813 and came to Minnesota in 1837. He became sutler of Fort Snelling in 1838; took a prominent part in the development of water power at the Falls of St. Anthony, and of logging and lumbering there. (See Chapter 41 for sketch of Captain Throckmorton).

SMITH BROTHERS & CO.,

WHOLESALE DEALERS IN GROCERIES;

ALSO, FORWARDING, COMMISSION AND PRODUCE MERCHANTS,

NO. 17 FRONT STREET, ST. LOUIS.

Shipped, In good order and condition, by **SMITH BROTHERS & CO.,** on account and risk of whom it may concern, on board the good Steamboat, called the *Senator* whereof *Harris* is Master for the present voyage, now lying at the port of St. Louis, the following packages or articles, marked or numbered as below, which are to be delivered, without delay, in like good order, at the Port of *Stillwater & Lake Pepin* (the dangers of the river and fire only excepted,) unto *Churchill & Nelson & Nelson Gilbut FG* or to _____ assigns, he or they to pay freight for the said goods at the rate of _____ *75 ₹ 100* and charges.

IN WITNESS WHEREOF, the Owner, Master or Clerk of said Steamboat hath affirmed to three Bills of Lading, all of this tenor and date; one of which being accomplished the others to stand void.

Dated at ST. LOUIS, this _____ 9th _____ day of _____ October _____ 1848   Chambers & Knapp, printers, Republican office.

Marks:	Articles.	Weight.
Churchill & Nelson Stillwater	10 Boxes Candles 2 Bbls Peaches 8 Sacks Dry Apples 1 Roll Line A. C. Monfort	
Nelson Gilbut FG Lake Pepin —	3 Sacks Dry Apples 6 Boxes Candles 1 Bbl Dry Apples 4 Grind Stones A. C. Monfort	

SENATOR

The *Senator* was built at Wheeling, Virginia, in 1846 and was 144 feet long, 22 feet breadth of beam, 4 feet depth of hold, and measured 121 tons. She was originally designed for the St. Louis and Keokuk trade and was owned by St. Louis and Quincy interests. A bill of lading, which was dated at St. Louis on August 13, 1847, showed the *Senator* captained by Daniel Smith Harris with A. C. Monfort as clerk. The same names appear on the above bill of lading issued by Smith Brothers & Company of St. Louis on October 9, 1848. The *Senator* ran in opposition to the *Dr. Franklin* until the close of the season of 1848 when Captain Harris sold the *Senator* to his opponents and agreed to remain in the Galena-St. Louis lead trade. The creation of the Territory of Minnesota in 1849 completely changed the picture and Captain Harris bought the *Dr. Franklin No. 2* to run in opposition to the "Old Doctor" *Franklin* and the *Senator.*

L. CHURCHILL & CO,
DEALERS IN HIDES, FURS, AND PELTRIES,
No. 2 Pine Street, St. Louis, Mo.

Shipped, IN GOOD ORDER AND CONDITION, BY L. CHURCHILL & CO.,

On board the good Steamboat called the *Doct Franklin* whereof _Lodwick_ is Master for the present voyage, now lying at the port of *St. Louis*, the articles marked and numbered as below, which are to be delivered, in like order and condition, (the dangers of river navigation and fire, only, excepted,) at the Port of _Stillwater & Nelsons Landing_ unto _Churchill & Nelson & McG_ or to their assigns, he or they paying freight for said goods at the rate of _Twenty five cents per 100 pounds_.

In witness whereof, The Owner, Master or Clerk of the said Steamboat hath affirmed to all of this tenor and date, one of which being accomplished, the others to stand void. _4_ Bills of Lading,

Dated at St. Louis, this _3_ day of _April_ 184 _9_

MARKS.	ARTICLES.	WEIGHT.
C & N Stillwater	1 Boxes Boots & Shoes	385
	2 " Tin Ware —	456
	1 Double Box Axes	120
	1 Box Merchandise	50
	1 Box G Sea	
	1 Bunk Oven —	
N. G Mc. Nelson Landing	5 Cases Boots & Shoes	280
1 Box G Sea	1 Box Tin Ware —	287
1 Bunk Oven	1 " Axes	60
	12 pc Castings	258
	1 noaly of Lighter	
	R F Blakely	

DR. FRANKLIN

The *Doctor Franklin* was the first boat of what developed into the Minnesota Packet Company. Built in Wheeling, Virginia, in 1847, she was 156 feet long, 24 feet breadth of beam, 4 feet 2 inches depth of hold, and measured 149 tons. The *Dr. Franklin* was owned by Captain M. W. Lodwick together with Orrin Smith, Ben H. Campbell, Russell Blakeley, and Nicholas Corwith of Galena. The bill of lading of April 3, 1849, shows M. W. Lodwick as master and Russell Blakeley as clerk. The freight—boots and shoes, tin ware, axes, and other merchandise—was destined for Nelson's Landing at the foot of Lake Pepin and Stillwater on the St. Croix. When Captain D. S. Harris brought out the *Dr. Franklin No. 2*, the first *Dr. Franklin* was referred to as the *"Old Doctor"* but never as the *"No. 1."* The *Dr. Franklin* was rammed by the *Galena* in 1854 and proved a total loss.

DAVID BARTLEY,

Dealer in Wines, Liquors, Habana Cigars, Tobacco, &c.

NO. 61 MAIN STREET, GALENA.

Shipped, *in good order and condition, by* David Bartley, *on account and risk of whom it may concern, on board the good Steamboat called the* ___Dr & e Franklin___ *whereof* ___P. Lodwick___ *is Master for the present voyage, now lying at* ___Galena___ *and bound for* ___Stillwater___ *the following articles, marked or numbered as below, which are to be delivered, without delay, in like good order, at the port of* ___Stillwater___ *(unavoidable dangers of the river and fire only excepted,) unto* ___Short Proctor & Co.___ *or to their assigns, he or they paying freight for said goods, at the rate of* ___Seventy five cents per cwt Barrel and twenty five cents per 100 lb___

In Witness Whereof, *The Owner, Master or Clerk of said boat has affirmed to* ___Three___ *Bills of Lading, all of this tenor and date, one of which being accomplished, the others to stand void. Dated at Galena, this* __14__ *day of* ___May___ *185* __3__

MARKS.		ARTICLES.	WEIGHT.
B. S. W. Taylors Falls	3	Barrels Whiskey	
	1 "	Brandy	
	1 "	Old Rye Whiskey	
	1 "	Crackers	100
Care of Short Proctor & Co. Stillwater	1 Keg (10 Galls)	Gin	80
	1 " "	Port Wine	80
	1 " "	Dark Brandy	80
	1 " "	St. Croix Rum	80
	1 " "	Peach Brandy	80
	1 " (5 Galls)	Holland Gin	50
	1 " "	Lemon Syrup	50
	2 Boxes	Tobacco	50
	1 "	Pint Flasks	40
	1 "	Smoking Tobacco	30
	1 "	Bar Tumblers	70
	1 "	Oysters	55
	1 "	Decanters	40
	1 "	Cigars	30
	1 Jug	Peppermint	15
	1 "	Bitters	15
			945

Geo. C. Blish

DR. FRANKLIN

The quantity of hard liquor listed might prove disconcerting until one notes that David Bartley was a Galena dealer in wines, liquors, Havana cigars, and tobacco. Destined for Stillwater, much of it was doubtless consumed by St. Croix River lumber jacks. Preston Lodwick, a brother of M. W. Lodwick, served as master and George C. Blish was chief clerk.

NICHOLAS DOWLING,

Importer and Wholesale Dealer in Hardware, Copper, Tin Plate, Steel, Iron, Nails, Stoves, Castings, &c. and Manufacturer of Tin, Copper and Sheet Iron Ware,

No. 3 DIAGONAL AND No. 213 MAIN STREETS, GALENA, ILLINOIS.

Shipped, In good order, and well conditioned, by

NICHOLAS DOWLING,

for account and risk of whom it may concern, on board the good Steam Boat called the Doctor Franklin *whereof is Master for the present voyage,* P. L. Lunicke *now lying at the Port of* Galena, *and bound for* St. Alexander *the following packages or articles, marked as below, which are to be delivered, without delay, in like good order, at the Port of* Stillwater, *(the dangers of river navigation, fire and unavoidable accidents excepted,) unto* Messrs Short Proctor & Co *or to their assigns; he or they paying freight for the said goods at the rate of* 50 ¢ hund.lb. ~ ~paid on Cp lighting & ferry.

Haven, print. 50 Third St. Pittsburgh.

In Witness Whereof, The Owner, Master or Clerk of said boat has affirmed to 3 *bills of lading, of this tenor and date, one of which being accomplished, the other to stand void.*

Dated at Galena, this 15th *day of* October 1853

MARKS.		WEIGHT.
S.P.& Co	1 Cook Stoves & Contents	
	3 Oval Heaters	
	1 Pots	
	12 Joints of Pipe	
	3 Bake Ovens	
	3 Oven Lids } 12)	
	8 Pieces of Sleigh Shoes 130	
	2 Boxes Mdse	
	40	113

CHARGES.

DR. FRANKLIN

That Galena was still an important entrepot on the Upper Mississippi is attested by the variety of hardware being forwarded by Nicholas Dowling aboard the *Dr. Franklin* for Stillwater, Minnesota. Cook stoves, bake ovens, oval heaters, and oven lids bring to mind the bitter cold winters in the North Star State. Mid-October meant the closing of navigation was fast approaching and the Ice Gnomes would soon close the Father of Waters to steamboats for four or five months. The inclusion of "8 Pieces of Sleigh Shoes" in the shipment indicated that Minnesotians had to prepare for the only means of overland transportation that would be available. Note the three *Dr. Franklin* bills of lading quote 25¢, 50¢, and 75¢ per hundred pounds for the same destinations, the lower figures actually being for the entire trip from St. Louis to Stillwater. The more than five thousand bills of lading in the writer's possession present a colorful picture of pioneer needs, and how they were supplied by steamboats more than a century ago.

JESUP AND COMPANY,

COMMISSION AND FORWARDING MERCHANTS,

DUNLEITH, ILLINOIS.

THE NORTH-WESTERN TERMINUS OF THE ILLINOIS CENTRAL RAILROAD ON THE MISSISSIPPI RIVER.

No. _____   Dunleith, _____ 1855

Shipped, in good order, by JESUP & CO. on board the Steamer _____ bound for _____ following described articles, marked and numbered as per margin, which we agree to deliver in like good order, dangers of Fire and Navigation excepted, unto _____ he or they paying freight on same at the rate of _____

In Testimony Whereof, the Master, Mate or Clerk of said boat hath affixed his signature unto _____ bills of lading, all of this tenor and date, one of which being accomplished the others to be of no effect.

MARKS AND NUMBERS.	ARTICLES.	WEIGHT.

ALHAMBRA

The *Alhambra* was a 187-ton sternwheeler built at McKeesport, Pennsylvania, in 1854 and claimed Pittsburgh as her first home port. She entered the Upper Mississippi trade in 1854 and appeared regularly in that trade for seven years through 1861. She was captained by Preston Lodwick in 1854 and bought by the Minnesota Packet Company in 1855 with William H. Gabbert as her master.

The bills of lading from Galena and Dunleith merchants reveal the *Alhambra* as a very busy boat. In 1860, the *Alhambra* and the *Fanny Harris* carried 500 delegates from the Chicago Convention that nominated Lincoln for president on an excursion from Dubuque to Clinton whence they returned to Chicago by rail. During the fall of 1860, William H. Seward was accompanied by Charles Francis Adams and his son on a campaign tour of the Upper Mississippi. On their return trip from St. Paul they were forced to take the *Alhambra* downstream. "Old and bad at the best," the *Alhambra* was crowded with passengers. The elder Adams declared the condition of the berths so "dubious that I deemed it most prudent not to risk the reception of vermin. Hence I was awake most of the night." A reasonably speedy boat, the *Alhambra* made a great deal of money for the Minnesota Packet Company. She was burned on the Cumberland River after being sold south and disappeared from the record in 1863.

The commission and forwarding merchants, Jesup and Company, were intimately associated with the organization and construction of the Dubuque and Sioux City Railroad. Thus, J. P. Farley was elected first president and F. S. Jesup the treasurer of a railroad that later became the Iowa Branch of the Illinois Central.

The B. H. Campbell firm, wholesale grocers of Galena, together with the Corwiths, Galena bankers, were the principal stockholders in the Minnesota Packet Company, then called the Galena & Minnesota Packet Company.

B. H. CAMPBELL.   J. R. JONES.

B. H. CAMPBELL & CO.

Wholesale Grocers, Commission and Forwarding Merchants,

No. 35 LEVEE, GALENA, ILL.

Shipped *in good order,* by **B. H. CAMPBELL & CO.** on board the *good Steamboat* *Alhambra* Capt. *Laurel* the following articles, marked as below, which are to be delivered, without delay, in like good order (the unavoidable dangers of navigation and fire excepted,) to *Short Carreter & Co.* at .... paying freight for the same at the rate of ....

In Witness Whereof, The Owner, Master or Clerk of said boat has affirmed to ...... Bills of Lading, all of this tenor and date, one of which being accomplished, the others to stand void. Dated at Galena this *13* day of *Oct* 1854

MARKS.	ARTICLES.	WEIGHT.

(handwritten ledger of shipped articles)

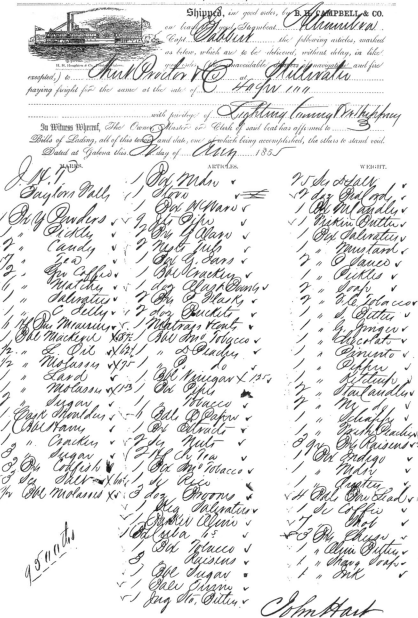

Shipped, *in good order, by* B. H. CAMPBELL & CO. *on board good Steamboat* _____ *Capt.* _____ *the following articles, marked as below, which are to be delivered, without delay, in like good order, (the unavoidable dangers of navigation and fire excepted,)* to _____ *at* _____ *paying freight for the same at the rate of* _____

_____ *with privilege of* _____

In Witness Whereof, *The Owner, Master or Clerk of said boat has affirmed to* _____ *Bills of Lading, all of this tenor and date, one of which being accomplished, the others to stand void.*

Dated at Galena this _____ *day of* _____ 185__

MARKS.	ARTICLES.	WEIGHT.

BURNS & RENTGEN,
WHOLESALE GROCERS, FORWARDING & COMMISSION MERCHANTS
LEVEE, KEOKUK, IOWA.

April 4, 185*7*

Shipped, In Good Order, by **BURNS & RENTGEN,** on the good Steamboat *Die Vernon* whereof _____ is Captain, now lying at **Keokuk,** the following articles, to be delivered without delay, in like good order, at *St. Louis* (unavoidable dangers of the river and fire only excepted,) unto *Wm. Megren* freight *as below + chgs. $9.15.*

Bills of Lading.

Clemens, Printer, Keokuk, Iowa.

MARKS.	ARTICLES.	WEIGHT.
Jooks. Branch & Trust St. Louis Mo From Dutch & Cox Eddyville	1 Box Saws 1 Circular Do Frt. 1.00 Chgs — 1.00	$1.00
T. S. Briggs Boston Mo Care Mudd & Hughes St. Louis	1 Cask Mdse 2 Boxes Do Frt. 1.00 Chgs — 0.15	2.00
Cutter & Tirrell St. Louis Mo From White & Coplan Oskaloosa	2 Boxes Mdse Frt. 1.00 Chgs 3.00	$1.00

DIE VERNON

The *Die Vernon* (second) was built at St. Louis in 1850 to replace the *Die Vernon* (first). She was a speedy 455-ton craft designed for the Keokuk trade but she did achieve considerable fame for several exciting excursions to the Falls of St. Anthony. (See Chapter 31.) The *Die Vernon* carried many Iowa troops from Keokuk to St. Louis during the Civil War.

Shipped, In good order, by **Crooks & Sanford,** on board the good Steamboat called the *Golden Era* .... Captain *Laughton* the following articles, marked or numbered as below, which are to be delivered without delay, in like good order,--the unavoidable dangers of navigation and fire only excepted,--to *Walcott & Conkey* .... at *Capoli Iowa* .... paying freight for the same at the rate of *One Dollar for Lot* .... Charges $ ....

with the privilege of Lighting, Towing ....

In Witness Whereof, The Owner, Master or Clerk of said Boat has affirmed to Three Bills of Lading, all of this tenor and date, one of which being accomplished the others to stand void.

Dated at Galena, Ills., this *31st* .... day of *Oct* 1859

MARKS.	ARTICLES.	WEIGHT
McDevitt & Ward Waukon Iowa Care Walcott & Conkey Capoli	8 Rolls Leather 1 Box Hrdwr Hrdw &c	400

GOLDEN ERA

The *Golden Era* was built at Wheeling, Virginia in 1852. She plied the Upper Mississippi for ten years. Her enrollment record in St. Louis shows that Captain Hiram Bersie owned one-half interest, Dan V. Dawley of Scott County one-sixteenth interest, and James Carter & Co. of Galena seven-sixteenths interest. The *Golden Era* was 180 feet long, 29 feet beam, 5 feet depth of hold, and measured 247 tons. The Lytle List makes her a 275-ton craft, which could well be after rebuilding her hull after an accident or perhaps to increase her speed or carrying capacity. The *Golden Era* had the honor of carrying ex-president Millard Fillmore on the Grand Excursion of the Rock Island Railroad to the Falls of St. Anthony in 1854. (See Chapter 32). The destination of the leather and hardware to Capoli would pose a problem to most students in 1968. A post office was established at Capoli in 1852 and discontinued in 1866. Although Capoli itself was not destined to develop, Allamakee County had grown from 277 population in 1849 to 10,843 in 1859. Known today by river men because of beautiful Capoli Bluff, Capoli itself has long disappeared, like more than a hundred other river towns between St. Louis and St. Paul that once aspired to greatness. The classic story in Minnesota is Rollingstone—a so-called paper town that held out dazzling albeit worthless opportunities for many a gullible pioneer.

The growth of Capoli and Allamakee County coincides with the rapid growth of Minnesota to the north—from Territorial status in 1849 to Statehood in 1858. The golden prospects forecast for many an Upper Mississippi townsite by such men as Albert Miller Lea, John Plumbe, Jr., and John B. Newhall in the period prior to Statehood had withered and died, sometimes even before the outbreak of the Civil War.

FRANK SMITH & CO.,

WHOLESALE AND RETAIL GROCERS,

AND FORWARDING AND COMMISSION MERCHANTS,

Steamboat Landing, Clayton, Iowa.

SHIPPED IN GOOD ORDER AND WELL CONDITIONED, by **FRANK SMITH & CO.**, *for account and risk of whom it may concern, on board the good Steamboat called the* .... *whereof* .... *is Master for the present voyage, now lying at the Port of* CLAYTON, *bound for* St Paul *being marked and numbered as below, and are to be delivered without delay, in like good order, at the port of* Stillwater *(unavoidable dangers of the River, and Fire, only excepted,) unto* Short Proctor & Co *or to* .... *assigns, he or they paying freight at the rate of* 40 cts *........................ for Bll*

In Witness Whereof, *the Master or Clerk of said Steamboat hath affirmed to three Bills of Lading, all of this tenor and date, one of which being accomplished, the others to stand void.*

DATED AT CLAYTON, *this* 1 *......... day of* ....August...... 1854

MARKS.	PACKAGES.	ARTICLES.	WEIGHT.
Elkader Extra H. Thompson & Co	25	Bbls Flour Windle Clk	

A visitor to Clayton in 1968 (population 130 in 1960) might marvel at the fact that this diminutive settlement could boast a "Steamboat Landing" in 1854.

The first settler was Frank Smith, a native of Massachusetts and the man who issued the bill of lading. Smith arrived in 1849, a roving Dubuque editor declared ten years later after visiting Clayton. At that time Smith was one of the proprietors of a steam saw and flouring mill, which was built in 1854. The Dubuque editor continues:

"Thompson, Whittemore & Co. have a steam flouring mill, which has been in operation three or four years, which turns out a hundred barrels of flour per day. The mill is similar to the water mill at Elkader, owned by Thompson & Davis. The arrangements of both for cleaning grain, for dusting bran &c., are excellent. Clayton flour stands well in the St. Louis market. Messrs. T. W. & Co. have twenty or thirty thousand bushels of wheat in store. J. A. Brown & Co. have also a large amount, together with other grain. It is estimated that 60,000 bushels of wheat, 25,000 corn, and about the same amount of oats, have found a shipping port here since the last harvest.

"Clayton has one foundry; one turner's shop; one cooper's shop; one cabinet shop; two wagon and two blacksmith shops; one butcher shop; one tin shop; one bakery; one grocery; three general variety stores . . . two hotels . . . one public school and two religious organizations, Methodist and Presbyterian.

"A steam ferry boat runs hourly across the river at this point.

"The population of Clayton is between five and six hundred."

The rise and fall of Clayton, like that of Capoli, was reenacted in a hundred river towns along the Upper Mississippi.

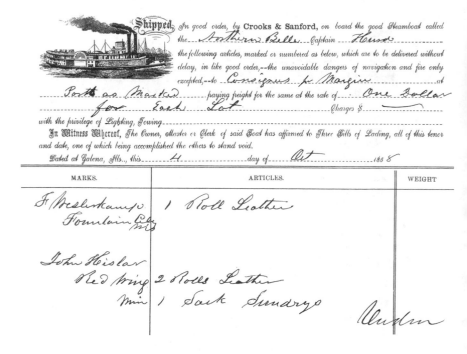

NORTHERN BELLE

The *Northern Belle* was a 498-ton sidewheeler that was launched at Cincinnati, Ohio, in 1856. She promptly entered the Minnesota trade with Galena as her home port. Preston Lodwick captained the *Northern Belle* her first season, and J. Y. Hurd served as her master the next four seasons. The *Northern Belle* was light of draft which made up in part for her lack of speed. She was a beautifully finished, very popular boat, and was a good money-maker during the fourteen seasons she churned the waters of the Upper Mississippi. During the winter of 1869-1870, according to George B. Merrick, the *Northern Belle* was dismantled, her cabin going into the new *Belle of La Crosse*. On June 22, 1861, the *Northern Belle* took five companies of the First Minnesota Regiment from Fort Snelling to La Crosse, on their way to Washington and the war front. The *Northern Belle* illustrates the confusion existing in steamboat tonnage. Merrick puts it at 298 tons, Lytle at 329 tons, and the *U.S. Supervising Inspectors of Steam Vessels* at Galena placed it at 498.23 tons, exactly 200 tons more than Merrick.

CANADA

The *Canada* was a 400-ton sidewheel packet built at Brownsville, Pennsylvania, in 1857. A popular boat in her early years, the *Canada* passed Dubuque in July of 1860 with $3,672 in passenger fares (both cabin and deck) and an immense amount of freight in her two barges. The *Canada* performed yeoman service during the Civil War. In June of 1861 she carried 300 recruits downstream from McGregor. On her next trip the *Canada* brought three companies from farther upstream. In 1866 the *Canada* won the unenviable title of "pest boat" because it was claimed she had several cholera deaths aboard who were tossed in the Mississippi before her arrival at Dubuque. The charge of cholera appeared to be unfounded but it lost the *Canada* many passengers in the years that followed. The *Canada* was also noted for having transported 756 Winnebago Indians down the Mississippi from their Minnesota homes in 1863. Bound for their new homes in Nebraska the "Injins" were described as a "squalid, wretched looking set."

Shipped, IN GOOD ORDER AND WELL CONDITIONED, BY **RAFFAUF & GEIGER,**

Grey Eagle's Barge FOR ACCOUNT AND RISK OF WHOM IT MAY CONCERN, on board the good Steamboat called the whereof *Harris* is Master for the present voyage, now lying at the Port of CASSVILLE, WIS., and bound for *St Louis*

being marked or numbered as below, and which are to be delivered, without delay, in like good order and condition, at the Port of

St Louis _____ (the unavoidable dangers of river navigation and fire only excepted,) unto

Wm L Ewing & Co or to *their* assigns, he or they paying freight for the said

goods at the rate of (9) *Nine cents pr. Bush. Wheat & (6) Six cent*

pr Bushel Oats *Priviledge to light, tow & Reship*

In Witness Whereof, the Owner, Master or Clerk of said Boat hath affirmed to __*3*__ Bills of Lading, of this tenor and
date, one of which being accomplished, the other to stand void.

Dated at CASSVILLE, WIS., this __*Eight*__ day of __*May*__ 18 *61*

MARKS.	ARTICLES.	WEIGHT.
R & Co Cassville Wis	348/ Three hundred & forty Eight Bags Wheat Seamless Bags 353) Three hundred fifty three Bags Oats, Osnaburg Bags Cooley CCR The above is a duplicate, the Original having been forwarded to the St Louis Insurance Co, the Grey Eagle having been a total Loss, and no B/L forwarded Raffauf & Geiger	

GREY EAGLE

The *Grey Eagle* was one of the fastest boats that ever turned a wheel on the Upper Mississippi. She was the darling of her colorful skipper, Daniel Smith Harris, who had incorporated all his ideas for a speedy craft into her construction. (See Chapters 42 and 43). When the *Grey Eagle* was wrecked on the Rock Island bridge in 1861, the disconsolate Captain Harris retired from the river. The above bill of lading is a duplicate of one made for shipment on the *Grey Eagle* which went down when she rammed into a pier of the Rock Island bridge on May 9, 1861.

11

The Story of the Western Engineer

ON THE EVE of the American Revolution Daniel Boone led a party of pioneers out of the Yadkin Valley in North Carolina and into the blue grass region of Kentucky, where one might live the life of a backwoodsman. By 1795 Boone found Kentucky becoming too crowded for comfort. Disliking to have a neighbor so close that he could see the smoke from his cabin, Boone once more moved westward, this time building a cabin fifty miles up the Missouri River in Spanish territory. He was then sixty years old. During the next twenty-five years he hunted and trapped along the Missouri. He died at the home of his son Nathan Boone in St. Charles County, Missouri, in 1820.[81]

At the time of Boone's death pioneer cabins were sprinkled for two hundred miles along both banks of the Missouri as far as Franklin and Chariton. Beyond lay a wilderness expanse inhabited by red men and dominated by the straggling trading posts of such empire builders as the Chouteaus of St. Louis and John Jacob Astor and his American Fur Company. Kansas City was yet unborn; and Joseph Robidoux did not found St. Joseph until 1826. Even in the settled area below Franklin, Jefferson City had not been laid out and six years were to pass before it became the permanent capital of Missouri. But hope and enthusiasm were not lacking among the pioneers. "Almost every settler, who has established himself on the Missouri", an eye-witness relates, "is confidently expecting that his farm is, in a few years, to become the seat of wealth and business, and the mart for an extensive district." [82]

St. Louis had waited five long years after the voyage of the *New Orleans* before the arrival of the first steamboat at her port. But the mushroom settlements along the lower Missouri welcomed their first steamboat only two years after the *Zebulon M. Pike* reached St. Louis. It was on May 21, 1819, that the departure from St. Louis of the steamboat *Independence* for Franklin and Chariton, Missouri, was announced by the *Missouri Intelligencer*. A week later the same newspaper recorded "with no ordinary sensations of pride and pleasure", the arrival of the *Independence* with passengers and a cargo of flour, whiskey, sugar, and iron castings. The *Independence* required only seven "sailing days" to reach Franklin : she was joyfully received by the inhabitants of that enterprising frontier community. Heavy artillery roared a salute of welcome from the shore and the *Independence* boomed a triumphant reply with her cannon.

The captain and passengers aboard the *Independence* were regaled with a grand dinner, and toasts were drunk in honor of the first steamboat to ascend the Missouri. "The grand *desideratum*, the important *fact* is now ascertained, *that steam boats can safely navigate the Missouri river*", declared the *Intelligencer* exultantly. "At no distant period may we see the industrious cultivator making his way as high as the *Yellow Stone*, and offering to the enterprising merchant and trader a surplus worthy of the fertile banks of the Missouri, yielding wealth to industry and enterprise." [83]

But this enthusiasm was short lived. The Missouri River was not yet conquered : the *Independence* may have arrived at Franklin in seven "sailing days", but she had actually been thirteen days en route. At that very moment a fleet of steamboats was steaming down the Ohio and up the Mississippi bent on conquering the Big Muddy. The expedition was financed by the government and had the backing of the army. Yet only one of these steamboats (the *Western Engineer*) was destined to stem the swift current of the Missouri successfully, as far as present-day Council Bluffs.

The story of the *Western Engineer* is linked with the expansion of the military frontier on both the Missouri and the Upper Mississippi. Late in 1817 President James Monroe appointed John C. Calhoun as his Secretary of War. Calhoun immediately dispatched expeditions to establish what later became Fort Snelling on the Upper Mississippi and Fort Atkinson on the Missouri. During the winter of 1818-1819 preparations went on apace. To Colonel James Johnson of Kentucky went three contracts : the first to transport clothing, ordnance, and military stores from Pittsburgh to St. Louis; the second to furnish supplies; and the third to transport supplies and troops by steamboat up the Missouri. It was the first time the government had dared to charter steam craft, and Calhoun was bitterly criticized for risking the success of the expedition on such a new and untried means of transportation.[84]

While James Johnson was securing steamboats to carry out his part of the contract the government suddenly decided to construct a steamboat at the United States Arsenal on the Allegheny River near Pittsburgh. It is not known whether this rash project was condemned as unfair to private capital. At any rate the new boat was launched on March 28, 1819, and christened the *Western Engineer* in honor of the engineering corps and her ultimate destination. Eye-witnesses declared she "embraced the watery element in the most graceful manner, under a national salute." She was a dingy looking craft, measuring only thirty tons and drawing but nineteen inches of water light. Her equipment was calculated to strike terror in the hearts of the Indians. In form she resembled a black, scaly serpent, rising out of the water, with waste steam escaping from her sculptured figurehead.

A mineralogist, a botanist, a geographer, and a painter, together with a considerable force of troops were aboard with Major Stephen H. Long when the boat steamed down the Ohio from Pittsburgh on May 5, 1819. The diminutive craft had no difficulty in descending the Falls of the Ohio; and she reached St. Louis on June 9th, thirty-six days after her departure from Pittsburgh. The *Western Engineer*, according to a St. Louis account of her arrival, anchored at the upper end of the town. "In passing the Independence and St. Louis, then at anchor before the town, she was saluted by these vessels . . . Her equipment is at once calculated to attract and to awe the savage. Objects pleasing and terrifying are at once before him : — artillery; the flag of the republic; portraits of a white man and an Indian shaking hands; the calumet of peace; a sword; then the apparent monster with a painted vessel on his back, the sides gaping with port-holes, and bristling with guns. Taken altogether, and without intelligence of her composition and design, it would require a daring savage to approach and accost her".[85]

The boat left St. Louis on June 21st and entered the mouth of the Missouri the following morning. In ascending to Fort Bellefontaine, a distance of four miles, she twice grounded on sandbars and had difficulty in getting afloat. Retarded by the strong current, impeded by sandbars and rafts of driftwood, the valves of her crude engine worn by the fine sand which hung suspended in the yellow, turgid Missouri, the *Western Engineer* toiled past Charbonniere, St. Charles, Cote sans Dessein, and on to Franklin. At Franklin the Indians recoiled in horror at the "monster of the deep" that smoked with fatigue and lashed the waves with violent exertion. Said one red man: "White man bad man, keep a great spirit chained and build fire under it to make it work a boat".

Leaving Franklin the *Western Engineer* churned past Chariton, Fort Osage, and on to the mouth of the "Konzas" River where Kansas City now stands. Nearby they found a party of "abandoned and worthless" white hunters whose deportment and dress appeared to surpass in uncouthness those of the rudest savages living in the vicinity. Puffing bravely up the sandbar-studded Missouri, the boat glided past Cow Island and the Nodaway River. She reached the mouth of Wolf River on September 1st. Here some hunters were sent ashore and returned with a "deer, a turkey, and three swarms of bees." Three days later many large catfish were caught, some of them weighing as much as fifty pounds. Finally, on September 17, 1819, the *Western Engineer* arrived at Fort Lisa, a trading post of the Missouri Fur Company located on the west bank of the Missouri a few miles above present-day Omaha. Here she went into winter quarters at a point which was designated as Engineer Cantonment — having ascended the Missouri farther than any other steamboat.[86]

Meanwhile the *Johnson*, the *Calhoun*, the *Expedition*, and the *Jefferson* had failed in their efforts to ascend the Missouri for any considerable distance. Despite his failure to fulfill his contract, Colonel Johnson estimated the cost of this service at $256,818.15. The amount staggered the committee appointed to investigate the bill; but it was endorsed by Quartermaster General Thomas S. Jesup. For the forty-day detention of the *Expedition* at the mouth of the Missouri, Johnson demanded of the government $13,333.33, or more than double the value of the boat. At the same time he asked $7200 for the thirty-six day delay of the *Johnson*. Such sums received the support of the Monroe administration, but drew a stern rebuke from the House Committee appointed to investigate this "Tea Pot Dome" of the "Era of Good Feeling". The committee

The Story of the *Western Engineer*

actually passed a resolution directing the Attorney General to "use all legal means" to recover $76,372.65 due the government.[87]

The difficulty of navigating the Missouri and the failure of the other steamboats to follow the *Western Engineer* necessitated a change in plans, and Lieutenant James D. Graham was ordered to steam down the Missouri to St. Louis with the *Western Engineer*, thence up the Mississippi to the "De Moyen rapids", and then down the same stream to Cape Girardeau, "taking such observations and sketches on the voyage as are requisite in constructing a chart of that part of the river and the adjacent country." [88]

If the ascent of the Missouri thwarted Colonel Johnson's steamboats in 1819, the problems of navigating the Upper Mississippi were hardly less difficult. During 1819 the War Department had ordered Major Thomas Forsyth to ship $2000 worth of goods by steamboat to the Sioux Indians above Prairie du Chien in payment for the site on which Fort Snelling was to be established. But at that time it was believed that the rapids could not be stemmed by steamboats, and so keelboats were used. The conquest of the Mississippi as far as the Des Moines Rapids would be no mean feat and would bring hope to an area even less populated than the banks of the Missouri.[89]

Little is known of this voyage on the Upper Mississippi, for in making his report Major Long merely states the results of the surveys of those aboard the *Western Engineer*. "The bottoms on the Upper Mississippi", Long reported, "contain less woodland, in proportion to their extent, than

[87]

those of the Missouri. The prairies upon this river also become more numerous and extensive as we proceed upward." The land was fertile, though hilly, and timbered in spots with cottonwood, blue and white ash, hackberry, black walnut, cherry, mulberry, hickory, and several varieties of oak. The population was located almost exclusively in the river valley and extended upwards about 160 miles. Especially numerous were the Salt River settlements around Louisiana, Missouri; but Long felt that the scarcity of timber, mill sites, and springs of water would prove a serious impediment to settlement in that region.[90]

It was left for Captain Stephen Watts Kearny to record the presence of the first steamboat known to have ascended the Upper Mississippi River as far as Keokuk. In his journal of August 15, 1820, Kearny wrote:

"At 8 A. M. we embarked on board our canoe & descended one mile, to the mouth of the Des Moines, where we found the Steam Boat, "Western Engineer", commanded by Lieut. Graham, who came here a week since, for the purpose of taking observations, &c. Put our baggage on board, & fastened the canoe to her. Near this saw a coffin containing the bones of an Indian tied fast to the centre of a large tree which was done at the request of the deceased to preserve his fame after the extinction of his body.

"Proceded at 10 & run about 15 miles when about 1 P. M. we found ourselves on the Sand bar & from which we endeavored, but without success, to extricate ourselves.

The Story of the *Western Engineer*

The boat has but few hands & those sick with fevers.
August 16th

"At 8 A. M. we succeeded after much exertion in getting off the Sandbar & in endeavoring to cross to the opposite shore to reach the channel, we ran on another bar about 200 yards from the one we left, & found ourselves even faster than before.

"At 2 P. M., aware of the uncertainty of the Steam Boat reaching St. Louis, and our party being desirous to proceed without loss of time we took to our canoe, & having a favorable breeze hoisted sail." [91]

Such unfavorable reports were doubtless responsible for the failure of steamboats to attempt the navigation of the Mississippi above the Des Moines Rapids before the voyage of the *Virginia*. Indeed the land was so sparsely populated below the rapids that there was little cause for steamboats to ascend above the mouth of the Missouri. Quincy and Keokuk were still unborn and even the site of Hannibal was beyond the fringe of settlement. Fifteen years were to pass before Mark Twain saw the light of day at Florida, Missouri; and it was not until 1839 that the four-year-old lad was to view the Mississippi at Hannibal.

12

The Voyage of the *Virginia*[92]

A MOTLEY crowd had gathered on the St. Louis levee on April 21, 1823. Squalid Indians intermingled with roughly clad immigrants, levee loungers, lead miners, and fur traders. A sprinkling of soldiers and officials added color to the general confusion and bustle. All eyes were centered on the steamboat *Virginia* which lay at the levee with steam in her boilers, preparing to carry government supplies to the posts on the Upper Mississippi.[93]

Built at Wheeling, Virginia, in 1819, the *Virginia* was a small stern-wheeler of 109.32 tons, owned by Redick McKee, James Pemberton, and seven others. She was 118 feet long, 18 feet 10 inches beam, and her depth was 5 feet 2 inches. She had a small cabin on deck but no pilot house, being guided by a tiller at the stern. James Pemberton acted as master occasionally, and John Crawford, it seems, held the official position of captain.[94]

Among the passengers aboard the boat was Major Lawrence Taliaferro, the Indian Agent at Fort St. Anthony (renamed Fort Snelling in 1824). Taliaferro superintended the movement of supplies. He no doubt imparted a great deal of information about the trip to Giacomo Constantine Beltrami, the Italian exile and explorer who was the sole chronicler of the events of the journey.[95] Another passenger was Great Eagle, a Sauk Indian chief,

The Voyage of the *Virginia*

whom William Clark had induced to come on board while his less fortunate tribesmen made their way along the banks. A Kentucky family bound for the lead mines at Galena was on board "with their arms and baggage, cats and dogs, hens and turkeys; the children too had their own stock." A woman missionary bound for the lead mines to work among the Indians completes the list of known passengers.

Finally all was in readiness : the last passenger had hastily scrambled aboard. Amid cries of farewell and the good wishes of those gathered on the levee to see her off, the *Virginia* swung gracefully out into the channel on an "enterprise of the boldest, of the most extraordinary nature; and probably unparalleled." Many skeptics shook their heads, doubtful of the practicability of steamboats crossing the rapids of the Mississippi. For days after the departure of the boat "there was a great speculation as to whether the steamboat would ever return".[96]

The current of the Mississippi seemed to grow swifter as the *Virginia* entered the Chain of Rocks channel a few miles above St. Louis. "We were approaching the mouth of the Missouri, which is only eighteen miles from that town", Beltrami remarked, "and notwithstanding the power of our steam-boat, we did not come in sight of this river before eight o'clock the following morning." The ease with which the boat passed the mouth of the Missouri was attributed to the presence of an island which obstructed the flow of that mighty stream, thereby breaking the pressure of its enormous volume.

Steamboating on Upper Mississippi

Sixteen miles above the mouth of the Missouri a series of towering bluffs attracted the attention of the venture-some Italian. "The eastern bank of the Mississippi, opposite the village called *Portage des Sioux*, leading from the Illinois to the Missouri", he noted, "rises in abrupt rocks, hewn by nature into perpendicular pillars." Piasa Bluff gave him an illusion of viewing the palaces of Pompey and Domitian on Lake Albano.

A few miles above the mouth of the Illinois, the *Virginia* entered the great bend of the Mississippi. Leaving picturesque *Cap au Gris* rock behind, she churned on past Clarksville to Louisiana, "two pretty rising villages" on the Missouri shore — the latter being about a hundred miles from St. Louis. With the exception of the forts along the way, Louisiana was the "last vestige of civilization" before Prairie du Chien was reached.

Beltrami designated the woodland region about present-day Quincy, Illinois, as the *Prairie des Liards* because of the extensive growth of poplar and cottonwood. He was amazed by the thick masses of trees which covered the islands and flood plains and stretched as far as the eye could see to the low-lying hills beyond. It would be a bad country in which to get lost, he thought.

One day while the *Virginia* was wooding up, Beltrami ventured alone into the forest. A flock of wild turkeys having eluded his pursuit, he continued his walk, soliloquizing on the beauty of the plant and animal life about him. Suddenly realizing that considerable time had elapsed, he hurried back to the river only to find the boat gone. Panic-stricken, he discharged his gun frantically, hoping to attract attention. The echoes resounded vainly in the great forest. Fortunately the boat struck a sandbar and Beltrami's absence was discovered. A canoe, sent to the rescue, brought him back completely exhausted from his mad rush through the heavy underbrush along the muddy bank in pursuit of the boat.

When Beltrami returned to the *Virginia* he found that Great Eagle and the pilot had quarreled because the Indian had recommended taking a certain channel while the pilot insisted on taking another. When the boat struck the sandbar Great Eagle was so vexed that without further ado he plunged into the stream, swam ashore, and joined his fellow tribesmen who were making their way along the bank. This incident probably occurred in the "Channel of the Foxes" a short distance below Fort Edwards.

The following day the *Virginia* arrived at Fort Edwards, where Great Eagle was found surrounded by members of his tribe. They had arrived before the boat, had set up a temporary encampment, and "were exchanging furs with the traders of the South-west Company." Great Eagle came aboard to get his bow, quiver, and gun. He was still exasperated with the officers of the boat but greeted Beltrami warmly. The latter, coveting the scalp of a Sioux chief that Great Eagle carried "suspended by the hair to the handle of his tomahawk", took advantage of this favorable moment to secure the much prized trophy. Upon visiting the Sauk lodges, Beltrami was struck by the perfect equality exhibited by the Indians : even their dogs and their young bears and otters were treated as belonging to the community.

Beltrami carefully observed the position of the fort, "built upon a promontory on the eastern bank of the Mississippi; its situation, which is very pleasant, commands a great extent of the river and the surrounding country, as well as the mouth of the river Le Moine [Des Moines] which descends from the west and is navigable for three hundred miles into the interior. The banks of this river are inhabited by the Yawohas [Iowas], a savage people, who have been almost entirely destroyed by the Sioux."

At the time of the voyage of the *Virginia* the land west of the Mississippi and north of the Missouri boundary line was "distinguished only under the name of *Savage Lands*". No traces of white civilization existed in what is now Iowa and Minnesota, other than a few scattered huts belonging to half-breed traders.

After being pleasantly entertained by the officers of the garrison, the visitors boarded the *Virginia* and continued on their journey to the foot of the Des Moines or Lower Rapids, a hitherto impassable barrier for steamboats. In 1820 the steamboat *Western Engineer* had proceeded to this point, but even the conqueror of the Missouri did not dare venture farther. Indeed, she had repeatedly grounded in the channel below Fort Edwards and had returned to St. Louis only with the greatest difficulty.

In spite of an excellent stage of water, the *Virginia* proceeded cautiously, since the sharp jutting rock could easily crush the hull of the stoutest steamboat. For nine miles

The Voyage of the *Virginia*

the perilous ascent continued, until the boat succeeded in squirming her way up to the "Middle of the Rapids of the Moine". There she was forced to return, her heavy load and draught being too great to effect the passage; it was only by sheer good luck that the vessel escaped a rock and was saved from being dashed to pieces. Fortunately the damage was slight. Two days later, with a considerably lightened cargo, the *Virginia* succeeded in reaching the head of the rapids, where a party of Sauk Indians was encamped on the east bank of the river, near the present site of Nauvoo, Illinois.

Nine miles farther upstream the ruins of old Fort Madison on the west bank attracted Beltrami's attention. It had been established in 1808 as an entrepôt for the Indian trade of that region. The government had abandoned its factory system in 1822, thus leaving the field open to the "South West Company" which, together with a rival organization, monopolized the commerce of almost the whole Indian region.

A short distance above Fort Madison the *Virginia* glided by the mouth of the "Bête Puante" or Skunk River. The Indian name for the precipitous "Yellow Hills" on the east bank of the river is perpetuated in the town of Oquawka, Illinois. Not far above the yellow banks, the mouth of the "Yahowas" or Iowa River came in view on the west side. From this point on the beauty of the Mississippi held Beltrami spellbound. "Wooded islands, disposed in beautiful order by the hand of nature, continually varied the picture : the course of the river, which had become calm and smooth, reflected the dazzling rays of the sun like glass; smiling hills formed a delightful contrast with the immense prairies, which are like oceans, and the monotony of which is relieved by isolated clusters of thick and massy trees."

Leaving the Grande Prairie Mascotin in her wake, the *Virginia* rounded a bend in the river just in time for Beltrami to gain a "distant and exquisitely blended view" of Rock Island. Fort Armstrong stood at the foot of this island on a plateau about fifty feet above the level of the river. The eastern bank of the Mississippi above the mouth of Rock River was lined with an encampment of Fox Indians, allies of the Sauk and resembling them in features, dress, weapons, customs, and language. On the western shore of the Mississippi "a semicircular hill, clothed with trees and underwood", enclosed a fertile spot carefully cultivated into fields and kitchen gardens. The fort saluted with four discharges of cannon, and the Indians paid the same compliment with their muskets.

While the *Virginia* lay at Fort Armstrong preparing for the ascent of the Upper Rapids, Beltrami paid a visit to the Indian village of Saukenuk. Situated about three miles to the southeast on the north bank of the Rock River, this was the largest village of the Sauk tribe in the Mississippi Valley.

Beltrami was astonished at the skill exhibited by the youthful Sauk Indians with their bows and arrows : they almost exhausted his supply of coins by hitting with ease small pieces twenty-five paces distant. To prevent the utter depletion of his purse he was forced to remove these costly targets to a distance of thirty-five paces. Smoked bear and highly flavored roots served as welcome refreshments during this sport.

The Sauk had never heard of any people other than the French, English, Spaniards, and Americans. They were surprised to learn that Beltrami was of a different nationality; their surprise turned to veneration when he told them that he had come from the moon; but when the wily Italian attempted to gain a "clandestine entrance" to the medicine dance he was promptly ejected. Nor did his celestial homeland enable him to secure a medicine bag until he had made a present of "good whiskey" both to the person who gave it to him and to the high priest whose sanction was necessary to secure it.

The following day, with the assistance of Colonel George Davenport and his "Patroon Debuts" or steersman, the *Virginia* began the ascent of the Rock Island or Upper Rapids, which Beltrami observed were longer and swifter than the Des Moines or Lower Rapids.[97] Suddenly the boat struck a rock and stuck fast. Every hand was instantly at work endeavoring to free the stranded craft. The fact that the river had been rising for two days helped the boat, which Beltrami believed would otherwise have remained "nailed" fast.

The crew was entirely exhausted by the labor involved in getting the boat over the rapids, so the captain held her over for a few hours near the present site of Le Claire, Iowa, in order to give the men an opportunity to recover from their fatigue. Beltrami went ashore and succeeded in shooting a large rattlesnake with which he returned in triumph to his fellow travelers.

Six miles above the rapids the *Virginia* passed a village of Foxes on the west bank of the river. A little higher up she passed the Wapsipinicon River flowing into the Mississippi from the west and the "Marais d'Ogé" or Marais Dosier Slough on the east bank. Steaming on past the present site of Clinton, Beltrami observed the "Potatoe Prairie" on the west side known today as Pomme de Terre Prairie. Higher up, after passing the rivers *La Pomme* and *La Garde* which ran westward, he "saw a place called the Death's-heads; a field of battle where the Foxes defeated the Kikassias [Kaskaskia], whose heads they fixed upon poles as trophies of their victory." This was at Têtes des Morts Creek, which empties into the Mississippi at the northern boundary of Jackson County.

The *Virginia* stopped at the mouth of the Fever (Galena) River and Beltrami considered its name "in perfect conformity with the effect of the bad air which prevails there." The family from Kentucky and the woman missionary debarked, while the other passengers spent a few hours visiting the lead mines.

Twelve miles above the mouth of the Fever River the lead mines of Dubuque came into view. The Italian visitor was again obliged to resort to the use of "all-powerful whiskey" to obtain permission to see the mines. He found that the Indians were carrying on just enough mining to satisfy their needs in trade. They melted the lead in holes

The Voyage of the *Virginia*

dug in the rock and reduced it to pigs in this manner. It was then carried across the river, for they would permit no white man to come to the mines to get lead. Despite these precautions Beltrami considered the mines so valuable and the Americans so enterprising that he doubted whether the Indians would long retain possession of them. His canny forecast was realized exactly a decade later.

Leaving the mines of Dubuque, the *Virginia* wound her way through a country of ever increasing beauty. Beltrami's pen was "struck motionless" as for forty miles the variety of scenes and objects attracted his attention and excited his astonishment. Rude and unkempt in its pristine grandeur, Eagle Point opened the way to "Prairie Macotche", as Beltrami labelled present-day Maquoketa Chute. At length a place which he felt might be called *Longue Vue* [Buena Vista?], elicited this description:

"Twelve small isolated mountains present themselves in defile, and project one behind another, like side-scenes. They are intersected by small valleys; each has its rivulet, which divides it, and reflects from its limpid streams the beauty of the trees by which its banks are adorned. These hills exhibit a mixture of the gloomy and the gay, while those which appear at the back of the scene are veiled with magical effect in the transparent mist of the horizon. On the eastern bank a verdant meadow rises with gentle slope to a distant prospect, formed and bounded by a small chain of abrupt mountains. Little islands, studded with clumps of trees, among which the steamboat was winding its course, appeared like the most enchanting gardens."

Steamboating on Upper Mississippi

A deserted Fox village was seen on the banks of the Turkey River. Eight miles farther up, the *Virginia* passed the "Old Village de la Port" where Guttenberg now stands. There the pretended territorial jurisdiction of the Foxes was said to terminate, but these red warriors often hunted beyond their domain, thus frequently precipitating bloody wars with the Sioux.

The importance of the Wisconsin River as a highway for the fur trader was noted as the *Virginia* passed the confluence of that stream with the Mississippi. Six miles above this point the boat hove in sight of Prairie du Chien. She had traveled almost five hundred miles, and this little French settlement was the only village to present any of the earmarks of white civilization. South of Prairie du Chien stood a "wretched wooden fort, named fort Crawford".

The passengers lost no time in poking about the interesting French settlement. Some "gloomy and ferocious" Winnebago Indians caught Beltrami's eye, but he refused to shake hands with "Mai-Pock" upon learning that he had regaled his friends with human flesh. This was "an expression of contempt the most severe and humiliating an Indian" could receive. The industrious and friendly Menominee were commended for their refusal to join the English in the War of 1812.

Bidding farewell to Prairie du Chien, where Joseph Rolette had politely entertained them, the voyagers began the last lap of the long journey to the northernmost military post on the Upper Mississippi. An uncharted channel fully two hundred miles in extent remained to be traversed before Captain Crawford could discharge the last of his cargo and once more turn the bow of his gallant little craft downstream.

About six miles from Prairie du Chien, near the mouth of the Yellow River, stood a rock which was painted red and yellow every year and which the Indians looked upon with veneration. The Mississippi at this point presented scenes of peculiar novelty. "The hills disappear, the number of islands increases, the waters divide into various branches, and the bed of the river in some places extends to a breadth of nearly three miles, which is greater by one half than at St. Louis; and, what is very remarkable, its depth is not diminished".

Conspicuous landmarks were noted as the boat threaded this network of channels. At the foot of Winneshiek Slough a mighty rampart called "Cape Winebegos" still stands guard over what is now Lynxville, Wisconsin. Cone-shaped Capoli Bluff, a few miles below present-day Lansing, was described as Cape à l'Ail Sauvage. The whole region is known to-day as the Winneshiek Bottoms and forms an important section of the Upper Mississippi Wild Life Refuge.

The *Virginia* usually stopped at dusk, since it would have been foolhardy to proceed in an unknown channel hitherto unnavigated by a steamboat. But one evening as they were about to tie up for the night it was found possible to go on, for suddenly the entire river was illuminated by the distant glow of a gigantic forest fire.

Steamboating on Upper Mississippi

"It was perfectly dark, and we were at the mouth of the river Yahowa [Upper Iowa]", wrote Beltrami, "when we saw at a great distance all the combined images of the infernal regions in full perfection . . . The venerable trees of these eternal forests were on fire, which had communicated to the grass and brushwood, and these had been borne by a violent north-west wind to the adjacent plains and valleys. The flames towering above the tops of the hills and mountains, where the wind raged with most violence, gave them the appearance of volcanoes, at the moment of their most terrific eruptions; and the fire winding in its descent through places covered with grass, exhibited an exact resemblance of the undulating lava of Vesuvius or Ætna . . . This fire accompanied us with some variations for fifteen miles . . . Showers of large sparks, which fell upon us, excited terror in some, and laughter in others. I do not believe that I shall ever again witness such astonishing contrasts of light and darkness, of the pathetic and the comic, the formidable and the amusing, the wonderful and the grotesque."

The *Virginia* traveled all night by the aid of this superb torch. During the night she passed the Bad Axe and Raccoon rivers, but at dawn the tired craft ran aground "by way of resting herself".

A few miles above the river *Aux Racines* [Root], Beltrami noticed a place called "Casse-Fusils" (broken muskets) from the fact that a party of Indians, jealous of another band armed with English guns, attacked them and broke their muskets. This incident probably occurred

[102]

The Voyage of the *Virginia*

opposite the present site of La Crosse, Wisconsin, near a point now known as Broken Arrow Slough.

Puffing on past the mouth of the Black River, the *Virginia* entered the beautiful and romantic country around what is now the city of Winona. The majestic bluffs were likened to those on the Rhine between Bingen and Coblenz. All Beltrami's powers of expression were exhausted by mighty Trempealeau, the mountain that walks in the water. "Amid a number of delightful little islands, encircled by the river, rises a mountain of conical form equally isolated. You climb amid cedars and cypresses, strikingly contrasted with the rocks that intersect them, and from the summit you command a view of valleys, prairies, and distances in which the eye loses itself. From this point I saw both the last and the first rays of a splendid sun gild the lovely picture. The western bank presents another illusion to the eye. Mountains, ruggedly broken into abrupt rocks, which appear cut perpendicularly into towers, steeples, cottages, &c., appear precisely like towns and villages."

A Sioux Indian encampment was observed at *"la Prairie aux Ailes"* [Winona], and here the *Virginia* landed. Wrapped in a wretched buffalo skin, Chief Wabasha came on board followed by a motley array of warriors. Major Taliaferro greeted Wabasha with "plenty of shakes by the hand", and smoked the calumet of peace while Beltrami acted as "ape" to this "troop of comedians". Wabasha was greatly impressed with the construction and performance of the white man's boat. The intricacy of the engine especially appealed to him. When members of the Stephen H. Long expedition passed his village in keelboats a short time later he expressed deep interest in the *Virginia* and was particularly curious about the construction of the engine and the principle on which it worked.[98]

Leaving Chief Wabasha behind, the *Virginia* entered a section of the Mississippi that was "diversified by hills, plains, meadows, and forests." The Buffalo and Chippewa rivers were seen flowing into the Mississippi from the east. Below modern Wabasha the Embarras or Zumbro River drained a region called the Great Encampment.

Just above the mouth of the Chippewa, the boat entered an "elliptical amphitheatre" known as Lake Pepin. Encircled by little hills and varying from one to three miles in width throughout its course of twenty-two miles, Lake Pepin is so deep that boats have no difficulty in navigating it even during seasons of low water. In stormy weather its waters are lashed into a fury and steamboats seldom venture upon it. As the *Virginia* was plowing her way through, a terrific squall struck the lake and it was only by means of skillful navigation on the part of Captain Crawford that she was able to wallow her way to safety. Staring Indians, transfixed with astonishment upon the bank, were the only spectators of this thrilling and almost fatal incident.

On the eastern shore near the head of Lake Pepin towers romantic Maiden Rock. Another Sioux village hove in sight at the Mountain of the Grange, now known as Barn Bluff at Red Wing. Here again the chief and his leading

The Voyage of the *Virginia*

warriors came on board. After the travelers solemnly smoked the peace pipe and gave ear to some long and woefully dull speeches, the *Virginia* continued upstream.

Above the mouth of the Cannon River the Mississippi became narrower and less studded with islands, while the bluffs were steeper and more imposing. All on board must have experienced a thrill as they passed the St. Croix River and realized that the long journey was almost at an end. Medicine Wood, Pine Bend, and Little Crow's Village at the Grand Marais were soon left behind. While the boat was wooding up, the passengers were told of a small valley of cedars, firs, and cypresses leading to a cavern named in honor of Jonathan Carver.

On May 10, 1823, the *Virginia* nosed her way into the St. Peter's or Minnesota River and came to a well-earned rest under the frowning cliffs upon which Fort St. Anthony was built. When the Indians saw the boat "cut its way without oars or sails against the current of the great river, some thought it a monster vomiting fire, others the dwelling of the Manitous, but all approached it with reverence or fear." When the tired boat began to blow off steam the frightened Indians "took to the woods, men, women, and children, with their blankets flying in the wind, some tumbling in the brush which entangled their feet as they ran away — some hallooing, some crying, to the great amusement of the people on board the steamboat."

The *Virginia* made the long journey of seven hundred miles in twenty days. She met with many delays. During the course of the journey she struck five sandbars, four below Prairie du Chien and one above. Approximately five days had been spent in getting over the Des Moines and the Rock Island rapids. Wood was burned for fuel, and since none had been prepared in advance the boat had been forced to lay over while fresh supplies were cut by the crew. Several days must have been lost in the process of wooding up. Moreover, with the exception of the night of the forest fire, the engines had stopped each day at sundown.

The voyage of the *Virginia* established the practicability of navigating the Upper Mississippi by steamboat. Later in the year she completed two more trips above the rapids, one to the mouth of the St. Peter's and another to Fort Crawford. After these trips the government did not hesitate to utilize this quicker and more reliable way of moving troops and supplies.

With the advent of steam navigation it became evident that the Mississippi provided the most expeditious and natural outlet for the huge quantities of lead that were just beginning to be produced and were soon to reach enormous volumes. The river was to become also the main artery along which the great waves of immigration moved steadily northward into the Upper Mississippi Valley. No other means of transportation before the advent of the railroad was capable of serving this region so well.

13

The Indian and the Steamboat

THE PROGRESS of the *Virginia* up the Mississippi was viewed with alarm by the Indians. Beltrami was impressed by the fright they displayed at Fort Snelling : "I know not what impression the first sight of the Phoenician vessels might make on the inhabitants of the coast of Greece; or the Triremi of the Romans on the wild natives of Iberia, Gaul, or Britain; but I am sure it could not be stronger than that which I saw on the countenance of these savages at the arrival of our steamboat." [99]

If the Indians at Fort Snelling were frightened, their white brothers who first saw such steamboats were equally startled. In Europe the peasants of Walachia fled (in 1830) at the sight of the first steamboat on the Danube, believing it to be the work of Satan. These same Walachians, like Beltrami himself, traced their lineage back to Imperial Rome and gloried in it. Less than six years later, in the spring of 1836, the Walachians anxiously awaited the arrival of the first steamboat. Eight craft then plied on the Danube, and little colonies were springing up at each steamboat landing. In 1836 a score of steamboats were churning between St. Louis and the mineral region. [100]

But the Indians soon became accustomed to the steamboats puffing up and down the Mississippi. They even came to look on with characteristic apathy while these boats discharged troops and supplies, and loaded up with furs and passengers for below. As the years rolled on and the Indians came to associate the steamboat with the arrival of their yearly annuities, they became even more strongly attached to the craft which plied regularly in the trade. They were especially fond of such steamboats as the *Lynx*, the *Otter*, the *Osprey*, and the *Argo*. Indeed, when the *Argo* sank in 1847, the Indians felt it was as much their loss as the owners'. "It became known", Captain Blakeley relates, "that we had bought the Dr. Franklin, called by them the *Great Medicine*, before that steamboat arrived. When she landed at Red Wing on her first trip, the traders sung out that the Great Medicine was coming. This cry raised everyone in the village, men, women, and children, and all rushed to the bank of the river and onto the boat, shouting 'How! how! how!' " [101]

The arrival of the steamboat at an Indian village was always a signal for a rush to meet her. On July 16, 1847, Harriet E. Bishop, a woman missionary, arrived at Kaposia on the *Lynx*. "The ringing of the bell", declared this badly frightened servant of the Lord, "occasioned a grand rush, and with telegraphic speed, every man, woman, and child flew to the landing.

"To an unsophisticated eye like mine, the scene on shore was novel and grotesque, not to say repulsive; blankets and hair streaming in the wind; limbs uncovered; children nearly naked, the smaller ones entirely so, while a papoose was ludicrously peeping over the shoulder of nearly every squaw." [102]

The Indian and the Steamboat

During the removal of the Winnebago from Iowa in 1848 an incident occurred which was remembered with deep chagrin by the Winnebago for several years. It appears that the *Dr. Franklin* was the first boat on the Upper Mississippi to have a steam whistle. On one occasion, after the boat had discharged her red passengers, the whole tribe gathered on the bank to watch the "Great Medicine" back out. Sensing the possibilities for some fun, the engineer, Bill Myers, pulled the cord of the whistle "which gave a terrible screech, and instantly every Indian man, woman, and child jumped, shed their blankets, and rushed for the top of the bank or some place to hide."

This incident made the poor Winnebago the laughing stock of the tribes on the Minnesota River. But in 1851 they had their revenge. When the *Dr. Franklin* went up to Traverse des Sioux, the Winnebago plotted with Captain Russell Blakeley to frighten the Sioux. The *Dr. Franklin* snorted up to the Sioux village under a full head of steam, and as the boat touched the shore a hideous blast sent every Sioux flying for cover. Indeed, so great was their fright that the Winnebago poked no little fun at their former mockers and thanked Captain Blakeley for squaring accounts.[103]

Steamboats played an important part in the relations of the Indian and the white man for almost half a century. The Indian even found courage to travel by steamboat. He seldom traveled alone, however, but factors other than fear and distrust accounted for this. Only on rare occasions did the Indian have funds to procure a passage; the desire for whiskey, generously diluted with river water, proved more tempting to his fancy. Moreover, by the time the steamboat had become common, the reservation system and the trading house, both under the close supervision of the Indian Agent, tended to discourage travel by the red men.

Despite this fact the Indian played an important rôle, both directly and indirectly, in the development of steamboating on the Mississippi River and its tributaries. Steamboating was stimulated directly by the necessity of transporting delegations to treaty grounds, by the delivery of annuity goods as provided by these treaties, and by the ultimate removal of whole tribes to new reservations. Each of these processes tended to weaken the Indians' hold on the lands of the Upper Mississippi Valley and to stimulate the advance of white settlers into the region. Indirectly, the Indian stimulated steamboating through the presence of the fur trader and the soldier on the Indian frontier.

14

To Treaty Grounds by Steamboat

A FOX WARRIOR was stealing furtively down the Mississippi below Prairie du Chien. Desperately wounded and half-starved, he staggered along, wading streams and skulking through the underbrush. His strength was ebbing fast as he approached the Fox village at the mouth of Catfish Creek below present-day Dubuque. Fortunately he managed to reach his kindred and friends just in time to tell of the ambuscade and massacre of their principal chiefs and headmen by the Sioux and Menominee. Then the lone survivor himself departed to the happy hunting grounds.[104]

A paroxysm of fear gripped the leaderless Fox Indians, and they fled precipitately to Rock Island. When the news of the bloody tragedy reached Washington, the government ordered General William Clark, Superintendent of Indian Affairs, to assemble the warring tribes at Prairie du Chien. William Clark (of Lewis and Clark fame) was deeply venerated by his many red children in the Mississippi Valley. They trusted this courageous "red-haired chief" with "iron in the blood and granite in the backbone". And well might they trust him as a friend, for as early as 1826 Clark had urged the Secretary of War to adopt a more humane policy toward his red charges : "While strong and hostile", Clark wrote, "it has been our obvious policy to weaken them; now that they are weak and harmless, and most of their lands fallen into our hands, justice and humanity require us to befriend and cherish them." [105]

Clark set out from St. Louis on the steamboat *Planet* with a motley cargo of Indians from the Missouri River. When the steamboat reached Rock Island, the Sauk and Fox, with recent atrocities still fresh in their minds, stubbornly refused to attend the peace negotiations. But Clark had learned the subtle techniques for the successful cajoling of red men. Long years before he had once remarked: "It requires time and a little smoking with Indians if you wish to have peace with them." The recalcitrant Foxes, their grief assuaged with a liberal supply of presents to the friends and relatives of the victims, finally agreed to proceed to Prairie du Chien on the *Planet*. When the boat reached Galena, she had some three hundred members of the Sauk, Fox, Iowa, and Oto tribes jammed aboard. In addition to these, a small delegation of Missouri, Sioux, and Winnebago lent color and confusion to the heterogeneous array of Indians that swarmed over Captain Butler's diminutive craft.

At Prairie du Chien "time and smoking" finally brought the warring factions to an understanding after two weeks of negotiations. On July 15, 1830, the Sioux and the confederated tribes of Sauk and Fox agreed to mark off between them a neutral strip forty miles in width in what is now northern Iowa and southern Minnesota. Shortly afterwards Clark returned the Indians to their homes

aboard the steamboat *Red Rover*, Joseph Throckmorton
commanding. A total of $24,265.83 was appropriated for
this treaty, and only $840.94 was left unspent.[106]

Before 1823 the Indian had traveled long distances by
canoe or on foot to attend a treaty meeting. With the
arrival of the steamboat the red man was transported to
the scene of the council and fed while away from his village. He found the Great White Father quite willing to
do this, particularly when spurred on by the hope of more
land cessions. Prior to the Black Hawk War most of the
councils in the Upper Mississippi Valley were called at
some point near a military post. Fort Crawford and Fort
Armstrong were favorite treaty grounds, but a number of
councils were also held at Fort Snelling.

The gradual withdrawal of the Indians northward to
the land of the sky blue waters can be measured by the
points at which the treaties were signed. In 1842 the Sauk
and Fox Indians gave up all claim to land in the Territory
of Iowa by a treaty signed at Agency, six miles east of
Ottumwa on the Des Moines River. Nine years later, at
Traverse des Sioux and Mendota, the Sioux ceded large
tracts of land in the Territory of Minnesota and smaller
patches in northern Iowa.[107]

Despite accounts found in contemporary newspapers of
the palatial appointments and speed of Upper Mississippi
craft, the journeys of the commissioners, clerks, and inter-
preters were seldom pleasant. Thus, in 1829 Caleb Atwater, a resident of Ohio, was appointed commissioner to
act with Brigadier General John McNeil and Colonel

Pierre Menard. After a tiresome journey down the Ohio and up the Mississippi, Atwater finally reached St. Louis where he busied himself for days in securing quantities of food and supplies. These he sent on by steamboat as quickly as they were purchased. When all was in readiness Atwater boarded the steamboat *Missouri* (John Culver commanding) and set out for Prairie du Chien. It took the *Missouri* almost a week to reach the Lower Rapids. Here the journey was interrupted by the low stage of the water. While making his way on foot along the river from Fort Edwards to the head of the rapids, Atwater found many of the packages, which had been forwarded several weeks before, scattered along the bank and exposed to the elements. A large part of these were stowed aboard Captain Throckmorton's *Red Rover* which lay at the head of the Lower Rapids, hopefully waiting for a cargo with which to return upstream.[108]

Fort Armstrong was not reached until noon of the third day. Here a delegation of two hundred Winnebago surrounded Atwater and demanded "flour, hog meat, and whisky." Eleven barrels of pork, two hundred pipes, and a plentiful supply of tobacco appeased their anger, and the *Red Rover* continued upstream. Learning at Galena that an unprecedented number of Indians had gathered at Fort Crawford, Atwater purchased an additional five hundred bushels of corn.

The Indians at Prairie du Chien greeted the commissioners warmly. According to Atwater : "As soon as we were discovered by our red friends, a few miles below the fort, opposite to their encampment, they fired into the air, about fifteen hundred rifles to honor us. Our powder had become wet, and, to our extreme mortification and regret, we could not answer them by our cannon. Having fired their arms, some run on foot, some rode on their small horses furiously along over the prairie to meet us where we landed." As soon as her cargo was discharged, the *Red Rover* departed downstream for the remaining annuities and treaty supplies.[109]

Orations were followed by unrestrained feasting; favorite Indian games were interspersed with murders. All the tribes appeared contented, save the Winnebago whose chief grievance was that $20,000 in annuity goods had not been delivered. They demanded that this debt be wiped out before the government enter into new obligations. Low water had delayed the delivery of these annuities, but this explanation did not placate the Winnebago who, even after the goods did arrive, threatened to murder every white man present.

At this crucial moment the two chiefs, Keokuk and Morgan, appeared with two hundred Sauk and Fox warriors and began their war dance for the United States. They informed the unruly Winnebago that thirty steamboats with cannon and troops and four hundred of their own warriors were close at hand. This silenced the Winnebago and brought the negotiations to a close. The successful termination of the treaty of 1829 may be attributed to the timely arrival of the long delayed annuities and to Keokuk's extravagant fabrication of the approach of thirty steamboats loaded with well armed white troops.[110]

In 1837 Governor Henry Dodge of the Territory of Wisconsin set out on the steamboat *Irene* for Fort Snelling to negotiate a treaty with the Chippewa, whereby they surrendered their choicest lands to the white man. Among the signatories to this treaty were Henry H. Sibley and Hercules L. Dousman of the American Fur Company; J. N. Nicollet, the noted French scientist; and Joseph Emerson, Assistant Surgeon, U. S. A., owner of the famous slave, Dred Scott.[111]

The signing of the Treaty of Traverse des Sioux on July 23, 1851, was the prelude to the final extinction of Indian land title in the Upper Mississippi Valley. Many steamboats were required to carry the Indians to and from the treaty ground and in transporting food and gifts. Thirty braves from Red Wing's band went up on the *Dr. Franklin*, while the *Nominee* carried Wabasha's warriors.

The steamboat *Excelsior* (James Ward commanding) arrived at St. Paul on June 20, 1851, with Commissioner Luke Lea on board and the next morning proceeded to Mendota where the party was joined by a number of traders and chiefs of the lower Sioux bands. According to a passenger, the Sioux managed "to conform here on the boat without murmuring to our pernicious habit of eating three meals a day." A drove of cattle and a supply of provisions were taken on board at Mendota to furnish subsistence for the Indians expected at the treaty.

Leaving Mendota, the *Excelsior* steamed over to Fort Snelling where Governor Alexander Ramsey came on board. But a company of dragoons who were to accompany the commission as a guard was not ready so the *Excelsior* departed without them. Among the passengers were James M. Goodhue, the first editor in Minnesota, and Frank B. Mayer, a Maryland artist whose famous painting of the Treaty of Traverse des Sioux has been preserved to this day. On July 20th, the *Dr. Franklin* brought a party from St. Paul to witness the signing of the treaty.

The year 1851 marks the last time a large body of Indians was carried by steamboat to sign a treaty in the Upper Mississippi region. Henceforth the activity of steamboats, so far as Indian councils were concerned, shifted to the Missouri River.[112]

15

Visiting the Great White Father

INDIAN COUNCILS in the West were never exclusive gatherings of the chiefs and headmen : the whole tribe attended. Braves came accompanied by their squaws and dirty-faced papooses. Old men and women, bent and withered with age, hobbled about the treaty grounds and scolded crossly at the slightest pretext. Even the dogs, half-starved on account of the lack of food, accompanied the tribe : they barked incessantly during the day and howled so dismally at night that the Indian orators called attention to their pitiful condition, the better to illustrate their own sad plight.[118]

Bitter quarrels among the Indians or with the commissioners and the interminably long speeches, together with the cost involved in transporting and feeding whole tribes of hungry Indians, led the government to inaugurate the policy of transporting small delegations to Washington. Limiting the number of orators tended to bring negotiations to an earlier conclusion. The amount saved on food and presents, it was estimated, would actually pay the cost of transportation; at the same time the bewildered Indians would be overawed by the power of the government. Such methods, it was hoped, would hasten the extinction of Indian land titles and work to the advantage of the white man.

Visiting the Great White Father

The payments to steamboat captains formed no small portion of the expense of taking the Indian delegations to Washington. William Clark's estimate of the cost of taking his delegation of Sauk, Fox, Iowa, and Piankashaw Indians to Washington in 1824 was $2,908.80. Included in the party was one agent, three interpreters, one servant, one hired man, and eighteen Indians. Transportation from St. Louis to Washington required $1,231.75; while provisions and tavern expenses amounted to $772.74.

Lawrence Taliaferro estimated $857.23 for transporting his Sioux, Chippewa, and Menominee Indians from St. Peter's to Washington in 1824. He figured $482.00 for transportation, $149.84 for provisions, $199.00 for hired men, $24.39 for sundries, $19.00 for presents, and $13.00 for medicine. It would be difficult to explain this difference. Still more confusing is Taliaferro's estimate of $2,992.00 for the journey home — especially since only $150 of this was needed to make the trip from Prairie du Chien to Fort Snelling. The difference can hardly be attributed to up and downstream tariffs.[114]

For the Indian, a trip to Washington was like the first visit of a country boy to a big city. But it was no easy task for the Indian Agent. Even aboard the steamboat it was necessary to be constantly on the alert to prevent the Indians from securing firewater : vigilance had to be redoubled whenever the steamboat landed and the Indians went ashore. On one occasion, Marcpee, a Sioux from the Fort Snelling district, had a bad dream while ascending the Ohio River, dived overboard, and swam ashore. He

[119]

reached St. Charles, Missouri, in safety, but there the thrust of a Sauk dagger changed the course of his journey to the happy hunting grounds.[115]

Amusing incidents were without number. In 1831 Colonel Samuel C. Stambaugh departed from Washington with a group of Menominee warriors. The journey home was to be made after visiting the principal cities of the East. At Philadelphia a theater party was arranged with a special section reserved for the warriors. During the course of the program a gigantic elephant from Siam was led on the stage. The astonished Menominee gave one loud, discordant shriek which almost precipitated a riot. Terrified whites and blacks hastily sought cover. But the Indians were not without a defender : a local newspaper declared that such a reception was no worse than the custom of fashionable gentlemen in Philadelphia theaters who beat boxes with their canes.[116]

Somewhat different was Black Hawk's visit to the Great White Father in 1833. At the conclusion of his ill-fated war he was carried in chains aboard the steamboat *Winnebago* and taken to Jefferson Barracks. On his journey downstream, the defeated Sauk leader was placed in charge of Lieutenant Jefferson Davis (the man who later became President of the Southern Confederacy). Of his treatment by Davis aboard the *Winnebago*, Black Hawk afterwards declared : "We remained here [Prairie du Chien] a short time, and then started to Jefferson Barracks, in a steam boat, under the charge of a young war chief [Davis], who treated all with much kindness. He is a good and brave young chief, with whose conduct I was much pleased. On our way down, we called at Galena, and remained a short time. The people crowded to the boat to see us; but the war chief would not permit them to enter the apartment where we were — knowing, from what his own feelings would have been, if he had been placed in a similar situation, that we did not wish to have a gaping crowd around us." [117]

Black Hawk and his two sons, the Prophet, and nine braves were aboard the *Winnebago* when she arrived at St. Louis. Fifty warriors had been landed at the foot of the Lower Rapids upon pledging to remain at peace. [118]

Held with ball and chain Black Hawk languished in Jefferson Barracks until spring. Then he made a steamboat journey by way of the Ohio to Pittsburgh, and thence overland to Washington. The trip was arranged to impress the fallen chieftain with the power of the white man : it turned out to be somewhat of a triumphant tour as related by Black Hawk in his *Autobiography*. [119]

"In a little while all were ready, and left Jefferson barracks on board of a steam boat, under charge of a young war chief, whom the White Beaver sent along as a guide to Washington. He carried with him an interpreter and one soldier. On our way up the Ohio, we passed several large villages, the names of which were explained to me. The first is called Louisville, and is a very pretty village, situate on the bank of the Ohio river. The next is Cincinnati, which stands on the bank of the same river. This is a large and beautiful village, and seemed to be in a thriving condition. The people gathered on the bank as we passed, in great crowds, apparently anxious to see us.

"On our arrival at Wheeling, the streets and river's bank were crowded with people, who flocked from every direction to see us. While we remained here, many called upon us, and treated us with kindness — no one offering to molest or misuse us. This village is not so large as either of those before mentioned, but is quite a pretty village.

"We left the steam boat here, having travelled a long distance on the prettiest river (except our Mississippi,) that I ever saw — and took the stage. Being unaccustomed to this mode of travelling, we soon got tired, and wished ourselves seated in a canoe on one of our own rivers, that we might return to our friends. We had travelled but a short distance, before our carriage turned over, from which I received a slight injury, and the soldier had one arm broken. I was sorry for this accident, as the young man had behaved well."

Upon meeting President Andrew Jackson the red warrior said to his Great White Father : "I am a man and you are another." This may have been sufficient for sending Black Hawk to Fortress Monroe as the guest-prisoner of the government. Upon his release Black Hawk returned to his home in Iowa by way of the Great Lakes and Prairie du Chien.

Three delegations of Upper Mississippi Indians went to Washington in 1837. Unknown to the representatives of the American Fur Company who were attempting to force the Sioux to sign certain papers acknowledging their debts, Major Taliaferro arranged with Captain James Lafferty of the steamboat *Ariel* to be at Fort Snelling on a certain day. Luckily for the Sioux, the steamboat was on time and they set out downstream before the Fur Company became aware of their departure. At Kaposia the *Ariel* was boarded by Big Thunder and his pipe bearer. The great Wahkoota and his war chief clambered aboard at what is now Red Wing; and at the present site of Winona, Wabasha and Etuzepah joined the delegation. Twenty-one Sioux were on the *Ariel* when she reached Galena. An editor described them as a motley and curious set of "varmints". Leaving Galena on August 23, 1837, the *Ariel* made her way down the Mississippi and up the Ohio to Pittsburgh, whence the Indians journeyed overland to Washington.

Secretary of War Joel R. Poinsett met the Sioux at Washington. Henry Hastings Sibley, Alexis Bailly, Joseph Laframboise, and Alexander and Oliver Faribault were present to "protect" the interests of the American Fur Company. After solemn deliberations, a treaty was signed on September 29, 1837, by which the Sioux relinquished all claims to the pine forests of the St. Croix Valley, thus clearing the way for the organization of the future Territory of Minnesota. The representatives of the Fur Company were able to include a provision whereby a sum of $90,000 was set aside for the payment of the "just" debts which they claimed the Indians owed them.[120]

After viewing some of the wonders of the East, the Sioux returned by way of the Ohio and the Mississippi to

[123]

St. Louis where the steamboat *Rolla* was chartered to transport the delegation to Fort Snelling. Leaving Galena on November 7, 1837, the Indians began the last lap of their three thousand mile journey. About twenty miles below Pine River, the flue of the boiler suddenly collapsed. The fireman of the *Rolla*, a negro, and a valuable horse were killed; but the Sioux escaped without injury, and the delegation was safely landed at Fort Snelling the next day.[121]

Before the *Rolla* turned her nose downstream Major Taliaferro paid Captain Dwyer $1450 "for transportation & fare of a delegation of Sioux Indians & their Interpreters & attendants by contract from St. Louis to the Agency at St. Peters". The government paid $55 per passage for the twenty-six Indians and their attendants aboard the *Rolla*, which was almost double the amount usually charged for such a trip. Not even the late season could justify such a payment. This sum, added to the income from freight and passage received from other sources, probably yielded the *Rolla* her most profitable trip of the season. Even if Captain Dwyer had creditors before he reached Fort Snelling he must have left for St. Louis with a light heart.[122]

Two other Indian delegations went to Washington in 1837. The Sauk and Fox under Joseph M. Street signed a treaty on October 21st, relinquishing 1,250,000 acres of Iowa land. This is known today as The Second Purchase. Then, on November 1st, the Winnebago, under Agent Thomas A. Boyd, ceded all their lands east of the Mississippi, together with a portion of the Neutral Strip. Three delegations in one year, together with the special annuity goods usually provided for in the treaties, brought rich returns to the enterprising steamboat captains who plied the Upper Mississippi.[123]

16

The Transportation of Indian Annuities

A LARGE BAND of Chippewa had assembled on the St. Croix River near present-day Stillwater. A year before, in July of 1837, they had made a treaty at Fort Snelling with their Great White Father. They had been solemnly promised that their first yearly annuity would be paid on this very spot. A year had passed and the Chippewa, with child-like simplicity, had gathered to receive their supplies. But long-winded Congressmen, inefficient departmental employees, the stage of the water, and the season of the year often delayed the delivery of annuity goods. These factors, together with an inherent dislike of the Indians for raising their own crops, often led to distressing hardships.

Delay in the delivery of Indian annuities was common, but few tribes suffered more than did the Chippewa in 1838. By the middle of July the Chippewa began to feel genuine concern as their annuities still remained undelivered. Suddenly the steamboat *Palmyra* (W. Middleton commanding) was spied puffing proudly up the St. Croix. She was the first steamboat to churn the waters of that river. The assembled tribesmen dashed down to greet her and to receive their long-awaited annuities. Their stock of provisions was running low : indeed, many of the Chippewa were in dire need of food. But Captain Middleton carried no annuities for the Chippewa aboard the *Palmyra*. Instead he brought a party of workmen with equipment to erect the first mill in the St. Croix Valley. The red man might cede his home; land pirates might immediately enter and denude the rich valley of its wealth of timber; but the Indian must await the delivery of his annuities.

It was not until the first week of November that the steamboat *Gipsey* arrived with the Indian goods. By that time the plight of the red men was desperate. An account of the first payment has been left by Levi W. Stratton, a St. Croix lumberman:

"The old stern wheel Gipsey brought the goods and landed them on the beach. The Chippewas came there to the number of 1,100 in their canoes, nearly starved by waiting for their payment. While there receiving it the river and lake froze up, and a deep snow came on; thus all their supplies, including one hundred barrels of flour, twenty-five of pork, kegs of tobacco, bales of blankets, guns and ammunition, casks of Mexican dollars, etc., all were sacrificed except what they could carry off on their backs through the snow hundreds of miles away. Their fleet of birch canoes they destroyed before leaving, lest the Sioux might have the satisfaction of doing the same after they left.

"Many of the old as well as the young died from over-eating, they being nearly starved. Thus their first payment became a curse rather than a blessing to them, for their supplies soon gave out, the season for hunting was past, they were away from home and had no means of getting there, except by wading through the deep snow. Many perished in the attempt. As is usual in such cases, I suppose, no one was to blame, but the poor Indians had to suffer the consequence of somebody's neglect. The Old Gipsey had scarcely time to get through the lake before the ice formed." [124]

The delivery of Indian annuities formed an important cargo for enterprising steamboat captains. Each year steamboats churned up the Mississippi and its tributaries to deliver a varied assortment of Indian goods. Steamboat captains who secured contracts to deliver annuities were considered extremely fortunate for, while the movement of delegations and tribes usually required but one trip, the traffic in annuities called for many trips to the points designated.

Before the voyage of the *Virginia* the government frequently sent presents to the Indians by means of keelboats. Thus, when the keelboat *Amelia* stopped at the mouth of the Upper Iowa River in 1821 Indian Agent Lawrence Taliaferro was visited by Chief Wabasha and a band of seventy-eight warriors. After explaining the views of the government, Major Taliaferro gave the "respectable" Wabasha a present which brought "visible" pleasure to his eyes. Although the value of such presents was usually small they proved a tempting bait which produced the desired effect. His appetite whetted, the Indian asked for more; it was then but a short step to the actual sale of lands. The steamboat was the chief means of transporting such annuity goods before the coming of the railroad.[125]

It should be pointed out, however, that until the steamboat had become a means of communication with points on the Upper Mississippi it was not possible to deliver huge quantities of annuities at the very doors of the tribes. For example, in 1824 provision was made to convey the Sauk, Fox, and the Iowa Indian goods only as far as St. Louis; but later treaties called for the transportation of goods to designated points on the Upper Mississippi. In 1829 the Winnebago were to receive immediately $18,000 in specie and $30,000 in goods and presents at Prairie du Chien and Fort Winnebago. Three thousand pounds of tobacco and fifty barrels of salt were also to be delivered at the same points annually for a period of thirty years. Likewise the amount of iron, tools, and steel required by a blacksmith called for annual shipments during the next three decades. Three years later the Winnebago were granted additional annuities for a period of twenty-seven years. At the same time the Black Hawk Purchase provided that annuity goods be delivered yearly at the mouth of the Iowa River. Both treaties specified that the government defray the cost of transportation.[126]

While eastern markets furnished a considerable portion of the Indian goods carried by Upper Mississippi steamboats, it was bustling St. Louis that claimed the lion's share of the trade. Indeed, in 1829 Atwater observed that the Indian Department had expended millions of dollars in St. Louis.[127] Ten years later a Davenport newspaper viewed with envy the departure from St. Louis of the steamboat *Pizarro* which was bound up the Missouri River to its confluence with the Kansas with 20 spinning wheels, 20 looms and their "appendages", 300 axes, 100 plows, and $10,000 in specie. This "pretty little outfit" was destined for the Iowa and other Indians.[128]

While the entire western country was included in this commerce no small share belonged to the Upper Mississippi. In the thirties, especially, with Sauk and Fox, Winnebago and Potawatomi, Chippewa and Sioux, and other tribes gradually giving way before the westward tide of immigration, treaties called for an ever increasing shipment of annuities. By 1844 four tribes alone were being supplied annually with goods valued at $218,910 : the Sioux received $40,510; the Sauk and Fox $85,540; while the Winnebago rejoiced over annuities valued at $92,860.[129]

The importance of the Indian trade is further illustrated by a comparison with the commerce from the white settlements on the frontier. "About $80,000", declared a St. Paul newspaper in 1852, "has been paid out to the lower bands of Indians in accordance with the treaty stipulations for the purchase of their land : also about $20,000 worth of goods. The Governor has gone to Traverse des Sioux, where he is to meet the upper bands of Indians, and will pay them, it is said, over $300,000. The effect of the payment is easily observed in St. Paul. The merchants are reaping a rich harvest. The Indians are as plentiful in town as mosquitoes in summer; but they are more welcome, for they bring the cash, while mosquitoes settle

The Transportation of Indian Annuities

their bills in another way." [130] At St. Paul the trade in general merchandise during the year 1853 was estimated at $390,000. This represented the goods purchased by the citizens of St. Paul and by white settlers throughout the surrounding country. But the government trade during the same year amounted to fully $400,000.[131]

Each flourishing community between St. Louis and St. Paul made strong bids for a portion of this trade and often received a generous share. For a long time Galena played a leading rôle; but in the decade preceding the Civil War other river towns cut deeply into her trade. In 1857 Davenport and the surrounding territory in Iowa furnished goods for the Sioux of the Minnesota River to the value of $28,000.[132]

The delivery of Indian annuities was usually a colorful spectacle. Captain Edwin Bell recalls a particularly dramatic episode following the arrival of the steamboat *Globe*.[133]

"In 1855 I had command of the steamer Globe, making trips on the Minnesota river, and in the early fall of that year we carried supplies to the Sioux at Redwood Agency. The Indians would come down the river several miles to meet the boat. They were like a lot of children, and when the steamboat approached they would shout, 'Nitonka pata-wata washta', meaning, 'Your big fire-canoe is good.' They would then cut across the bend, yelling until we reached the landing.

"In the fall of that year, 1855, their supplies were late, when I received orders from Agent Murphy to turn over to the Indians twelve barrels of pork, and twelve barrels of flour. As soon as we landed, we rolled the supplies on shore. I was informed that the Indians were in a starving condition. It was amusing to see five or six of them rolling a barrel of pork up the bank, when two of our deck hands would do the work in half the time.

"When the flour and pork were on the level ground, the barrel heads were knocked in, and the pork cut in small strips and thrown in a pile. Two hundred squaws then formed a circle, and several Indians handed the pieces of pork to the squaws until the pile was disposed of. The flour was placed in tin pans, each squaw receiving a panful.

"Later, in the same season we had an unfortunate trip. The boat was loaded deep. Luckily Agent Murphy and Capt. Louis Robert were on board. We had in the cabin of the boat ninety thousand dollars in gold. About three miles below the Agency, we ran on a large boulder. After much effort, we got the boat afloat. Major Murphy gave orders to land the goods, so that they might be hauled to the Agency. We landed and unloaded, covering the goods with tarpaulins. There were about fifty kegs of powder with the goods. While we were unloading, the agent sent for a team to take Captain Robert and himself, with the gold, to the Agency. Then we started down the river. We had gone only a few miles, when we discovered a dense smoke, caused by a prairie fire. The smoke was rolling toward the pile of goods which we had left in charge of two men. When we reached the ferry at Red

Bank, a man on horseback motioned to us to land, and told us that the goods we left were all burnt up and the powder exploded. This was a sad blow to the Indians."

Late in April, 1857, the *Fire Canoe* (R. M. Spencer commanding) lay at the foot of Lake Pepin loaded with three hundred tons of flour, pork, and lard for the Indian Agency at Redwood. This consignment, which was part of a contract of $28,000, had been produced in Iowa. William Wood of Davenport, a member of the firm of Wood and Barclay of St. Paul, was the successful bidder for these annuities. The *Fire Canoe* arrived at the St. Paul levee on May 6, 1857, with two barges in tow and 1800 barrels of flour, 600 barrels of pork, 100 barrels of lard, and 3000 bushels of corn. The voyage to Redwood took thirteen days; the Indians were almost starved when the *Fire Canoe* arrived. Averaging barely fifteen miles per day upstream, the *Fire Canoe* returned to St. Paul after an absence of twenty days.[134]

The yearly delivery of Indian annuities gave steamboat captains a rich source of revenue during the early years of steamboating on the Upper Mississippi. But the coming of the railroad, together with the removal of the tribes westward across the Missouri, had well nigh destroyed this traffic by the opening of the Civil War.

17
The Last Red Cargoes

THE DRAMATIC migration known as the westward movement reached what is now Keokuk on the Upper Mississippi in the decade preceding the Black Hawk War. By 1860 both banks of the Mississippi between St. Louis and St. Paul were well populated. The scattered Indian tribes that had occupied the area had been carried back on the crest of the immigrant waves, first across the Mississippi and then across the Missouri. A generation of pioneers witnessed the removal of the Winnebago from Wisconsin to Iowa and to northern Minnesota. During the same period the Sauk and Fox moved from Illinois to Iowa and thence on to Kansas.

Weary and vanquished, bewildered and embittered, the Indians trekked westward. Sometimes the movement was made on foot, sometimes by wagon teams, and not infrequently by steamboat. Late in 1832 over two thousand Choctaw Indians arrived at Memphis and embarked on a steamboat for Rock Roe on the White River : wagon trains carried them west of Arkansas Territory. A delegation of Seminoles arrived at Memphis in 1832 on the steamboat *Little Rock*, and from there set out overland for Fort Gibson. Four years later 511 Creek Indians arrived at Little Rock on the steamboat *Alpha*. The tragic story of the dispossession of the red men was reënacted over and over again on a frontier more than two thousand miles in extent.[135]

Not all the Indian tribes of the Upper Mississippi Valley were removed to their new homes by means of steamboats. Many tribes were forced to migrate overland. But steamboat captains reaped a harvest whenever whole tribes were transported on their boats. The removal of the Winnebago during the summer of 1848 was one of the most colorful incidents in Upper Mississippi steamboat history. It was a difficult task; but, if newspaper accounts can be relied upon, the profits accruing to the owners of the *Dr. Franklin* amply repaid them for their work.

By the treaty of 1846 the Winnebago had agreed to cede their claims and privileges in the Neutral Ground and remove northward to a spot provided by the government. A strip of land at the mouth of the Crow Wing River was finally designated. Since over two thousand Winnebago were involved in this transfer, a detachment of troops from Fort Atkinson was ordered to accompany them. Five hundred head of cattle were taken along for subsistence; while three hundred teams were required to haul the baggage which made up this Indian camp. At Wabasha's village the party was to be picked up by steamboat and carried as far as St. Paul, but when the Indians assembled on the prairie just below Wabasha's village, they refused to move another foot. Captain Russell Blakeley has left a report of the episode.

"After the agent had nearly despaired of success, the only alternative left was to send to Capt. Eastman of Fort

Steamboating on Upper Mississippi

Snelling for additional troops, which, with a six-pounder, were sent under the command of Lieut. Hall, to see whether he could encourage the fellows to go. In canvassing the situation, Lieut. Hall became suspicious that the chief, Wabasha, whose village was just above the prairie upon the Rolling Stone creek, had in some way encouraged the Winnebagoes not to go. He arrested Wabasha and brought him on board the Dr. Franklin, and chained him to one of the stanchions of the boat on the boiler deck, evidently with the intention of frightening him; but after a short time he thought better of it, and released him. This was regarded as a great outrage to this proud chief, and it was not regarded in favorable light by those having charge of the Winnebagoes, who numbered over two thousand souls, besides Wabasha's band; but it finally passed without trouble. All the men in charge of the Indians were constantly urging them to consent to the removal, and talks were almost of daily occurrence, which would always end in Commissary Lieut. J. H. McKenny's sending down to the camp more flour, sugar, meat and coffee, realizing that when their stomachs were full they were more peaceable.

"One morning the troops, agent, and all in charge, were astounded to find the Indian camp deserted; not an Indian, dog or pony was left. The canoes that had brought part of them were gone as well. Everything in camp that could hunt was started to find them. The Dr. Franklin was sent down the river to overtake them if they had gone in that direction, and I think it was three days before they were found. They had taken their canoes and gone down

[136]

the river to the mouth of the Slough, and thence had gone over into Wisconsin and were comfortably encamped on the islands and shores of the river, but were nearly starved. They promised to return to their camp the next day in their canoes. About ten o'clock the next day those on watch saw them coming out of the head of the Slough some three miles above the steamboat landing. It was one of our beautiful summer mornings, with not a ripple on the water; and when these two thousand men, women, children, and dogs, passed down, floating without even using a paddle, except to keep in the stream, all dressed in their best, they presented such a picture as I have not seen equaled since. They were disposed to show themselves at their best. Lieut. McKenny met them at their camp with provisions, and the old *status quo* was reëstablished."

The Winnebago were fearful lest the Sioux should object to this removal into their country, and so it was decided to send the *Dr. Franklin* to St. Paul for the purpose of picking up the principal Sioux chiefs to meet the Winnebago in council. When the Sioux were gathered together they presented a colorful spectacle. Each chief was fitted out from head to foot with a new suit consisting of blue frock coat, leggins, moccasins, silk plug hat, white ruffled shirt, and a small American flag. After several days of orations the Winnebago finally agreed to go. Several trips were required to remove the whole tribe and its equipment.[136]

But some of the Indians were obdurate and steadfastly refused to leave their homes and migrate with the rest of the tribe. An old Winnebago settled on the bank of the Wisconsin River, denied any relationship to his tribe, and presented three land office certificates for forty acres of land. Despite every effort on his part to remain behind, the *Dr. Franklin* carried him northward.[137]

During the exodus the newspapers in the mining district were filled with reports of the progress of the *Dr. Franklin*. Charges were made that the Winnebago were carried back and forth several times and the government assessed with the cost. The Indians, it appears, enjoyed the novelty of the steamboat trip : it was said they rode up the river, disembarked, sprang into their canoes, and paddled back to Wabasha, a distance of over one hundred miles, in order to enjoy the excellent food and accommodations of the steamboat.

Some of the Indians, however, remained behind; in 1849 the *Senator* picked up at Prairie du Chien one hundred Winnebago who had refused to leave the preceding year. They were a motley array of braves, squaws, papooses, lean and battered ponies, dogs, traps, and tin kettles. When the *Senator* reached St. Paul the squaws set to work unloading the goods while their indifferent braves looked on. The following spring Governor Alexander Ramsey was again bitterly assailed for estimating the cost of removing the Winnebago at $5000 and then demanding $100,000.[138]

Following the uprising of the Sioux in 1862 the government contracted with the Minnesota Packet Company to remove some of the Indians from Mankato to Fort Snelling. Captain Joseph B. Wilcox was sent by the packet

The Last Red Cargoes

company with the steamboat *Flora* to transport the Indians. Commodore William F. Davidson also contracted
to remove a part of the Sioux on the *Favorite*.

At Mankato the *Flora* took aboard several hundred Sioux
with their camp equipment and headed down the Minnesota. Near Carver she struck a piling that had been
driven into the river for bridge purposes and sank in
about three feet of water. The *Flora* was an open hull
boat, and much of the Indian equipment which lay in
her hold was damaged. Since there were no siphons in
those days the ship's carpenter had to repair the break as
best he could with his men working up to their waists
in water in the hold of the boat. The hole was finally
patched and the crew commenced bailing out the water.
This was slow work. Captain Wilcox asked the Indians
to help, but they refused.

"Bill" True, the engineer on the *Flora*, believed he could
frighten the Sioux into helping. He ordered the firemen
to raise steam in the boilers, and motioned to the Indians
to watch him as he dramatically lifted the safety valves.
The Sioux trembled, but remained firm. Not to be denied,
True again appealed to the Great Spirit and opened the
mud-drum valves which roared so hideously and shook the
Flora from stem to stern so violently that the Sioux capit-
ulated and set to work with their huge camp kettles.
They soon tired, however, and it was not long before the
braves were seen signaling their squaws to take their places.
The squaws bailed with a will while their dusky mates
looked on approvingly. The *Flora* was soon able to steam

to St. Paul where the Indians were landed temporarily.[139] From St. Paul, the Northern Line contracted to carry the Sioux down the Mississippi to Davenport where they were taken to Camp McClellan and occupied a part of the area later known as Camp Kearny. Here they remained until March 29, 1866, when they were ordered removed to Fort Randall, Nebraska. This was perhaps the last time a large body of Indians was transported by steamboat down the Mississippi River.[140]

The removal of Indian tribes elicited considerable comment in the local press. News of the arrival of a steamboat at a river town with its picturesque red cargo was the signal for a rush to the levee.

Fifteen years after their removal into Minnesota a portion of the Winnebago were transported to Fort Randall in Nebraska. It was a scant two hundred miles overland in a southwesterly direction to the new home, or no farther than the Winnebago might go on a summer's hunt. It was well nigh ten times as far by steamboat down the Minnesota and Mississippi rivers and up the Missouri. But the Winnebago enjoyed the easy motion and good food of the steamboat, and so the government agreed to transport them in this way. Proceeding down the Minnesota River from Mankato, the Winnebago boarded the steamboat *Canada* at St. Paul. A local editor has left this impression of the Winnebago:

"Their looks indicate anything but the 'good Indians' that we read about in missionary works, and it is probable that Satan would not have great difficulty in selecting and officering at *least* a full company, who would be admirably adapted for his body-guard. It is very charming, indeed, to read in Hiawatha verse of the 'noble Indian,' but we acquit Longfellow of any intention to personify the Winnebagoes. He must have alluded to some tribe now extinct, as that class of Indians don't roam in this region at present. — The only nobility we could discover consisted of half-dressed bodies with ugly, devilish faces, hideously daubed with paint.

"As usual, the squaws were occupied with housework, washing, cooking, &c., while the men and boys participated in various kinds of amusements, a large number being industriously engaged in doing nothing. The 'moccasin game,' as it is called, was their favorite sport, though occasionally a deck of cards would be called into requisition to while away the hours. We saw none of the devotional exercises for which the Sioux are so celebrated, and fear that they were not able to bring their religion away from the reservation.

"Near the centre of the encampment they had placed a young sapling and fastened to this the keep-sakes that had been captured from the Sioux who were murdered by them last week. They consisted of two scalps stretched upon hoops and attached to long poles, the skins of fingers with nails pendent, tufts of hair, pieces of flesh, &c., fastened upon bushes, all ornamented with fancy colored bits of cloth. Some of the half breeds and 'good Sioux' who are at the Fort examined them and gave it as their opinion that the scalps were taken from Sioux who were living with the Winnebagoes, as those upon the plains never wear such short hair. They looked savage when viewing the relics of their brethren and vow vengeance.

"During the forenoon they participated in one of their grand scalp dances, forming a circle about the sapling, the men beating upon drums and sticks, while the squaws carried the scalps and other relics, and all shouted and sung their wild war cadence as they moved in the 'misty maze of the dance'." [141]

There were 756 Winnebago aboard the *Canada* when she arrived at Davenport. An editor who visited the boat while in port described them as a "squalid, wretched looking set" of "Injins". Unfortunately history has not left a record of the Winnebago opinion of the citizens of that thriving Iowa community. [142]

The removal of whole tribes does not compare in importance with the transportation of delegations or the delivery of annuities. The three combined, however, were a constant source of profit to steamboats. When the season was dull in the settled areas below the lead mines or when competition became keen, a tramp voyage to Fort Snelling or the tributaries of the Mississippi always brought with it a handsome return. Furthermore, captains became familiar with the channel of the Mississippi and its tributaries — a fact which was to stand them in good stead a little later. More important still, Atwater and other Indian Commissioners wrote glowing accounts of the rich lands of the Upper Mississippi which were eagerly read by the discontented in the more settled areas of the United

States. It was such accounts that turned the tide of immigration northward. The news that the Indians had been removed from this region so suited to agriculture and industry also encouraged white settlement.

18

Facts, Figures, Furs, and Buffalo Robes [143]

THE FUR TRADER on the Upper Mississippi created a lucrative steamboat traffic. Supplies and equipment for traders and goods to be used in the Indian trade formed the principal upstream cargo, while large quantities of furs and peltries were shipped downstream. In 1822 the United States factory system was abolished. A St. Louis newspaper noted a marked activity in the fur trade : "Those formerly engaged in it, have increased their capital and extended their enterprize, many new firms have engaged in it, and others are preparing to do so. It is computed that a thousand men, chiefly from this place, are now employed in this trade on the waters of the Missouri, and half that number on the Upper Mississippi." [144]

Trading posts were planted at strategic points along the Upper Mississippi and its tributaries. Those on the Mississippi were usually established at the confluence of a tributary stream, such as the Des Moines, the Skunk, the Iowa, the Rock, the Fever, the Wisconsin, the Chippewa, and the St. Peter's rivers. Late in the fall of 1824 Thomas Forsyth, Indian Agent at Rock Island, appointed six licensed traders in his district; David G. Bates and Amos Farrar were granted permits to trade with Sauk, Fox, and Winnebago Indians at the Fever River settlements; Russell Farnham received a license to trade with Sauk and Fox at

Facts, Figures, Furs, and Buffalo Robes

Flint Hills on the site of Burlington, Iowa; Maurice Blondeau procured the right to traffic with the same Indians at Dirt Lodge on the Des Moines River; George Davenport obtained the privilege of bartering with the Sauk, Fox, and Winnebago at Rock Island; and Antoine Gautier, at the special request of the Winnebago, was located at a point fifty miles east of Davenport's post on the Rock River.[145]

Few places exhibited a greater activity than the region about the Falls of St. Anthony. In 1826 Lawrence Taliaferro, Indian Agent at Fort Snelling, reported that he had made seven locations on the waters of the Mississippi alone : "one at the mouth of Chippeway River, one at the Falls of S^t. Croix, one on Crow Island, one at Sandy Lake, one at Leaf Lake, one at Leach Lake and one at Red Lake." At the same time ten other posts of the Columbia, the Cheyenne American, and the American Fur companies were located at strategic points within Taliaferro's jurisdiction. Fort Snelling served as the entrepôt for most of these posts, and from there the seasonal catch was shipped downstream.[146]

Each decade witnessed the abandonment of posts along the Mississippi as the northerly tide of immigration gradually pushed back the fur traders. By 1829 the country which Giacomo C. Beltrami described as wasteland in 1823 seemed to Caleb Atwater to be growing populous. What was considered a wilderness by Captain Frederick Marryat in 1837 had become a thriving settled area when Fredrika Bremer visited it in 1851. By the turn of the half century the posts which formerly extended from Galena almost to St. Louis had disappeared. St. Paul and Prairie du Chien alone remained the chief fur centers on the Upper Mississippi.[147]

Abundant and colorful information about Upper Mississippi steamboats is entombed in the correspondence between Hercules L. Dousman and Henry H. Sibley. The former was born at Mackinac in 1800 and educated in New Jersey. He entered a mercantile house in New York in 1818, but returned to Mackinac two years later to assist his father who was a fur trader. In 1826 he removed to Prairie du Chien and became an agent of the American Fur Company and a partner of Joseph Rolette. When the latter died in 1844, Dousman put the final stamp on his reputation as a shrewd business man by marrying his partner's widow. Steamboats puffed up to the wharf at Dousman's home, "Chateau Brilliante", discharging cargoes of goods and luxuries for Wisconsin's wealthiest citizen before the Civil War. Dousman was the outstanding representative of the American Fur Company on the Upper Mississippi.[148]

Sibley, the other representative of the American Fur Company, was located after 1834 at Mendota directly across the Minnesota River from Fort Snelling. He played an important rôle in the district about the Falls of St. Anthony. Franklin Steele, Joseph Laframboise, Martin McLeod, Alexis Bailly, and Norman W. Kittson also were important characters in the fur trade of this district. Dousman, Sibley, and Steele were especially interested in encouraging steamboating : each held shares in Upper Mississippi craft.[149]

While no record is known which would indicate that the *Virginia* and the *Rambler* in 1823, or the *Mandan* and the *Indiana* in 1824, carried the employees or cargoes of the fur companies to the Upper Mississippi, it is altogether possible that they did. On April 2, 1825, Captain David G. Bates took the *Rufus Putnam* to Fort Snelling. Four weeks later this craft carried goods to the Columbia Fur Company's post at Land's End, about a mile above the fort on the Minnesota River. The *Rufus Putnam* is the first steamboat known to have carried such supplies upstream to Fort Snelling, as well as the first to ascend the Minnesota River.[150]

St. Louis was the entrepôt for the fur trade on the Upper Mississippi, as well as on the Missouri. "The American Fur Company", noted Atwater in 1829, "have here a large establishment, and the furs, skins and peltry cannot amount to less than one million dollars annually, which are brought down the Mississippi and Missouri rivers . . . The Indian goods sold by this company, all come from England, and are of the best quality." [151]

Not all the furs from the Upper Mississippi, however, went to St. Louis. Before 1840 the trading posts below Prairie du Chien shipped their pelts downstream, but the seasonal catch of the American Fur Company on the Wisconsin and Minnesota rivers was concentrated in Dousman's warehouse, counted and sorted, loaded on keel or Durham boats, and forwarded to New York by way of the Wisconsin and Fox rivers and Green Bay. This was a difficult course to travel, for the boats were so badly battered by snags and sandbars on the Fox and Wisconsin rivers and from being dragged across the portage at Fort Winnebago that they were generally worthless at the close of the first season. Provisions were often wasted and spoiled. The route lessened the receipts of Upper Mississippi steamboats, since they usually carried the furs only from St. Peter's at the mouth of the Minnesota River to Prairie du Chien and were obliged to depend on lead and miscellaneous cargoes of freight for the remainder of the trip to St. Louis. Each year it became more apparent to traders on the Upper Mississippi that St. Louis was the logical point from which to ship furs eastward.

In 1835 Dousman informed Ramsay Crooks, president of the American Fur Company, that it was almost impossible to ship pelts by way of Green Bay because of the damage to the furs and the great expense involved in transporting them over this route. To reduce the cost of transportation, Dousman proposed that Prairie du Chien be made the entrepôt for the inspection of furs, that he be granted the "privilege of the St. Louis markets, previous to sending them on to New York", and that Crooks should set a fair price on the furs shipped to him.

No immediate action was taken on this proposal, but the subject was revived each year. In 1838, for example, Dousman urged Crooks to ship trade goods by way of St. Louis, Pittsburgh, and the Pennsylvania Canal and railroad; and he recommended that certain heavy articles be purchased in St. Louis. Dousman considered the New Orleans route too long; and he asserted that "from Green Bay here the conveyances are so uncertain that it will not do to trust to them."

As the traffic on the Upper Mississippi increased, shipments to St. Louis by steamboat became more certain and the wisdom of Dousman's suggestions was soon recognized. Bundles of furs were a part of almost every steamboat cargo after 1840. The *Malta* left St. Peter's on June 8, 1840, in command of William P. Gorman, with ten packs of skins for St. Louis. According to a bill of lading signed by E. F. Chouteau, clerk of the *Malta*, the downstream tariff was a dollar a pack.[152]

Since the traffic above Galena occasioned by the presence of Indians, fur companies, and military posts was small, it rarely warranted the services of more than one or two boats. Moreover, a goodly portion of the supplies for the Upper Mississippi Valley was taken from St. Louis and the Ohio River by transient craft, although regular boats plying between Galena and St. Louis captured an occasional cargo.

Such a consignment was carried by the *Bellview* to Sibley in 1836 for the Sioux Outfit. Besides the customary assortment of blankets, cloth, and strouding, the *Bellview* took to the Upper Mississippi a number of other items of dress, including three blue cloth frock coats and six pairs of cloth pantaloons, presumably intended for some of the notable Sioux chiefs. Then there were also aboard two dozen common horn combs, a dozen dressing combs, 1600 pairs of earbobs, 400 large and 2000 small common broaches, 160 pierced broaches, 14 bunches of garnets, 27,000 white and 25,000 black wampum, 14 pairs of arm bands, and 15 pairs of wrist bands.

Hunting and war equipment included 20 North West guns four feet long, 10 North West guns three and one-half feet long, 16 kegs of gunpowder, 3000 percussion caps, 53 pigs of lead, 6 dozen cartouche knives, and 24 dozen scalping knives — the latter possibly to be used on the crowns of luckless Chippewa braves. Firewater, in the form of a basket of champagne, four kegs of Spanish Brown, and five gallons of old port wine, probably disappeared all too soon. Four kegs and three boxes of tobacco may have enabled the Sioux to spend many hours in reverie over the delightfully "civilizing" sensations resulting from an intimate and perhaps too liberal use of the wines.

Foodstuffs included 18 barrels of pork, 25 barrels of flour, 2 kegs of lard, 3 barrels of New Orleans sugar, 50 bags of corn, a chest of tea, and 12 bags of peas. The miscellaneous material included 12 boxes of soap, square irons, nail rods, flat irons, steel, a set of wagon harness, 4 kegs of white lead, a stove and pipe, a barrel of linseed oil, 10 bars of iron, an ox plough, 4 kegs of nails, 5 brass kettles, a coil grass rope, and a trunk.[153]

The cost of transporting such consignments from St. Louis to Prairie du Chien and St. Peter's on Upper Mississippi steamboats was slight compared with the expense incurred in bringing the goods to St. Louis. Although trade goods were less bulky than food supplies, the amount paid for importing goods from England to Prairie du Chien almost equaled the original price of the goods in England. In 1835, for example, the cost of a single shipment of goods in England was $11,238.53. The itemized bill for conveying this merchandise from England to Prairie du Chien was as follows : packing, shipping, and other charges, $935.29; exchange and insurance to New York, $1,241.49; duties and other charges in New York, $5,228.95; commission at five per cent, $904.94; freight to New Orleans and charges there, $204.85; freight to St. Louis and charges there, $229.50; freight to Prairie du Chien, $105.78; and the total, including five per cent interest, was $9,050.80. When the goods reached Prairie du Chien the cost was $20,289.33, or almost double the original price.[154]

The tariff on the English goods shipped from St. Louis to Prairie du Chien was slightly more than a hundred dollars. But imported trade goods were insignificant compared with the commodities such as flour, sugar, corn, dried fruit, meats, liquor, powder, and lead (all products of the Mississippi Valley) which made up the bulk of the shipments. Steamboats obtained a generous return on freight of this kind, since charges of a dollar and more per hundred pounds was the general rule.[155]

After goods arrived at Prairie du Chien, Dousman took the portion belonging to his outfit and forwarded the remainder to Sibley at St. Peter's. In 1835 Captain Joseph Throckmorton carried Sibley's supplies upstream on the

Warrior. Foodstuffs aboard included 33 barrels of New Orleans sugar, 12 kegs of lard, 11 barrels of molasses, a barrel of dried peaches and another of apples, 2 bags and 12 sacks of coffee, a barrel of crackers, a box of bacon hams, 10 shoulders of bacon, 33 barrels of "One Hog Pork", 200 sacks and 400 bushels of corn, and 4 barrels of salt. Two dozen bales of blankets, strouding, and pieces of gaudy colored cloth were also stored aboard. The cargo included 2 "Chiefs Guns", 10 North West guns, 129 kegs of gunpowder, 170 pigs of lead, 310 rat traps, and 36 beaver traps. A box of Cavendish tobacco, 2 boxes and 2 kegs of common plug tobacco, 4 boxes of British soap, 6 boxes of glass, 12 barrels of porter, 10,000 pine shingles, a barrel of tallow, 5 demijohns of sperm oil, a crate and a cask of tinware, a bundle of square irons and another of round irons, and a bundle of German steel made up the miscellaneous articles that were shipped to Sibley on the *Warrior* in 1835.[156]

After the trip of the *Rufus Putnam* in 1825, the arrival at Fort Snelling of the first steamboat of the season was awaited with impatience. Under date of March 31, 1826, Taliaferro noted that the weather was moderate and the ice firm. Six days later the ice was still thick but weak. Flocks of wild geese flew honking over Fort Snelling on April 14th, but the ice remained intact despite a twelve foot rise in the river. The following day the Minnesota River broke up, but the Mississippi remained firm. A bateau carrying peltries, the first boat of the season, arrived from Lac qui Parle on April 17th. With the Mississippi twenty feet above its normal level, the ice finally started out from above Fort Snelling on April 21st, sweeping away the crude huts that stood clustered along the bank. A second bateau arrived from the Minnesota River on April 26th; but still no steamboat appeared. Finally, on May 2nd, the steamboat *Lawrence* (Captain D. F. Reeder commanding) arrived with a heavy cargo of freight and a considerable number of passengers.[157]

Steamboat captains (whether they were the first to arrive, the last to depart, or simply made flying mid-season trips) were always held in high regard by the pioneers — especially on the fur-trading frontier. If a captain arrived twice during a season he was welcomed as a friend; if he made several trips he was looked upon as a brother; and if he appeared in the trade two successive seasons he was almost deified. Such men as Daniel Smith Harris, Joseph Throckmorton, John and George W. Atchison, David G. Bates, James Lafferty, Orrin Smith, and Hiram Bersie made several trips during the course of a season or plied in the trade more than one year. By 1850 Harris and Throckmorton had each averaged about fifteen years on the Upper Mississippi, and the combined record of the Atchison brothers was equally good.[158]

Before the creation of Minnesota Territory in 1849, arrivals of steamboats at Fort Snelling were extremely irregular; while the arrivals at Prairie du Chien were likened by a settler to "angel's visits, 'few, and far between'." The scarcity of cargoes often led captains to demand exorbitant rates : in 1840 Dousman "blackguarded" Captain James

Lafferty for charging Sibley excessive freight rates for goods shipped on the *Omega*. Trips were made only when a sufficient cargo was offered. In 1844 forty-one craft reached Fort Snelling, while in the five years preceding 1849 an average of forty-four boats docked there. The exact number of trips to St. Peter's between 1835 and 1844 is unknown, but it is not likely that the average was more than twenty-five a year.[159]

When Stephen R. Riggs, a missionary to the Sioux, arrived in St. Louis in 1837 he was told that less than a half dozen craft reached Fort Snelling each season. Riggs was horrified to learn that the steamboat *Pavilion* left St. Louis every Sunday : he hoped to avoid breaking the Sabbath by boarding a boat at Alton. When the *Olive Branch* arrived he took passage on it. Saturday night found the *Olive Branch* near Davenport, and Riggs, refusing to travel on the Lord's Day, got off and spent the night in a room where his slumber was broken by intermittent volleys of profanity from an adjoining "doggery". The missionary reached Galena without mishap; but there he was forced to await the arrival of a boat destined for Fort Snelling. The *Pavilion* arrived at Galena on a Saturday night, where fervent prayers, coupled with a dearth of freight, held the boat over until Monday. The remainder of the journey was made by the missionary without interruption.[160]

Some regularity of service might have been attained had one or two boats taken over the trade of the Upper Mississippi and transient craft remained below. Since, however, captains of "tramp" vessels were not imbued with any such altruistic spirit, much rivalry resulted. The American Fur Company was interested in encouraging regular service, and so found it necessary to make a choice of captains. Both Throckmorton and Atchison were of a temperament more tractable than that of the fiery "Smith" Harris, and the lion's share of the fur trade traffic went to them. This was a bitter blow for Harris; but he continued in the trade throughout the forties with the *Otter*, the *War Eagle*, the *Senator*, and the *Dr. Franklin No. 2*. His skill and daring, his genial disposition, and his dogged and often ruthless determination in the face of competition were a constant source of annoyance to his competitors. During the forties Throckmorton ran the *Malta*, the *General Brooke*, the *Nimrod*, the *Cecilia*, and the *Cora*, while John Atchison commanded the *Lynx* and the *Highland Mary*. Throckmorton withdrew from the Upper Mississippi in 1848 and Atchison died of cholera in St. Louis two years later.[161]

For four or five months each year the Mississippi froze over, leaving the fur traders almost completely isolated in their frozen northland until the following spring. Whenever the steamboats failed to bring them their winter supplies the plight of the fur traders became desperate.

The importance of steamboats to the fur-trading frontier is graphically revealed in a letter of Dousman dated November 20, 1838, and replying to Sibley's plea for aid.

"I sent off another Boat with Provisions for you on the 6th Inst but the Ice commenced running in the river the next day & they only got a few miles above Painted Rock — [mouth of Yellow River] the cold weather came on so suddenly that the Boat could not even get back here and she now lies frozen up a few miles above this place — from below I hear that the Burlington left St. Louis on the 2nd Inst with our supplies & that the Ariel would meet her at the Lower Rapids to bring the loading here & St. Peters if the weather permitted — how far the[y] got up we have not learnt — the[y] have not yet reached Du Buque as we have heard from there — the River is now completely closed so as to preclude all hope of seeing a Boat here this fall — Horses now cross the River on the Ice and the weather continues cold. We are not the only persons who have been disappointed by the extreme low water on the Rapids & the Winter closing in on us So early and unexpectedly — there is not a pound of Pork, Sugar, Tea, Coffee, Lard, Butter for sale in this place — all the merchants are entirely destitute of groceries & have all been caught with their supplies on the way up — Galena, Dubuque &c are even worse off than this place — the People in the mining country will have to kill all their Cattle & eat Corn Bread — luckily the Corn Crop is good this year — I was fortunate in getting from the Winnebagos 250 Bbls Flour which they did not want till Spring, as otherwise we should have actually been in a starving condition at this time — You will see that I had put on board of the two Boats near 100 Bbls out of this quantity for you — You will naturally enough say, all this does not fill our Bellies".[162]

Facts, Figures, Furs, and Buffalo Robes

Since the fur-trading frontier was dependent upon the steamboat, Dousman, Sibley, and other members of the American Fur Company did not hesitate to assume heavy financial interests in the Upper Mississippi craft. Perhaps the earliest boat in which the fur company had an interest was the *Burlington*, which was built at Pittsburgh in 1837. She was owned by Throckmorton, Pierre Chouteau, Jr., and the firm of Hempstead and Beebe — all of St. Louis. These men, with Captain George McNeil and Isaac Newton Waggoner who hailed from Illinois, had an interest in the *Ariel*, also built at Pittsburgh in 1837. Two years later the *Malta* slid from the "ways" at Pittsburgh. She was owned by Throckmorton and Chouteau.[163]

Dousman seems to have taken his first financial interest in an Upper Mississippi steamboat in 1840, when he and Throckmorton bought the 107-ton *Chippewa*. In 1844 Sibley, Franklin Steele, B. W. Brisbois, and Captain William H. Hooper each owned an eighth in the *Lynx*; Dousman possessed the remaining half. The American Fur Company held an interest in the *Nimrod* and the *General Brooke*, but Throckmorton was the sole owner of the *Cecilia* and the *Cora*. In 1850 Brisbois, Dousman, and Henry M. Rice of St. Paul had a part interest in Captain Orrin Smith's *Nominee*.[164] Dousman continued his interest in Upper Mississippi steamboating until his death. In 1857 he owned a hundred and sixty shares of stock in the Prairie du Chien, Hudson, and St. Paul Packet Company, and was making payments on three hundred additional shares. The members of the Northern Outfit were instrumental in organizing the Minnesota Packet Company, which twenty years later absorbed almost all the other steamboat lines on the river.[165]

Throckmorton was a great favorite with the agents of the Northern Outfit. In 1839 Dousman notified Crooks that he had authorized Throckmorton to draw on him for a thousand dollars.[166] Six years later he wrote Sibley that Throckmorton (then in command of the *General Brooke*) wished to form a steamboat line between St. Louis and Fort Snelling with Captain John Atchison of the *Lynx*. "I am in favor of it", concluded Dousman, "& shall encourage him to do so, as it will be of benefit to the Outfit & hurt the Harris's which I desire very much. I want you to give Throckmorton a part of your Freight so as to encourage him to run regular. He is just off and I have not time to say more at present." [167]

Atchison was also a favorite with the fur company, although he was by no means so popular as Throckmorton. In 1845 Dousman wrote Sibley that Captain Harris had just gone up to St. Peter's with the *Otter* and urged him to restrain his people from buying anything from this boat, as Atchison had left St. Louis with the *Lynx* and would arrive shortly with "every thing you stand in need of." [168]

It is not likely that either Dousman or Sibley, anxious as they were for supplies from below and news from the outside world, would expect Atchison or Throckmorton to make a trip when no freight was offered. Nevertheless, the opening of spring navigation always found the two

traders hopefully awaiting the arrival of their yearly shipment of supplies. In the spring of 1838 Dousman wrote
Sibley that Throckmorton was at Prairie du Chien with
the *Burlington*, that he had just left for below to procure
a cargo of supplies for Sibley, but that none of the regular spring stock had come up. The following April he
informed Sibley that the *Ariel* was expected shortly with
all their goods and provisions.[169] Sometimes it was necessary to offer special inducements to persuade a captain to
make a trip.[170]

Competitors of the American Fur Company often sent
buyers north to attempt to break the company's monopoly.
On such occasions steamboat captains often carried letters
warning members of the Northern Outfit of the presence
of such buyers. In 1844 S. W. McMaster gave Captain
Harris a note for Franklin Steele informing him that competitors were going up on the *Otter* for the purpose of
buying furs and advising him of a rising market in which
most furs had gone up fifty to a hundred per cent.[171]

It would be impossible to estimate the earnings of steam
boats directly engaged in the fur trade. Governed largely
by the amount of freight on hand, the stage of the water,
the season of the year, and the number of craft in the
trade, rates varied greatly; but as a rule they were high.
Before 1850 the cost of transportation between Galena
and Fort Snelling was generally higher than it was a decade later between St. Louis and St. Paul. Charges from
Galena upstream were seldom less than fifty cents a hundred pounds; usually more was asked. In 1840 the *Malta*

demanded a dollar a barrel for transporting five barrels of beer from Prairie du Chien to Fort Snelling. The *Demoine* charged seventy-five cents a hundred pounds for transporting the freight of the *Agnes* from Galena to St. Peter's. In June, 1845, the *Otter* carried a trundle bed, a tin boiler, and a musket bar for one dollar. Captain Throckmorton in October of the same year conveyed six kegs of powder from Galena to Fort Snelling on the *Cecilia* at the rate of a dollar per keg.

Captains sometimes collected the amount due on an article as well as the regular transportation fee. In 1845 the *Agnes* took 75 kegs of butter from Louisiana, Missouri, to St. Peter's at the rate of $1.75 per hundred pounds. Clerk B. F. Wood was required to collect $1,375.00 from Franklin Steele in payment for the butter. A sum of $205.82 was paid Captain W. P. Gorman of the *Chippewa* for 4989 pounds of miscellaneous freight, 16 pigs of lead, 5 barrels of apples, and the passage of a man and servant from St. Louis to St. Peter's. Pound freight was transported at the rate of $2.50 per hundred.[172]

Despite such exorbitant prices, Upper Mississippi steamboats did not always reap rich profits. In 1844 the *Lynx* netted only $161.04 for the season, after deducting losses sustained by injury to the boat. The following year, however, the same boat earned $11,194.73 with a considerable amount still due her from tardy shippers. This was probably near the average yearly earnings. Since the fur company had a seven-eighths interest in the *Lynx*, it shared in the dividends. While Captain John Atchison delayed in

apportioning the earnings of the *Lynx,* Dousman frequently suggested to Sibley that a final settlement be made.
This misunderstanding was a subject of much written and
verbal controversy over a period of several months.[173]
Important as was the Mississippi traffic in furs, it nevertheless dwindles into insignificance when compared, both
in value and bulk of shipments, with the lead trade.
Neither was it as profitable as the government shipments
to the Indian and military frontiers. Then, too, the
shipment of a large portion of the furs by way of the Wisconsin and Fox rivers and Green Bay route deprived steamboats of a considerable cargo. The fur trade, however,
was significant because it offered a supplementary cargo
to the stores shipped by the government to the Indians and
troops of the Upper Mississippi. Likewise the financial
encouragement of the American Fur Company was of
importance, supplying a subsidy that neither the Indian
nor the military frontier offered to steamboat captains.
Finally, it should be pointed out that the considerable
stimulus given by the fur trade to steamboating on the
Upper Mississippi and its tributaries contributed to the
spread of general information about the region. This in
turn played its part in attracting the settlers and immigrants who were soon to transform the fur-traders' frontier into an agricultural and industrial domain.

19

Freight for Red River Oxcarts

MORE UNIQUE than the Upper Mississippi fur traffic was the trade which resulted from the planting of a settlement on the Red River of the North by the Earl of Selkirk. In 1811 this philanthropic Scotchman acquired from the Hudson's Bay Company a tract of about 116,000 square miles. Here in the immense inland empire, known as Assiniboia and comprising roughly Manitoba and the northern part of Minnesota and North Dakota, Selkirk planned to establish colonies of evicted Scotch peasants. On August 30, 1812, an advance guard of Scotch, with a few Irish, arrived at the confluence of the Assiniboine with the Red River, where Winnipeg now stands. The colony grew despite many hardships and adversities. By 1821 a company of Swiss mechanics and tradesmen had been induced to seek their fortunes in this frontier land.

A more remote site for a settlement could scarcely have been chosen. Fully five hundred miles from the Falls of St. Anthony, the Selkirk colonies were so isolated that the Upper Mississippi offered the best means of transportation to and from the outside world. When news of the arrival of the steamboat *Virginia* at Fort Snelling reached these lonely colonists it was hailed with delight.[174]

As early as 1819 a party of men had left the Selkirk settlement for Prairie du Chien to buy seed grain. After making the desired purchases they began their homeward journey on April 20, 1820, in three Mackinaw boats loaded with two hundred bushels of wheat, a hundred bushels of oats, and thirty bushels of peas. Ascending the Minnesota River to its source, they dragged their boats and supplies over the portage to Lake Traverse, descended the Bois des Sioux and Red rivers, and reached the Selkirk colony sometime in June.[175]

The advent of the *Virginia* on the Upper Mississippi in 1823 ushered in a new era for the Red River settlements. When the *Rambler* left St. Peter's in 1823 she took down two Swiss families from the Selkirk colony to St. Louis. They had left because of the constant dread of Indian attack and the severe winters and short summers; but with uncanny foresight they prophesied the development of a lucrative steamboat traffic in provisions from St. Louis to be exchanged for furs and peltries. A herd of two hundred cattle had been driven to the Red River settlement in 1823 and sold for six thousand dollars. The drovers made the round trip in five months.[176]

The people in the Red River area drew a large portion of their incomes from furs and peltries — especially from buffalo hides. Indeed the prowess of the Pembina group in the chase became proverbial : they were often referred to as the Red River hunters. Fort Snelling, and later St. Paul, became the entrepôt for the Red River Valley trade. Heavily loaded with the spoils of the chase, long caravans of oxcarts jolted southward each spring to the head of navigation, there to await the arrival of supplies on Upper

Mississippi steamboats. Several months were required to make the round trip overland. The creaking of the lumbering oxcarts could be heard for miles. On July 10, 1847, a caravan of 120 carts arrived at St. Paul in single file, "wearily moving along by the moonlight". The caravan had been nineteen days on its way through a region abounding with buffalo : and so the hunters had a choice assortment of "well dressed" buffalo robes which they sold in St. Paul by the lot at $3.50 each. The caravan remained in St. Paul several days awaiting the arrival of a steamboat load of flour and groceries.[177]

Before 1850 St. Louis, Galena, and Dubuque were termini for the trade of the Red River Valley. Galena furnished goods valued at fifteen thousand dollars to the settlements in 1848. At the same time the traders from the Red River were urged to take buffalo packs farther south if Henry Sibley and Henry Rice did not offer fair prices. In 1849 the steamboat *Senator* arrived at Galena with a hundred packs of buffalo robes from the Red River hunters.[178]

In 1853 it took thirty-two days for a caravan of 133 oxcarts to make the journey from "Grant Cote" in Pembina County to Traverse des Sioux. Norman W. Kittson, Joseph Rolette, and Peter Hayden were among the traders who went to Mendota on the *Clarion*; Charles Cavileer, the United States collector at Pembina, also was a passenger. Kittson had over four thousand buffalo robes as his share of the spoils of the chase. The number of buffaloes on the plains (said to be unprecedented) seemed almost to verify the Indian theory that they sprang from out of the earth.[179]

After 1850 St. Paul sought a complete monopoly of the Red River trade. The *Minnesota Democrat* of July 22, 1851, complained bitterly of a duty of twenty or thirty per cent on goods of the Red River settlers and urged that it be speedily removed or a valuable trade would be lost. Interest in the Red River country became national in character; and during the winter of 1857-1858 arrangements were made with the U. S. Secretary of the Treasury to enable the Hudson's Bay Company to ship its goods in bond through the United States to St. Paul. The St. Paul Chamber of Commerce paid Anson Northup two thousand dollars for putting a steamboat in operation on the Red River in 1859. At the same time the Hudson's Bay Company asked Burbank and Company of St. Paul for aid in transporting across the Minnesota country one hundred and twenty tons of goods from England and thirty tons of tobacco, sugar, and other commodities from New York. Two hundred tons of freight were carried by the steamboat *Enterprize* on the Mississippi to St. Cloud, whence it was teamed to Georgetown and thence taken on the Red River to Fort Garry on the *Anson Northup*. In 1862 the *Enterprize* contracted to carry seven hundred tons of freight for the Hudson's Bay Company from St. Paul to St. Cloud.[180]

Steamboats on the Upper Mississippi continued to transport goods destined for the Red River country after the Civil War. An item in a Dubuque newspaper in 1866 reads : "There is stored in the depot at Dunleith, 1,600 packages of goods for the Hudson Bay Company up the Red River, in the British American possessions. They are the neatest and best done up packages ever seen in that depot, and Americans could learn something by inspecting them. They consist of teas, sugars, dry goods, clothing, hardware, shot, and a general assortment of articles of use for the comfort of men. An agent accompanies them on their transit, pays the freight bill over each road, in British gold, sees that they are not molested, and keeps the articles together. They were shipped from London to Halifax, from thence to Dunleith, and will be shipped this week to St. Paul on a packet. Each package has the duty stamped upon it, and is covered with sealing wax to detect fraud, and all packages encased with cloth are bound firmly with cords tied in a flat knot and the ends connected together with lead. Any of the goods could be bought in Dunleith or Dubuque for half what the freight has cost."

Later an additional shipment of one hundred tons of goods arrived at Dunleith, destined for the Red River country.[181] Although the Red River freight transported by Upper Mississippi steamboats was of little consequence when compared with the traffic in lead or grain or with the passenger trade; it made, nevertheless, one of the most picturesque of steamboat cargoes by virtue of its nature and destination.

20

Steamboats on the Military Frontier

SHORTLY BEFORE the opening of the War of 1812 the Sauk and Fox Indians were at war with the Winnebago, and the life of every fur trader was endangered. Robert Grant, a friend of the Sauk and Fox, made his headquarters at Prairie du Chien but traveled much through the lead district. Seldom sleeping two nights in the same place, Grant traversed the hilly, heavily wooded country in quest of furs. Stream and forest supplied this self-reliant trapper with food prepared in a brass bowl tucked unceremoniously under his fur cap when not in use.

One day Grant met a party of Winnebago who instantly recognized him as a friend of the Sauk and Fox. Grant fled, but was overtaken by a Winnebago who drew his tomahawk and struck a terrific blow on Grant's head. A sharp, metallic click was the only result. Sensing the situation, the hardy pioneer calmly turned around and confronted the astonished Indians who recoiled in terror crying "Manitou! Manitou!" Henceforth Grant went his way unmolested. Grant County, Wisconsin, bounded for sixty miles along its western border by the Mississippi, is named in honor of hard-headed Robert Grant.[182]

Long before the arrival of the first steamboat, the constantly recurring outbreaks between the various Indian tribes and friction between Indians and fur traders made necessary the erection of military posts at strategic points along the Upper Mississippi.[183] As early as 1808 the first American fort on the Upper Mississippi had been erected in what was to become Iowa. It was named Fort Madison but was abandoned and destroyed during the War of 1812. At the conclusion of that struggle, three new forts were erected along the Upper Mississippi. Fort Edwards was constructed on the east side of the Mississippi at the mouth of the Des Moines River near the foot of the Lower Rapids. Fort Armstrong was situated on Rock Island at the foot of the Upper Rapids. Fort Crawford was located on the outskirts of the little French village of Prairie du Chien, six miles above the junction of the Wisconsin and the Mississippi. In 1819, Fort Snelling was built on a towering bluff on the west bank of the Mississippi at its junction with the St. Peter's or Minnesota River : a site almost seven hundred miles from what was to be its chief source of supply and reënforcement — Jefferson Barracks, Missouri.

Equally dependent on the Upper Mississippi steamboats were the posts situated on the various tributaries of the Mississippi. The second Fort Des Moines (at the Raccoon Fork of the Des Moines River), Fort Atkinson in northeastern Iowa, Fort Ridgely and Fort Ripley in Minnesota, and Fort Winnebago in Wisconsin were important military posts in the period which preceded the Civil War.[184] Approximately four decades intervened between the erection of Fort Armstrong and Fort Crawford and such posts as Fort Ridgely on the Minnesota River and Fort Ripley on

Steamboats on the Military Frontier

the Mississippi River above the Falls of St. Anthony. As the Indian and fur trader frontier receded before the oncoming waves of immigration, the military frontier followed and the distance which steamboats had to travel was consequently increased.

The presence of troops on the frontier gave steamboating its initial impetus. Both the *Virginia* and the *Rambler* carried public stores as far north as Fort Snelling in 1823. Prior to this time keelboats were used to transport troops and supplies to the newly erected forts. To complete the entire journey upstream to Fort Snelling (the most remote point on the Upper Mississippi) the keelboat sometimes took only forty days, but often as many as sixty were required. As early as 1819 the War Department ordered Major Thomas Forsyth to ship $2000 worth of goods by steamboat to the Sioux Indians above Prairie du Chien in payment for the site on which Fort Snelling was to be established. But at that time it was believed that the rapids could not be navigated by steamboats, and so keelboats were used. By the summer of 1826 fourteen steam boats had followed in the wake of the *Virginia* and the *Rambler*: each had ventured northward primarily because of the traffic in troops and military supplies.[185]

The advent of the steamboat on the Upper Mississippi was of strategic importance to the government. Transportation by keelboat had been slow, uncertain, and expensive; and the risk was great. For example, in 1819 James Johnson charged three cents per pound to transport goods from Bellefontaine, Missouri, to Fort Crawford. At

Steamboating on Upper Mississippi

$3.00 per hundred the 389,946 pounds (194 tons) netted $11,699.28. Despite the fact that St. Peter's was only two hundred miles farther upstream the rate from Bellefontaine to that place was seven cents per pound : $9,810.50 was paid for the transportation of seventy tons of provisions to that post. This was more than seven times the usual charge later made by steamboats.[186]

Steamboats on the Upper Mississippi were afforded several ways of reaping profits. Scientific and exploring expeditions were generally dependent on steamboats for transportation of equipment and supplies. Three years before the voyage of the *Virginia*, the steamboat *Western Engineer* had ascended the Upper Mississippi as far as the present site of Keokuk. This was not only the first steamboat to ascend to the Lower Rapids; she was also the first steamboat to ascend the Mississippi on a scientific expedition.[187]

Despite the expenses incurred, scientific expeditions were frequently undertaken. Indeed, the same year (1820) that the *Western Engineer* was ascending the Upper Mississippi to the Des Moines Rapids, Henry R. Schoolcraft set out in a canoe to discover the source of the Mississippi. In 1823 William H. Keating led a division of one of Stephen H. Long's expeditions down the Wisconsin in keelboats and up the Mississippi to the source of the St. Peter's River. Engineers were constantly dispatched to make surveys, soundings, and maps of the river, and for these equipment was provided. The Upper and Lower rapids were especially troublesome : in 1837 Lieutenant

Steamboats on the Military Frontier

Robert E. Lee was sent to report on the best means of eliminating them.[188]

In 1852 a Dubuque newspaper announced the departure of the steamboat *Lamartine* with a large party of surveyors employed in establishing the northern boundary of Iowa. The men were under the personal direction of Captain Andrew Talcott who performed his work under instructions from the United States Surveyor General for Wisconsin and Iowa. The *Lamartine* carried the surveyors, with supplies sufficient for six months, to Lansing in Allamakee County. Active field operations began at the monument "heretofore established by Captain Lee a few miles from Lansing." It was expected that with "great exertions" the survey might be completed that very season.[189]

When the northern route for a transcontinental railroad was surveyed by Isaac I. Stevens in 1853, steamboats carried members of the expedition, scientific equipment, food, clothing, and scores of draft animals to St. Paul. Stevens arrived at St. Paul on May 27, 1853, on board the *Nominee*, having purchased all the draft mules offered in the ports along the way. Such expeditions offered a lucrative income to steamboat captains.[190]

Another source of profit came from the frequent tours of inspection of the various military posts. In the spring of 1824 Brigadier General Winfield Scott left St. Louis for the Upper Mississippi on the steamboat *Mandan* (Captain William Linn commanding). It was on this trip that Scott recommended that the name of Fort St. Anthony be changed to Fort Snelling. Six weeks later the *Mandan* returned to St. Louis in sixty-two and one-half hours running time. Captain Linn expressed the belief that he could make the round trip of fifteen hundred miles in ten days. Shortly afterwards the *Mandan* ascended the Missouri River to Fort Atkinson.

Jefferson Barracks was the entrepôt for such expeditions. The trips were made when a good stage of water was assured. In the fall of 1831 Brigadier General Henry Leavenworth and his officers (having completed their inspection of the posts on the Upper Mississippi) left St. Louis on board the *Enterprise* for Cantonment Jesup near Natchitoches, Louisiana. Though the number of passengers carried was small, such trips afforded a welcome addition to the business of the Upper Mississippi steamboats.[191]

Troops escorted Indian delegates to treaty grounds and conducted tribes to new reservations. Bound for the conference at Prairie du Chien, a detachment of troops under Colonel Willoughby Morgan accompanied the three hundred Indians on board Captain Butler's *Planet* when she arrived at Galena in 1830. Dragoons and regulars were aboard the *Dr. Franklin* as she steamed back and forth from Wabasha's prairie to St. Paul during the removal of the Winnebago in 1848. Troops were also aboard the *Excelsior* when she conveyed the lower tribe of Sioux to Traverse des Sioux in 1851. After the massacre at New Ulm, Minnesota, in 1862, a heavy military force escorted the Sioux prisoners down the Minnesota and Mississippi rivers to Davenport.[192]

Steamboats on the Military Frontier

Surveys and scientific expeditions, tours of inspection and military escorts for the red man, all afforded profitable returns to the enterprising steamboat captains. More important, however, was the transportation of troops in time of war, the yearly movement of troops from post to post during times of peace, and the transportation of supplies and equipment. From these three sources steamboat captains secured their richest gains.

21

Wars and Rumors of War

THE TRANSPORTATION of troops by steamboats during war times was usually more profitable than during times of peace, because the work was done under pressure when no time could be lost in obtaining competitive bids. The first military sortie transported by steamboat occurred in July, 1827, when the *Hamilton*, the *Indiana*, and the *Essex* departed from Jefferson Barracks with a detachment of five hundred soldiers under Brigadier General Henry Atkinson to chastise the Winnebago for attacking white settlers. The progress of this formidable flotilla up the Mississippi was interrupted by the low stage of water at the Des Moines Rapids; the remainder of the journey was made by keelboat. Four years later (in 1831) six companies from the Third and Sixth Regiments left Jefferson Barracks on Captain James May's *Enterprise* to quell disturbances of Sauk, Fox, and Winnebago Indians at Rock Island.[193]

In addition to serving the nation well during minor disturbances, Upper Mississippi steamboats played an important rôle in three major conflicts — the Black Hawk War, the Mexican War, and the Civil War. During the Black Hawk and Mexican wars the Mississippi was the chief avenue of transportation and communication; while throughout the Civil War steamboats conveyed thousands of troops to the war zone and brought back the wounded.

◆━━◆◆◆━━◆

With the outbreak of the Black Hawk War in 1832 the Indian question became a national problem. Steamboats were promptly pressed into the service of the government. Early in April, 1832, the Sixth Regiment of United States Infantry left Jefferson Barracks on board the *Enterprise* and the *Chieftain*, with strict orders to force the Sauk and Fox to surrender the murderers of twenty-eight Menominee Indians in the village of Prairie du Chien. Undeterred by this movement, Black Hawk and his followers started up the Rock River where the defeat of the militia at Stillman's Run was followed by Governor John Reynolds' proclamation asking for two thousand mounted volunteers. Thoroughly aroused by this reverse, both State and national governments moved frantically to crush the uprising.[194]

Throughout the hostilities, conflicting reports trickled into St. Louis from steamboats running on the Illinois and Upper Mississippi rivers : crowds lounged about the levee awaiting each arrival. Anxious wives and mothers lingered patiently, hopeful for news from passengers and newspapers brought down on the steamboats. Captains and clerks, always extolled for their kindness and gentlemanly virtues, became more popular than ever. While the pilots received fabulous salaries, the lowly clerk received the plaudits of the press. Editors spared neither space nor ink in extolling him.[195]

Steamboating was not without its attendant thrills in

[175]

those days. Dangers of snags, explosions, or fires now became of secondary importance. Passengers and crews lived in constant fear of attack by bands of Indians. While making her way downstream from Galena to St. Louis the steamboat *Dove* was suddenly attacked by Indians hidden along the bank of the river. Her sides and upper works were splattered with lead, but she managed to run safely through the gauntlet of fire without serious injury. Piloting under such conditions became a real art. To lose one's head and run the boat on a sandbar or into the bank might easily invite a massacre. Throughout the struggle, however, pilots and captains exhibited a skill and daring indicative of the character of the men who operated Upper Mississippi steamboats.[196]

That steamboating was perilous in war times is revealed by the fact that fewer boats ventured on the Upper Mississippi during the year 1832. But the services of the steamboat *Warrior* during the Black Hawk War entitle her to be ranked among the dozen most historic boats to ply the waters of the Upper Mississippi. Launched at Pittsburgh in the summer of 1832, the *Warrior* was commanded by Joseph Throckmorton. A veteran of four years service on the Upper Mississippi, Throckmorton brought the *Warrior* and her safety barge to St. Louis in mid-summer of 1832, and set out immediately for the war zone.[197]

The *Warrior* arrived at Prairie du Chien just as Black Hawk and his band were retreating toward the Mississippi. She was pressed into service and Throckmorton was given orders to patrol the river above the fort to prevent the

Early navigation by barge on Western Waters.

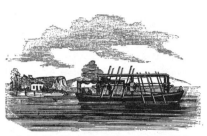

John Fitch's Philadelphia Boat—1786.

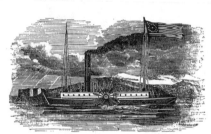

Robert Fulton's *Clermont*—1807. The first truly successful steamboat.

The *New Orleans*—the first boat built on Western Waters—1811.

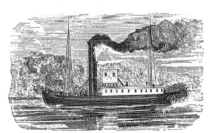

The *Enterprise*—the first boat to ascend Mississippi from New Orleans to Louisville: Time—25 days! She aided General Jackson in the defense of New Orleans.

Reproduced from Lloyd's Steamboat Directory.

The *Washington*—designed by Capt. Henry M. Shreve, this first double-deck steamboat made the round trip between Louisville and New Orleans in 41 days. Blew up-1816.

A painting by Clyde O. Deland depicting the trial trip of John Fitch's first steam-boat at Philadelphia on July 27, 1786.

The Centennial Celebration of steamboat navigation on inland waters. The scene is the Pittsburgh levee on October 31, 1911. The replica of the *New Orleans,* that had been built at Pittsburgh for the occasion, is the small launch-

The replica of the steamboat *New Orleans* stops at Marietta, Ohio, on her way to New Orleans in 1911, one of the many ports visited along the way.

like craft wedged in between two larger boats, and the sixth vessel over from the left. This *New Orleans* made the trip downstream from Pittsburgh to New Orleans and was greeted by cheering multitudes at every port along the way.

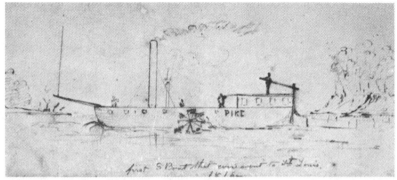

The *Zebulon M. Pike* was the first steamboat to reach St. Louis—August 2, 1817. The 31-ton craft took six weeks to go from Louisville to St. Louis.

The *Western Engineer* was the first steamboat to ascend the Missouri to present-day Omaha (1819); the following year she blazed the trail up the Mississippi to Keokuk.

Artist's concept of the *Virginia* passing the Dubuque lead mines in 1823—the first steamboat to ascend the Upper Mississippi to Fort Snelling.

Steamboats from many ports on Western Waters visited the Upper Mississippi heavily laden with freight and passengers. Hordes of immigrants, both native-born and foreigners, came by way of the Ohio River. Countless numbers of foreigners, however, reached the five states of the Upper Mississippi Valley by way of New Orleans and the palatial Lower Mississippi craft that plied regularly between the Crescent City and St. Louis. At bustling St. Louis, the immigrants lingered but a short time before boarding one of the many steamboats advertised for various points upstream. Prior to the Civil War more than a hundred different steamboats were being recorded at St. Paul. Even more impressive, perhaps, was the registering of more than a thousand steamboat arrivals at that busy port. Most of the Upper Mississippi steamboats during this period were built on the Ohio River—at Pittsburgh and its environs, at Wheeling, at Cincinnati and Louisville, and at New Albany and Jeffersonville in Indiana. It is significant that 99,000 out of 674,000 people living in Iowa in 1860 had migrated from Ohio.

The following eight pages from William Cullen Bryant's *Picturesque America* depict with great detail and accuracy some of the highlights travelers might have seen between 1850 and 1870 as they journeyed down the Ohio and up the Mississippi to St. Louis, or by way of colorful New Orleans to St. Louis, and thence to the Ultima Thule of navigation—the Falls of St. Anthony. (See Chapters 30 through 39)

View of Cincinnati—The "Queen City of the West."

New Albany (above) with her neighbor, Jeffersonville, Indiana, as well as Louisville, Kentucky, across the Ohio, were thriving boat building centers.

SOUTHWEST PASS— NEW ORLEANS

Thousands of immigrants, most of them foreigners, entered the mouth of the Mississippi and proceeded to New Orleans where the ocean vessels discharged their human cargoes for the long trip upstream to St. Louis. Here many boarded Upper Mississippi steamboats for points in northern Missouri, Illinois, Iowa, Wisconsin, and Minnesota.

New Orleans was a colorful seaport, as well as a Mississippi River terminal for steamboats carrying their argosies from all the tributaries of the Father of Waters.

The Mississippi at New Orleans.

Eads Bridge at St. Louis was almost completed when the artists were making their sketches for *Picturesque America*. The Centennial of the Declaration of Independence and the completion of Eads Bridge were events that were looked forward to with eager enthusiasm by St. Louisans and thousands of American visitors.

The levee at St. Louis was jammed with river craft throughout the steamboat era.

The cities of Rock Island, Illinois (above) and Davenport, Iowa, (below) were thriving steamboat and railroad towns. The railroad bridge linking the two cities was a bone of contention between steamboatmen and railroadmen following the wreck of the *Effie Afton* on one of its piers in 1856, a short time after the bridge was completed. Abraham Lincoln served as a railroad lawyer in the legal suit brought against the bridge company by St. Louis steamboatmen.

Shot Tower and bridges at Dubuque showing three states—Iowa, Wisconsin and Illinois.

Eagle Point—a splendid bluff and landmark for the pilot north of Dubuque. Rafting, steamboating, and railroads are depicted in the foreground. The Iowa-Wisconsin high bridge and the Diamond Jo Boatyards were located at this point.

A steamboat passing a floating raft at the mouth of the Wisconsin.

The levee at La Crosse. "Here we begin to see rafts coming down the stream, with often twelve men tugging away at the clumsy, huge oars, battling against the swift current."

"Queen's Bluff, a fragmentary pyramidal bluff, is one of the landmarks by which the pilots know that they are approaching the fairy region of Trempealeau."

Chimney Rock, near Fountain City, Wisconsin.

Approach to Trempealeau—the "Mountain which dips in the Water." "It rises sheer out of the water in the centre of the channel . . . nothing can be conceived more beautiful than the approach to this most romantic and picturesque spot, which . . . exceeds in positive beauty the far-famed scenery of Lake Pepin."

Lake Pepin, described as "truly charming" in *Picturesque America,* extends for twenty-two miles northward from the mouth of the Chippewa River. "A superb amphitheatre of bluffs encloses the lake, many of which have an elevation of five hundred
feet. These present every variety of form, some of them being square masses, like the
keep of an old castle; others flow out in a series of bosses; others are angular, others
conical."

MAIDEN'S ROCK, LAKE PEPIN

"Winona was a young Sioux Indian maiden. She loved a hunter . . . but her parents
wished her to marry a warrior . . . The day before the union she ascended a bluff of
great height, whose upper part is a sheer precipice, and began chanting her deathsong.
Soon the base was surrounded by the tribe, and all those who possessed any influence
over the girl shouted to her to descend, and that all should be well. She shook her head
in disbelief . . . upbraided them bitterly, not only for wishing to marry her against her
will, but for their folly in preferring the claims of a warrior, who did nothing but fight,
to those of a hunter, who fed the tribe. Then she continued her interrupted chant, and
threw herself, at its conclusion, from the height, being dashed to pieces . . . below."

St. Paul from Dayton's Bluff.

Falls of Minnehaha.

Minneapolis, St. Anthony, and St. Anthony's Falls.

The *Robert E. Lee-Natchez* race of 1870 is famous in song and story. An artist in *Every Saturday* magazine for September 2, 1871, records something of the spirit and excitement when a fast steamboat left port. The firing of the canon, the crowded decks, and the cheering crowds on shore were never to-be-forgotten scenes that were enacted almost daily at the New Orleans levee as at other ports.

Cabin passengers enjoying the excitement of a steamboat race. But after breakfast there commences "the regular business of the day, which is loafing on cool chairs on the forward guards. Perhaps two out of the two or three hundred will be reading; the rest gossip and smoke and flirt and sleep in their chairs till dinner-time. . . . Supper and sardines come again with the sunset; smoking, gossip and flirting succeed in the evening; and then it is bedtime once more. The chairs upon the guard become gradually vacant, and silence and hot weather reign in the cabin. At last the whole boat seems asleep; you hear nothing but the steady snoring of the engines and the irregular nightmare shrieks of the steamwhistle."

"About the regions of the boiler deck," according to the writer in *Every Saturday*, "we find the furnaces, the engines, the boilers, the kitchen, and the human *potpourri*, known as the deck passengers. Poor whites, negroes, and Chinamen are stretched, bent, and sprawled over boxes, bales, and barrels, some asleep, some smoking, some eating fat meat, and all sweltering in the heat."

"The firemen on the river are white men; the coal-heavers are negroes; the deck hands, who have charge of the freight, are white men; the roustabouts, who load and unload it, are negroes. . . . They get from forty-five to sixty dollars a month, and invariably spend their wages on the night they are paid off. They would scorn to leave port with a cent of money. Such are the roustabouts, the happiest and most worthless of wretches."

The *John A. Scudder* nosed her bow up to the New Orleans levee with her largest trip of cotton on November 28, 1878. She carried 4,484 bales of cotton; 10,055 sacks of cotton seed; 1,069 barrels of cotton seed oil; and 3,059 sacks of oil cake. The *John A. Scudder* was built at Cincinnati in 1873 and measured 1,747 tons. The boat was named for a prominent St. Louis citizen.

The *Henry Frank* arrived at New Orleans on April 2, 1881, with the largest cargo of cotton ever floated on one bottom—9,226 bales. The 1,169-ton *Henry Frank* was in her fourth season, having been built in Cincinnati in 1878. Although double the tonnage of the average Upper Mississippi steamboat in the 1860's, she in turn was dwarfed by comparison with such boats as the *Robert E. Lee*—1,467 tons, the *Natchez*—1,547 tons, the *Great Republic*—1,727 tons, the *J. M. White*—2,027 tons, and the *Grand Republic* —2,600 tons. The last mentioned boat could carry a cargo of 4,000 tons.

Indians from crossing. Lieutenants James W. Kingsbury and Reuben Holmes, with a detachment of fifteen regulars and six volunteers, were sent aboard; and a small six-pounder was placed on the bow.

The *Warrior* first steamed north to Wabasha's village where about one hundred and fifty Winnebago Indians were enlisted to help patrol the river. Proceeding downstream Throckmorton reached the spot where De Soto now stands just as Black Hawk and his warriors were pouring out through the hills to the river. A white flag was raised by Black Hawk, and Throckmorton was invited to land. Fearing treachery upon the part of the wily Sauk chief, Throckmorton refused to leave the boat. Black Hawk in turn refused to board the *Warrior*; whereupon hostilities began. During the brief engagement the Indians fired hundreds of shots, only sixty of which reached their mark. One white man was wounded. Four shots of grape sent the Indians scurrying for shelter.

Having halted the retreat of the Indians the *Warrior* steamed down to Fort Crawford for a fresh supply of fuel. While this brief skirmish was of no great significance in itself it served to check the Indians sufficiently to allow the troops to come up a little later and completely rout them at Bad Axe. Shortly afterwards the Winnebago Indians captured Black Hawk and brought him to Prairie du Chien whence he and eleven of his warriors were taken down to Jefferson Barracks on the steamboat *Winnebago*.[198]

Throughout the Black Hawk War the picturesque commanders and their forces used steamboats. Inscribed in the cabin registers of such boats as the *Chieftain*, the *Dove*, the *Enterprise*, the *Warrior*, the *Winnebago*, and the *William Wallace*, were the names of Colonel Zachary Taylor, who was to become President of the United States, and Lieutenant Jefferson Davis, who achieved the same distinction in the Confederacy. After the battle of Bad Axe, Brigadier General Henry Atkinson took passage on the *Warrior* to Jefferson Barracks; while Brigadier General Winfield Scott in forwarding Atkinson's two reports of the battle, dated the letter "steamboat Warrior, near Galena, Aug. 10".[199]

◆━━◆

There were other wars. On May 15, 1846, the *Tempest* whisked up to the Galena levee with news of the outbreak of the Mexican War. The *J. M. White* had brought this news from New Orleans to St. Louis, whence the *Tempest* had steamed upstream to spread the news throughout the Upper Mississippi Valley. Four days later the *Red Wing* brought newspaper accounts of the destruction of Matamoros and the killing of seven hundred Mexicans; while the *Atlas*, the *Uncle Toby*, and the *Prairie Bird* arrived almost in her wake with further dispatches.

Since the telegraph did not reach the Upper Mississippi around Galena and Dubuque until 1848, and since the railroads were not destined to reach Chicago from the East for another six years, the Upper Mississippi Valley relied on the steamboat to transmit the latest news from the front. Many river towns had contributed young men to the struggle, and so the levee was constantly thronged with people awaiting the arrival of steamboats. There was general rejoicing at Galena when in the spring of 1847 the *War Eagle* came snorting up the Fever River with news of Major General Zachary Taylor's victory at Buena Vista.[200]

The outbreak of hostilities with Mexico demanded a hasty concentration of troops throughout the Mississippi Valley. Steamboats were immediately pressed into service. Almost every downstream craft was crowded with regulars and volunteers. Early in June, 1846, the dragoons stationed at Fort Crawford and Fort Atkinson passed down on Captain Throckmorton's *Cecilia*. Shortly afterwards volunteers from Galena and Jo Daviess County, composed chiefly of young miners, departed for Alton on the *St. Anthony*. During the winter it was necessary for troops to march overland; on February 2, 1847, a company of weather-beaten but healthy soldiers arrived at Galena after a four hundred mile tramp from St. Peter's.

Spring brought a revival of traffic on the river : Captain John H. King recruited sixty-four men in Galena and departed immediately on the *War Eagle*. Two weeks later one hundred Illinois volunteers left Galena and Savanna for Cairo. Of the sixty and more craft which plied the Upper Mississippi during the period of the Mexican War, few failed to secure a fair share of the troops and supplies moving southward.[201]

During the winter of 1860 the importance of the impending struggle to Upper Mississippi steamboats was quickly recognized. Eastern newspapers sympathized with the northwestern States because they felt that the Confederates would close the Mississippi River and prevent western products from moving southward. But a Dubuque newspaper editor thought this unlikely : he believed that the South would grant free trade at both New Orleans and Mobile, which was exactly what the East did not want. A week later the same editor observed that the prospect of being blocked by the South was a problem of less importance for Senator James W. Grimes and other Iowa Congressmen to solve than was the urgent need of appropriations for improving the Upper and Lower rapids.[202]

Excitement was at a fever pitch during the early days of the Civil War. Galena citizens were thoroughly alarmed when the steamboat *La Crosse* arrived at their levee with 224 kegs of powder from the Platteville powder mills, presumably destined for Pike's Peak. Fearful lest the powder should fall into the hands of Confederates at Hannibal or St. Louis, the mayor of Galena forbade the captain of the *La Crosse* to take it downstream. This was in accordance with the Illinois Governor's telegram to "detain it by all means". A little later the powder was ordered to be forwarded to La Salle, Illinois.[203]

Thousands of regulars and volunteers were transported by steamboat during the Civil War. Generous quotas of troops were contributed by the various towns along the Mississippi and its tributaries as far north as St. Paul. Late in April the *Sucker State* left Dubuque with a dozen members of the Governor's Greys on board; while her sister ship, the *Hawkeye State*, carried a portion of the First

Wars and Rumors of War

Iowa Regiment from Davenport to Keokuk. Eight boxes of uniforms for the Dubuque "Greys" were shipped to Keokuk on board the *Key City.* Early in June the *Canada* passed Dubuque with three hundred recruits from McGregor. On her next trip she brought three companies of volunteers from further upstream. Met at the levee by the Dubuque volunteers, they made a "grand appearance" parading through the streets. Shortly afterwards the Washington Guards of Dubuque, the Pioneer Greys of Black Hawk County, and the Union Guards of Butler County left Dubuque on the *Key City.* Throughout the season the *Jeanie Deans,* the *Denmark,* the *Henry Clay,* the *Pembina,* the *Bill Henderson,* and two score other craft took companies of volunteers to the various points below. So gratifying were the returns from such employment during the first few months of the war that the Northern Line Packet Company of St. Louis did an unprecedented thing : it reduced the fare for transporting troops![204]

A unique upstream traffic developed during the early months of the Civil War as steamboats brought north ward hundreds of Southern refugees. A Davenport editor noted:

"Coming in from the South yesterday afternoon the steamer Key City came up loaded to the guards with Southern passengers fleeing from the wrath to come. They were mostly of the laboring class, and probably some of those which left this country for the South when hard times came on here. The *Key City* left not less than *one hundred* men, women and children at the levee. Every boat coming up brings along good numbers of Southern folks. Capt. Marden [Worden] says he left about fifty at Muscatine on this trip up. A few weeks of such arrivals will make change in our population. We are glad to see it. This is the country for the laboring people — and we welcome them back to Iowa soil where there is abundant chance for them to earn an honest living and something besides. Unless martial law goes into effect soon on the Lower Mississippi, our city and other cities along the Iowa shore will receive large additions to their population in the course of a few days. The arrival yesterday was made up of hardy looking chaps with their families and household goods. Let them come. They are all wanted here." [205]

Despite the activity in transporting troops, the war had at first a depressing effect on steamboating. In commenting on an item in the Keokuk press the Dubuque *Herald* of June 2, 1861, declared that a similar situation would soon exist all along the river if the war continued. The Keokuk dispatch commented:

"To sustain a river news column with the business that's now doing and the number of boats running, would be an impossibility. If our soldiers were not daily exercising on the Levee we would see grass grow there in abundance. The public can judge what business there is when six regular liners do the whole of it from St. Louis to the upper Lakes. Only for the mail the Keokuk and St. Louis Packet could not make expenses to run one boat and make weekly trips. The Northern Line boats bring up a great many passengers but little freight, and their return freights are equally meagre, and totally destitute of passengers. Produce finds no outlet below us, and merchants just order sufficient to keep their stock assorted."

So many steamboats lay idle at the various ports that the Dubuque *Herald* of June 11, 1861, proposed that an excursion be run to Keokuk to allow the relatives and friends an opportunity to visit the three hundred volunteers encamped at that point.

Navigation slowly revived as the summer wore on : a better stage of water and the movement of grain southward once more called steamboats into action. Captain Datus E. Coon's company of sixty-five cavalrymen was given a rousing farewell when the *Denmark* departed from Dubuque in August. The cheers of the company from the hurricane deck of the *Denmark* were heard on the bluffs of the city half a mile distant.[206]

In November, 1861, a flotilla of steamboats carried the Third Regiment of Minnesota Volunteers southward from St. Paul. Throngs of cheering people gathered at the various towns along the Mississippi to see the troops. The levee at Red Wing was "jammed" with the largest crowd that ever gathered there. Each boat was greeted with cheers and salutes. When the steamboat with the Goodhue County volunteers arrived, an immense bonfire was lighted near the point where the boat landed. The soldiers were allowed half an hour ashore, which was spent in hurried greetings and farewells to relatives and friends.[207]

Keokuk was a grand rendezvous for the army during the Civil War : scores of steamboats departed from this

Iowa town for St. Louis and points below. In addition to receiving raw recruits from the various points above, Keokuk almost daily dispatched companies southward aboard such boats as the *Jeanie Deans*, the *Die Vernon*, the *Hannibal City*, and the *Jennie Whipple*.[208] The first casualty for the Seventh Iowa Volunteer Infantry occurred while the *Jennie Whipple* was en route from Keokuk to St. Louis : during the night a member of Company A while sleeping rolled off the boat into the river and was drowned.[209]

When the South finally blocked the Mississippi a severe blight was cast on the commerce of Keokuk, Davenport, Dubuque, and other upriver ports. Davenport chronicled 73 steamboat arrivals in March and 134 in April, 1861. By the latter part of April, however, freight became so scarce that even such regular steamboats as the *Denmark* and *Henry Clay* laid up until times became better. Early in May business was described by a Davenport editor as "extremely dull and unprofitable". It was believed that a "general stagnation in freight" would follow for an indeterminate period. "The effect this will have on producers, shippers, grain and produce dealers, and business generally will be ascertained too soon, and its realization will be anything but agreeable." [210]

The resentment of northern towns grew more bitter with each passing month. As early as May, Captain J. W. Parker of the steamboat *Canada* reported that the mayor of Burlington had issued a proclamation compelling all steamboats to hoist the stars and stripes when passing that city. The same hatred was manifested in the South where the captain of the *Adelaide Bell* sued the editors of the New Orleans *Crescent* for $50,000 damages for alleging that the boat had unfurled a "Black Republican flag". By July of 1861 it was announced that 20,000 steamboatmen were out of work at St. Louis.[211]

The departure of cheering volunteers was in sharp contrast to the return of the sick and wounded, the dying and the dead. A single illustration will suffice. The frontier State of Iowa furnished 78,000 men out of a population of less than 700,000. This represented half the able bodied men in the State, or more than Washington had in his armies during the American Revolution. Twelve thousand Iowans were killed in the Civil War, or almost one-fourth the total losses of the United States during the World War. In addition, nearly nine thousand were wounded in battle and almost ten thousand were discharged because of ill health. Steamboats bound upstream during the Civil War carried gruesome cargoes as mute evidence of the bloody struggle that was being enacted to prove that all men are "created equal".[212]

On April 19, 1862, the steamboat *Express* arrived at Keokuk with about 300 sick and wounded soldiers, including four who had died en route. Four days later the *D. A. January* came up with 300 wounded; and a month later the same steamboat put into port with 311 more. In three trips the *City of Memphis* brought 928 sick and wounded soldiers to Keokuk. When the steamboat *Decatur* docked in mid-July, Keokuk had opened its fourth hospital in a public school house. Twice within a week in October the *Fanny Bullitt* arrived carrying almost 700 patients.

By the close of the year 1862 it was estimated that more than seven thousand men were being treated in Keokuk. The same scenes were reënacted in 1863 : the *Diligent*, the *Schuyler*, the *Glasgow*, the *Sunnyside*, and the *Gladiator*, came in jammed to their guards with the sick and wounded. On December 24, 1863, the record showed that 7396 sick and wounded soldiers had been brought by steamboats from the South to Keokuk. Of these, 617 had already died.[218]

Early in April, 1863, the regular Keokuk packet *Sam Gaty*, while carrying government supplies and passengers up the Missouri River, was overtaken by a band of fifty-six guerrillas at Sibley's Landing, thirty-seven miles below Kansas City. Led by George Todd, Dick Yager, and Cole Younger, the guerrillas ordered the pilot to land his boat, threatening to fire into her if they were not obeyed. Since the *Sam Gaty* was only fifty feet from shore, the pilot was compelled to "round to" and land his boat. The officers and passengers left the following composite picture of the episode:

"They ordered the Captain ashore, and then rushed aboard, presenting pistols to the heads of the passengers and demanding all their money and valuables. They drove all the soldiers and negroes ashore, killing nine negro men, two soldiers, and wounding a third, who escaped to Independence. They then rifled all the baggage and public and private property, exchanged coats and hats with some of the passengers, and ordered all the women and children ashore, with the intention of burning the boat, but were finally prevailed upon by the Captain to spare her on condition that all the government freight would be destroyed, which was consented to.

"The crew and passengers were compelled to assist in throwing overboard 300 sacks of flour, 48 wagon-beds and considerable private property. The boat was then released and allowed to proceed on her way up at 8 o'clock in the morning."

The guerrillas had intended to capture the *Sam Gaty* at Napoleon; but having arrived too late, they chased her all the way to Sibley's Landing. Fully $2285 was taken, of which $600 belonged to the boat. One passenger lost $1000.[214]

Upper Mississippi steamboats did heroic work during the Civil War. Many of the boats were requisitioned into service by the government. In this group were such well known steamboats as the *Kate Cassel*, the *Jennie Whipple*, and the *Ad Hine*. In this way transportation was often crippled — at least temporarily. There was general rejoicing when General Grant permitted the *Jennie Whipple* to continue plying between Fort Madison and Rock Island.[215]

The news of the surrender of Vicksburg was hailed with delight. "The Father of Waters flowed peacefully to the sea, free and untrammelled", wrote Admiral David D. Porter. "The great chain of slavery was broken, never to be again united. The work of setting free the great artery of the North and South, so essential to our nationality, had been accomplished, and the foul blot of human slavery had disappeared forever from our escutcheon. The squadrons of the Upper and Lower Mississippi had shaken hands in New Orleans, and the great highway between Cincinnati and the Queen City of the South was once more open to the commerce with the North and with foreign countries." [216]

By 1864 the movement of steamboats was again in full swing up and downstream. On April 18th more than one hundred soldiers from the Keokuk hospitals left on the steamboat *Lucy Bertram* to rejoin their regiments. Nine days later the *Die Vernon* took the Fifteenth Iowa to the front; and a month later the *Lucy Bertram* took the Forty-fifth Iowa Regiment downstream. On July 10th the *Kate Kearney* arrived with over a hundred invalid soldiers. Throughout the year steamboats brought wounded soldiers to Keokuk and the ports above. They departed with fresh troops for below. [217]

At the close of the war the reception accorded the war-weary troops was as heart-felt as it was tumultuous. Joy reigned supreme in the various Upper Mississippi ports. Cannon roared, bands blared, and flags waved as the boys in blue marched firmly down the stage of the steamboat. But their thinned ranks left many a welcoming eye tear-dimmed for those who would not return. As troop transports and hospital boats, as conveyors of ammunition and supplies, and as auxiliary forces in the battles which re-opened the Mississippi to commerce, Upper Mississippi steamboats had played a dramatic rôle. With the return of peace, commerce, industry, and agriculture resumed their normal place in the life of the people. The Mississippi River again furnished a peaceful waterway from St. Paul to the Gulf of Mexico.

22

Movement of Troops in Peace Times

THE MOVEMENT of troops during times of peace was more profitable to steamboats than in times of war, when viewed over a period of three or four decades. Before the voyage of the *Virginia* troops had been transported by keelboat — a method which was as costly as it was slow. Thus, in 1821 it took the keelboat *James Ross* sixteen days to convey a detachment of the Fifth United States Infantry from Prairie du Chien to St. Peter's. Although no rapids impeded its progress the keelboat averaged but thirteen miles per day for the two hundred and twelve miles between Fort Crawford and Fort St. Anthony.[218]

Keelboats generally descended the river with great facility. On October 13, 1821, the *Saucy Jack* left St. Peter's with Colonel Snelling on board. Gliding along at a rate of eight miles an hour, the *Saucy Jack* traveled throughout the night and by sunrise reached the foot of Lake Pepin, a distance of eighty miles. Four days were required to reach Prairie du Chien. This exceptionally good time meant that wind and water were favorable. The *Saucy Jack* probably consumed about sixty-five hours running time, so that the average rate of speed was approximately three miles per hour downstream. Three years later (in 1824) the steamboat *Mandan* ran from St. Peter's to St. Louis in sixty-two and one-half hours running time, an average of almost twelve miles per hour downstream.[219]

That keelboat transportation was unsatisfactory as well as costly and slow is demonstrated by the efforts of a celebrated army officer to facilitate the transportation of troops and supplies. A new type of boat, invented by Brigadier General Henry Atkinson in 1824, made the trip from St. Louis to St. Charles on the Missouri River in two days or half the time usually consumed by the keelboat. It was estimated that General Atkinson's boat could average twenty miles a day, and make thirty in an emergency. A description of Atkinson's strange craft has been preserved: [220]

"The machinery consists of a shaft, thrown across the centre of the boat, with a water wheel at each end — a five feet cog wheel in the centre of the shaft, and put in motion by another cog wheel, three feet four inches, resting on an iron shaft, which supports a fly wheel at one end, of eight feet in diameter. The fly and small cog wheel are moved by a crank, projecting from an arm of the fly wheel, with two pitmans, which are impelled by soldiers, seated on from eight to ten benches, four abreast, with a succession of cross bars before each bench, contained in a frame that moves on slides, with a three feet stroke of the crank. The men are comfortably seated under an awning, sheltered from the sun and rain — the labor much lighter than rowing with a common oar, and the boats are propelled with a velocity sufficient to stem the most rapid current of the Missouri."

After the successful navigation of the Upper Mississippi

[191]

by the *Virginia* it was only on rare occasions that the army resorted to keelboats and similar craft. Thus, in 1826, thirty-five keelboats arrived at St. Louis from Green Bay bringing the Third Regiment of Infantry. During the driest season the flotilla had to portage only twenty-five hundred yards between the Fox and Wisconsin rivers. Again, the low stage of water in 1827 forced the troops under Brigadier General Atkinson to disembark from the steamboats *Missouri* and *Illinois* at the foot of the Lower Rapids and complete the remainder of the journey to Prairie du Chien by keelboat. With only a few such exceptions the transportation of troops after 1825 was accomplished by steamboat.[221]

Attacks were often made in Congress against the expenditure of large sums yearly for transporting soldiers from post to post; but Major General Jacob Brown warmly defended the policy. He asserted that the army looked to the government for "justice and impartiality" in the distribution of troops, some of whom would (if no changes were made) be located in unhealthy surroundings for long periods with no hope of a transfer. The occasional movement of troops was also necessary for the "preservation of discipline and efficiency": it was held that the morale and general condition of the troops was kept at such a high level that the good results more than compensated for the expenditures involved in transportation.[222]

Despite these occasional outbursts in Congress the movement of troops continued, and the steamboats reaped rich

Movement of Troops in Peace Times

profits. The steamboats *Missouri* and *Illinois* were particularly busy in the spring of 1828 transporting troops to the various military posts on the Upper Mississippi and Missouri rivers. When the season came to a close four companies of the First United States Infantry had been transferred to Fort Crawford and four additional companies from the same regiment had been carried to Fort Snelling. At the same time eight companies of the Fifth Regiment were taken from these two posts. Two companies of the Third United States Infantry were left at Fort Armstrong and the two seasoned companies of the Fifth removed. The steamboat *Illinois* ascended the Missouri River for Cantonment Leavenworth where eight companies of the Third Infantry were posted under Colonel Henry Leavenworth.[223]

In 1837 the entire First Regiment of Infantry stationed at Fort Crawford and Fort Snelling was ordered south to the Red River where a half dozen regiments had already been concentrated.[224] Two years later the *Pike* arrived at Galena bound for Fort Snelling with eighty new recruits from Covington, Kentucky. Shortly afterwards the *Pike* returned to Prairie du Chien to pick up one hundred troops destined for Fort Snelling. At that time there were two hundred soldiers at Fort Crawford and three hundred at Fort Snelling.[225]

Steamboats engaged in conveying troops on the Upper Mississippi occasionally met with accidents, but the casualties were only minor in character. In April, 1842, the *Illinois* sank on the Lower Rapids while ascending the

Mississippi with troops from Jefferson Barracks. At the same time the *Galena* passed upstream with 358 soldiers on board, 130 of whom were destined for Fort Snelling while the remainder were to be discharged at Fort Crawford. The *Galena* broke her machinery on the way up, and blew a cylinder while bound downstream. She was towed from Galena to St. Louis by the *New Brazil*. On April 27, 1865, the *Sultana* exploded on the Lower Mississippi with a loss of 1647 lives — the worst disaster ever to befall a steamboat on western waters. Most of those aboard were exchanged Union soldiers who were homeward bound.[226]

The profit reaped by steamboats transporting soldiers in time of peace sometimes exceeded that gained from the regular passenger trade. The *Canada* passed Dubuque in July of 1860 with the largest load of the season : she had on board deck passengers who had paid $1672 in fares and cabin passengers whose fares amounted to $2000; and at the same time towed two barges loaded to the water's edge with freight. On her way up from St. Louis the *Canada* was obliged to refuse both freight and passengers at every port below Dubuque. Most of her passengers were United States troops bound for some point upstream.[227]

Two factors are essential in estimating the cost of transporting troops during the times of peace preceding the outbreak of the Civil War : the number of troops carried and the distance traveled. Although the exact number of soldiers conveyed is not known, it would seem fair to assume that on an average at least five hundred troops were

[194]

moved about each year to the half dozen posts in existence at one point or another throughout this period. In estimating the distance traveled one must take into consideration the fact that the steady influx of immigrants swept back the frontier line. Fort Edwards, two hundred miles distant from St. Louis, was the post closest to Jefferson Barracks in 1823 and was beyond the settled area. By 1861 Fort Snelling was the fort on the Upper Mississippi nearest to Jefferson Barracks; while Fort Ripley and Fort Ridgely were located on the outer fringe of settlement. With this in mind the average distance traveled was possibly about six hundred miles. If the government were to pay Upper Mississippi steamboats $40 a round trip fare, it would expend approximately $20,000 annually for transporting five hundred soldiers six hundred miles. At this rate about three quarters of a million dollars might well have been expended in transporting troops by steamboat in the decades preceding the Civil War.[228]

23

Transportation of Supplies

MORE PROSAIC than the movement of troops, but equally important, was the transportation of supplies and equipment to the various posts on the Upper Mississippi. Each year newspapers carried advertisements inviting merchants to submit bids for furnishing huge quantities of pork, flour, whiskey, beans, soap, candles, vinegar, and salt to the forts on the frontier. Separate bids were also solicited for furnishing fresh beef on the hoof. Sometimes the cattle were driven overland, but usually they were transported northward in pens constructed on the lower decks of steamboats. Even though such stock was not seen, its presence was otherwise noticed by the deck and cabin passengers who were forced to locate near the cattle pen.

In 1823 the *Missouri Republican* advertised for bids for the posts at New Orleans, Pensacola, Baton Rouge, Natchitoches, Fort Smith (Arkansas), Council Bluffs, Green Bay, Saginaw Bay, Superior, Mackinac, Pittsburgh, Niagara, Fort Edwards, Fort Armstrong, Prairie du Chien, and St. Peter's. The provisions were to pass St. Louis for their ultimate destination by April 15, 1824; and if destined for posts above St. Louis, such as St. Peter's, they were to be aboard the boat and ready at that time. A definite time limit was set for final delivery at each post. Thus, Fort Edwards and Fort Armstrong were to receive

[196]

Transportation of Supplies

their goods by May 15th, Fort Crawford by June 1st; while June 15th was set as the date for final delivery at St. Peter's.[229]

The amount of provisions and supplies was of course governed by the number of troops at each post. In 1824 Fort Edwards received 60 barrels of pork, 125 barrels of fine fresh flour, 700 gallons of good proof whiskey, 55 bushels of good sound beans, 880 pounds of good hand soap, 220 pounds of tallow candles with cotton wicks, 14 bushels of salt, and 225 gallons of cider vinegar. The consignments that year for the posts above were as follows: [280]

		ARMSTRONG	CRAWFORD	SNELLING
Pork	(barrels)	60	120	360
Flour	(barrels)	125	225	750
Whiskey	(gallons)	700	1400	4200
Beans	(bushels)	55	110	330
Soap	(pounds)	880	1760	5280
Candles	(pounds)	430	860	
Salt	(bushels)	14	28	84
Vinegar	(gallons)	225	450	1350

Similar announcements were made in succeeding years. The *Missouri Republican* of July 26, 1827, requested bids for supplies and provisions for Upper Mississippi posts; and on October first the same paper called for separate and sealed proposals for furnishing 35,000 pounds of fresh beef to Fort Snelling, 30,000 to Fort Crawford, and 15,000 to Fort Armstrong. The beef was to be delivered on the hoof before June 1, 1828.

Early each spring Upper Mississippi steamboats began

transporting military supplies. On April 1, 1824, Captain William Linn, commanding the *Mandan*, arrived at St. Louis from New Orleans. After spending five days in port loading a cargo of military supplies, the boat departed on April 5th for St. Peter's with her guards dripping. She returned to St. Louis on May 17th, having taken forty-two days for the round trip. A low stage of water on the rapids, an ice-locked Lake Pepin, some unforeseen engine trouble, or a channel studded with sandbars must have delayed the *Mandan* on her voyage upstream, since she required less than three days running time to return. On her way down she met the *Indiana* bound for St. Peter's with a cargo of provisions and supplies from Louisville. The *Indiana* left St. Louis on May 13th, commanded by S. Craig, and returned on June 5, 1824, having consumed twenty-three days in making the round trip. The *Virginia* had taken twenty days to complete the journey upstream the previous year.

Low water made the passage over the rapids difficult and often dangerous. The time of arrival and departure of steamboats was extremely uncertain under such conditions, since their speed was reduced by one-half; while the delay occasioned by sandbars tended to quadruple the time of a trip. Early in April, 1824, the *Indiana* carried military supplies to Fort Edwards. It took sixteen days to complete the round trip of four hundred miles. Late in June she departed for the same post with an immense cargo and returned in six days! On a previous voyage, the *Indiana* had made the run to Fort Armstrong and back

Transportation of Supplies

to St. Louis in the astonishing time of five days, running two hundred miles farther and picking her way up and back over a fourteen mile stretch of the Lower Rapids! [281]

By July 31, 1824, four steamboats (the *Virginia*, the *Rambler*, the *Mandan*, and the *Indiana*) had visited Fort Snelling. Two years later, under date of May 17, 1826, Major Lawrence Taliaferro recorded three of these together with the *General Neville*, the *Rufus Putnam*, the *Lawrence*, the *Scioto*, the *Eclipse*, the *Josephine*, the *Fulton*, the *Red Rover*, the *Black Rover*, the *Warrior*, the *Enterprise*, and the *Volant*. Most of the goods received at Fort Snelling on these steamboats consisted of supplies and provisions for the military. Taliaferro notes that the steamboat *Scioto* arrived on Friday, May 26, 1826, with public stores and some Indian goods for him and the Columbia Fur Company. Among the passengers were Mr. Langham, the Sub-Agent at St. Peter's, and Major John Fowle of the Fifth Infantry. The *Scioto* left for Prairie du Chien the next day to bring up the balance of the public stores : she returned on June first, having made the round trip in six days. [232]

During the thirties the steamboat *Warrior* (Joseph Throckmorton commanding) was one of perhaps a dozen craft that carried large quantities of military supplies to Fort Snelling and the various posts on the Upper Mississippi. "These supplies", as Colonel John H. Bliss later recalled, "were chiefly clothing, salt beef and pork, flour and beans." Bliss, as a lad of nine, had accompanied his father, Major John Bliss, to Fort Snelling. He relates that besides the regular supplies for the post the steamboats carried also the personal luxuries of the officers of the post. In 1832, for example, before setting out for Fort Snelling, Major Bliss, the newly appointed commandant, purchased "quantities of hams, dried beef, tongues, rice, macaroni, family groceries in general, furniture, crockery, and what in these days would be considered a huge supply of wines and liquors".

After leaving the port of St. Louis, young Bliss recalls stopping at "Hannibal, Quincy, Des Moines [Rapids] and Galena, all very small places". At Prairie du Chien he found Colonel Zachary Taylor in command of Fort Crawford. At that time Colonel Taylor was very much upset because a dashing young army officer, Lieutenant Jefferson Davis, was "violently in love" with his daughter Sarah Knox. Old "Rough and Ready", it seems, " 'would none of it' — he did not like a single bone in his [Davis'] body." His objections, however, seem to have been no more effective than those of modern parents.

Before leaving Prairie du Chien, young Bliss relates that all "available space" in the *Warrior* was "filled with cord wood, and when that gave out we were obliged to lay by and cut fresh supplies, for not a house or a white man did we see until our arrival at Fort Snelling, so the trip of course was a long one ... At Lake Pepin, on account of a heavy wind, we were obliged to tie up for nearly two days in sight of 'Maiden Rock,' or 'Lovers' Leap,' as in those days it was unromantically called. I shall never forget the clear transparency of the waters, and beautiful wild shores of that lovely river, long before its charms were ruined and outraged by hard practical civilization. On our way we overhauled and took on board a canoe with five soldiers, conveying the monthly mail to Fort Snelling, and thus saved the boys many a weary pull. A sight never to be forgotten was when on turning a point in the river there suddenly appeared, a mile or so before us, the imposing and beautiful white walls of Fort Snelling, holding, as though by main force, its position on a high precipitous bluff, and proudly floating the stripes and stars. It was a fortified oasis of civilization in a lovely desert of barbarism." [283]

According to an estimate made by Secretary of War William Wilkins on March 22, 1844, the public property transported annually on the waters of the Upper Mississippi was valued at $272,213.90. The clothing and quartermaster's stores furnished annually to the troops on the Mississippi and its tributaries above the mouth of the Missouri amounted to $25,000. Clothing and equipment for Fort Snelling was valued at $4,041.93; for Fort Crawford $5,389.24; for Fort Des Moines $3,579.78; for Fort Atkinson $3,579.78; and for Fort Winnebago $1,347.31; or a total of $17,938.04. The quartermaster's stores for the same posts amounted to $7,061.98. Small arms, ammunition, and paints for gun carriages, to the amount of $5,910.00, were also sent to the companies stationed at Fort Atkinson, Fort Des Moines, and Prairie du Chien in 1844. The quantity and value of the subsistence shipped to the same posts in 1844 were as follows:

Steamboating on Upper Mississippi

Post	Companies	Bulk in Barrels	Value
Fort Snelling	3	822	$ 5,992.30
Fort Crawford	4	1073	7,481.40
Fort Atkinson	2	530	3,757.40
Fort Des Moines	2	530	3,791.20
Fort Winnebago	1	270	2,371.60
Total	12	3225	$23,393.90

In concluding his report, Commissioner of General Subsistence George Gibson complained bitterly that the rapids made it necessary to ship a whole year's supply early each spring during a good stage of water.[234]

While steamboats continued to be actively engaged in transporting troops and supplies in the decade before the Civil War, their trips were confined chiefly to Fort Snelling and the posts above. Destined for service among the Indians on the Des Moines River where Fort Clarke was being established, 150 soldiers embarked from Fort Snelling on the *Highland Mary* in May of 1850. Three years later the *Ben Campbell* arrived at St. Paul with a cargo of five hundred tons of freight, most of which was consigned to the government. Fort Madison and Burlington provided these goods — the largest cargo to reach St. Paul that season. On August 1, 1857, the *Northern Light* came booming up to the St. Paul wharf with Company L of the Second Artillery in command of Major William (?) Hays. The troops had traveled sixteen hundred miles in six days, "giving a fair impression of the celerity with which troops can be concentrated in exposed parts of the country, by means of railroads and steamboats." [285]

It would be difficult to overestimate the relative importance of the trade for which the presence of the military was responsible. In 1853 the St. Paul trade in government supplies actually exceeded that of supplying goods to settlers.[286] Although the exact amount is not known, the receipts from transporting supplies was perhaps as great as those derived from conveying troops during times of peace; so one might estimate that approximately $1,500,000 was earned by steamboats engaged in this work. An additional sum of $500,000 was probably netted during the Black Hawk War, the Mexican War, and the Civil War. The total income from transporting scientific expeditions, assisting in engineering projects, and conveying United States Army officers on tours of inspection of the military posts was perhaps $750,000.

The commerce arising from the military frontier before the close of the Civil War may have yielded Upper Mississippi steamboats almost $3,000,000. While the trade arising from the Indian and the fur trader did not equal this steady traffic in military forces and supplies, the three combined were significant factors in stimulating steamboating on waters far beyond the settlers' frontier.

24

Pigs of Lead

THE FABULOUS wealth of John Jacob Astor, the boundless
energy and endurance of Manuel Lisa, and the matchless
strength and courage of hairy-chested Hugh Glass are
dramatic chapters in the epic of the American fur trade.
No less colorful are the exploits of William Becknell and
Josiah Gregg in the Santa Fé trade. But the story of the
lead traffic on the Upper Mississippi has yet to be told.
Even that prince of raconteurs, the benevolent, kindly
George Merrick, failed to chronicle the hardworking, tur-
bulent steamboatmen who plied in the lead trade for a
quarter of a century.

The lead miners, like the men on the fur-trading frontier, were "laughers at time and space". Fully a decade
before the northern half of Indiana and Illinois began to
receive settlers, lead miners formed an island of population
far beyond the fringe of settlement. Lead was found in
abundance in northwestern Illinois, southwestern Wisconsin, and in that portion of eastern Iowa immediately
adjoining these two States. More precisely, it was found
in what are now Jo Daviess and Carroll counties in Illinois; Grant, Iowa, and Lafayette counties in Wisconsin;
and Dubuque County in Iowa.[287]

The first white man known to have mined lead in the
Upper Mississippi Valley was Nicolas Perrot. This French

Pigs of Lead

soldier had been named "Commander of the West" in 1685; and it was at the urgent request of the Miami Indians in 1690 that he had hastened to the lead mines. A century later (in 1788) Julien Dubuque secured permission from the Fox Indians to work the mines west of the Mississippi. When Lieutenant Zebulon M. Pike arrived at these mines in 1805, Dubuque told him that he manufactured from 20,000 to 40,0000 pounds of lead yearly. Pike considered this a very low estimate and thought that the wily Frenchman was merely trying to keep secret the real wealth of his land.[238]

At the time of Dubuque's death in 1810 the Fox Indians were melting 400,000 pounds of mineral annually at Fever River. That same year Henry Miller Shreve won for himself the distinction of being the first American to take a barge of lead out of Fever River. Five years later there were twenty rude Indian furnaces in the neighborhood of Galena. In 1816 the first flatboat cargo of lead to emanate from the Fever River mines was sent to St. Louis by George Davenport; and by 1821 it was not an uncommon sight to see these unwieldy craft heavily laden with lead slowly making their way down the Mississippi.[239]

The movement to the lead mines in the vicinity of Galena had begun as early as 1819. A government agent was soon appointed to supervise the district. When the *Virginia* arrived at the mines in 1823 the region was still in a wild state, populated only by Indians roaming about at will. In the Iowa country they held undisputed sway; while in the Wisconsin and Illinois areas all land north of a line drawn due west from the southern tip of Lake Michigan to the Mississippi belonged to them — with the exception of one or two small tracts in the vicinity of Prairie du Chien and Chicago. In 1828 the right to the lead district was secured from the Indians for a consideration of $20,000. Then, in the following year at Prairie du Chien, the whole territory east of the Mississippi River between the Rock and Wisconsin rivers was ceded to the United States by the Chippewa, Ottawa, Potawatomi, and Winnebago Indians. Finally, the last Indian barrier to the settlement and development of the entire lead region was removed by the Black Hawk Purchase of 1832.[240]

The establishment of a government mineral agent at Fever River was the signal for a slow but steady influx of squatters from Tennessee, Kentucky, Missouri, and southern Illinois. While many of these pioneers came up the Mississippi in keelboats, a considerable number came overland from the South through Fort Clark (Peoria), Illinois. The first mining lease was granted on January 4, 1822. Later in that same year three more leases were granted. Nine leases were given in 1823. At the same time those who operated without license could be numbered by the score. As a rule the lessee was granted 160 acres for the period of three years, during which time the government was to receive one-tenth of all the mineral mined. This was reduced to five per cent in 1830. But the whole system proved very unsatisfactory, and by an act of Congress of July 11, 1846, the lands were brought into the market and sold.

Pigs of Lead

From the very start, the growth of population in the mining region was phenomenal. On July 1, 1825, there were 100 miners at the Fever River mines. On August 31, 1826, there were 453, with the number steadily increasing. The population of Galena alone (in 1830) was almost 1000; while that of the surrounding lead district was about 10,000. Of the total population of 11,683 in Wisconsin in 1836, 5234 were in the lead district. The population of the whole lead mining region that year was about 16,000. The paralyzing effect of the tariff law of 1829 upon lead production makes this growth all the more remarkable.[241]

The history of lead mining from 1823 to 1848 may be divided into three distinct stages. The period from 1823 to 1829 is one of beginnings in which the whole mineral region witnessed a rapid and steady growth both in population and in production. A period of decline and uncertainty is noted from 1829 to 1835, with the production far below normal but with a steady influx of people to the district. The years 1835 to 1848 may be termed the stage of greatest activity when the annual production rose from 11,000,000 to 55,000,000 pounds with a total valuation of $1,654,077.60.[242]

Enthusiasm was at a fever pitch as production rose by leaps and bounds. In 1824 it appears that 175,220 pounds of lead were taken from the mines; but by 1829 the amount had increased to 13,994,432 pounds. The total production down to March 31, 1829, was 31,764,862 pounds. Then a deep gloom shrouded the mineral region:

the unfavorable tariff of 1829, together with a glutted market, led to a period of depression. Both miners and steamboat captains felt the withering effects of hard times. But one man, at least, retained his enthusiasm. Hidden away in a yellowed lead book for the years 1828 to 1830 appears the following wager between John Atchison, noted lead miner and steamboatman, and Colonel William S. Hamilton, the son of Alexander Hamilton, who was mining lead near present-day Wiota, Wisconsin:

A Bett between J. A. [John Atchison] & W S H [William S. Hamilton] of a suit of Cloaths for [from] Head to foot that there will not be 6,000,000 of Lead made at Fever River Lead mines.

J. A. affirmative

The records do not tell whether Colonel Hamilton paid the "bett"; but in 1829 and 1830 the production of lead far exceeded the amount in the wager.[243]

The total amount of lead produced from 1829 to September 20, 1834, was 34,901,205 pounds. Had conditions been more favorable, the same proportionate increase in production prior to 1829 would have made this amount close to 100,000,000 pounds by the end of 1834. After 1835 the production of lead steadily increased : the total lead mined to 1844 was 192,000,000 pounds; and in the following four years the total equaled 204,000,000 pounds — an amount almost equal to that produced during the preceding twenty years.

Within the brief space of a quarter of a century approximately 472,000,000 pounds (6,728,000 pigs) of lead had been mined and shipped down the Mississippi River —

cargoes which must have brought much gain and comfort to steamboat captains and owners. The value of the lead mined from 1841 to 1848 was $8,676,647.39; while the total of the lead mined throughout the quarter century was approximately $14,178,000. Compare this with the trade in furs and produce. In 1848 the value of the fur trade at St. Louis was estimated at $300,000, while the value of the produce on the Santa Fé Trail amounted to $500,000. For the year 1847 alone, the total value of lead mined was $1,654,077.60.[244] No other single factor during the quarter century between 1823 and 1848 was so important in developing steamboating on the Upper Mississippi as the shipment of lead.

25

The Fever River Settlement

EARLY IN THE month of April, 1823, a band of forty-three men, women, and children, with three dogs, assembled on the levee at Cincinnati. Led by Moses Meeker, an enterprising lead manufacturer and mining prospector, they were prepared to board the keelboat *Colonel Bomford* headed for the Fever River lead mines eleven hundred miles distant. During the preceding winter they had purchased their supplies, which all together totaled fully seventy-five tons of freight. Meeker's outfit alone had cost $7000.

Everyone waited patiently while the last of the trappings were safely stored in the hold of the keelboat. Flushed and stimulated by a liberal draught of whiskey (the usual prelude to a day's work) each rugged boatman stood nonchalantly at his post on the runway with pole "set" awaiting the signal of the captain or steersman. Finally all was in readiness. The last passenger had scrambled hastily on board. As the poles of the boatmen bit deep into the river bottom the *Colonel Bomford* slipped slowly from its moorings and glided downstream. Among the passengers was one James Harris. He was accompanied by his son Daniel Smith Harris, a pleasant-faced youth of fifteen who was destined to become the most picturesque of Upper Mississippi steamboat captains.

The Fever River Settlement

Propelled by the skill of the boatmen, the *Colonel Bomford* sped down the Ohio River. Numerous villages dotted the banks and newly erected, rough-hewn farmhouses studded the shores. But the country became more sparsely populated as the keelboat proceeded up the Mississippi.

At Grand Tower, about eighty miles above the mouth of the Ohio River, the steamboat *Virginia* passed the *Colonel Bomford*. Meeker tried to get the *Virginia* to tow his keelboat, but Captain John Crawford refused because the swift current often brought his own craft to a standstill. Despite these difficulties the *Virginia* was able to complete her trip to Fort Snelling, return to St. Louis, reload, and steam northward again before the *Colonel Bomford* reached Fever River.[245]

At that time St. Louis, with its five thousand nondescript inhabitants, was the point of departure for all expeditions destined for the Missouri, the Illinois, or the Upper Mississippi. At Hannibal (which was to become the boyhood home of Mark Twain) a solitary backwoodsman deserted his shack and boarded the *Colonel Bomford*. Quincy, Illinois, boasted of one lone settler (John Wood) who subsequently became Governor of Illinois. With the exception of a few government posts and fur-trading establishments the country above St. Louis was uninhabited by white men.

From dawn till dusk the crew of the *Colonel Bomford* toiled up the broad expanse of the Mississippi, sometimes pushing with their poles and at other times pulling the boat along by means of the brush growing along the bank.

This latter method of making headway was called "bush-whacking". When these methods failed the crew resorted to "warping" to stem the swift current : a rope was attached to a tree or anchor some distance ahead, and then each boatman would grasp the rope, or warp, as it was called, and walk to the stern, pulling as he went. As each man reached the stern he would "break off" and run to the bow for a new grip. In this fashion the men continued until the tree or anchor was reached. It was hard work, and progress was so slow that dusk frequently found the boat barely out of sight of the previous night's stop. Occasionally a breeze would enable the boat to sail for a few miles; but since the wind did not shift with the bends of the river such respites from labor were all too brief. It took thirty-one days for Moses Meeker and his companions to travel the four hundred miles from St. Louis to Galena — an average of but thirteen miles a day, or less than one mile per hour.[246]

When the *Colonel Bomford* arrived at Fever River with her passengers there were less than one hundred miners and traders and only one white woman at this pioneer settlement. Prominent among the settlers were Dr. Samuel C. Muir, Thomas H. January, Amos Farrar, Jesse W. Shull, Francois Bouthillier, A. P. Vanmatre, David G. Bates, James Johnson, and John and Cuyler Armstrong. The real beginning of Galena is usually associated with the advent of the Meeker colony at the Fever River mines.

The increase in population and in the production of lead at the Fever River settlement had a pronounced effect

The Fever River Settlement

upon the number of steamboats arriving at the lead mines. During the course of the year 1823 the *Virginia* made three trips above the rapids. Late in the same year the *Rambler* (Captain Bruce commanding) after making a hasty trip to St. Peter's returned to St. Louis early in September. The *Virginia* and the *Rambler* are the only boats known to have passed the rapids that year : their trips mark the beginning of steamboating on the Upper Mississippi.[247]

During the next three years only a small quantity of lead was produced and steamboats plying the Upper Mississippi were engaged chiefly in transporting troops and supplies. Indeed the steamboats usually carried only such lead on their downstream trips as keelboats were unable to move. In 1824 only 175,220 pounds had been mined; and this had increased to but 958,842 pounds two years later. Prior to the year 1827 scarcely a dozen different steamboats frequented the waters of the Upper Mississippi, and not one of the number was engaged solely in the lead trade.[248]

But Moses Meeker and other enterprising lead miners were not long in realizing the retarding effect of so foreboding a name as Fever River. Despite their efforts to point out that Fever was really a corruption of the French word Febre, meaning bean, the story persisted that a band of Indians had perished miserably of the smallpox at that point. Even Beltrami alluded to the stench around the lead mines. Considerable alarm was therefore manifested when a post office was established on June 4, 1826, and

[213]

called "Fever River". The following year the name was changed to Galena after the mineral deposits found there. Prior to 1850 no other Upper Mississippi town was more widely known than Galena — the metropolis of the mineral region.[249]

26

The Port of Galena

A WILD STAMPEDE for the Fever River lead mines began in the spring of 1827 : the traffic at the St. Louis levee was immense. By March 15th one steamboat had already left for the mines, three were advertised, and it was estimated that at the rate people were pouring into the city several thousand would head northward before navigation ceased. By the close of the week ending April 19th, restless knots of determined men thronged the levee, anxious to reach the mines and try their fortunes. Prominent among the men who arrived in Galena in 1827 were H. H. Gear, John G. Hughlett, Horatio Newhall, James G. Soulard, Thomas Ford (a future Governor of Illinois), John Atchison, William Hempstead, D. B. Morehouse, and Lucius and Edward Langworthy.[250]

The influx of lead miners was reflected in the number of steamboats engaged in the trade. The *Indiana* and the *Shamrock* arrived at St. Louis on April 19th heavily freighted with lead. Several keelboats arrived the same day with similar cargoes. Before the close of navigation almost 7,000,000 pounds of lead had been mined and transported down the river. During the season the steamboats *Lexington, General Hamilton, Indiana, Lawrence, Mexico, Muskingum, Mechanic, Pilot, Shamrock, Scioto, St. Louis and Galena Packet,* and *Velocipede* had visited the Upper

Mississippi, and practically all of them had plied fairly regularly in the lead trade. This was a larger number than had visited the Upper Mississippi during the preceding four years.[251]

Galena became the great entrepôt for the lead traffic. St. Louis lay over four hundred miles downstream, and Fort Snelling nearly three hundred miles above. On July 8, 1828 (more than five years before Chicago was born and could boast its first newspaper), citizens of Galena were reading the first issue of the *Miner's Journal*. The astonishing growth of this rough little mining community was aided by the number of steamboats in the trade.[252]

In 1828 and again in 1829 some 13,000,000 pounds of lead were produced. Galena already boasted a weekly paper and seven hundred aggressive pioneers. "There are forty-two stores and warehouses; twenty-two porter cellars and groceries; a goodly number of lawyers and physicians, and a general assortment of mechanics, &c. The number of dwelling houses and stores is 195; and 46 new buildings are going up. There have been 75 steamboat and 38 keel boat arrivals since 1st. March. Almost *eight million pounds* of lead were exported during the year ending 1st of June last. The population in the neighborhood of the mines is estimated at 10,000." [253] Goods were constantly being dumped upon the Galena levee by incoming steamboats; and a cargo of lead was soon loaded aboard each one, sinking the boat to her guards. Five steamboats heavily laden with lead left the city in one day during the month of March, 1828.[254] When the season came to a close

The Port of Galena

almost one hundred trips had been made to Fever River.²⁵⁵
About the same number of steamboats appeared in the
lead trade during 1829. By the end of that year approximately thirty different boats had visited the mineral region since the trip of the *Virginia*. Many of these had gone
as far north as Prairie du Chien, and even to St. Peter's.
During the period from 1823 to 1829 inclusive, approximately three hundred trips had been made by steamboat
to the Upper Mississippi. Between October 1, 1823, and
July 1, 1824, there had been only fifty-one arrivals at St.
Louis from all ports on western waters; while during the
year 1828, some ninety-nine steamboat arrivals were recorded at the lead mines.²⁵⁶
From 1830 to 1834 the unfavorable tariff held down
lead production, but despite this fact there was an average
of about eleven different steamboats each season. During
the Black Hawk War only six boats ventured above the
Upper Rapids into the war zone. The defeat of Black
Hawk at Bad Axe brought more promising conditions, and
the number quickly rose to eighteen the following year.
In 1834 there were 127 steamboat arrivals at Galena;
while Cassville chronicled 52 the same year. The *Galenian*, the *O'Connell*, the *Olive Branch*, the *Warrior*, the
William Wallace, the *Winnebago*, the *Wisconsin*, the *Veteran*, the *Yellowstone*, and the *Springfield* appeared in the
trade that year. Approximately 35 steamboats made about
550 trips during this period; while from 1823 to 1834 inclusive, about 65 steamboats made approximately 850
trips above the rapids.²⁵⁷

[217]

Steamboating on Upper Mississippi

In 1835 a Galena editor complained of the difficulty of keeping a correct list of boats; but 176 steamboat arrivals were chronicled for the season. Seven boats were plying regularly in the trade, with no serious accidents during the season of navigation. Emigrants from below were highly pleased with the upward trip and were loud in their praise of the splendid facilities afforded.[258] With the exception of periods of extreme low water, the number of steamboats continued to show a healthy increase after 1835.

So dependent was the lead district upon the steamboat for its supplies that after the long winter months the opening of navigation was awaited with impatience. There was much discussion and wagering as to the exact date when the ice would break up. Not infrequently the local paper would entertain hopes for the great day late in January. From the middle of February the weather conditions were watched with eager eyes.

"Contrary to our expectations", observed the *Northwestern Gazette and Galena Advertiser* of April 1, 1837, "the River opened earlier this season than usual. On Tuesday afternoon, the 28th [of March], the joyful cry of 'a boat! a boat!' was echoed through town, making glad the hearts of our citizens — sure enough, upon casting our eyes down the river, the splendid steamer Palmyra, Capt. Gleim, was observed booming her way up to town laden with freight and passengers. Immediately in her wake came other boats thick and fast — the next was the Du Buque, Capt. Atchison — the Pavillion, Capt. Lafferty — the Adventure the same evening and the Emeral[d] the morning after. The arrivals have filled our town with people, and gives a very animated appearance to Galena."

Thirty different steamboats appeared in the trade during 1837 (a number equal to the total during the first seven years of steamboating on the Upper Mississippi), while the total arrivals for that year exceeded by fifty the total from 1823 to 1829.[259]

By 1847 approximately forty different steamboats were visiting the lead mines, thirty of which were regulars in the trade. In that year, nine steamboats arrived at the Galena levee on June 29th; during the week a total of twenty arrivals were registered; and thirty-two different boats were recorded by the end of June. A total of 662 steamboats docked at St. Louis from the Upper Mississippi in 1846 — fully one-fourth of the total reaching that port. During the same year 395 steamboats came from New Orleans and the Lower Mississippi River, 420 from the Ohio, 446 from the Illinois, 256 from the Missouri, while 232 arrived from other ports. In 1847 the total from the Upper Mississippi was 717, with the same approximate ratio to the other ports and rivers. An aggregate of 697 steamboats reached St. Louis from the Upper Mississippi in 1848.[260]

Thus, within the brief space of a quarter of a century the activity of steamboats on the Upper Mississippi River far surpassed that of either the Ohio or Lower Mississippi rivers when measured by the total arrivals at St. Louis from the port of Galena.

Not all the steamboats listed in the last figures came to

Galena : a few were employed in plying between St. Louis and Keokuk or points below the Upper Rapids. The great majority, however, represented steamboats which had run as far north as Galena, Dubuque, Potosi, and Cassville, and were engaged in the lead trade. Thus, the total number of boats reaching Bloomington, now Muscatine, in the Territory of Iowa during the first week in May, 1846, was nineteen. Of this number one was engaged between St. Louis and St. Peter's, three were in the St. Louis and Bloomington trade, while fifteen were plying between St. Louis and the Galena lead district. The total arrivals and departures from Bloomington during the month of May numbered 124, of which approximately 100 risked both the Upper and the Lower rapids in order to engage in the lead trade.[261] In 1847 the number of boats regularly visiting the mining region was thirty.

During the period from 1823 to 1848 approximately 365 different steamboats made their way above the Lower and Upper rapids. About 200 of these had been engaged primarily in transporting lead; while the remainder, which included either transient or excursion boats, must have carried a fair proportion of the lead on their downstream trips. During this same quarter of a century approximately 7645 trips were made to the lead mines of the Upper Mississippi by steamboats.[262]

While the activity on the Upper Mississippi was greater than that on either the Lower Mississippi or any of its tributaries, the tonnage of boats on the larger waterways was greater. The impediment which the rapids presented during low water was an important factor in governing the size of the boats in the Upper Mississippi trade. The average tonnage of the first fifty-one steamboats built and documented on western waters up to 1819 was 198. The smallest of this group was the *Pike* of 31.76 tons; while the largest was the *Columbus* of 450 tons.[263] A list of twenty-two steamboats which engaged in the Galena trade during the years 1841 to 1843 inclusive shows a tonnage varying from 92 to 200, with an average for the total number of 129 tons. The *Agnes*, the *Otter*, and the *Jasper* varied from 92 to 98 tons, while the *New Brazil* and the *Amaranth* measured 200 tons each.[264]

Thus, the Upper Mississippi steamboats of the early forties actually showed a decrease, both in average tonnage and size, over the boats which plied the Ohio and the Lower Mississippi River a quarter of a century before. On the other hand, a list of 146 steamboats which docked at St. Louis during the year 1848 reveals ten boats whose tonnage exceeded 500. The *Autocrat* was of 847 tons burden, the *Missouri* of 886 tons, while the *Sultana* measured 924 tons. These figures indicate that a steady increase in the size of steamboats had taken place on the Ohio and the Lower Mississippi.

Forty-five of the 146 steamboats which landed at St. Louis in 1848 were either regular or transient visitors to the region above the Upper Rapids. They ranged in size from the little *Pearl* of only 64 tons to the *Highlander* of 346 tons, with an average tonnage for the group of 160.[265] The higher average is due to the greater size of the transient steamboats which were able to visit the Upper Mississippi during seasons of high water. But for most practical purposes the boats which averaged about 140 tons were best suited to the lead-carrying trade.

Keelboats were used in order to facilitate the passage of steamboats over the rapids and also to increase their carrying capacity. These were lashed to the sides or bow of the steamboat, and while they impeded the speed and added to the difficulty of piloting, these disadvantages were more than counterbalanced by the additional cargoes carried. Almost all captains engaged in the lead trade made use of keelboats, especially when the water was low or when the amount of freight required an increase in the carrying tonnage.

Keelboats usually bore names. In May, 1826, the arrivals of the *John Adams*, the *Belvidere*, and the *Rock Island* were chronicled at St. Louis. These engaged in the Fever River trade in competition with the few steamboats which then visited the mining region. Early in the spring of 1828 a steamboat successfully towed two keels of forty tons burden — a feat heralded with joy by the St. Louis paper, which immediately urged the improvement of the rapids as a further aid to steamboating. This event was the final blow to keelboating, and in July of that year the *Belvidere* was listed for sale at a low price.[266]

On June 7, 1827, the steamboat *Indiana* advertised its regular departure for Fever River during low water on Sunday morning of each week, emphasizing the fact that a sufficient number of keels would be on hand to transfer passengers and cargo from the Lower Rapids to the mining region. On February 1, 1827, Captain John Newman of the *Indiana* was the first to advertise a steamboat for the lead mines.[267] A distinct innovation on the Upper Mississippi was noted the same year when Captain S. Shallcross of the steamboat *St. Louis and Galena Packet* advertised his boat for Prairie du Chien with the safety barge *Lady Washington*. The latter drew but eleven inches light.[268]

On March 4, 1828, Captain Culver of the steamboat *Missouri* advertised for Fever River with a safety barge which allowed him to carry and tow 200 tons and run light on twenty-two inches of water.[269] A third safety barge was introduced in 1832, when Captain Joseph Throckmorton brought out the steamboat *Warrior* and safety barge.[270] While the safety barges were introduced primarily because of the large number of steamboat explosions which were occurring on western waters, they fill an important place in the evolution of Upper Mississippi steamboating since they demonstrated the value of flat-bottomed boats as a means of overcoming the dangers of navigating the rapids.

Despite the precautions on the part of steamboat captains many keelboats were lost on the Lower and Upper rapids. In 1842 the steamboat *New Brazil* sank two keels of lead on the Sycamore chain of the Upper Rapids, and the *Northwestern Gazette and Galena Advertiser* bitterly complained that the losses incurred would have sufficed to improve the entire rapids.[271] In July, 1846, the *Fortune* sank a keel with 1800 pigs of lead at the mouth of Fever

River in eighteen feet of water.[272] In April, 1848, the barge of the steamboat *Montauk* sprang a leak on the Upper Rapids and damaged about $25,000 worth of goods.[273] While accidents such as these were common, the keels not only increased the carrying capacity of steamboats but also served as a means of protection to the latter. Nearly 400 tons of lead left Galena in 1839 — carried by the steamboat *Ione* and her three keelboats.[274] Such cargoes often paid the cost of a steamboat in one round trip and helped to make up the deficit incurred when keels were sunk on the sharp-toothed rocks of the rapids. By the middle of the century, the keelboat was discarded and the barge took its place as the auxiliary of the steamboat.

But Galena's days, like those of the keelboat, were numbered. As early as 1848 a Galena editor had pointed out that the Fever River must be improved or other cities would get Galena's trade. The rapid flow of settlers into the Upper Mississippi Valley was calling for larger steamboats and it was becoming increasingly difficult, if not impossible, for steamboats to squirm up the narrow Fever River.[275]

When Mrs. Elizabeth Fries Ellet arrived at Galena in 1852 she described it as a "rough-looking place 'jammed in' between rocky hills" with houses looking "like a drove of sheep going down to water." According to Mrs. Ellet: "It was a novel amusement in the evenings to sit by the window and see rushing under it, with the noise made by the Western high-pressure boats, steamers so large as apparently to fill up the little river that skirts the city, and is now shrunken by the drought into half its accustomed limits." [276]

The arrival of the railroad at Galena in 1854 brought momentary prosperity; but its construction to the Mississippi opposite Dubuque the following year was the death blow to any hopes Galena may have entertained for her future growth and prosperity. [277]

After the turn of the half century Dubuque surpassed Galena. Nor did the "Key City" of Iowa let Galena forget this fact. In 1858 a Dubuque editor referred to Galena as the "Niobe of the West", pointing out that Dubuque was shipping to Galena on the Galena packets because the St. Louis boats found it "inconvenient to go out of their way in order to reach Galena." [278] Two years later (in 1860) Dubuque poked more fun at Galena and branded her as an "inland town" because the steamboat *W. L. Ewing* had been "unable to get up the Fever River on account of the mud." At a meeting of the Dubuque city council a suggestion was made in the form of a resolution that the bed of Fever River "be plowed up and potatoes planted." It is asserted this resolution would have passed had not someone in the council chamber remarked that the ground was too dry. [279]

To such an end came the "Port of Galena". Once acclaimed as the mighty commercial emporium of the northwest, the home of General Ulysses S. Grant and eight other Civil War generals, the community made famous by the visits of Abraham Lincoln and Jenny Lind, the chief port of call for scores of steamboats from points as far flung as Pittsburgh and New Orleans, this once flourishing metropolis of 9241 souls had dwindled to 3878 inhabitants by 1930. Like many another mining community Galena today finds her greatest comfort in a glory that is past. Such dreams must be as pleasant as her history was great.[280]

27
Steamboat Bonanzas

STEAMBOATING ON the Mississippi under a blistering hot sun was not always pleasant. Frederick Marryat knew something about the trials of steamboat captains. This adventurous British sea captain and author, who traveled several thousand miles aboard steamboats on the western waters, arrived in the mineral region on the *Burlington* in 1837.

Of steamboating in the summer time the observative Marryat records : "I have often heard the expression 'Hell afloat' applied to very uncomfortable ships in the service, but this metaphor ought to have been reserved for a small high pressure steam-boat in the summer months in America; the sun darting his fierce rays down upon the roof above you, which is only half-inch plank, and rendering it so hot that you quickly remove your hand if, by chance, you put it there; the deck beneath your feet so heated by the furnaces below that you cannot walk with slippers; you are panting and exhausted between these two fires, without a breath of air to cool your forehead. Go forward, and the chimnies radiate a heat which is even more intolerable. Go — but there is no where to go, except overboard, and then you lose your passage. It is, really, a fiery furnace, and, day or night, it is in vain to seek a cool retreat." [281]

Steamboating on Upper Mississippi

Galena, it is said, became infernally hot in the summer. Particularly in July and August the life of a roustabout became well-nigh intolerable. Pigs of lead piled along the banks of the Fever River were exposed to the merciless rays of the sun. These became so hot it was impossible to pick one up and the luckless rousters would, instead, go into the warehouses and shoulder a seventy pound ingot that had lain in the shade. "He would start on the run for the boat, but the lead would melt and run down his back so that when he got on board he would have to cool the lead, after which the engineer would cut it off his person with a cold chisel." [282]

Despite the torrid weather the lead traffic afforded a veritable bonanza in freight earnings for steamboat captains. Sometimes a single trip paid for the original cost of a steamboat. On the other hand, unforeseen circumstances sometimes made the labors of a whole season profitless. For one thing the earnings of steamboat captains were dependent upon freight rates that were constantly fluctuating. These rates were governed in the main by four factors: the amount of freight on hand, the number of steamboats in the trade, the stage of the water, and the season of the year.

The first two factors were subject to competition and the law of supply and demand. With a plentiful supply of lead on hand and a good stage of water, the regular boats usually charged a rate sufficiently high to yield a handsome return. Thereupon transient, or "wild boats" as they were commonly called, would put in an appearance and seek

[228]

to capture a share of the trade. So long as freight was plentiful and competition did not prevail, the traffic remained normal. But when freight became scarce either the regular or the "wild boats" would begin to "cut under". Cut-throat competition would then become the order of the day; and a season which might have started out with a normal downstream tariff of twenty-five cents per hundred pounds would soon find the rate as low as five or six cents per hundred. While this price was ruinous to steamboat owners, it was hailed with joy by the shipper who pocketed the savings. On April 15, 1843, for instance, the rate was eighteen cents per hundred pounds. By June 15th it had dropped to the low figure of six and one-fourth cents.[283]

The St. Louis *Reveille* comments that "During the last three years, there has been a regular declension in the rates of freight to this port, from above. In 1841, *ninety-two* cents per 100 lbs. were paid for freight on lead from Galena, and now, we hear of lots being brought from Galena for three cents."[284] For a period of two months, the rate per hundred pounds averaged less than eight cents.[285] The captains and owners who had the most capital survived, but their less fortunate competitors were either bought out or wisely withdrew from the trade. After such withdrawals the old rates were immediately resumed.

Nor was competition limited merely to rate wars. Rivalry often became so intense that serious altercations sometimes put the lives of innocent people in danger. In October, 1843, the whole lead district was aroused by a quarrel between two regular participants in the trade. During the season a feud had existed between Captain Thomas Culbertson of the steamboat *Potosi* and Captain Charles Ross of the *St. Louis Oak*, and each trip served to increase the bitterness. Late in September the two boats left St. Louis for Galena only a few hours apart. They did not enter a port together until Montrose, Iowa, was reached. Between Montrose and Savanna, Illinois, the *Potosi* passed the *St. Louis Oak* several times. By the time Muscatine was reached, both captains realized that it would be a lively port-to-port race and that the first boat to arrive would secure the lion's share of the freight and passengers.

A desperate contest ensued, in the course of which the passengers of both steamboats crowded the decks and urged the crews of their respective ships to redouble their efforts. About thirty-five miles below Galena the *St. Louis Oak*, while endeavoring to pass her rival at a bend in the river, rammed the *Potosi*, tearing away her wheel and a part of her guards. Proceeding on her way, the *St. Louis Oak* reached Galena first and departed downstream before the badly crippled *Potosi* came into port. The incident created much bad blood between the partisans of the two boats and brought about an exchange of bitter recriminations in the press.[286]

The third factor influencing freight rates was the stage of the water. The average downstream rate from Galena to St. Louis, over a period of eight years from 1836 to 1843, was thirty-two cents per hundred-weight. The upstream rate during the same period averaged sixty-three cents. Six of these years were normal, with the rate averaging around thirty-two cents for the season; only the stage of the water and the season of the year caused any deviation from that figure. In 1839, however, the water in the Mississippi was very low, and the average downstream rate was fifty cents per hundred for the year, while the upstream figure reached one dollar per hundred. The highest rate that year for shipment from Galena to St. Louis was about eighty cents, with $1.50 prevailing for upstream freight.[287]

The chief difficulties in navigating the Mississippi during low water were the cost of lighting the cargo over the rapids and time spent on sandbars in the river and the reefs of the rapids. "The river has risen 15 inches in the last 48 hours", noted an editor in the spring of 1847. "Several boats have been stuck fast on the rapids for a number of days. They will now be able to get off, likely".[288] During low water the rapids at times became so treacherous that even the cost of lighting did not always save the steamboat from being grounded indefinitely or from being sunk by some hidden rock. In July, 1846, the *Saint Anthony* struck a rock on the Lower Rapids and was sunk. The *War Eagle* experienced the same misfortune on the Upper Rapids, but was raised after much difficulty and towed to Rock Island for repairs.[289] When two such accidents occurred within the space of a week, the larger boats usually withdrew from the trade and awaited a more favorable stage of water.

The final factor which might affect freight rates was the

[231]

season in which the shipment was made. A slightly higher price prevailed during the first month in spring when navigation opened. This was due to the unusually large amount of lead left over from the preceding fall or mined during the winter months. The spring thaw, with the consequent rise in the river, sent the price slowly down, although the fluctuation during the first three months of navigation was comparatively small. During August and September the low stage of the water brought out the much-feared sandbars and the navigation of the rapids became so difficult that the freight rate rose rapidly. A slight drop in October, during the fall rise in the river, was followed by extremely high rates as the season of navigation came to a close in November or early December.

Last-minute shipments were hurriedly sent on their way, while belated travelers scurried home before the river should freeze. At such times the freight and passenger charges often reached fabulous figures — frequently exceeding the low water rates. Over a period of four years, the average rate in the month of November was higher than for any other month of the year. In 1841 the downstream rate from Galena to St. Louis went as high as sixty-five cents per hundred-weight, or double the average charge for the season.[290] The *Otter* (Captain Daniel Smith Harris commanding), the last boat to depart that year, left the Galena levee on November 22nd.[291] Late in November, 1845, the *Iron City* battered her way up the ice-choked Mississippi and succeeded in gaining the port of Galena. The cargo was quickly discharged, and at eleven o'clock on the night of November 23rd, the vessel departed. In the face of a biting wind she succeeded in plowing her way through a thin layer of ice on Fever River and entered upon a mad race with the weather for warmer and friendlier waters.[292]

With such conditions and the great risks which steamboat captains ran in making these hazardous trips, it is no wonder that freight rates reached high levels. Dangers from ice and the extravagant (though justifiable) wages demanded by crews in making the last trip of the season, together with the possibility of not completing the voyage, served to make the late season charges very high.

The returns reaped in transporting lead from Galena to St. Louis from 1823 to 1848 were enormous. With a knowledge of the amount of lead shipped and complete statistics on freight rates and averages for most of the years, a fairly accurate estimate of these receipts can be made. In 1826 a shipment of 150,000 pounds of lead was made from Galena to St. Louis for $600 which was forty cents per hundredweight.[293] The total amount of lead mined that year was 1,560,534 pounds; so that at the above rate the total receipts of the boats engaged in the traffic during the season were about $6000. The average rate for the period from 1823 to 1835 is not known, but it is safe to estimate it as slightly higher than that of the following eight years. The total receipts for the period must have been around $227,000.[294]

During the years 1836 to 1843, inclusive, the average rate was thirty-two cents per hundredweight, and the total amount shipped was 192,000,000 pounds. The receipts for these years, therefore, amounted to about $526,000. From 1843 to 1847 inclusive, the receipts on the 204,508,400 pounds shipped were $511,000, or an average yearly revenue of over $125,000. A total of $1,250,000 is a fair estimate of the amount paid to steamboat captains for hauling lead from Galena to St. Louis during the first quarter of a century of steamboating on the Upper Mississippi.[295]

The profits reaped by steamboat captains for a single trip were often immense. Early in 1835 the *Wisconsin* (Captain Henry Crossle commanding) arrived at Galena heavily laden with freight and passengers. She had two keels in tow, and after discharging a considerable amount of freight on the way up carried 234 tons of freight and 130 passengers. The *Wisconsin* departed downstream with a cargo consisting of 9000 pigs of lead. The *Heroine* (Captain Orrin Smith commanding) also brought up a large freight cargo and some 300 passengers. The *Heroine* broke her shafts just below the mouth of Fever River and had to be towed up by the *Wisconsin*.[296]

The following summary of the earnings of the steamboat *Ione* for a single trip is preserved : "She arrived here with three keels in tow, and with 240 tons freight, having discharged 110 tons on her way. The probable amount received for freight on her trip up, after paying expenses and dividing with other boats, was about $5,000. This morning the *Ione* leaves for St. Louis, with her three keels loaded with near 400 tons of lead, and one hundred thousand dollars in specie. Her freight-bills will amount to $5,200 more." [297]

Perhaps one of the largest freights ever carried by a steamboat on the Upper Mississippi during this period was that of the *Amaranth* in command of Captain George W. Atchison. This boat left the Galena levee on May 1, 1843, crowded with passengers and with a freight of 13,000 pigs of lead amounting to 910,000 pounds or 455 tons. Since the *Amaranth* was a boat of only 200 tons burden, a trip such as this would ordinarily have brought a profit almost sufficient to pay for its original cost. Unfortunately for Captain Atchison, the freight rate on that day was only fifteen cents per hundredweight. His receipts for the lead alone amounted to $1265 for the trip down. Two months later competition had become so intense that this immense cargo would have netted him less than $500. On the other hand, the same cargo would have netted him $4550 during the season of low water in 1839. [298]

The receipts of twenty-two regular and eleven transient steamboats on freight and passengers of all kind for the period from 1841 to 1843 inclusive were $610,000. Of this amount about $236,000 was made by transporting lead, $156,000 by upstream freight (which usually doubled the tariff of downstream freight), and $228,000 in upstream and downstream passenger traffic. The receipts of steamboats from the lead trade were, therefore, about two-fifths of the total gross receipts. Assuming that this proportion held throughout the period from 1823 to 1848, the total revenue of steamboats was about $3,000,000. [299]

Steamboating on Upper Mississippi

In 1841 the *Otter* (Captain Daniel Smith Harris commanding) made fifteen trips from Galena to St. Louis, towing nine keelboats up the river during the season. At its close, the receipts were found to be $15,000 from freight and $7000 from passengers. Her small size and light draught enabled the *Otter* to ply the Mississippi at all seasons of the year; and when navigation finally closed she had cleared an amount equal to over four times her value. During 1842 the *Otter* made eleven trips, towed six keels, and cleared $13,000 on freight and passengers.

The season of 1843 witnessed a period of competition in which freight was carried for less than half the price of former years. The *Otter* squirmed out of the Fever River nineteen times during the season, with her keels and lower deck creaking under the heavy lead freight and with passengers crowding the upper decks. When the boat was laid up for the winter in the slough near Galena, her profits for the season were found to be only $6000 on freight and $4000 on passengers. Had the rates of 1841 been in force, Captain Harris would have cleared close to $30,000; while a profit of almost $45,000 would have resulted from the low water rate of 1839.

During the same season the *Iowa*, a 112-ton steamboat in command of Captain D. B. Morehouse, made twenty-three trips from Galena to St. Louis, towed ten keels, and cleared $10,000 on freight and $8000 on passengers. From 1841 to 1843 inclusive, the *Iowa* made a total of sixty-two trips, towed thirty-eight keelboats, and cleared $43,000 on freight and $28,000 on passengers.[309]

[236]

Steamboat Bonanzas

A gradual increase in the average number of trips by steamboats is noted during these years, while the number of keels towed shows a decrease of over fifty per cent. The average receipts for sixteen steamboats during 1841 were about $11,118, while the average trip netted about $1446. Although the length of time taken for a trip varied with each boat, the approximate time required for a round trip under ordinary circumstances was, let us say, eight days. About two days were required for the down trip, four days for the upstream passage, and the remaining two days were spent in port loading and unloading cargoes.[301]

A colorful pageant of steamboats plied between St. Louis and the ports of Galena, Dubuque, Potosi, and Cassville in the mineral region. In 1846 fully thirty-eight different steamboats squirmed up the Fever River to Galena; in the following year thirty-seven were recorded. These two years marked the peak when measured by the number of different boats; by 1849 the number of different craft had dropped to twenty-eight. In that year the *Anthony Wayne*, the *Cora*, the *Dubuque*, the *Montauk*, the *Revenue*, the *St. Peters*, the *Time and Tide*, and the *Senator* had been plying three years in the trade; the *Bon Accord* and the *Red Wing* had seen four years of service; the *War Eagle* had snorted up and down the Mississippi for five seasons; while the archaic *St. Croix* and the decrepit, wheezing *Uncle Toby* had toiled six years in the lead traffic.[302] Their services were manifold : they provided the mineral region with its best means of transportation and communication; they left their tribute of passengers and freight at the many river ports along the way; and they provided rich bonanzas to many enterprising steamboat captains. The fortunes reaped in the lead traffic laid the foundation for a still more picturesque pageant of the packets which began in the fifties.

28

Race Horses in the Lead Trade

The names of such steamboats as the *J. M. White*, the *Sultana*, the *A. L. Shotwell*, the *Eclipse*, the *Natchez*, and the *Robert E. Lee* bring memories of the halcyon days of steamboating on western waters. Their great races, against each other or against time, were talked of throughout the Mississippi Valley : they even attracted national and world-wide attention. The records of fast time established by the boats in the lead trade have been neglected, although many of them compare favorably with those of the race horses of the lower river. It was not until the middle forties that steamboats began to reach that point of perfection in construction both of hull and of engine which allow them to be compared with the splendid models of a later day.

It was a combination of a famous lower river and an upper-river boat which established a record from New Orleans to St. Louis to Galena of seven days, three hours, and twenty minutes. In April, 1844, the *J. M. White* made the run from New Orleans to St. Louis in four days and eighteen hours. The *Lewis F. Linn* took her cargo and passengers at St. Louis and carried them on to Galena in two days, nine hours, and twenty minutes. Thus the entire time was a little more than one week. A little later the *J. M. White* lowered her time between New Orleans and St. Louis to three days, twenty-three hours, and nine minutes — a mark which stood until 1870.[303]

Fast time on the Upper Mississippi was inaugurated by Captain Daniel Smith Harris and his long string of race horses. In July, 1836, Harris ran the *Frontier* from St. Louis to Galena in three days and six hours, having stopped between twenty and thirty hours on the way up. In 1840 the *Omega* was able to negotiate the distance between the two points in an even three days. The following year, the *Indian Queen* ran the distance in three days and twelve hours with a keel in tow; while the *Little Ben* surprised the citizens of the mining community on July 3rd by bringing up St. Louis papers of June 29th. The *Little Ben*, an Ohio River boat, made the run in two days and twelve hours — the fastest time on record to that date. In the same year the steamboat *Iowa*, commanded by Captain D. B. Morehouse, made the round trip between Galena and St. Louis in six days and fifteen hours. This feat was beaten in 1845 by Captain Young of the *Monona* who made the trip in four days and twelve hours — the fastest time on record.[304]

All previous records between St. Louis and Galena were broken in quick succession during a few months of the year 1845. On March 28th Captain Harris's *War Eagle* arrived at Galena from St. Louis in fifty-six hours, and in the following month lowered this to forty-nine hours. Within a month the *St. Croix* came panting up to the Galena levee from St. Louis in forty-five hours and forty-five minutes. Undaunted by this feat, Captain Harris set out from St. Louis almost in the wake of the *St. Croix* and brought his *War Eagle* to Galena in the astonishing time of forty-three hours and forty-five minutes — a record which was not surpassed for many years. Some of the passengers on this trip expressed dissatisfaction with the treatment accorded them. Upon inquiry it was found that Captain Harris was considered too parsimonious with the meals, since only one dinner had been served on the trip. Further examinations showed that the *War Eagle* had left St. Louis after dinner on Tuesday and had reached Galena before noon on Thursday. The disgruntled passengers were immediately informed that if they were traveling for dinners they would have to take a slower boat.[305]

In May, 1843, the *Iowa* made the trip from Galena to St. Louis in forty-four hours. This was lowered by Captain Harris and his famous *War Eagle* in 1849 when the distance was run in thirty-three hours.[306]

Record runs such as these were not the rule, however, for some captains refused to race their boats even though they were capable of making high speed. Most of the boats were comparatively slow, since they were built primarily for the transportation of freight. It was only after the admission of Iowa and Wisconsin as States and the creation of the Territory of Minnesota that the Upper Mississippi steamboats began to reach a point in construction where speed and beauty became as important as capacity. Although no hard and fast line can be drawn, it seems safe to say that the turn of the half-century marks this transformation period.

29

Rival Trade Routes

BITTER RIVALRY sprang up as the Great Lakes cities jealously watched the lead traffic glide down the Mississippi to fatten the pocket-books of St. Louis and New Orleans merchants. Because of the high and unstable freight rates and the dangers of ascending and descending the rapids, it was quite natural that a cheaper and more certain route should be sought. Indeed, as early as 1822 a cargo of 12,000 pounds of lead reached Detroit from Green Bay : with the exception of a short portage between the Wisconsin and Fox rivers, it had been transported the entire distance by water.[307]

With the practicability of navigating the Mississippi by steamboat established by the *Virginia*, agitation began for a general improvement of the channel of the river and for the elimination of the Upper and Lower rapids as obstacles to navigation. In his recommendation to the Secretary of War, Lieutenant Martin Thomas, the Superintendent of Mines, estimated that this work could be done at a cost of not more than $30,000. Not only would these improvements be of inestimable benefit in the transportation of lead, but they would also be important in facilitating the movement of troops and supplies. While the strategic importance of the latter was not lost sight of, the improvement of the rapids was not immediately undertaken.[308]

Rival Trade Routes

In 1829, Henry Dodge decided to convey a portion of his lead via the Wisconsin-Fox rivers and Green Bay route. Huge oxcarts were employed to carry the lead from Dodgeville to the Wisconsin River where it was conveyed as far as Fort Winnebago, hauled across the portage, and transported down the Fox River on the little twenty-five-ton steamboat *Winnebago Chief* to Green Bay.[309]

Naturally the people of Galena were opposed to this route which, if successful, would have a disastrous effect on their prosperity. "Considerable quantities of lead", said the *Miner's Journal* of Galena, "have been brought down the Ouisconsin [Wisconsin], in flat-boats, and thence down the Mississippi to St. Louis. Steam boat navigation will be difficult in the Ouisconsin river, if not impracticable. The steam boat St. Louis and Galena packet, bound for the portage, made an attempt, in April last, to ascend the Ouisconsin; but was not able to make more than 6 or 7 miles up, when she was compelled to return. The river is full of sand bars, and has been somewhat compared to the Missouri, as the channel frequently shifts."[310] By such unfavorable reports Galena hoped to discourage any attempts to adopt the Wisconsin-Fox route.

A further stimulus to this route was given by the erection of a shot tower near Helena on the Wisconsin River. In 1831 it was purchased by Daniel Whitney, a merchant of Green Bay, and held by him until 1836. While it was natural for him to favor this route, a more significant factor was that the older and more strategically located shot tower at Herculaneum, Missouri, controlled the market of the Lower Mississippi Valley. The Green Bay route continued to be favored after the Helena shot tower was purchased by merchants from Buffalo, New York, but the amount of lead sent by this route was negligible when compared with the vast quantities sent down the Mississippi. A poor river channel, the circuitousness of the route, and the number of necessary rehandlings doomed it to failure from the start.[311]

A second route lay by land over rough corduroy roads to Milwaukee. In 1841 the Milwaukee *Courier* heralded the arrival of four wagons loaded with ten tons of lead from Muscoda, Grant County, Wisconsin. The cost of conveying lead overland had been ninety-three cents per hundred pounds. An additional fifty cents per hundred would be required to ship it by way of the Great Lakes and the Erie Canal to New York. The total cost per hundred was $1.50 or $30 a ton, while shipment by way of New Orleans cost around $40 per ton. The wagons had returned loaded with salt which was bought at $2.50 a barrel and sold at the mines for $7 a barrel. No difficulty had been experienced in getting over the roads despite the fact that each wagon contained over two tons of lead. The route was not so favorable, however, as its advocates claimed. It was not until the railroad was built that an overland route gained any share of the trade.[312]

A third route clamored for by Great Lakes cities was the Illinois-Lake Michigan Canal. As early as 1836 Chicago had developed a plan to increase her future prosperity by constructing a railroad to Galena and a canal to connect with the Illinois River. To aid this project 120 merchants of St. Louis and Alton went so far as to sign a contract to import their goods by means of a transportation company which had been formed to develop the new route.[313] The *Wisconsin Herald* (Lancaster) warmly endorsed the Illinois River route — a further mark of the indifference with which towns located almost on the Mississippi viewed that great waterway as a means of transportation.[314] The canal was not completed until 1848, but the interest manifested in it for fifteen years prior to its completion and the quantity of goods shipped overland to and from the Illinois River made it a logical route. By 1848 the number of steamboat arrivals at St. Louis from the Illinois River was almost equal to those arriving from the Upper Mississippi.[315]

Strenuous efforts were made by the lake cities to divert the course of lead eastward over these routes. Milwaukee and Chicago were especially active; but in spite of their best efforts only a very small amount of lead trickled through. On January 21, 1842, Governor James Doty of Wisconsin urged and obtained the reduction of Erie Canal tolls in order to encourage shipments of lead by that route. But even this failed to divert the trade, and the Buffalo *Advertiser* bewailed the fact that the number of pigs of lead received at that port had dropped from 23,926 in 1844 to 6276 in 1846 and acknowledged that all efforts seemed to have been in vain.[316]

Over ninety-five per cent of the lead shipped eastward

during the period which followed the year 1823 made its way down the Mississippi River to New Orleans, and thence by ocean to the eastern markets.[317] Notwithstanding the objection to high and fluctuating freight rates, the obstructions and difficulties which confronted the steamboat, and the comparatively short season for transportation, the Mississippi offered the most logical route and the best facilities for transporting the lead output.

The influence of the lead mines upon the development of steamboating on the Upper Mississippi in the first quarter of a century of navigation on the river is apparent. First, it encouraged the immigration of thousands of hardy and adventurous settlers, most of whom came up the Mississippi from St. Louis to a point far in advance of the frontier line and thereby caused it to be extended. Secondly, the influx made necessary an ever-increasing supply of importations to a region which, for a large part of the period under survey was not self-sufficient. Thirdly, it created an article for exportation which gave to the steamboat owners approximately two-fifths of the total revenue from upstream trade. Finally, the large number of steamboats which were required on the Upper Mississippi for the lead trade prepared them for an even more lucrative traffic — the transportation of the steady waves of immigrants which poured into the region after the creation of the Territory of Minnesota, the commodities required by them for consumption, and the vast quantities of agricultural products which found their way to markets down the broad highway of the Mississippi.

Rival Trade Routes

Had the steamboat failed to establish itself as the dominant factor in transportation and in communication with the Upper Mississippi as early as it did, the construction of railroads might have taken place a decade earlier and a picturesque phase of Upper Mississippi Valley life would have been lost to posterity. After 1848 the steamboat was so strongly intrenched in the economic life of the region that it was able to wage a thrilling, albeit a losing, battle against the railroad.

30

Catlin and the Fashionable Tour

PRIOR TO THE Civil War no steamboat excursion was so popular as that which George Catlin designated as the "Fashionable Tour". It represented a colorful phase of Upper Mississippi steamboating that stood in sharp contrast to the drab though lucrative lead trade. George Catlin, who was born in Pennsylvania in 1796, studied and practiced law as a young man; but his greatest renown was achieved as an artist. In 1823 Catlin shoved aside his law books and moved to Philadelphia to devote himself to portrait painting in oil and miniatures. During the next five years he painted portraits of such notables as De Witt Clinton and Dolly Madison. Upon seeing a group of red men from the western wilds in Philadelphia, Catlin resolved "to use my art and so much of the labors of my future life as might be required in rescuing from oblivion the looks and customs of the vanishing races of native man in America."

Between 1829 and 1837 Catlin was almost constantly in the West, during which time he painted some six hundred Indian sketches, including portraits, pictures of villages, domestic habits, games, mysteries, and religious ceremonies of the red men. By exhibiting his original collection of paintings in many cities of the United States and Europe he achieved an international reputation.[318]

Catlin and the Fashionable Tour

During the course of his wanderings in the West, Catlin made several steamboat trips on western waters. Thrilled by the wild beauty of the Upper Mississippi, he wrote from Fort Snelling in 1835 : "The Upper Mississippi, like the Upper Missouri, must be approached to be appreciated; for all that can be seen on the Mississippi below St. Louis or for several miles above it, gives no hint or clue to the magnificence of the scenes which are continually opening to the view of the traveller, and riveting him to the deck of the steamer, through sunshine, lightning or rain, from the mouth of the Ouisconsin to the Fall of St. Anthony."

From day to day Catlin stood with eyes transfixed in "tireless admiration, upon the thousand bluffs which tower in majesty above the river on either side". As the enraptured artist later relates : "The scenes that are passed between Prairie du Chien and St. Peters, including Lake Pepin, between whose magnificently turretted shores one passes for twenty-two miles, will amply reward the tourist for the time and expense of a visit to them. And to him or her of too little relish for Nature's rude works, to profit as they pass, there will be found a redeeming pleasure at the mouth of St. Peters and the Fall of St. Anthony. This scene has often been described, and I leave it for the world to come and gaze upon for themselves; recommending to them at the same time, to denominate the next 'Fashionable Tour,' a trip to St. Louis; thence by steamer to Rock Island, Galena, Dubuque, Prairie du Chien, Lake Pepin, St. Peters, Fall of St. Anthony, back to Prairie du Chien, from thence to Fort Winnebago,

Steamboating on Upper Mississippi

Green Bay, Mackinaw, Sault de St. Mary, Detroit, Buffalo, Niagara, and home." [319]

But Catlin was not the first to extol the beauties of the Upper Mississippi. The first to visit the Falls of St. Anthony by steamboat and to describe them was Giacomo Constantine Beltrami. Arriving at Fort Snelling aboard the *Virginia* on May 10, 1823, the picturesque Italian exile and explorer quickly set out to view the scene which Hennepin had described 143 years before. "What a new scene presents itself to my eyes", Beltrami exclaimed. "Seated on the top of an elevated promontory, I see, at half a mile distance, two great masses of water unite at the foot of an island which they encircle, and whose majestic trees deck them with the loveliest hues, in which all the magic play of light and shade are reflected on their brilliant surface. From this point they rush down a rapid descent about two hundred feet long, and, breaking against the scattered rocks which obstruct their passage, they spray up and dash together in a thousand varied forms. They then fall into a transverse basin, in the form of a cradle, and are urged upwards by the force of gravitation against the side of a precipice, which seems to stop them a moment only to encrease the violence with which they fling themselves down a depth of twenty feet. The rocks against which these great volumes of water dash, throw them back in white foam and glittering spray; then, plunging into the cavities which this mighty fall has hollowed, they rush forth again in tumultuous waves, and once more break against a great mass of sandstone forming a little island in the midst of their bed, on which two thick maples spread their shady branches." [320]

Perhaps the earliest and shortest pleasure-seeking trip on record to the Falls of St. Anthony was that of the steamboat *Lawrence* in 1826. With Captain D. F. Reeder in command, this 120-ton craft reached Fort Snelling on the second of May. The following day Captain Reeder invited all the ladies and gentlemen of Fort Snelling to take a pleasure trip to the Falls. The offer was accepted by a large party. Accompanied by a band, the *Lawrence* steamed up the swift current to within three and one-half miles of the Falls : she did not dare to venture nearer. While some of the party played games, others danced to the music of the military band. Staring Indians came to view the *Lawrence* with mingled wonder and astonishment. [321]

In later years other craft may have ventured near the Falls on similar excursions from Fort Snelling. Before 1850, however, the season of low water (during which excursions were made) together with the swift current and jagged rocks immediately below the Falls forced steamboats to discharge their passengers at St. Peter's. From there they were carried to the Falls in such vehicles as a straggling frontier community was able to provide. Often an eight mile tramp was made across the plains.

Finally, in May of 1850, the *Lamartine* (Captain J. W. Marsh commanding) stemmed the Mississippi to Steele's Point, a quarter of a mile below the Falls. Captain Daniel Able followed almost in the wake of the *Lamartine* with the *Anthony Wayne*, ascending to the city of St. Anthony, directly at the foot of the Falls. Governor Alexander Ramsey was among the invited guests and a number of notables were picked up at Fort Snelling. The *Anthony Wayne* employed a band which provided lively dance music throughout the trip. Captain Marsh received a purse of $200 for reaching Steele's Point; while Captain Able rejoiced over a purse of $250 for venturing to the Falls.[322]

Although the *Lamartine* and the *Anthony Wayne* demonstrated the possibility of navigating the Upper Mississippi from the mouth of the Minnesota to the Falls during a good stage of water, steamboats continued to discharge tourists at St. Paul. Indeed, in 1854 it was necessary to convey twelve hundred eastern visitors to the Falls in every conceivable form of vehicle. Throughout the decade St. Paul mocked the citizens of St. Anthony for claiming to be at the head of navigation.[323]

Steamboats made occasional trips from Galena, St. Louis, and from points below, but only a few tourists were among their regular passengers. Until the Black Hawk War had eliminated the danger of Indian attack, only transitory voyages were made during the summer months. Even as late as 1835 trips were governed by the cargoes offered. Thus, when Charles Augustus Murray, a noted English traveler, reached Prairie du Chien early in October, he was unable to secure a steamboat passage to the Falls. Murray had to content himself with a hunting expedition from Fort Crawford to the headwaters of Turkey River before descending the Mississippi to St. Louis.[324]

Catlin and the Fashionable Tour

Generally speaking, however, steamboats arrived more regularly at Fort Snelling after 1832 and a number of pleasure-seekers were usually found on every boat. Colonel John H. Bliss recalls that whenever the steamboat *Warrior* appeared she had her hold filled with military supplies and her cabins crowded with "delightful and delighted tourists who were making an excursion, considered more wonderful in those days than would be a trip to the Hawaiian Islands now." [325] On June 24, 1835, Captain Joseph Throckmorton arrived at Fort Snelling with a cargo of supplies and a lively throng of excursionists aboard the *Warrior* and her safety barge. Among the passengers were Captain William Day, George W. Jones, a member of Congress from the Territory of Michigan, J. Farnsworth and daughter, Mrs. Felix St. Vrain, and the renowned artist, George Catlin, and his wife. [326]

If travelers were thrilled by the scenic splendors of the Upper Mississippi, their joy upon reaching St. Peter's was limited only by the brevity of their visit. Most of those who made the Fashionable Tour were obliged — either through their own limited time or the anxiety of the steamboat captain to depart downstream — to confine themselves to a fleeting glimpse of St. Anthony and Minnehaha Falls and an even more hurried glance about the fort. To miss a boat prior to 1850 might entail a sojourn of a week or more before another craft appeared. So the joy of the pleasure-seekers was always tempered by the constant dread of failing to hear the last bell of the steamboat, calling belated stragglers aboard.

Steamboating on Upper Mississippi

Other excursionists who were fortunate enough to spend several days or weeks about Fort Snelling were amply rewarded. After a day of viewing St. Anthony in all its moods, and another near Minnehaha, the tourist could turn his attention to the activities about Fort Snelling. Officers and soldiers were always communicative (their ladies equally if not doubly so), and so a social hour would quickly run into two. The Indian Agency and the American Fur Company post also attracted visitors. Here fur trader and voyageur vied with Chippewa and Sioux in entertaining the pleasure-seekers. The traders always made amiable and valuable guides to some nearby stream or lake where fish might be caught; the Indians were equally delighted to dance, sing, and play their games for a small consideration.

The Fourth of July, 1835, was memorable for the excursionists who, with Catlin, awaited the return of the *Warrior* to Fort Snelling. Major Lawrence Taliaferro, the Indian Agent at Fort Snelling, had informed the Sioux and Chippewa that Catlin was a great medicine man, and he promised to fire the *"big gun"* twenty-one times (the customary salute of the day) if they would come and entertain the tourists with a ball game and some of their dances. Highly flattered by this compliment, hundreds of Indians appeared at Fort Snelling where Catlin presented them with a barrel of flour and a quantity of pork and tobacco.

For two hours Sioux and Chippewa exerted every effort to demonstrate to Catlin that they were as skillful at ball

as any tribe he had ever seen in the West. They then performed the beggar's dance, the buffalo dance, the bear
dance, the eagle dance, and the dance of the braves which
Catlin felt was "peculiarly beautiful, and exciting to the
feelings in the highest degree." When Major General Robert Patterson arrived on the *Warrior* a short time later the
games and dances were repeated. "The greater part of the
inhabitants of these bands", Catlin records, "are assembled
here at this time, affording us, who are visitors here, a fine
and wild scene of dances, amusements, &c. They seem to
take great pleasure in 'showing off' in these scenes, to the
amusement of the many fashionable visitors, both ladies
and gentlemen, who are in the habit of reaching this post,
as steamers are arriving at this place every week in the
summer from St. Louis." [327]

Next to the scenery the Indian offered the most interesting entertainment and diversion to the visitors, and
as late as 1845 a Dubuque newspaper urged the trip as the
most convenient and certain way of seeing the red man
as he actually lived. [328] Catlin painted many pictures of
the Sioux and Chippewa at their games and dances; of
chiefs and warriors; of squaws and papooses; of canoes,
snowshoes, and other equipment. Then, while his wife
journeyed downstream on the *Warrior*, he paddled leisurely along in a canoe to record with his brush such pictures
as the Falls of St. Anthony, Fort Snelling, Maiden Rock,
the Winona hills, Capoli Bluff, and Cornice Rocks; Pike's
Peak at McGregor; Fort Crawford and the island-studded
Mississippi; and Dubuque's grave and the lead mines above

Steamboating on Upper Mississippi

Catfish Creek — a panorama of the Upper Mississippi.[329]
The yearly arrival of steamboats loaded with excursionists became more marked following Catlin's return to the East from this trip. Early in June, 1836, the *Palmyra* arrived at Fort Snelling with a party of pleasure-seekers. A journal kept by one of the party described the scenery en route, the Falls of St. Anthony, and a three mile excursion up the Minnesota River. Two months later Captain Throckmorton carried a pleasure party on board the *St. Peters* — a 119-ton craft built at Pittsburgh the previous winter. She was owned by Throckmorton and the firm of Hempstead and Beebe of St. Louis. One of the ladies on board the *St. Peters* wrote a letter to a friend in Buffalo describing the beauties of the Upper Mississippi and the rapid growth of population in the country between Dubuque and St. Louis.[330]

By 1837 Upper Mississippi steamboat captains advertised excursion trips in the various river towns throughout the summer months. Early in May, Daniel Smith Harris informed citizens of Galena, Dubuque, and Belmont that he would make a trip to the Falls of St. Anthony in the *Smelter*, should a sufficient number of passengers present themselves. A week later Captain James Lafferty advised Galenians that he expected to run a similar excursion on the *Pavilion*.[331]

Despite the panic of 1837 the Fashionable Tour attracted hundreds of pilgrims : indeed their number sometimes exceeded the immigrants on board the steamboat. A card of thanks signed by over forty passengers aboard

Catlin and the Fashionable Tour

the *Missouri Fulton* commended Captain I. Perrin on the success of the trip and the kind attention and gentlemanly treatment of the officers and the crew. Seven of the signers came from New York State; while Pennsylvania, Maryland, Virginia, Kentucky, and Ohio were represented by one or more. A number hailed from Illinois. Missouri and Wisconsin Territory were strongly represented. John Plumbe, Jr., claimed by some to be the first man to conceive the need for a trans-continental railroad, was among the Dubuque tourists.[332]

Not only did many notable Americans grace the deck of Upper Mississippi steamboats, but travelers from England, France, Italy, Russia, Switzerland, and other countries were attracted by the tour. The season of 1837 found George Catlin and his wife again with Captain Throckmorton on board the *Burlington* with Colonel John Bliss and family as fellow pasengers. During the same year J. N. Nicollet, John C. Frémont, Henry Atkinson, and Franklin Steele, together with many other prominent personages took passage with Throckmorton. Captain Frederick Marryat, the English novelist and sea captain, also paced the deck of the *Burlington*. Sweet and serene in the dignity of her eighty years came Elizabeth Schuyler Hamilton, the widow of Alexander Hamilton, braving the wilderness with its many discomforts to visit her son, Colonel William S. Hamilton, then located in the Wisconsin lead district at Wiota. Her visit elicited a warm reception wherever the *Burlington* stopped. Many other notables were carried aboard such craft as the *Pavilion*, the

Missouri Fulton, the *Irene*, the *Rolla* and the *Smelter*.[333]

Before 1840 none of the embryo cities above St. Louis had a sufficient number of wealthy citizens capable of chartering a vessel for a private excursion. Since boats were generally limited to a score or two of excursionists, captains reserved the right to pick up such freight and passengers as would not interfere with the comforts of the pleasure-seekers. Even as late as 1847 the *Lynx* carried a heavy consignment of government supplies and transient passengers along with a merry party from New Orleans.[334]

The decade of the "Fabulous Forties" witnessed many excursions from thriving towns on the Ohio and the Lower Mississippi. In 1840 the Louisville *Journal*, in expressing delight at the prospects of a large and fashionable excursion party on the *Dayton*, declared the trip to be the most interesting in the United States. A similar excursion left St. Louis on the *Valley Forge*, the first iron-hulled steamboat on the Ohio and Mississippi. Built at Pittsburgh in 1839, the *Valley Forge* was 150 feet long, had a 25-foot beam, a 5½-foot hold, and measured 199 tons. She was owned by William Robinson, Benjamin Mines, and Reuben Miller, Jr., of Pittsburgh. Thomas Baldwin served as skipper in 1840. During the same year a large party bound from Pittsburgh to the Falls of St. Anthony stopped at Cincinnati to greet General William Henry Harrison.[335]

Daniel Stanchfield found St. Louis sweltering hot following the sale of a lumber raft in 1847. This pioneer Upper Mississippi lumberman accordingly joined a merry party from New Orleans aboard Captain John Atchison's

Catlin and the Fashionable Tour

Lynx. A brass band entertained the excursionists by day, while an orchestra provided excellent music for dancing at night. At Fort Snelling the group was met by Franklin Steele with carriages for transporting the party across the plains to the Falls where the steward of the *Lynx* served a tempting dinner on the grass. The ladies had also prepared delicacies which were distributed to the tourists. Wines flowed freely for two hilarious hours when a storm sent the excursionists racing for shelter beneath the ledge of Minnehaha Falls.[336]

While steamboats brought tourists from points as widely separated as Pittsburgh and New Orleans, the budding towns along the Upper Mississippi began to contribute a greater volume of passengers each year. By carefully advertising excursions several weeks in advance in such towns as Alton, Clarksville, Louisiana, Hannibal, Quincy, Keokuk, Fort Madison, Burlington, Muscatine, Davenport, Rock Island, Clinton, and Galena, the captains engaged in the trade usually made several profitable voyages each season.[337]

Newspaper editors, with personal motives often outstripping their civic pride, encouraged their readers to patronize certain boats making excursions. Thus, when Captain Orrin Smith announced in the *Iowa News* that the *Brazil* would leave Dubuque for St. Peter's on June 10, 1838, an editorial in the same issue praised Captain Smith and recommended the *Brazil* to all. A little later, after the *Brazil* had steamed past Dubuque on her way to the Falls, the editor spoke wistfully of the gay crowd aboard, the music and dancing, the "splendor" of the new boat, and expressed a hope that an invitation might be extended to him for a similar frolic. "Who'll invite us to take a trip . . . don't all speak at once", this weary editor pined. "Yet the first one who asks us is a gentleman of the pure water, and a scholar and a dancing master into the bargain." If the lavish use of printer's ink was any inducement, he probably received an invitation.[338]

In later years many steamboats paddled northward with gaily attired vacationists promenading their decks by day and dancing, visiting, and courting by night. The *Rosalie*, the *Knickerbocker*, the *Malta*, and the *Brazil* announced trips from Galena in 1839; while the *Malta, Loyal Hanna, Brazil, Ione, Monsoon*, and *Valley Forge* ran similar notices during the year following. Within the space of three weeks in 1845 the *Lynx* (Captain John Atchison commanding), the *St. Croix* (Captain Hiram Bersie commanding), the *Iowa* (Captain D. B. Morehouse commanding), and the *War Eagle*, commanded by Daniel Smith Harris, advertised trips for the Falls. Crowded with happy excursionists, the *War Eagle* and the *Time* left the mouth of Fever River and proceeded briskly upstream with their bows lashed together.[339]

Little attention was paid to passenger accommodations until the late thirties, for steamboats were engaged primarily in hauling lead, supplies for military posts and Indian agencies, goods for the fur traders, and such cargoes as the steady infiltration of immigrants required. Strange M. Palmer described the steamboat *Adventure* bound for

Catlin and the Fashionable Tour

Prairie du Chien in 1836 as "a very small, dilapidated and filthy boat". Measured by the standards of that day, however, most captains probably tried to keep their boats clean and comfortable.[340]

The regular upstream craft upon which Theodore Rodolf, a pioneer in the lead region, found himself in 1834 was "a high-pressure steamer, whose puffing could be heard miles ahead. The cabin was plainly but substantially furnished, and kept very clean. There were no state rooms; but two tiers of bunks, containing the beds, ran along the side of the boat and were separated at night from the saloon by curtains. The fare was substantial, plentiful, and good, and the officers were pleasant and gentlemanly." [341]

No factor was so important in bringing about a change in steamboat accommodations as the "Fashionable Tour" which George Catlin had urged Americans to make in 1835. Realizing that most tourists would patronize those boats which offered the best facilities, Captain Daniel Smith Harris and his brother Robert Scribe Harris built private staterooms in the *Smelter* — a speedy side-wheeler launched at Cincinnati in the spring of 1837. She was described as the fastest, the most luxurious, and the largest craft on the Upper Mississippi. According to W. H. C. Folsom the Harris brothers were "greatly delighted in her speed, decorated her gaily with evergreens, and [when] rounding to at landings, or meeting with other boats, fired a cannon from her prow to announce her imperial presence." [342]

Steamboating on Upper Mississippi

Two years later the Harris brothers (Smith and Scribe) brought out the *Pizarro*, a 107-ton craft built at Cincinnati at a cost of $16,000. While her cabin was not so spacious as those in some of the other crafts, this boat was "commodious" and had the usual staterooms. She also boasted a fire engine and hose attached to her main engine and ready for immediate use in case of fire.[343]

Captain Orrin Smith was also responsible for many improvements in steamboat architecture. In 1838 he brought out the *Brazil* "completely fitted up with staterooms, two berths in each, with doorways leading both into the cabin and out upon the deck." The rooms were said to be sufficiently spacious, and each had a "wash-stand and other necessary articles of toilet", besides the regular "sleeping apparatus". When the *Brazil* struck a rock on the Upper Rapids in the spring of 1841, Smith built the light draught *New Brazil* at Cincinnati. She was 144 feet long, had a 22-foot beam, a 5-foot hold, and measured 166 tons. Her cabin contained 30 staterooms, and her 22-foot paddle wheel was propelled by a double engine with three boilers.[344]

Always a leader in new ventures, Captain Joseph Throckmorton is credited with introducing spring mattresses on his beautiful $18,000 craft, the *Malta*. Launched at Pittsburgh in 1839, the *Malta* was 140 feet long, had a 22-foot beam, a 5-foot hold, measured 114 tons, and had a fire pump and hose attached to her double engine.[345]

A novel improvement, generally adopted by other captains, was introduced in 1845 by Robert A. Reilly of the

Wiota. Instead of locating the stairs which led to the boiler deck on each side of the boat, as was customary in all the old side-wheelers, Reilly had a flight placed in front. The *Wiota* was built at Elizabethtown, Pennsylvania, in 1845, and was owned by Captain Reilly, Henry Corwith, and William Hempstead of Galena. She was 170 feet long, twenty-five feet and six inches broad, five feet and three inches hold, and had a displacement of 219 tons. Her two engines had three boilers, each twenty-six feet long and forty inches in diameter; the cylinders were eighteen inches in diameter and had a seven foot stroke; and her wheels were twenty-two feet in diameter with ten foot buckets.[346]

Although steamboat captains felt they were keeping apace with the times some of the traveling public did not think so. As late as 1852 a Minnesota editor complained : "One of the first reforms needed on steamboats in the west, is good comfortable beds, with so much clothing that you do not have to spread a newspaper over you at night, to prevent freezing. Why should a boat spread an extra table and fine carpets, and then send a poor fellow to a hard straw mattress, to shiver all night and take a severe cold, under a dirty sheet and a narrow comforter?" [347]

Increasing competition forced captains to offer still other inducements. By the middle of the century few steamboats dared compete without the aid of a band or orchestra — usually comprised of cabin boys, deck hands, and roustabouts. These were modestly heralded as the finest musicians on the Upper Mississippi and equal to any

Steamboating on Upper Mississippi

in the United States. Stewards were ever mindful that tables must be supplied with the best that money could buy, and vacationists soon learned which craft served the best meals. Furthermore, excursionists liked nothing better than a chance to prowl about historic or legendary spots, such as Maiden Rock. Tourists who were so inclined had numerous opportunities, since steamboats "wooded up" about every thirty miles. Besides a Sunday lay-over at St. Peter's, Captain Hiram Bersie promised that the *St. Croix* would stop at points of interest on the downstream trip.[348]

A typical notice apprised the citizens of Dubuque of such an excursion in 1845.[349]

PLEASURE EXCURSION
From Dubuque to St. Peters and
The Falls of St. Anthony.
Passenger Steamer

WAR EAGLE

D. S. HARRIS, MASTER

Will leave for the above and intermediate Ports on Friday the 27th inst. at 10 o'clock A. M.

The War Eagle is a new and Splendid Boat, and will be two weeks making the trip. Capt. Harris intends to make a pleasure excursion in *reality*, and will stop at all places of curiosity or amusement as long as the passengers may desire. A Band of Music will be on Board. Strangers and Travelers will have a fine opportunity of visiting one of the most beautiful and romantic countries in the world. *For Freight or Passage, apply on Board.*

For more than a generation the pioneers of the Upper Mississippi Valley enjoyed steamboat excursions to the

Falls of St. Anthony. In 1849 the *Clermont* carried a large pleasure party upstream from Quincy. Two years later the *Die Vernon* ran several excursions to the Falls from St. Louis. Commenting on these excursions a Galena editor pointed out that such a "summer jaunt" answered the onerous problems of those harassed as to where to go on a vacation. In 1853 the *Die Vernon*, the *New St. Paul*, and the *Dr. Franklin* arrived at the St. Paul levee with merry excursionists who were carted off to the Falls in buggies. Captain Preston Lodwick invited the leading citizens of St. Paul to join his party aboard the *Dr. Franklin* for two hours of recreation and dancing.

Four years later (in 1857) the masters of the *Henry Clay* and *Northern Belle* brought pleasure parties from St. Louis and Dubuque and tendered a "grand ball" for the principal citizens of St. Paul while in port. The *Harmonia*, the *Rescue*, the *Rosalie*, the *Orb*, the *Sam Young*, the *Conewago*, the *Denmark*, and the *Key City* were only a few of the boats that gladdened the hearts of excursionists that year. In good times and bad, the Fashionable Tour provided an enjoyable and inexpensive outing for travelers on Upper Mississippi steamboats.[350]

31

The West Newton vs. the Die Vernon

AN ERA OF intense rivalry began in 1848 and did not end until the Minnesota Packet Company was formally organized at the close of the season of 1852.[351] The Fashionable Tour became more popular each year for vacationists who found traveling on steamboats cheaper than living in hotels. "The boats continue to come loaded with passengers, many of them seeking only recreation", declared a St. Paul editor in 1852. "Boats are crowded down and up. Some travel for the sake of economy and save the expense of tavern bills at home. Who that is idle would be caged up between walls of burning brick and mortar; in dog-days, down the river, if at less daily expense, he could be hurried through the valley of the Mississippi, its shores studded with towns and farms, flying by islands, prairies, woodlands, bluffs — an ever varied scene of beauty, away up into the lands of the wild Dakota, and of cascades and pine forests, and cooling breezes?"[352]

Nor was rivalry limited to the packets running above Galena. During the summer of 1852 the Keokuk Packet Company extended its operations to Galena and occasionally ran an excursion to the Falls. Realizing that a death struggle was in the offing for its boats — the *Nominee*, the *Ben Campbell*, the *Dr. Franklin No. 2*, and the *Black Hawk* — the Minnesota Packet Company invited

The *West Newton* vs. the *Die Vernon*

Daniel Smith Harris to join their line with his speedy *West Newton*. It was a wise move, for in addition to being the most popular skipper on the river, Harris was a skillful pilot, a demon in competition, and, what was most important, he was perhaps the only man whose boat could always be counted on to out-race an opponent.[353]

Pitted against the *West Newton* was the *Die Vernon*, floating palace of the Keokuk Packet Line and, perhaps, the fastest craft on western waters. Built at St. Louis in 1850 at a cost of $50,000, the *Die Vernon* was 255 feet long, thirty-one feet two inches beam, five feet nine inches hold, and measured 455 tons. She had over 100 berths and was more than a match for any boat owned by the Minnesota Packet Company.[354]

The round-trip fare on the *Die Vernon* for the excursion was fixed at $25. There was no free list : even Commodore John S. McCune and the directors of the line paid their passage. An "army" of waiters was hired, and the steward was ordered to spare no luxury, including Longworth's Sparkling Cabinet and Still Catawba wine. A brass band was to render martial music — especially when in port or in passing rival boats. Twenty-five firemen were shipped aboard the *Die Vernon* to ensure hot boilers. The ever watchful steward had a barrel of old butter — presumably for soap grease — but actually for extra fuel should the emergency arise.[355]

Late Monday afternoon, June 13, 1853, the *Die Vernon*, commanded by Rufus Ford, left St. Louis as handkerchiefs waved and the band blared "Yankee Doodle". Alton was passed in record time. Every craft below Keokuk gave the boat a brush just to see her run. And run she did. The Lower Rapids were crossed on Tuesday afternoon. Twenty-five cords of white oak were taken aboard at Bellevue on Wednesday afternoon. At dusk she came snorting up the Fever River to Galena where the *West Newton* lay awaiting her arrival.

Captain Harris did not conceal his intention of either outstripping the *Die Vernon* or of blowing up his boat in the attempt. All the tar and rosin in Galena was aboard the *West Newton*, and every wood boat for 150 miles up the river was pledged to sell only to him. Galenians offered bets at heavy odds that the *West Newton* would pass the *Die Vernon* under way and lead her to St. Paul.

When the *Die Vernon* backed out of Fever River the *West Newton* followed, "blowing off steam and making more noise than a stalled freight train", intent on passing her rival on the Mississippi before she was fairly under way. But half the "niggers" on the *Die Vernon* were hanging on the safety valves and Captain Ford had the boilers so hot that his boat led the way to Dubuque. The *Die Vernon* stopped a few moments at Dubuque, but the *West Newton* continued upstream and was soon out of sight. It was evidently Harris's intention to lead the way to Lake Pepin, one hundred and ninety miles above, and there await the *Die Vernon* for a twenty-two mile race through the lake. It would then be but fifty-five miles to St. Paul with the victory in favor of the winner through Lake Pepin.

The *West Newton vs.* the *Die Vernon*

Captain Ford tarried but a moment in Dubuque, hoping to pass Harris within a few hours. Despite the fact that her twenty-five firemen worked frantically throughout the night and were plied with "whisky toddies to assist them in making steam", the *West Newton* was not sighted until after breakfast the following morning a short distance above La Crosse. A bitter race ensued. The *Die Vernon* fairly trembled under the terrific pressure of steam, but she slowly closed the gap between the two boats until only a few scant yards separated them. According to a passenger aboard the *Die Vernon*, the *West Newton* was finally forced to land to keep from being passed under way, a fact which Harris's friends vigorously deny. Be that as it may, the *Die Vernon* did pass the *West Newton*, and, what was worse, for it was still anybody's race, she obtained through the connivance of Louis Robert, at that time master of the *Greek Slave* and a bitter enemy of Captain Harris, possession of two wood flats loaded with choice dry fuel for the *West Newton*. Harris drew abreast of the *Die Vernon* while she was towing the flats; it was then that the crew quickly tossed the wood aboard and cast the flats loose before the *West Newton* was able to forge ahead. It is perhaps as well that history does not record Captain Harris's remarks when he learned how Louis Robert had tricked and probably beaten him.[356]

While he ran a gallant race against a boat which was much faster than his own, Harris took the defeat bitterly and departed from St. Paul without leaving the hurricane deck. The *Die Vernon* made a record run of eighty-four hours counting all stops from St. Louis to St. Paul. Her time from Dubuque was twenty-eight hours for 265 miles or nine and four-tenths miles per hour upstream. The *West Newton* averaged nine and one-tenth miles per hour upstream from Galena to St. Paul, covering the 288 miles in thirty-one hours and forty-six minutes. She returned to Galena in twenty-one hours and seven minutes, averaging thirteen and seven-tenths miles per hour downstream.[357]

It was left for the pious and temperate *Nominee*, commanded by Russell Blakeley, to take the measure of the *Die Vernon* and avenge the defeat of the *West Newton*. While the St. Louis excursionists were celebrating their victory at Maiden Rock with Sparkling Cabinet and Still Catawba, the *Nominee* hove in sight and blew a shrill challenge. Although her owner, Orrin Smith, was a strict Sabbath observer and follower of the Maine Law, the *Nominee* was a fast boat and led the *Die Vernon* all the way, disappearing around the bend at Catfish Creek as the latter reached Dubuque. Despite the fact that the Keokuk Packet Company received almost $4000 in cabin passages, the excursion of the *Die Vernon* left a deficit of $1100.

The spirited fight of the Minnesota Packet Company forced a compromise, and when the season of 1854 opened its boats carried the celebrated excursion of the Chicago and Rock Island Railroad — probably the most colorful gathering of notable Americans that had assembled in the West before the Civil War.[358]

32

The Grand Excursion of 1854

THE FIRST railroad to unite the Atlantic with the Mississippi River reached Rock Island on February 22, 1854. To celebrate this event leading citizens of the country were invited by the firm of Sheffield and Farnam, contractors for the construction of the Chicago and Rock Island Railroad, to participate in a joint railroad and steamboat excursion to the Falls of St. Anthony. The response was so hearty and the requests for passes were so numerous that the Minnesota Packet Company was obliged to increase the number of steamboats chartered from one to five.[359]

So lavish were the preparations that an eastern paper declared the affair "could not be rivalled by the mightiest among the potentates of Europe." The account continues: "Without bustle or noise, in a simple but grand manner, like everything resulting from the combined action of liberty and association — guests have been brought hither free of charge from different places, distant thousands of miles, invited by hosts to them unknown, simple contractors and directors of railroads and steamboats." [360]

John H. Kinzie was chairman of the reception committee in Chicago, where the Tremont House served as headquarters for the assembled guests. There, Millard Fillmore, a President by accident, met Samuel J. Tilden, who later failed by accident to achieve the presidency. Prominent western leaders such as Ninian Edwards (former Governor of Illinois) and Edward Bates of Missouri (later Attorney General in Lincoln's cabinet) exchanged views with notable Easterners such as John A. Dix, John A. Granger, J. C. Ten Eyck, and Elbridge Gerry. Francis P. Blair of Maryland greeted his son, Francis P. Blair, Jr., of St. Louis. New Haven and Yale University sent Professors Benjamin Silliman, A. C. Twining, Leonard Bacon, and Eleazar Thompson to match wits with Judge Joel Parker of Harvard and Professor Henry Hubbard of Dartmouth. George Bancroft, a Harvard graduate and already a national historian, accepted an invitation to make the "fashionable tour": he was repeatedly called upon to address the crowds which gathered to greet the Easterners. Catherine M. Sedgwick was one of the more notable women to make the trip.[361]

No profession was so ably and numerously represented as was the press. Almost every metropolitan paper of the East had sent a writer to accompany the excursion. Charles Hudson of the Boston *Atlas* and Thurlow Weed of the Albany *Evening Journal* were seasoned and nationally known editors. Samuel Bowles of the Springfield *Republican* and Charles A. Dana of the New York *Tribune* were at the threshold of long and famous careers. Hiram Fuller of the New York *Mirror*, Epes Sargent of the Boston *Transcript*, Charles Hale of the Boston *Advertiser*, and W. C. Prime of the New York *Journal of Commerce* were other eastern reporters. The West was represented by such editors as William Schouler of the Cincinnati *Gazette* and

The Grand Excursion of 1854

C. Cather Flint from the staff of the Chicago *Tribune*.[362]

Early on the morning of June fifth the excursionists assembled at the Rock Island station in Chicago. Shortly after eight o'clock two trains of nine coaches each, gaily decorated with flowers, flags, and streamers, and drawn by powerful locomotives, left the city. Speeches, military parades, and the discharge of cannon greeted the excursionists on every hand. A free lunch was distributed at Sheffield, Illinois. Notwithstanding frequent stops, the trains reached Rock Island at 4 P. M. There the *Golden Era* (Captain Hiram Bersie commanding), the *G. W. Spar-Hawk* (Captain Montreville Green commanding), the *Lady Franklin* (Captain Le Grand Morehouse commanding), the *Galena* (Captain D. B. Morehouse commanding), and the *War Eagle*, in command of Daniel Smith Harris, lay waiting to take the excursionists aboard.[363]

So large was the number of unexpected or uninvited guests that the five boats were quickly jammed, and it was necessary to charter two additional craft — the *Jenny Lind* and the *Black Hawk*. But accommodations still proved insufficient. According to Dana "state-rooms had been allotted at Chicago, where the names had been registered; but many of the tickets had been lost, and many persons had none at all. Besides there had been some errors — husbands and wives were appointed to different boats, and several young fellows were obliged to part from the fair ladies about whom they had hitherto revolved with the most laudable devotedness." The lack of berths caused fully one-third of the guests to renounce the steamboat trip and return to Chicago. Despite this fact at least twelve hundred remained aboard the boats, where they were served a "sumptuous feast" that was said to equal any afforded by the best hotels in the country.[364]

After listening to brief speeches at Rock Island and Davenport (including two addresses by Fillmore on internal improvements and the Great West), the passengers were entertained with a brilliant display of fireworks from Fort Armstrong. Bells rang and whistles sounded as the boats, decorated with prairie flowers and evergreens, left Davenport at ten o'clock "and sailed with music on their decks, like birds by their own song, lighted by the moon, and saluted by the gay fireworks from the Old Fort." Captain Harris led off with the *War Eagle*; while the *Golden Era*, with the former President aboard, brought up the rear.[365]

Everyone was delighted with the bright moonlight and the refreshing river breeze which greeted the boats as they puffed upstream against the powerful current. Shortly after midnight a violent thunderstorm occurred. According to one passenger : "Impenetrable darkness enshrouded us, and nothing could be seen of our fleet of seven steamers, save the lurid glare of their furnaces shining upon the agitated waves, and their red and blue lights suspended from their bows. A sudden flash of vivid lightning would illumine the entire scene for a moment, and then as suddenly would it be blotted from view. At such moments, so intense was the light, and so vivid the impression produced, that each separate leaf upon the trees on shore, each crevice in the bank, the form of each steamer, and even the countenances of those upon the guards, could be seen as plainly as if printed upon a canvas." After a few hours the storm subsided and the weary travelers were soon lulled to rest.[366]

The night was spent with varying degrees of comfort, for many of the young men were obliged to "rough it" on mattresses on the cabin floors. But none of them was heard to complain; Miss Sedgwick praised them for their good-natured and manly attitude. Another passenger, less optimistic, declared : "Through the whole trip many gentlemen who should by all means have had comfortable places have had no opportunity to sleep, except on mattresses on the cabin floor. As these could never be laid down before midnight, and must be removed before 5 o'clock in the morning, and were never very favorable to repose, their occupants have had but from two to four hours sleep at night, while sleeping by day was even more out of the question." [367]

Dawn found the boats a few miles below Bellevue, whence the *War Eagle* led the fleet booming up Fever River to Galena. A trip to the lead mines was followed by a picnic dinner in the woods. "Wines of Ohio and of France stood upon the board, sparkling Catawba the favorite, and glasses were drained to the health and prosperity of Galena and its citizens." Dana noted with regret "that total abstinence is not the rule of the Mississippi Valley, everybody feeling it to be a sort of duty to temper the limestone water of the country with a little brandy, or other equally ardent corrective." [368]

After leaving Galena the boats proceeded to Dubuque where, despite a heavy downpour, they were met by a throng of people. Fillmore, Silliman, Bancroft, Bates, Hudson, and others addressed the citizens of Dubuque. La Crosse was described by Dana as "a wooding-place on the eastern shore, with two or three frame houses." A dozen excursionists climbed a lofty cliff overlooking the embryonic settlement while the boats were "wooding up". According to Dana "Wide prairies, marked by Indian trails, or dotted with the plowed patches of here and there a chance settler, interrupted by oak forests, or by inland ranges of lower bluffs and knolls, made up the scene, with the river, its shores and islands, for the center of the whole." [369]

Frequent landings were made at the scattered settlements along the river, and wherever the boats stopped to "wood up", the excursionists invariably trooped ashore. "Our light boats", notes Miss Sedgwick, "skimmed the surface of the water like birds; and, with the ease and grace of birds, they dipped down to the shore, and took up their food, their fiery throats devouring it with marvellous rapidity." The process of "wooding up" always attracted the attention of passengers who were not inclined to go ashore and wander about. President Fillmore's daughter (while her steamboat was "wooding up" at Trempealeau) mounted a horse and scaled that "mighty rampart". Her appearance at the summit was greeted with a salvo of steamboat whistles and the prolonged cheers of those aboard.[370]

Amusements aboard the boats were as varied as human ingenuity could devise. Racing was prohibited; but the boats were often lashed together, and passengers enjoyed the opportunity of visiting with old friends and making new ones. Promenading on deck and allowing the ever-changing landscape on shore to "daguerreotype new pictures on the mind" formed the principal pastime for most of the travelers. When the boats were lashed together "dancing in one cabin would draw together the dancers or a *conversazione* in another, the listeners and talkers."

Slavery was probably the chief topic of conversation, for the Kansas-Nebraska bill had just been passed, and abolitionists were deeply aroused by the Boston slave case as a result of which a Negro named Burns had been sent back into slavery. The closing of stores in Boston, the hanging of effigies, the tolling of bells, the festooning of buildings in black, and the floating of the flag with the Union down were events that doubtless made the Boston newspapermen (Hale, Sargent, and Hudson) centers of attraction. The Austrian alliance, reciprocity or annexation with regard to Canada, and the influence of the discovery of gold in California and Australia in maintaining high prices elicited editorial comment in the New York *Tribune* of the day. Rioting of native Americans and Irishmen in Brooklyn, and the wreck of the *Powhatan* with a loss of over three hundred passengers were news items featured in the newspapers. The scientifically inclined probably found special interest in such inventions as a compact and almost frictionless steam engine, Ralston's portable saw-mill, a new patent for making nails, and gas for country use — all of which were on display at the Crystal Palace Exhibition in New York. The distinguished Yale scientist, Professor Silliman, had a large audience one evening; but Dana was "attracted by gayer sounds from another boat" and was unable to report Silliman's speech to the readers of his paper.[371]

When Lake Pepin was reached at eleven o'clock on Wednesday night four boats were lashed together; and they then proceeded upstream shooting brilliant shafts of light that streamed and danced on the waters and shores of the lake. The remainder of the night was spent in "dancing, music, flirtations, *et cetera.*"[372] Then as now there were romantic souls who found their greatest joy on the upper deck with only the moon to disturb a tryst.

A mock trial was held in the cabin of the G. W. *Spar-Hawk* one rainy and disagreeable evening. Schouler of the Cincinnati *Gazette* was tried for assault and battery on the person of Dr. Kennedy. The prisoner pleaded not guilty, and Moses Kimball of Boston was selected to defend him. Prime of the New York *Journal of Commerce* acted as prosecutor. Both Kimball and Prime appeared before the court heavily armed with dueling pistols and bowie knives. The closing speech of Kimball lasted three-quarters of an hour and was listened to with profound attention. Both attorneys attempted to bribe the jury. Happily the evidence showed that the plaintiff had been injured when a berth broke down while both he and the defendant were asleep. The case was promptly dismissed.[373]

The appearance of the fleet when it rounded the bend below St. Paul was described as "grand beyond precedent". The steamboats approached like an armed squadron taking its position in line of battle. "Two full bands of music were on board, both of which struck up lively airs as the boats neared the landing. This, with the rays of the bright June sun which broke forth in all his glory after three days' storm; the animation of the company on board the boats, and the enthusiasm of the assembled hundreds on shore and on the decks of the Admiral, then lying at the landing, produced a scene of excitement which St. Paul has never before witnessed, and perhaps will not again for many years." [374]

Although little more than six years old, St. Paul boasted six thousand inhabitants and made a fine appearance from the decks of the approaching vessels. According to Dana there were "brick dwellings and stone warehouses, a brick capitol with stout, white pillars, a county court-house, a jail, several churches, a market, school-houses, a billiard-room, a ten-pin alley, dry goods' stores, groceries, confectioners and ice-creamers, a numerous array of those establishments to which the Maine law is especially hostile, and a glorious, boundless country behind." [375]

Shortly after the excursionists arrived they were bundled into every conceivable class and variety of vehicle and trundled away at various rates of speed to the Falls of St. Anthony. Three prominent New York editors were seen perched precariously upon a one-horse water cart. The editor of the Galena *Jeffersonian* declared that "The 'March to Finley' was nothing compared to our motley cavalcade. Here was a Governor bestride a sorry Rozinante of which even the Great Don would have been ashamed; here an U. S. Senator, acting the part of footman, stood bolt upright in the baggage boot of a coach, holding on by the iron rail surrounding the top, here the historian of which the country is justly proud, squatted on his haunches on the top of a crazy van, unmindful of everything but himself, his book, his hat and spectacles; there a hot house flower, nursed in some eastern conservatory, so delicate and fragile that a falling leaf might crush it, but a beautiful specimen of the feminine gender, withal, would be seated over the hind axle of a lumber wagon, supported on either side by opera glass exquisites, who only wondered 'why the h — l the people in this country didn't send to New York for better carriages.' " [376]

After viewing the Falls of St. Anthony, the excursionists visited Lake Calhoun, Minnehaha Falls, and Fort Snelling. In the evening a reception was held in the Capitol, where Henry H. Sibley welcomed the visitors. Fillmore thanked the citizens of St. Paul for their cordial reception, and pointed out the significance of the city as a central point on one of the routes leading from the Atlantic to the Pacific. Bancroft responded on behalf of the railroad directors and bade Minnesota become "the North Star of the Union, shining forever in unquenchable luster." At eleven o'clock the tired tourists returned to the landing, where the boats lay illuminated and with steam hissing from their boilers. Shortly after midnight the fleet cast off from St. Paul, whose hills and lighted windows disappeared as the boats rounded Dayton's Bluff.[377]

While speeding downstream at the rate of ten miles an hour, the passengers found time passing all too fast. In addition to the usual dances, lectures, and musical entertainments in the cabins, meetings were called for the purpose of drawing up resolutions of thanks to the railroad directors and steamboat captains. Not only were many toasts drunk to the directors, captains, and boats, but generous contributions were made for the presentation of loving cups and gold plate to the officers. Fillmore presided over a meeting on the *Golden Era* where three hundred dollars were raised to purchase a silver pitcher for Captain Bersie.[378] According to the Chicago *Tribune* the pitcher bore the following inscription : "Presented to HIRAM BERSIE, Master of the Golden Era, by the passengers of that Steamer, on their Excursion to the Falls of St. Anthony, while guests of the Chicago & Rock Island Railroad Company, as a slight testimonial of their respect and their grateful appreciation of his urbanity, vigilance, and professional abilities, June, 1854."

A cup of solid gold, beautifully engraved, was awarded to Henry W. Farnam (then a well-behaved baby in his mother's arms) who many years later became professor of economics in Yale University. John A. Rockwell of Norwich, Connecticut, made the address of presentation, and Professor A. C. Twining responded for the six-months-old infant : "I, Henry W. Farnam, being young in years, and wholly unaccustomed to public speaking, feel incompetent to discharge in suitable terms the duty imposed upon me on this interesting occasion. When I came on board this boat, it was farthest from my expectation to make a speech. 'Man wants but little here below,' and babies still less. All my wants may be confined within this little cup which you propose to give me. Its contents are a baby's world — his universe. Heaven and earth and ocean plundered of their sweets may be compressed within the golden rim of this little measure. Some babies might cry for joy over my good fortune, but I am as unused to crying as to public speaking. I give you my best smile of thanks for your kindness, while I rely upon my interpreter for a further and more mature expression of the grateful emotion of my joyful little heart." [379]

Resolutions gave unstinted praise to the lesser officers and to the crews for their efforts to make the travelers comfortable and happy. Miss Sedgwick was delighted with the courtesy of Captain Morehouse and the "civil lads" aboard the *Lady Franklin* who performed their work as if it was "a dainty task, to be done daintily." Nor did Dana forget Captain Bersie and Clerk Dawley of the *Golden Era*, whose "many civilities and attentions" were gratefully acknowledged in the New York *Tribune*.[380] The other captains probably received similar recognition from the writers who graced the decks of their boats.

The responsibility for providing varied and well-prepared meals fell upon stewards who never before had been called upon to serve such an array of notable guests. Since the floors of the cabins were covered with sleepers, it was the stewards' duty to awaken them gently and diplomatically in order that the mattresses might be removed and the tables set for breakfast by seven o'clock. (No deck hand or roustabout could perform so delicate a task.) Breakfast over, the cooks were given the menu for dinner. Meats and vegetables were prepared in one kitchen, while pastry and desserts were made ready in another. When needed, fish, game, eggs, and vegetables were bought at the various towns along the way. At Trempealeau, two bushels of speckled trout were purchased; the fish proved a rare treat for the excursionists. Supplies of fresh meat (a dozen lambs or pigs) were picked up from time to time.

James F. Babcock of the New Haven *Palladium* described the meals aboard the *Golden Era* : "We have had oysters and lobsters daily, though two thousand miles from the sea. These, of course, were brought in sealed cans. Hens, turkeys, and ducks have given their last squeak every morning. Two cows on the lower deck furnish us with fresh milk twice a day. Beets are cooked, and every variety of stuff, and the dessert consists of all kinds of fruits, nuts, cakes, confection ices, and other things too numerous to mention. Such is our daily fare. Then there are meats for supper, with tea and coffee, with toast, dry and wet, cold bread, warm bread, Indian bread, biscuits, rolls, etc." [381]

The excursionists were never invited to visit the meat

and vegetable kitchen, for the scenes enacted there might well have caused a loss in appetite : they were cordially urged to drop into the pastry and dessert kitchen at any time. The number and variety of puddings, pies, ice creams, custards, and jellies was astonishing. Miss Sedgwick declared : "Morning, noon and night a table was spread, that in most of its appointments and supplies would have done honor to our first class hotels, and its confections would not have disgraced a French artiste with all the appliances and means of a French cuisine. By what magic art such ices, jellies, cakes, and pyramids, veiled in showers of candied sugar, were compounded in that smallest of tophets, a steamer's kitchen, is a mystery yet to be solved." [382]

The notables who made the fashionable tour of 1854 were almost unanimous in their praise of the Upper Mississippi steamboats. Only one adverse (but by no means harsh) criticism was made by an anonymous writer in the New York *Tribune*. He observed : "As the Upper Mississippi must now become a route for fashionable Summer travel, it is only proper to say that those who resort here must not yet expect to find all the conveniences and comforts which abound on our North River steamers. Everything is very plain; the staterooms are imperfectly furnished, but the berths are roomy; the table is abundant, but butter-knives and sugar-tongs are not among its luxuries. But those who know how to overlook these little deficiencies cannot hope anywhere to behold nature in such multiform loveliness and grandeur as on the waters of the Mississippi, between Rock Island and St. Paul, nor in traveling to pass a week or fortnight of more genuine and constant enjoyment." [383]

But sugar tongs or no sugar tongs, the excursion of 1854 was by far the most brilliant event of its kind that the West had ever witnessed. Millard Fillmore declared it to be one for which "history had no parallel, and such as no prince could possibly undertake." Bancroft dwelt at length on the easy and agreeable manner in which more than a thousand people had been conducted a greater distance than from New York to Liverpool. The Chicago *Tribune* described the trip as "the most magnificent excursion, in every respect, which has ever taken place in America." [384]

On June 23, 1854, the New York *Tribune* urged travelers to follow "in the wake of the just completed Railroad Excursion, ascend the Upper Mississippi, the grandest river of the world, flowing for a thousand miles between shores of incomparable beauty — the boundaries of States destined to wealth, population and power almost without rivals in the Union." Miss Sedgwick observed that as a result of the completion of the railroad to the Mississippi, "the fashionable tour will be in the track of our happy 'excursion party, to the Falls of St. Anthony.' The foreign traveller must go there, and the song of the bridegroom, to many a 'Lizzie Lee' will be 'Ho! for the Falls of St. Anthony.' " [385]

In the years that followed, hundreds of excursions were made to this garden spot of the West. Solitary travelers, tired business men and their families, private parties, and various religious, political, and social organizations made pilgrimages to this Mecca of the Upper Mississippi. When the Milwaukee and La Crosse Railroad was completed to the Mississippi in 1858, a similar though less colorful party than that which constituted the excursion of 1854 was conveyed to the Falls aboard the *Northern Belle*, the *War Eagle*, and the *Northern Light*.

During the campaign of 1860 William H. Seward arrived at St. Paul with Charles Francis Adams and his son Charles Francis, Jr. Upon visiting the Falls, Adams complained that the beauty of former years was in danger of being spoiled because the sawmills had drawn off so much water. In the same year the "Governor's Greys", a unit of the Iowa National Guard from Dubuque, generously supplied with fiddles and champagne baskets, made the trip upstream on the *Milwaukee* and downstream on the *Northern Belle*. Four omnibuses and sixteen carriages were required to convey the "Greys" and their ladies to the Falls. Six years later (in 1866) the *Phil Sheridan* and the *Milwaukee* were but two of a score of boats which ran excursions to St. Paul and the Falls of St. Anthony. Probably no other single factor was so important in popularizing the fashionable tour with Easterners as was the grand excursion of the Rock Island Railroad in 1854.[386]

33

Mid Pleasures on Palaces

THE FLOATING palaces that churned the waters of the Upper Mississippi provided a vehicle for fun and frolic. Steamboats had engaged in the excursion trade from the start. Thus the voyage of the *Clermont* from New York to Albany in 1807 was an outing as well as a trial run. In 1811 the *New Orleans* carried excursions out of both Louisville and Cincinnati — Captain Nicholas Roosevelt charging one dollar "per head" for a short run from Cincinnati to Columbia.[387]

Perhaps the earliest excursion on the Upper Mississippi occurred in 1819 when the steamboat *St. Louis* "gratified the citizens of St. Louis with a sail to the mouth of the Missouri". The company on board the boat is said to have been "large and genteel" and the entertainment provided by Captain Hewes was described as "very elegant".[388] Almost every steamboat took one or more parties on a pleasure excursion up or down the river during the course of the season of navigation.

No holiday was more universally observed on the frontier than the Fourth of July. Steamboats played a leading rôle in the celebration of Independence Day. The first known Fourth of July steamboat excursion on the Upper Mississippi took place in 1828. A committee of Galenians issued special invitations to the leading citizens to join an Independence Day excursion on the *Indiana*. On the morning of July Fourth the *Indiana* slipped down the Fever River and steamed proudly up the Mississippi on what was probably the first Independence Day steamboat excursion above Alton. The excursionists disembarked at the mouth of the Catfish Creek in the shadow of Julien Dubuque's grave. These Galena excursionists were the first white settlers known to have observed the Fourth of July on Iowa soil. The American flag was raised opposite the "tepee" of an Indian maiden in the "aristocratic quarter" of the Fox village, which is said to be the first time the Stars and Stripes was floated by private citizens in what is now Iowa.[389]

Fourth of July steamboat excursions were always popular on the Upper Mississippi. In 1839 "Many Citizens" of Galena signified by an advertisement their intention of attending a Fourth of July excursion on the steamboat *Pizarro* from Galena to Cassville. "There will be a splendid band of music on board the boat, and arrangements will be made for dancing; — four sets of cotillions can be accommodated. A superb dinner will be served up, with the best lemonade and liquors. Every attention will be paid, to make the day one of comfort — and to celebrate the glorious day in a style worthy of the Far West." Tickets for the trip cost five dollars.[390]

Steamboat excursions were also sponsored by various civic, political, fraternal, and religious groups. Of these not one was more popular than those held by Sabbath Schools. Frequently Sabbath School excursions were held

Mid Pleasures on Palaces

on the Fourth of July. Captains reaped rich profits and warm praise — and none more than the skipper of the *Uncle Toby* who in 1849 expressed a "willingness" to take the Galena Sabbath Schools to Dubuque free of charge for the Fourth. A local editor observed that such a generous invitation would require more than one boat as both young and old would respond with alacrity.[391]

By 1856 youthful Winona sponsored its first annual Sabbath School outing when it chartered the *Tishomingo* to run a Fourth of July excursion to Minneiska and possibly to Wabasha. Tickets, which included dinner, were two dollars for single gentlemen or three dollars for a lady and a gentleman. After the expenses were paid the surplus (if any) was to be donated to the various Sunday Schools. The excursionists landed to listen to the reading of the Declaration of Independence and an oration. On the return journey the *Tishomingo* climbed a sandbar near Fountain City : the *Golden State* took off her passengers and was then able to pull the "noble" *Tish* off. A Winona editor heard many complaints about the poor food served aboard the *Tishomingo*.[392]

Late in the afternoon of July 4, 1860, some thirty couples of gay young Dubuquers set out for Cassville on the *Peosta* (Captain Tom Levens commanding). A lone Dubuque newspaperman accompanied the merry party. After the heat of the day the evening ride was "heavenly", enriched as it was by the "superb music" of Torbet's String Band. For two hours "fairy feet and lightsome forms moved in harmony with the most magnificent music ever produced from a conjunct of horse hair and cat gut."

The party reached Cassville about ten that evening and marched to the hotel where gay "Cassvillians" were dancing. "All hands took a cotillion, gave three hearty cheers for the citizens of Cassville and returned to the boat." The "stag at eve" found the return trip a "little different", as the full effects of the moonlight began to be felt by the romantic souls aboard the *Peosta*. Wistfully, this lone wolf records:

"Overcome by the delicious music, the crowd paired off, and in every shaded nook of the boat nestled a pair of turtle doves. More disconsolate and unsettled than Old Banquo in his ghostly life were we thereafter. Did we go forward to see where the boat had reached, we ran afoul of some couple about four feet apart, who of course were looking very stiff and unconcerned as if they had not spoken for a month — if we went aft to smoke a segar and watch the long sparkling wake of the boat, we were sure to be *malapropos* by again disturbing some cooing harmony — if we went aloft and went around the smoke stack, we again got our foot in it; if we rounded the wheel-house or ascended the texas we were always equally and severely unfortunate". When the *Peosta* docked at Dubuque at three o'clock in the morning the lone excursionist vowed to go prepared in the future "with a remedy against the frightful loneliness of the return."

The *Fanny Harris* took Dubuquers and the *Northern Light* carried citizens of both Dubuque and Galena on a Fourth of July excursion to Cassville in 1860. Upon arriving at Cassville the Reverend Mr. Mason was informed that a pair of excursionists aboard the *Fanny Harris* "needed his services. He immediately called upon the waiting ones, and was informed that they desired to cement a long existing friendship, by the inseparable process of matrimony. The Squire went ahead, and the couple were speedily reduced to one." A Dubuque editor doubted the wisdom of a man binding himself "with the fetters of matrimony" on a day of "universal freedom" but hoped the "fates" would "avert all harmful results." [393]

Fourth of July excursions continued popular after the Civil War. In 1866 the *Lansing* ran an excursion from Dubuque to Savanna at a charge of only one dollar for the round trip. Steamboats were usually chartered for such occasions. In 1867 the Dubuque chairman of a prospective excursion aboard the *Itasca* was obliged to inform Captain Webb that the party had "played out". It appears that the company asked $400 for the use of the boat and the local committee intended to secure a party of fifty couples at eight dollars per couple. This proved to be too high for most Dubuquers and the contract was cancelled. When the *Andy Johnson* reached Keokuk in May of 1874 she had less than a hundred aboard from Quincy. The "slim turnout" was attributed to the fact that the weather "was more suggestive of warm stoves and heavy wearing apparel than of steamboat excursions". [394]

A somewhat different type of excursion was sponsored in 1841 by W. A. Wentworth and P. M. Pinckard, two enterprising Alton citizens. Learning that four negroes were to be hanged "on the point of *Duncan's Island*, just below St. Louis", Wentworth and Pinckard chartered the steamboat *Eagle*, "repaired and fitted her up for the occasion", and offered for the sum of $1.50 to transport citizens to the scene of the gruesome affair. The obliging gentlemen guaranteed to "drop along side, SO THAT ALL CAN SEE WITHOUT DIFFICULTY" and "reach home the same evening".[395]

But the excursionists aboard the *Eagle* were by no means the earliest to witness the hanging of a criminal on the Upper Mississippi. On June 20, 1834, two steamboats brought passengers from Prairie du Chien and Galena to witness the execution of Patrick O'Connor by the Dubuque lead miners. The steamboats swelled the list of spectators at Dubuque to not "less than one thousand".[396]

Steamboats were also employed in carrying excursionists to fairs and celebrations in nearby river towns. In 1858 Captain R. C. Gray of the steamboat *Denmark* advertised in a Dubuque paper that he would run an excursion to the Missouri State Fair at St. Louis. A few days later the boat left loaded to the guards with freight and crowded with passengers. The *Metropolitan* also advertised an excursion for the same fair. Eleven years later (in 1869) Captain Abe Hutchinson of the *Phil Sheridan* advertised that he would take passengers to the St. Louis Fair at two-thirds the regular rate. "This is an opportunity", an editor remarked, "that no doubt many will improve." [397]

In 1867 steamboats carried excursionists from the various river towns to witness the Independence Day races at the

Mid Pleasures on Palaces

Dubuque Driving Park. The *Davenport* brought a merry throng from Davenport; the *Bill Henderson* carried visitors from Savanna, Sabula, and Bellevue; the *Bannock City* arrived at Dubuque with excursionists from De Witt and Clinton; and the *Milwaukee* steamed in crowded with passengers from above. Steamboats were important factors in giving Dubuque a larger crowd "than on any previous Fourth for years." In 1868 steamboats were busy carrying passengers to and from the State Fair which was held at Clinton that year.[398]

Despite the sobering effect of the Civil War a Dubuque editor declared that steamboat excursions were "great institutions" and that there were not "half enough of them". Ordinarily no expense or effort was spared to make a steamboat attractive for the occasion. In 1861 the *Canada* was chartered to take the Catholic Institute of Dubuque to Prairie du Chien on the Fourth. An editor described the *Canada* as "evergreened and summer-greened until she looked like a small wooded island with an undergrowth of Star Spangled Banners fluttering their little stars and turning their little faces this that and the other way to enjoy the breath of freedom. If the exterior of the *Canada* is pleasant to see, the interior is beautiful, decorated as the cabins are with evergreens and flags, almost lining the whole interior of the boat. A piano will pour forth its music under the hands of some of the fair musicians who will grace the party, and a vocal concert will be one of the afternoon attractions". Dance music was furnished by the Germania Band.

[293]

Steamboating on Upper Mississippi

Some steamboats carried material more exhilarating than flags and evergreens. "The *Adelia*", notes the Dubuque *Herald* of August 6, 1861, "took a large party to Guttenburg last Sunday, there being over 400 persons aboard. They consumed fifty half barrels of Lager, two whiskey barrels of Lemonade and twelve hundred pounds of ice, and wanted as much more. The party was too large for the boat, and all whom we have conversed with that went, say they never want to go again. A few got sunstruck, and when the boat was about to land on her return a couple of men walked overboard." Much more decorous was the excursion of a party of teachers from Dubuque to St. Paul in 1867.

If excursion parties were well-behaved the captain would frequently reward his passengers for leaving the boat intact. In 1868 the captain of the *War Eagle* invited a few couples to remain and participate in "the nicest little impromptu party of the season. Six sets of cotillions took possession of the cabin and danced until two o'clock, to the music of Steward Buckley's band, which has no superior, and few equals, ashore or afloat. Capt. Painter with other officers of the boat moved among the guests and did their best to make the party pleasant." [399]

Politics and politicians were responsible for some steamboat excursions. On August 25, 1858, the "spacious and finely fitted-up" steamboat *Peosta* took a large party of Dubuque citizens on an excursion to Galena to hear Stephen A. Douglas. A fare of one dollar was charged to hear the "little giant" who "personates all the elements of a masterly intellect, and is also the greatest orator of the United States".

In 1860 five hundred delegates from the Chicago Convention that had just nominated Abraham Lincoln came all the way by railroad to Dubuque to enjoy an outing on the Mississippi. All political parties joined in welcoming the distinguished visitors who departed the next day on the steamboats *Fanny Harris* and *Alhambra* for Clinton.[400]

The "Fashionable Tour" to the Falls of St. Anthony formed a unique phase of steamboating and did much to advertise the Upper Mississippi. But the hundreds of excursions which yearly were run from the various river ports afforded captains a richer profit. Socially, as well as economically, steamboats played a significant part in the Upper Mississippi excursion trade.

34

Paths of Empire

THE DRAMATIC migration known as the westward movement is a colorful chapter in American history. It took almost two hundred years to plant the thirteen original colonies along the narrow Atlantic seaboard. It took less than a century to span the two thousand miles of trackless wilderness between the Allegheny Mountains and the Pacific Ocean. Spurred on by hopes, enthusiasms, and ambitions that would not brook denial, the rugged pioneers trekked westward. Grim tragedy stalked them every mile of the way. Some who died of cholera on steamboats were flung into the muddy river or left to rot in shallow graves along the bank. Others sprinkled the desert with their bleached bones — a mute but somber warning to those who followed. Not infrequently the spring thaws disclosed the congealed bodies of pioneers who had been caught the previous winter in some snow-clad mountain pass. Only the strong, the resourceful, and the self-reliant were destined to survive in the conquest of a mighty empire.

Steamboats played a leading rôle in the settlement of the Upper Mississippi Valley — itself a distinct segment in the westward movement. Indeed, the growth in population of the counties adjoining the Mississippi between St. Louis and St. Paul before 1870 presents in miniature the development of the entire Upper Mississippi Valley. Thus, in 1820 the area around St. Louis was well-populated; by 1830 the frontier line had reached Keokuk; by 1840 it included the mineral region around Dubuque and Galena; and by 1850 it had reached the northern boundary of Iowa. During the fifties steamboats shoved the frontier line a short distance beyond St. Paul. By 1870 a fairly dense population extended for many miles inland along both banks of the Father of Waters.[401]

Although steamboating was important other modes of transportation were used. A large percentage of the American pioneers came overland in covered wagons — frequently using the Cumberland Road which extended to Columbus, Ohio, in 1833, and was completed to its western terminus in Illinois by the mid-forties. Those who came in covered wagons, however, were forced to use the ferries stationed at strategic points along the Mississippi. These ferries were so crowded at times that steamboats transported large numbers of covered wagons across the river.[402]

A smaller number of pioneers came by the Ohio and Lower Mississippi steamboats as far as St. Louis, whence they continued northward on Upper Mississippi boats. The completion of the Erie Canal in 1825,[403] the Welland Canal in 1847,[404] and the Illinois-Lake Michigan Canal in 1848[405] provided still another way of reaching the Upper Mississippi before the coming of the railroad.

Somewhat less numerous, but fully as interesting was the migration of foreigners. While most of the American-born pioneers probably came overland, it is equally true that the majority of the foreigners, who came to America and the Upper Mississippi Valley between 1830 and 1870, used the steamboat for all or part of their journey. Foreigners came westward over four highways : two of these, the St. Lawrence River and the Erie Canal, served as important arteries for the Great Lakes. The Pennsylvania Canal fed the Ohio River until the construction of the railroad across the mountains supplanted it. The Mississippi from New Orleans northward to the Falls of St. Anthony afforded a cheap highway for both Europeans and Americans who preferred a route that would not necessitate the constant transfer of trunks, baggage, and household goods. All of these routes to the Upper Mississippi were affected by the construction of the railroad westward to the Mississippi.[406]

Only six thousand miles of railroads had been constructed in the United States by 1848. It was not until 1852 that the Michigan Southern and the Michigan Central gave Chicago through rail service to the Atlantic seaboard. In the meantime, while Chicago was impatiently awaiting the coming of the railroad from the East, a number of railroads were projected westward to the Mississippi. On February 22, 1854, the neigh of the iron horse was first heard on the Father of Waters when the Rock Island was completed to the Mississippi opposite Davenport. This was the first railroad to link the Mississippi with the East, and there was general rejoicing throughout the country.[407]

During the year 1855 the railroad reached the Mississippi at three different points opposite Iowa. On March 17th the road was opened for traffic between Chicago and East Burlington. Ten "superb" passenger cars drawn by the "huge and gallant iron horse" arrived opposite Burlington on May 31st with Lewis Cass, Stephen A. Douglas, and Mayor Boone of Chicago aboard to help celebrate the completion of this second link with the East.[408]

Early in June, 1855, the Illinois Central reached Dunleith opposite Dubuque. By a previous arrangement the Illinois Central had agreed to construct the road from Freeport to Dunleith and use this track with the Galena & Chicago Union Railroad. The latter ran between Freeport and Chicago, providing direct communication between the mineral region and the Great Lakes. The following December the iron horse of the Galena & Chicago Union puffed proudly up to the banks of the Mississippi at Fulton to slake his thirst in the icy waters of the Father of Waters opposite Clinton. In the space of a single year this railroad (now known as the North Western) forged two links between the Mississippi and Chicago.[409]

The mad race of the "robber barons" to monopolize the trade of the country west of the Mississippi did not end in 1855. On January 31, 1856, the Burlington tapped the Mississippi at Quincy;[410] in 1857 Milwaukee and Prairie du Chien were welded together by iron rails;[411] and in 1858 a railroad linked Milwaukee with La Crosse.[412] Thus, by 1860 seven Upper Mississippi ports had been united with the Atlantic seaboard by the railroad. The withering effect of the panic of 1857 prevented the railroad from reaching other points along the Upper Mississippi until later. Meanwhile, only three points below Quincy (St. Louis, Cairo, and Memphis) had been joined to the East by rail. New Orleans had no direct connection with the Atlantic cities, being forced to secure access to the East by means of the lines tapping the Illinois Central at Memphis, Cairo, or Chicago.[413]

Between 1850 and 1870 the westward trek of immigrants was influenced by the unprecedented railroad construction in the Mississippi Valley. But steamboating on the Upper Mississippi continued to flourish, since no competitive north and south system had been constructed. St. Paul did not greet the iron horse until 1867, when it was linked through La Crosse with the Great Lakes.[414] Instead of hindering, the railroads actually augmented steamboating, transporting carloads of immigrants to the various ports along the Mississippi to be carried upstream. After the seventies, however, the railroads linked St. Louis with St. Paul, bracketed the river to gradually cut off southbound commerce, and absorbed the east and west bound traffic with a network of bridges which trussed the river at strategic points.

By 1890 the Diamond Jo Line (the lone survivor of twenty years of cut-throat competition for the freight and passenger trade) was unable to declare a reasonable dividend. But the heyday of steamboating between 1850 and 1870 witnessed a veritable Armada of palatial river craft, carrying their tribute of settlers to the States of the Upper Mississippi Valley.

35

They Crossed the Mississippi

"WESTWARD THE course of empire takes its way", said Bishop Berkeley as Englishmen sailed westward to found new homes and culture in America. But the exodus of Englishmen across the Atlantic pales before the American migrations into the Mississippi Valley a century later. Cold census figures for 1860 show that the main-traveled highway for this mighty army of occupation followed the Ohio River and the Great Lakes. Thus, between 1830 and 1860 the five States of the Old Northwest jumped in population from 1,470,018 to 6,926,884. In fact the gain in population in Ohio, Indiana, Illinois, and Missouri almost equaled the increase in population of the whole United States from the settlement of Jamestown in 1607 to the election of Jefferson in 1800.

The supremacy of the Upper Mississippi Valley is demonstrated by the fact that when the westward-bound pioneers reached the Mississippi at St. Louis they spread out fan-like in every direction : some continued westward; others moved south; but most of the migrants headed northward. By 1860 the 2,028,948 inhabitants of Missouri, Iowa, and Minnesota exceeded by almost four hundred thousand the total population of Arkansas, Texas, New Mexico, California, Oregon, Washington, Nevada, Utah, and Colorado. In 1860 Iowa surpassed Texas in population; while Minnesota could count more settlers than Kansas and Nebraska with Colorado thrown in for good measure.[415]

Visitors from foreign lands were amazed at the migratory tendencies of the Americans. "The American agriculturalists", observed Charles Augustus Murray in 1839, "seem to have little local attachment. A New Englander or Virginian, though proud and vain of his state, will move off to Missouri or Illinois, and leave the home of his childhood without any visible effort or symptom of regret, if by so doing he can make ten dollars where he before made eight. I have seen such repeated instances of this that I cannot help considering it a national feature." [416]

"The Americans are such locomotives themselves", said Captain Frederick Marryat, "that it is useless to attempt the incognito in any part except the west side of the Mississippi, or the Rocky Mountains. Once known at New York, and you are known every where, for in every place you will meet with some one whom you have met walking in Broadway." [417]

The "passion for turning up new soils and clearing the wilderness" appeared to increase with years. Basil Hall observed very little individual regard for "particular spots". "There is a strong love of country", Hall admitted, "but this is quite a different affair, as it seems to be entirely unconnected with any permanent fondness for one spot more than another." [418]

Nor was this tendency to migrate unnoticed by Americans. "What a restless, but enterprising spirit characterizes the American people!" exclaimed an editor of the forties. "They are ever ready to follow to the world's end the bright promises of ambition, or wealth, or charity." [419]

In 1843 James K. Paulding described this migratory tendency of the Americans in the following words : "Our people have more of the locomotive principle than any other not excepting the Israelites and Arabs. Our forefathers wandered here and their posterity have been wandering ever since. But the people of the 'Great West' beat all the rest together. I hardly met a man, or indeed a woman who had not traveled from Dan to Beersheba, and back again, and 'settled', as they are pleased to term it, in half a dozen places, some hundreds, perhaps thousands, of miles distant from each other." [420]

A bird's-eye view of this movement may be obtained from the musty newspaper files of the period. Since Illinois attracted the largest number of settlers one may examine the influx into that State. "The rapid tide of emigration — the rushing flood of population that is constantly pouring in upon our Western borders, has been to us, an oft-told tale", declared the editor of the Chicago *Democrat* in November, 1833. "To it we have never given full faith and credit. We have supposed it but the fruit of an overheated brain, or the offspring of uncontrolled exaggeration." Suddenly the "reality" of the westward movement was impressed upon this "Doubting Thomas". "Chicago, nay the very spot of ground where we are now writing", he wrote, "a few months since was the abode of the savage; and where are now seen a long line of

habitations for white men, a short time ago was unoccupied save by the wigwam of the Indian. The change
has been wrought by magic. More than eight hundred
souls may now be found within the limits that within a
few short months since included less than one tenth of
that number." Seven years later Chicago counted 4479
people within its limits; in 1860 the census revealed
108,206.⁴²¹

The editor of another Illinois newspaper, the Sangamo
Journal, was equally impressed by the rush of emigrants
into Illinois in 1833. "Emigrants are coming by thousands into Illinois, and from all quarters of the Union. —
On Friday last fifteen large wagons, from St. Lawrence
County, N. York, loaded with emigrants, arrived in our
village, and drove up in front of the market house, in
grand style. — These emigrants had been about ten weeks
on the journey, and enjoyed good health during the time.
They design to settle in Sangamo County — to which we
bid them welcome. — A few days previous a company of
emigrants from Vermont for Green County, passed thro'
this place. Our northern counties are daily receiving inhabitants from New York, Ohio, and the Eastern States.
Kentucky is pouring out her population upon us — which
generally passes over to the military tract. Tennessee also
contributes largely to the current of emigration; and even
some of the wandering sons of Illinois, who were driven
off to the Paradise of Arkansaw by a certain cold winter,
are bending their weary steps back to the sucker land. We
calculate that Illinois will increase her number of inhab-

itants the present season by emigration between 20 and 30,000." [422]

A Kentucky paper chronicled the passing of large numbers over the Ohio River into Illinois in 1833. "The number of persons that daily pass thro' this place, on their way to the State of Illinois is immense. Many of these people seem to be much more wealthy and respectable, than those we have observed moving to that State in former years. A company passed, in which were five large well built and heavily laden wagons, and six neat two horse carriages, filled with females. The fertile lands of Illinois must invite men of enterprise and capital; and e'er long we expect that this young State will take a conspicuous rank among her sisters of the Union." A few years later over two hundred wagons passed through Vevay, Indiana, from Kentucky "all full of emigrants, discouraged from continuing among these lawless people."[423]

Emigrant guides and books of travel yield similar pictures. Captain Marryat was amazed at the stream of emigration flowing from North Carolina into Indiana, Illinois, and Missouri during the thirties. "Every hour", he declared, "you meet with a caravan of emigrants from that sterile but healthy state. Every night the banks of the Ohio are lighted up with their fires, where they have bivouacked previously to crossing the river; but they are not like the poor German or Irish settlers; they are well prepared, and have nothing to do, apparently, but to sit down upon their land. These caravans consist of two or three covered waggons, full of women and children, furniture, and other necessaries, each drawn by a team of horses; brood mares, with foals by their sides, following; half a dozen or more cows, flanked on each side by the men with their long rifles on their shoulders; sometimes a boy or two, or a half-grown girl on horseback. Occasionally they wear an appearance of more refinement and cultivation, as well as wealth, the principals travelling in a sort of worn-out old carriage, the remains of the competence of former days." [424]

Not infrequently emigrants came by covered wagon to some port like Buffalo or Pittsburgh and there contracted for passage on a Great Lakes steamer or Ohio River craft. James Hall, editor of the *Illinois Monthly Magazine*, urged emigrants to travel by steamboat, particularly if they contemplated coming west in the spring. "The streams are then swollen. The largest rivers rise from thirty to fifty feet above the low water mark; rocks, snags, sawyers, and sandbars, those formidable obstacles to navigation, are now all buried far below the surface; the steamboat glides without interruption from port to port, ascends even the smallest river, and finds her way to places far distant from the ordinary channels of navigation. Business is now active; the number of boats are increased, to meet the demand for transportation; and the *traveller by water* meets with no delay; while the hapless wight, who bestrides an unlucky nag, is wading through ponds and quagmires, enjoying the delights of log bridges and wooden causeways, and vainly invoking the name of M'Adam, as he plunges deeper and deeper into mire and misfortune." [425]

They Crossed the Mississippi

James Baird observed that a family of five or six could go on the deck of a Great Lakes steamer in a comfortable manner during the summer for twenty dollars. A Maryland household of fifteen reached Wheeling after a three hundred mile journey in their four-horse wagon at a total cost of seventy-five dollars. The master of the only steamboat then in port demanded $250 for transporting the wagon, baggage, and horses, and the seven cabin and eight deck passengers to St. Louis. The head of the family finally secured passage for $160. Instead of a month's journey overland he was able to reach St. Louis in a week.[426]

Edmund Flagg watched with deep interest while the steamboat discharged emigrant families along the banks of the Ohio and Mississippi rivers. A party of emigrants from the State of Vermont were "landed near the mouth of the Wabash, one of whom was a pretty, delicate female, with an infant boy in her arms. They had been *deck-passengers*, and we had seen none of them before; yet their situation could not but excite interest in their welfare. Poor woman! thought I, as our boat left them gazing anxiously after us from the inhospitable bank, little do you dream of the trials and privations to which your destiny conducts, and the hours of bitter retrospection which are to come over your spirit like a blight, as, from these cheerless solitudes, you cast back many a lingering thought to your dear, distant home in New England; whose very mountain-crags and fierce storms of winter, harsh and unwelcome though they might seem to the stranger, were yet pleasant to you."

[307]

Steamboating on Upper Mississippi

A little farther on this compassionate pilgrim watched the boat discharge another group at a "desolate-looking spot" upon the Missouri shore. Flagg noted "men, women, and little ones, with slaves, household stuff, pots, kettles, dogs, implements of husbandry, and all the paraphernalia of the backwood's farm heaped up promiscuously in a heterogeneous mass among the undergrowth beneath the lofty trees." [427] Prior to 1850 an emigrant who was not blessed with considerable funds was more likely to jolt his family westward over the rough roads of the interior than to take passage by boat.

The overland trek of the covered wagon continued throughout the forties and fifties. "Hundreds of muslin-covered wagons, bearing wives and children, and household goods, and driven by stalwart men, seeking a new home in the mighty West, cross the Mississippi at this point weekly", declared the editor of the *Rock Islander* in 1855. "It is a tide which knows no ebb, but still keeps flowing, ever flowing, onward toward the rich prairies of Nebraska and the setting sun." [428]

The fording of streams and creeks was of almost daily occurrence : ferry operators were kept busy from dawn to dusk. During a single month in 1854 fully 1743 wagons passed a point beyond Peoria, Illinois, all bound for Iowa. [429] The following year a westward bound immigrant watched forty-nine wagons from Michigan, "bound for Iowa", cross an Illinois stream. This man, who had passed "oceans of wagons", declared that it was a "common occurrence to see twenty or thirty of these form an encampment at night". An Illinois editor viewed with no little alarm the departure of twenty-five wagons from a "single town in Northern Illinois" destined for the Iowa country across the Mississippi.[430]

Throughout the fifties the ferries were busy day and night transporting the emigrants across the Mississippi. St. Louis and Hannibal in Missouri, Alton and Quincy in Illinois, Keokuk, Fort Madison, Burlington, Davenport, Dubuque, and McGregor in Iowa, and La Crosse, Winona, and St. Paul farther upstream were favorite crossings. The ferry formed an important segment in facilitating the movement of pioneers westward. A few samples of their activity may be given.

A ferry had served the needs of Burlington since the opening of the Black Hawk Purchase in 1833. During the first two weeks of October, 1846, a total of 582 wagons were ferried across the Mississippi River at this place.[431] During the year 1854 the steam ferry at this point was kept "constantly in motion from morning till night and frequently till midnight". According to an eyewitness the Illinois bank was covered every evening with the "tents, wagons and cattle" of emigrants waiting to be ferried across to Iowa.[432]

During 1855 the Burlington *Telegraph* chronicled the passage of immigrant teams through that city at the rate of six or seven hundred a day. "We have these facts from the ferry folks", the editor declared, "who keep a sort of running register. About one team in a hundred is labelled 'Nebraska'; all the rest are marked 'Iowa'." [433]

[309]

Steamboating on Upper Mississippi

Late in the fall of 1855 a Muscatine editor designated Iowa as the "Canaan for the children of the eastern and middle states." Scores of covered wagons were noted lining the Illinois bank of the Mississippi awaiting the ferry as it puffed "to and fro, carrying westward at every trip five wagons" all bound for the Hawkeye State.[434]

Perhaps no point exceeded Davenport in ferry activity. "Our ferry is busy all hours in passing over the large canvas-backed wagons, densely populated with becoming Iowaians", observed the Davenport *Commercial* in 1854. "An army of mechanics have added 300 buildings to this city during the past season, yet every nook and corner of them are engaged before they are finished; but our hospitable citizens will not allow any to suffer for want of shelter. In several instances the citizens have, like true aborigines, withdrawn to close quarters, and given their parlors to those who have come to make their homes among us and were unable to find dwellings. There is not a vacant dwelling or business room in the city." [435]

The following year the Davenport levee presented an "unusually stirring appearance" to an eyewitness on the opposite shore. "We counted no less than twenty-five white-tented wagons ranged round near the ferry, while some twenty farm wagons stood here and there among a small sea of reposing cattle. All the way up Brady street was a row of these wheeled tents while some half dozen were visible on the steamer Davenport, just then crossing the river. And all these, so far as we could learn, were bound for Iowa." [436]

They Crossed the Mississippi

To the north, the westward rush of land seekers caused the Dubuque *Tribune* to exclaim : "Daily — yes, hourly — immigrants are arriving in this and neighboring counties from Ohio, Kentucky, Indiana, and Illinois. All are in raptures at the lovely sights which here greet their gaze; and they with one accord yield the palm to Western Iowa for lovely prairies, beautiful groves of timber, and meandering streams of water." Such items when printed in papers back East, although sometimes rather exaggerated, must have served as bait for those who were wondering whether they should follow Horace Greeley's advice and "Go West!" [437]

Of the rush of settlers into northern Iowa an account in the Dubuque *Reporter* reads : "Never before, in the history of this northwestern region of the United States, has there been a more gratifying spectacle than that now presented to those who take an interest in its progress and welfare. Viewing the almost countless throng of immigrants that crowd our streets, and learning that a similar scene is visible at every other point along the Mississippi border of Iowa, the spectator is naturally led to infer that a general exodus is taking place in the Eastern States of the Union, as well as in those that, but a few years ago, were denominated the West.

"Day by day the endless procession moves on — a mighty army of invasion, which, were its objects other than peace, and a holy, fraternal, cordial league with its predecessors, their joint aim to conquer this fair and alluring domain from the wild dominion of nature would strike terror into the boldest hearts. They come by hundreds and thousands from the hills and valleys of New England, bringing with them that same untiring, indomitable energy and perseverance, that have made their native States the admiration of the world, and whose influence is felt wherever enterprise has a votary or commerce spreads a sail; with intellects sharpened to the keenest edge, and brawny arms to execute the firm resolves of their iron will, and gathering fresh accessions, as they sweep across the intermediate country, from the no less thrifty and hardy population of New York, Ohio, and Indiana. Tarrying no longer amongst us than is necessary for them to select their future home, away they hie to the capacious and inviting plains, that spread themselves interminably, ready to yield, almost without preparation, their rich latent treasures.

"Soon will be seen innumerable the farmer's comfortable abode, and the frequent thriving village, with its 'people's college,' as its highest worldly pride, and close at hand the house of God, with spire pointing to heaven, as if to remind the worshippers of the source to which they are indebted for all the store of blessings they enjoy. And soon, too, in the wake of such a mighty rush and all its soul-swelling consequences, will follow the laying out and construction of those great works that will link us to the wide-spread members of our confederacy, over which the iron horse, more terrible in the fierceness of his strength than the war-steed of Job, will snort his triumphant ha, ha! as he bounds along in his tireless race. Science, in turn, will rear her loftiest fanes, and plant deep in the hearts of her disciples the seeds of a deathless devotion to the institutions of our common country." [438]

The same bustle and activity was noted in the interior counties of Iowa. Oskaloosa was overwhelmed with the influx of emigrants. "Our town is almost constantly thronged with mover's wagons and herds of cattle", exclaimed a resident in 1851.[439] Three years later the Oskaloosa *Times* noted the passing of covered wagons from "early morning till night-fall", and estimated at least a thousand persons passing through Oskaloosa every week.[440] The Galena *Advertiser* expressed surprise at the rapidity with which northern Iowa was increasing in population. "Allamakee and Winneshiek counties", it prophesied, "are destined to become among the most wealthy in the State." [441]

Some of these settlers had banded together in emigrant companies, hoping by lumping their resources to eliminate some of the hardships to be encountered on the frontier. Such a company was formed in Transboro, New Jersey, for the purpose of raising funds to enable fifty families to proceed to Iowa. Each family was required to pay three hundred dollars into the general treasury. Of the fifteen thousand dollars thus raised, the sum of twelve hundred and fifty dollars was allowed for transportation to Iowa. The company intended to purchase five thousand acres of government land and work it in common the first year, or until houses were built to accommodate all. Then each family was to receive one hundred acres.[442]

Steamboating on Upper Mississippi

In 1856 an advance agent for the Stafford Western Emigration Company of Massachusetts arrived at Muscatine to seek the "best points" for his company — an organization composed of 850 persons "equipped with sawmills, carpenter tools and farming implements of all kinds, fully prepared to establish themselves and build up a town in a few weeks." These emigrants were indeed well organized, "having a constitution and rules of business for carrying on all branches peculiar to the West. We can readily imagine", commented the Muscatine *Journal* of May 23, 1856, "the purchase of a large tract of land and the immediate erection of dwelling houses and a village of 850 inhabitants springing into existence as by magic."

Thoughtful observers were not slow to grasp the significance of this westward trend of population into the Upper Mississippi Valley. Perhaps Henry Clay would have felt genuine concern for his great Compromise of 1850 had he discussed the westward movement with a certain Iowa editor. After pointing out that the movement to the Hawkeye State was not made up of foreigners but of "the steady, well educated and industrious farmers of New York, Ohio, Pennsylvania and other northern states", the Muscatine *Democratic Enquirer* concluded:

"From the beginning of the century, the middle and the northern states have perverted the legislation to selfish ends. It will not be long, thank providence, ere the Valley of the Mississippi — the garden spot of the world — will wield a controlling influence in national affairs. Connected as the states are by fine navigable streams and social

and political ties, and extending through several degrees
of latitude, they will when the day of their predominance
comes, put an end to that system of local and partial
legislation which has done more to weaken the bond of
union and obliterate the reverence of the people for the
constitution, than all other causes combined." [443]

The exodus of native sons and daughters from the seaboard States into the Upper Mississippi Valley had a
salutary effect on steamboating. In the first place, a goodly number of emigrants used the steamboat for all or a
part of the way to their new homes. Secondly, steamboats
as well as ferries profited by transporting the covered
wagon pioneers across the Mississippi. Thirdly, many
American pioneers used the steamboat to "spy" out the
land before bringing their families and household possessions westward by covered wagon. Still others followed in
the van of the covered wagon to join those who had gone
before, and so the growth in population led to an ever
increasing passenger service for steamboats. Finally, the
sturdy American pioneer, together with the immigrants
from foreign lands, soon provided the heavy shipments of
golden grain which distinguished the last period of steamboating on the Upper Mississippi.

36

On the Trail of the Immigrants

"WHAT IS THE best Landing Port for the West?" queried a prospective immigrant of John Regan who had emigrated to northern Illinois from Ayrshire in 1842. "New Orleans", replied Regan, "if you wish the most direct route. But if not encumbered with much luggage or a family, by landing at New York, thence sailing up the Hudson, taking the Grand Western Canal through the state of New York, and then steaming it on the great lakes to Chicago, Milwaukie, or Detroit, you may no doubt get a better idea of the greatness and richness of the country. There is also another way by Montreal, up Lake Ontario, and through the Welland canal into Lake Erie, which is said to be as cheap as by New York. Another way still, is by Philadelphia, over the Alleghany Mountains to Pittsburg on the Ohio river. Still, New Orleans is by far the most direct and the cheapest route for the States of Iowa, Illinois, Indiana, Ohio, and Minnesota." [444]

The hordes of foreign immigrants that journeyed along the four routes described by John Regan provided Upper Mississippi steamboats with a colorful as well as a profitable cargo, although they were somewhat less numerous than native Americans. Since the passenger traffic was the dominant feature of steamboating between 1850 and 1870 the foreigner played a conspicuous rôle during these decades.

On the Trail of the Immigrants

The census of 1860 revealed 1,673,694 of the 4,136,175 foreign-born in the United States residing in the six Middle Atlantic States. Seven-eighths of these were in New York and Pennsylvania, where lay the great ports of New York and Philadelphia through which most of the foreigners passed. The port of Boston exerted the same influence on the population of the Bay State. Massachusetts attracted 260,114 of the 469,338 foreigners who had settled in the New England States. Thus, the twelve North Atlantic States retained fully one-half of the foreign immigrants. These usually were of the poorer class who arrived penniless and promptly availed themselves of the many jobs open to artisans, unskilled laborers, and servants. Later they might have saved enough to continue their migrations westward and purchase a tract of government land for one dollar and twenty-five cents an acre.[445]

The remainder of the immigrants moved westward: serving as laborers in canal and railroad construction; finding employment in the rapidly sprouting cities of the West; or squatting on the rich lands of the interior. During the late thirties Captain Frederick Marryat noted the small wooden shacks of newly arrived Irish workmen on the Erie Canal. A family dwelt in one of these "dog-kennels" that measured fourteen feet by ten. According to Marryat there was but "one bed, on which slept the man, his wife, and family." Above the bed were some planks where seven laborers slept "without any mattress, or even straw, to lie upon . . . I looked for the pig, and there he was, sure enough, under the bed."

[317]

Steamboating on Upper Mississippi

At Pittsburgh during the thirties Charles Augustus Murray was ever aware of the "proudly eminent" voice of the Irish whether raised in "fun, bargain, or wrath!" Murray also saw many "broad-faced and broad-sterned, fair-haired butchers" whose nationality he could easily guess without looking at the boards over their stalls bearing such names as Schmidt, Reinhardt, and Hermann.[446]

Immigrants came from England, Scotland, and Wales; from France and Switzerland; from Norway, Sweden, Denmark, and Holland; and from two score countries besides. But the Irish and Germans predominated. In 1860 Pittsburgh contained 30,000 Americans, 9297 Irish, 6049 Germans, and a scattering of others. The population of Cincinnati was almost equally divided between native and foreign-born, the Germans outnumbering the Irish more than two to one. St. Louis contained 61,390 Americans and 96,086 foreigners — 50,510 of the latter being German. In both Chicago and Milwaukee the foreign-born exceeded the native-born, with Germans predominating. Well might Captain Marryat remark that cities in the United States grew up to more importance in ten years than they did in Europe in a century.[447]

The westward flow of foreign immigrants is attested by the 1,197,100 found in the five States of the Old Northwest in 1860. "Do not the Alleghany Mountains and Niagara stand as giant watchers at its entrance, to open the portals of that new garden of Paradise, the latest home of the human race?" queried Fredrika Bremer in 1853. "The people of Europe pour in through the cities of the eastern coast. Those are the portals of the outer court; but the West is the garden where the rivers carry along with them gold, and where stands the tree of Life and of Death." [448]

The census of 1860 showed Missouri, Iowa, and Minnesota with 325,350 foreign-born within their borders. Minnesota attracted twice as many foreigners as the four South Atlantic States; Iowa's accretions almost equaled those of Virginia, Kentucky, and Tennessee combined; Missouri gained more than the total of Alabama, Mississippi, Louisiana, Texas, and Arkansas. The popularity of these eight States of the Upper Mississippi Valley is clearly demonstrated by the heavy influx of immigrants. [449]

The St. Lawrence was the most northerly migration trail to the Mississippi. From Quebec an emigrant might reach Montreal in fourteen hours at a cost of five shillings. An additional ten shillings carried him to Kingston. Passage over Lake Ontario in a regular mail line steamer to Toronto or Hamilton could be procured for around twenty-two shillings. Emigrants were warned to drink "sparingly" of the waters of the St. Lawrence, since they had a "strong tendency to produce bowel complaints in strangers." [450]

The crest of the immigrant wave swept up the St. Lawrence during the year 1847 when 74,408 arrivals were chronicled at the ports of Quebec and Montreal. It was estimated that fully one-fourth of those who adopted this route died of ship fever while crossing the ocean or in passing up the St. Lawrence. *Niles' Register* had this account of the tragic events in 1847 : "The poor creatures die as they pass up the river St. Lawrence; even such as appear healthy when they leave Quebec, often expire on their passage. Montreal, Kingston, Toronto, the various towns on the Bay of Quinte, and other towns with which there is regular communication, are filled with the sick and dying." On August 22, 1847, there were 2048 patients on Grosse Island alone. During the preceding week 288 had died and the number of deaths in the hospital and tents since the opening of the season totaled 2126.[451]

Many would-be settlers, however, traveled this route to reach the western States. At Buffalo they helped swell the endless stream flowing westward through the Erie Canal. "Day after day the train on the Buffalo and Niagara Falls Railroad has come in, stretched to the length of a monstrous serpent, and filled so full of German emigrants, that it seems like cruelty to compel a single engine to drag such enormous loads in such excessively hot weather. We learn that they choose the route, via Montreal, to evade the somewhat onerous requirements of the port laws and regulations at New York. From Montreal, they come up through Lake Ontario to Lewiston, thence to the city by the railroad. When they arrive here, they encamp any where on the street side, where they can find empty buildings, which they occupy during a few days detention; but their stay is generally short, as they seem to have made up their minds whither they were going before they left home." [452]

[320]

St. Louis & Keokuk Packet Company was organized in 1842. Its first steamboat, the 211-ton *Die Vernon*, plied between St. Louis and Keokuk for eight years before burning at St. Louis. The *Jeannie Deans* was one of several boats named for characters from Sir Walter Scott books. Built in 1852, she burned at St. Louis May 12, 1866.

LUCY BERTRAM

Two *Lucy Bertram* steamboats were owned by the Keokuk Packet Company. The first was a 268-ton sidewheeler launched at St. Louis in 1847. The second *Lucy Bertram* (shown above) was a 698-ton steamboat built in 1863. On April 18, 1864, she carried over one hundred recuperated Union soldiers from Keokuk to rejoin their regiments. A month later she took the 45th Iowa Regiment downstream. Disappeared in 1878.

ROB ROY

The *Rob Roy* was an 866-ton steamboat built at Madison, Indiana, in 1866. She served in the Keokuk trade for fourteen years, during which period she was snagged and sunk twice but was raised both times. She was dismantled at the close of 1880.

DIE VERNON (second)

The second *Die Vernon* was a sleek 445-ton boat that was built at St. Louis in 1850. Her excursions to the Falls of St. Anthony were widely heralded and added luster to Keokuk Packet Company fame. She was abandoned in 1858. (See Chapter 31)

ANDY JOHNSON

An 884-ton sidewheeler built in 1866 for the Keokuk Packet Company. She was sold to the St. Louis and New Orleans Packet Company in 1870. The *Andy Johnson* was "cut down" by ice at the St. Louis wharf on December 14, 1876, along with the *Jennie Baldwin, Bayard, Rock Island,* and *Davenport.*

BURNING OF STEAMBOATS AT ST. LOUIS

The *New Lucy,* the *New England,* and the *Brunette* caught fire at the Keokuk Daily Packet Landing at the St. Louis levee on January 18, 1853. The *New Lucy,* a 416-ton sidewheeler, went up in smoke six weeks after going into service. The *New England* was a Keokuk Packet boat while the *Brunette* made occasional trips to the Upper Mississippi.

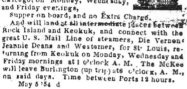
NEWSPAPER ADVERTISEMENTS — ADVERTISING CARDS

A key to the activity of steamboats and steamboat companies may be gleaned from two sources, viz: the advertisements carried in newspapers by individual boats and companies, and special advertising cards like the one listing the boats of the Keokuk Northern Line in the year 1874. The newspaper advertisements generally appeared in approximately the same columns of the press throughout the season of navigation. Sometimes they appeared as individual boats with twenty or more in a column. As the corporations grew they listed their boats, captains, and time of arrival and departure.

The company advertising cards had a more limited circulation but served their purpose well. In addition, the public was furnished with more detailed folders of steamboats, schedules, and passenger and freight tariffs charged.

TOM JASPER

The mighty Mississippi has been praised in song and story. The author has almost two hundred items of sheet music dealing with the Father of Waters, the cities and towns that line its banks, and the steamboats that plied its winding course. The above honors the *Tom Jasper,* a famous steamboat that was built at Madison, Indiana, in 1867. The *Tom Jasper,* named for a Quincy banker, was designed originally for the Quincy trade and opposed the Keokuk Packet boats. With the close of this competition, the *Tom Jasper* ran in the Keokuk and Upper Mississippi trade. The *Tom Jasper* gradually came under the control of the three major steamboat companies — the Keokuk Packet, the Northern Line, and finally the North Western Union Packet Company — in the year 1873. In 1875, Commodore Davidson dismantled her at St. Louis, converting her into the 1,112-ton *Centennial.*

GALENA AND MINNESOTA PACKET

Galena was the commercial entrepot of the Upper Mississippi throughout the Lead Period—1838-1848. The *General Brooke,* a regular in the Minnesota trade, appears in the picture. Fully thirty different steamboats were docking at Galena by 1845.

Four steamboats—the *Saint Paul,* the *West Newton,* the *Minnesota,* and the *Ben Campbell*—sets this Galena painting around 1852 or 1853. These steamboats, and two score other craft, were regular visitors to Dubuque and Galena.

At least five steamboats, with the *War Eagle* and the *City Belle* in the foreground, lie at the Galena levee. The two railroad trains (Illinois Central and the Galena & Chicago Union) together with the boats named, would indicate this picture was drawn between 1854-1857. At least eighty different boats were docking at Dubuque by 1856.

GREY EAGLE

Captain Daniel Smith Harris's sleek race horse—the *Grey Eagle*—lies at the Galena levee prepared to take on freight and passengers for Dubuque, La Crosse, and points north. The *Grey Eagle* was a 382-ton craft built at Cincinnati in 1857. (See Chapter 42)

DANIEL SMITH HARRIS

Arrived at the Galena lead mines in 1823 aboard the keelboat *Colonel Bomford.* He began his steamboat career in 1829 as a cub pilot on the *Galena.* During the next thirty years he owned and captained a score of steamboats. He ascended hitherto unnavigated streams, broke through ice-locked Lake Pepin on seven occasions to lead his rivals into St. Paul, and won many steamboat races against fast boats and experienced competitors. His career ended with the wreck of the *Grey Eagle* on the Rock Island Bridge in 1861.

ITASCA

The *Itasca* lies at a Minnesota levee discharging and taking on freight and passengers. In 1858 the *Grey Eagle* beat the *Itasca* in a race to St. Paul, thus winning the honor of delivering a copy of Queen Victoria's message to President Buchanan congratulating him on the successful laying of the Atlantic cable. (See Chapter 43)

Duplicate

Application for Inspection

No.

Galena April 11 1859

State of Illinois District of Galena

J. R. Prindervle & Tho. C. James

Local Inspectors of the Port of Galena

The Undersigned,

applied to have Steamer Grey Eagle
on the 15th Inst
INSPECTED under the provisions of Law of Congress relating
to Steamboats, approved August 30, 1852.

D. S. Harris. Master or Owner.

APPLICATION FOR STEAMBOAT INSPECTION

In 1859 the *Grey Eagle* and the *Henry Clay* collided causing considerable damage to both boats. After such an accident the law required that the captain must bring his boat in for inspection. The above is the form of application filled out by Captain Harris requesting inspection by the local inspector at Galena following the collision with the *Henry Clay*. The *Henry Clay* was destined to play a dramatic role in the siege of Vicksburg when she was chosen by Commodore Porter as one of eleven boats to attempt to run the batteries. The pilot of the *Henry Clay* had her pilothouse cut away, saying he preferred being hit by bullets rather than splinters of wood or glass.

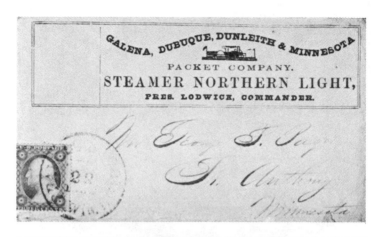

HISTORIC STEAMBOAT COVERS

Two outstanding Upper Mississippi steamboat covers from the *Risvold Collection*. Of the *Grey Eagle* cover Floyd E. Risvold declares: "It is considered by many to be the finest Minnesota Territorial cover known. Steamboat covers from the Upper River are real gems of Philatelic Americana and they are rare." While the dates do not appear on the postage cancellation, corporate titles on the paddle box plus the years of service (*Grey Eagle*—1857-1861) and (*Northern Light*—1857-1866) afford a partial clue to the year of mailing which was probably around 1857-1858.

THE NORTHERN LINE: THE *BURLINGTON*

The Northern Line was formed by steamboatmen who banded together in 1858 to run their boats on schedule between St. Louis and St. Paul. Many of their steamboats were named for river towns. The *Burlington* was a 359-ton sidewheeler built at Cincinnati in 1864 for the Northern Line. In 1866 she made nineteen round trips between St. Louis and St. Paul and cleared $70,000, or twice her original cost in one season.

DAVENPORT

The *Davenport* was a 340-ton sidewheeler built at Pittsburgh in 1863 for Captain Richard C. Gray of the Northern Line. She was one of six boats sunk in the heavy ice jam in the St. Louis harbor on December 14, 1876. Her value at the time—$3,000.

MUSCATINE

Another sidewheel packet built at Pittsburgh in 1863 for the Northern Line by Captain Gray. The *Muscatine,* a 298-ton craft, was a highly successful boat, netting $77,000 in the St. Louis and St. Paul trade in 1865. The *Davenport* netted $70,000 the same season. The *Muscatine* sold for $220 in 1881.

KEOKUK

The *Keokuk* (third) was a 300-ton craft built at Brownsville, Pennsylvania, in 1858. She was a fast boat that could challenge the best of the race horses that churned the waters of the Upper Mississippi. She was dismantled in La Crosse in 1879.

CLINTON

The *Clinton* was a 902-ton steamboat that was built for the Keokuk Northern Line at St. Louis in 1872 from the dismantled *Sucker State*. On April 19, 1876, she collided with the Hannibal bridge. She burned in Alton Slough about 1880 in Winter Quarters.

DUBUQUE

The *Dubuque,* third of that name, was a 602-ton sidewheeler built by Captain Gray for the Northern Line in 1867. Scene of a bloody race riot on July 29, 1869, above Davenport, the *Dubuque* was burned while in Winter Quarters in Alton Slough in 1876.

HENRY CLAY

The *Henry Clay* was a 400-ton sidewheeler that was built at McKeesport, Pennsylvania, in 1857. She was selected by Commodore Porter to be one of eight gunboats and three transports to run the Vicksburg batteries. She sunk a few miles below the city.

SUCKER STATE

The *Sucker State* was a 523-ton sidewheeler built at Pittsburgh for the Northern Line in 1860. She had the exact measurements of the *Hawkeye State* and was just as fast. The two race horses made the run from St. Louis to St. Paul in less than three days.

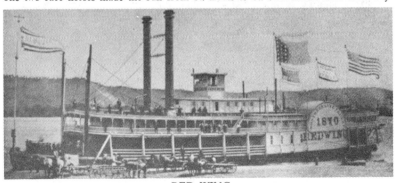

RED WING

The *Red Wing* (third) was a 670-ton sidewheeler built at Pittsburgh in 1870 for the Northern Line. She ran eleven seasons as a Keokuk Northern boat. Dismantled in 1880.

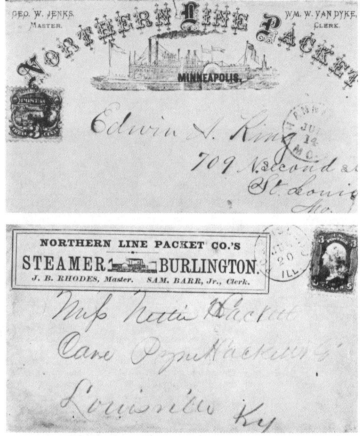

The above covers of two Northern Line Packets—the *Minneapolis* (1869-1883) and the *Burlington* (1864-1867)—are from the *Risvold Collection*. The inclusion of the names of the captain and the clerk are interesting but unfortunately, since the year does not appear, the exact date is not readily pinned down. At times, captains were shifted from one boat to another, but sometimes they remained on the same boat for several seasons. The *Minneapolis* was a 649-ton steamboat that was wrecked in the ice gorge of January 30, 1884, at the St. Louis levee. The handsome boat originally cost $50,000 but after fifteen years of service she was valued at only $15,000 when lost.

This Picture Of JOSEPH REYNOLDS

JOSEPH REYNOLDS (1819-1891)

Founder and sole owner of the Diamond Jo Line Steamers, Joseph Reynolds was a man of tremendous energy and business talent who, while engaged in other activities from gold mines to railroads, operated one of the most famous steamboat lines on the Upper Mississippi. The names of such steamboats as the *Lansing*, the *Diamond Jo*, the *John C. Gault*, the *Ida Fulton*, the *Bannock City*, the *Arkansas*, the *Tidal Wave*, the *Imperial*, the *Jeannette Roberts*, the *Josephine*, the *Mary Morton*, and the *Libbie Conger*, to mention the earlier ones, were household names familiar to young and old alike. The Diamond Jo Line continued to the year 1911 when the four remaining steamboats—the *Sidney*, the *Quincy*, the *St. Paul*, and the *Dubuque*—were sold to the Streckfus Line. Reynolds himself died at his Arizona gold mine in 1891.

LANSING
The *Lansing* was the first steamboat owned by Joseph Reynolds. She was an 83-ton stern-wheeler built near Prairie du Chien in 1862. The *Lansing* exploded a boiler while endeavoring to back away at Hampton, Illinois, on May 13, 1867. Six persons were killed, including the pilot. She was rebuilt at Dubuque into a 123-ton ferry that operated out of Clinton, Iowa, until 1874 when she was sold south.

DIAMOND JO WAREHOUSE AT GUTTENBERG
This well-built structure, with two other warehouses, is still standing in Guttenberg.

CABIN OF THE QUINCY

Although few of the Upper Mississippi steamboats could compare in furnishings and equipment with the "floating palaces" of the Lower Mississippi, the 806-ton *Quincy* would rank with some of the better boats. This handsome craft was formerly the *Gem City*, a boat which in turn had the engine of the *Alex Mitchell*. It is said the cabin of the *Gem City* was placed on the *St. Paul*.

DIAMOND JO

The *Diamond Jo* was a 193-ton steamboat built at Prairie du Chien in 1864. The four barges she has in tow are typical of those used in the grain trade that characterized steamboating following the Civil War. The large barges stand in sharp contrast to the small keelboats used during the Lead Period to transport pigs of lead downstream.

"Diamond Jo" Line Steamers

RUNNING ON THE UPPER MISSISSIPPI RIVER
——BETWEEN——

BURLINGTON AND ST. PAUL.

THROUGH FREIGHT ROUTE between the EAST and the NORTHWEST

BY JOINT ARRANGEMENT WITH

CHICAGO & NORTH-WESTERN R'Y from CHICAGO via FULTON,
GREEN BAY & MINNESOTA R. R. from GREEN BAY via EASTMOOR,

——ALSO BY JOINT ARRANGEMENT WITH——

ROCKFORD, ROCK ISLAND and ST. LOUIS RAIL ROAD

—BETWEEN—

ST. LOUIS and the NORTHWEST via ROCK ISLAND.

Also connecting with diverging Rail Roads at all the following points:

BURLINGTON,	SABULA,	EASTMOOR,
MUSCATINE,	SAVANNA,	WINONA,
ROCK ISLAND,	DUBUQUE,	READS LANDING,
DAVENPORT,	DUNLEITH,	LAKE CITY,
MOLINE,	McGREGOR,	RED WING,
PORT BYRON,	PRA. DU CHIEN,	HASTINGS,
CLINTON,	LANSING,	ST. PAUL,
FULTON,	GRAND CROSSING,	HUDSON,
LYONS,	LA CROSSE,	STILLWATER.

TO ALL POINTS

EAST, WEST, NORTH & SOUTH.

THROUGH CONTRACTS made and THROUGH BILLS LADING given from NEW YORK, BOSTON, BALTIMORE, PHILADELPHIA, PITTSBURGH, WHEEL-ING, CINCINNATI, LOUISVILLE, and all important points, to all River Land-ings, Burlington and above, and to all important interior points.

☞ RATES ALWAYS LOWER than All Rail Lines. ☞ NO TRANSFER CHARGES will be made from Eastern Roads or Lake Boats at Chicago or Green Bay on freights consigned to us.

☞ To prevent diversion and to insure speedy transportation and low rates it is *important* that all *packages* should be MARKED and all *shipments* CONSIGNED and Way-Billed as follows :

From CHICAGO, -	"Care ◆Jo◆	Line, Fulton."
From EAST via CHICAGO, "	"	" Chicago."
From GREEN BAY, - "	"	" Eastmoor."
From EAST via GREEN BAY, "	"	" Green Bay."
From MILWAUKEE, - "	"	" Fulton."
From EAST via MILWAUKEE, "	"	" Milwaukee."
From ST. LOUIS, "	"	" Rock Island."

STENCILS for marking furnished FREE on application to either of offices named on other side.

The above information was contained on the back of the stationery pro-vided passengers aboard its steamboats. The Diamond Jo Line was very successful in acquainting shippers and friends with its name and connection.

DIAMOND JO LINE STEAMERS

LANDINGS,
DISTANCES, ELEVATIONS,
POPULATIONS, ETC.

NAMES OF CITIES AND TOWNS ON ROUTE. (For names of landings, see opposite page.)	Miles Between Landings.	Miles from St. Louis.	Miles from Mouth of Mississippi.	Feet above Sea Level at Low Water, 1864.	Population, 1900
St. Louis, Mo........			1253	390	575,238
Alton, Ill..........	23	23	1276	399	14,210
Grafton, Ill........	16	39	1292	....	988
Cap au Gris, Mo....	27	66	1319	....	270
Hamburg, Ill........	22	88	1341	....	308
Clarksville, Mo.....	15	103	1356	427	843
Louisiana, Mo......	10	113	1366	431	5,131
Hannibal, Mo.......	28	141	1394	445	12,780
Quincy, Ill.........	20	161	1414	453	36,252
LaGrange, Mo.......	10	171	1424	....	1,508
Canton, Mo.........	7	178	1431	461	2,365
Alexandria, Mo.....	19	197	1450	470	660
Warsaw, Ill.........	1	198	1451	....	2,335
Keokuk, Iowa.......	4	202	1455	472	14,541
Montrose, Iowa.....	12	214	1467	494	748
Nauvoo, Ill.........	3	217	1470	....	1,321
Fort Madison, Iowa.	8	225	1478	497	9,278
Dallas, Ill..........	10	235	1488	....	970
Burlington, Iowa....	14	249	1502	505	23,201
Oquawka, Ill........	13	262	1515	510	1,010
Keithsburg, Ill......	12	274	1527	517	1,566
New Boston, Ill.....	6	280	1532	518	703
Muscatine, Iowa....	23	303	1556	524	14,073
Buffalo, Iowa.......	18	321	1574	....	372
Davenport, Iowa....	10	331	1584	....	35,354
Rock Island, Ill.....	1	332	1585	534	19,493
Moline, Ill..........	4	336	1589	....	17,248
Hampton, Ill........	6	342	1595	....	576
LeClaire, Iowa......	6	348	1601	555	997
Port Byron, Ill......	1	349	1602	....	732
Princeton, Iowa.....	5	354	1607	....	456
Cordova, Ill........	1	355	1608	....	414
Camanche, Iowa....	9	364	1617	....	713
Albany, Ill.........	2	366	1619	....	629
Clinton, Iowa......	9	372	1625	559	22,695
Fulton, Ill..........	2	374	1627	....	2,685
Sabula, Iowa.......	17	392	1645	....	1,029
Savanna, Ill........	2	394	1647	565	3,325
Bellevue, Iowa.....	21	415	1668	571	1,607
Dubuque, Iowa.....	24	439	1692	578	36,297
East Dubuque, Ill...	1	440	1693	....	1,146
Cassville, Wis.......	28	469	1722	588	979
Guttenburg, Iowa...	8	477	1730	....	1,630
Glen Haven, Wis....	3	480	1733	593	207
Clayton, Iowa......	7	487	1740	595	398
McGregor, Iowa....	11	498	1751	597	1,498
Prairie du Chien, Wis.	3	501	1754	....	3,232
Lynxville, Wis......	17	518	1771	....	322
Lansing, Iowa......	12	530	1785	605	1,438
DeSoto, Wis........	5	535	1788	....	387
Victory, Wis........	7	542	1795	609	131
Brownsville, Minn...	21	563	1816	615	453
LaCrosse, Wis......	10	573	1826	621	28,895
Dresbach, Minn.....	8	581	1834	....	250
Trempealeau, Wis...	18	592	1845	....	609
Winona, Minn......	12	604	1857	632	19,714
Fountain City, Wis..	8	612	1865	637	1,031
Minneiska, Minn....	11	623	1876	643	372
Alma, Wis..........	10	633	1886	649	1,201
Wabasha, Minn.....	9	642	1895	655	2,528
Read's Landing, Minn	3	645	1898	....	477
North Pepin, Wis....	5	650	1903	....	407
Lake City, Minn.....	6	656	1909	....	2,744
Stockholm, Wis.....	2	658	1911	....	185
Frontenac, Minn....	4	662	1915	....	176
Maiden Rock, Wis...	3	665	1918	....	304
Red Wing, Minn....	12	677	1930	658	7,525
Diamond Bluff, Wis.	9	686	1939	....	276
Prescott, Wis.......	13	699	1952	....	1,002
Hastings, Minn......	3	702	1955	664	3,811
Newport, Minn......	19	721	1974	....	306
St. Paul, Minn......	8	729	1982	678	163,065

USEFUL INFORMATION—Continued.

PASSENGERS should always purchase tickets at regular ticket offices in order to avoid obtaining expired, stolen and counterfeit tickets from unauthorized persons.

REDEMPTION OF TICKETS.—Bona fide holders of unused tickets over the Diamond Jo Line Steamers may have them properly redeemed when presented within thirty days of date of purchase, by mail or in person, at the General Passenger Office at St. Louis. If tickets are mailed, reason for their non-use at time of purchase should be given.

LOST TICKETS.—This company will not assume responsibility for loss of tickets by passengers. If ticket is lost, inform purser or agent, and pay fare, taking receipt therefor. If ticket is recovered without being used, the extra fare paid will be refunded by General Passenger Agent, St. Louis. Give number and form.

BAGGAGE.—Personal baggage, not exceeding 150 lbs. in weight, will be checked for each passenger presenting full ticket; 75 lbs. on each half ticket, except that porter of Steamer is allowed to charge 25 cents for each trunk for handling and placing same where it is accessible to passenger. No single piece of baggage exceeding 250 pounds will be checked

STORAGE.—Storage will be charged on each piece of baggage either in or out-bound, checked or not checked, remaining at a station over twenty-four hours, at the rate of twenty-five cents for the second day and 10 cents for each successive day, except that baggage received any time Saturday will be held until same hour Monday. Baggage received any hour Sunday will be held until midnight Monday without charge. This exception will also apply to legal holidays.

As a matter of ordinary precaution, owners should mark baggage with their names and addresses, and also make a note of the numbers of checks to aid in identification and recovery in case of loss.

A typical small brochure of a packet company like the Diamond Jo Line showed a map of the Mississippi, cities and towns along the route, miles between landings, and miles from St. Louis and the mouth of the Mississippi. It also showed the elevation and population of various towns.

On the Trail of the Immigrants

The opening of the Welland Canal in 1847 inaugurated a new era in transportation via the St. Lawrence. During the year 1848 the steamer *Free Trader* made several trips from Quebec to Chicago without trans-shipment, and Alice Mann believed emigrants proceeding to the western States would find this route "much shorter and cheaper" than any other. During the fifties, however, fewer travelers were recorded by this route, the peak for the decade being 53,180 in 1854.[453]

Most of the immigrants who docked at the port of New York steamed up the Hudson to Albany and then floated westward over the Erie Canal. During periods of intense competition the fare up the Hudson was sometimes as low as twenty-five cents. At Albany they were absorbed in the flow of settlers from New England and New York, who, according to Robert M. Baird, approached Buffalo by stage or wagon on the road from Albany or by the Erie Canal. Early in the thirties six transportation lines were in operation on the canal, besides a number of short-run lines and boats belonging to individuals. Immigrant could leave Albany for Buffalo almost hourly. The price of passage in a packet boat was about four cents per mile, and the common or "line" boats charged from two to two and one-half cents per mile. Immigrants generally paid much less.

At Buffalo the immigrant might set out by steamer for Detroit. Cabin passage for this trip cost eight dollars per person while a deck passenger paid only four dollars.

Steamboating on Upper Mississippi

During one week in June, 1833, seven steamboats arrived at Detroit from Buffalo with 2610 passengers.[454]

Ole Rynning believed the "best route" was by way of New York. "It is doubtless cheaper and quicker to go by way of New Orleans; but it is too warm and unhealthy there in the summer, and it is not advisable to immigrate at any other time of the year to unbroken land without houses. I must also remark that New Orleans is noted for having the worst people in the United States." Rynning declared that most Norwegians secured transportation from New York to Buffalo by steamer and canal boat for from three to four dollars, baggage included. The tariff from Buffalo to Chicago ranged from nine to twelve dollars.[455]

The most distant ports on the Great Lakes witnessed this colorful pageant of native Americans and foreigners. At Sault Ste. Marie, Lawrence Oliphant found two hundred strangers (chiefly European and American emigrants) seated upon "piles of boxes and carpet-bags" waiting to board the steamer. "Fragile, delicate-looking ladies, with pink and white complexions, black ringlets, bright dresses, and thin satin shoes, reclined gracefully upon carpet-bags, and presided over pyramids of band-boxes. Square-built German fraus sat astride huge rolls of bedding displaying stout legs, blue worsted stockings, and hob-nailed shoes. Sallow Yankees, with straw-hats, swallow-tailed coats, and pumps, carried their little all in their pockets; and having nothing to lose and everything to gain in the western world to which they were bound, whittled,

On the Trail of the Immigrants

smoked, or chewed cheerfully. Hard-featured, bronzed miners, having spent their earnings in the bowling saloons at the Sault, were returning to the bowels of the earth gloomily. There were tourists in various costumes, doing the agreeable to the ladies; and hardy pioneers of the woods, in flannel shirts, and trousers supported by leathern belts, and supplied with bowies, were telling tough yarns, and astonishing the weak minds of the emigrants, who represented half the countries of Europe." [456]

Few people except immigrants, according to Ole Raeder, were willing to be packed away in the hold of a Hudson River or Great Lakes steamboat.[457] But cramped quarters, declared Captain Marryat, meant little to Irish immigrants. "A single bed will contain one adult and four little ones at one end, and another adult and two half-grown at the other. But they are all packed away so snug and close, and not one venturing to move, there appears to be room for all."

At Dunkirk, New York, Marryat saw the boat put off a lone emigrant family. "I watched them carefully counting over their little property, from the iron tea-kettle to the heavy chest. It was their whole fortune, and invaluable to them; the nest-egg by which, with industry, their children were to rise to affluence. They remained on the wharf as we shoved off, and no wonder they seemed embarrassed and at a loss. There was the baby in the cradle, the young children holding fast to their mother's skirt, while the elder had seated themselves on a log, and watched the departure of the steam-vessel; — the bedding, cooking utensils, &c., all lying in confusion, and all to be housed before night. Weary did they look, and weary indeed they were, and most joyful would they be when they at last should gain their resting-place." [458]

But to many the Great Lakes proved a final resting place from whose bourne no migrant ever returned. "Not long since", Fredrika Bremer relates, "a vessel of emigrants, mostly Germans, was destroyed by fire on Lake Erie, and hundreds of these poor people found a grave in its waters. Among those who were taken up were seven or eight couples, locked in each other's arms. Death could not divide them." [459]

During the fifties William Ferguson saw a train of German immigrants who had just debarked from a Great Lakes steamer start for the West on the Michigan Central. "Their accommodation is very poor — merely common box freight-cars, with the rudest seats fitted up in them. There are no windows, so no light or air, unless they keep the sliding doors in the sides always open. I do not wonder that multitudes died from cholera in these trains last summer, or that they die still in numbers; coming into them, as they often do, from the foul holds of the ships, — disease already upon them." [460]

Immigrants by the thousands made their way westward over the Pennsylvania Canal. A Philadelphia newspaper noted with no little pride the following "Glorious Accession" to the Stars and Stripes. "Among a number of emigrants arrived at Philadelphia, was an old man in the fifty eighth year of his age, who had with him ten sons, four daughters, five daughters in law, three sons in law, twenty eight grand children, and two great grand children. He was smoking his pipe quite leisurely, and seemed happy. They intend to locate themselves in the western country and till the soil. Success to them." [461]

From Philadelphia or Baltimore the route lay by railroad to Columbia, Pennsylvania, thence by canal boat up the Susquehanna and Juniata rivers to Hollidaysburg. A portage railroad of inclined planes and stationary engines then crossed the Alleghenies to Johnstown. The journey of almost 400 miles to Pittsburgh was continued in canal boats by way of the Conemaugh and Allegheny rivers. The fare from Philadelphia to Pittsburgh ranged from seven to ten dollars and the time consumed from four to eight days. [462] To Iowa over the Pennsylvania Canal went the Dutch to establish Pella. [463] By this route also went many of the Swedes to found New Sweden in the Hawkeye State. [464] Let us follow a group of immigrants over this route.

On June 30, 1845, two hundred Swiss landed at Baltimore after a stormy voyage of forty-nine days. A kindly German gave some of the company lodging on the attic floor of his home for three cents a night and charged them twelve and one-half cents for meals. Competitive bids for transportation to Pittsburgh were secured from three shippers: the contract was awarded to one, Abraham Cuyk. The Swiss paid twenty francs for each passenger, children four to twelve going at half fare, while those under four went free. A hundred pounds of baggage was allowed each grown person, the residue being carried at the rate of $1.00 per hundred.

The Swiss enjoyed the novelty of their first railroad trip, traveling with the "speed of the wind" from Baltimore to Columbia. Here they clambered aboard canal boats to enjoy a good night's rest before setting out up the Susquehanna River. "One may imagine", wrote one of the party, "how 30 to 35 human beings were pressed like herrings into a space 12 by 7 feet, many had no room even to sit and were obliged to stand all night as if they were sentenced to the stocks."

The Swiss were astounded at the engineering involved in constructing the Pennsylvania Canal. Sometimes their boats were drawn up and let down steep inclines by a wire rope connected with a stationary steam engine. Locomotives or horses were used on the levels, while down easy inclines they sailed "fast enough" without assistance. Meals were procured while passing through the locks, the prices depending, apparently, upon the eagerness of the travelers to buy. It required a week to reach Pittsburgh. As they floated into the city the Swiss yodelled a few songs "which attracted hundreds of people to the border of the canal and to the windows of the adjoining houses."

A contract was made with a steamboat captain at Pittsburgh to carry the party to St. Louis. A fare of two dollars was charged for each person over fourteen. Children of eight to fourteen years went at half fare, while those under eight were to be carried free. On the eve of their departure the wife of one of the colonists was "safely delivered in greatest quietness of a boy. Mother and child were well, although they lay in a berth near the boilers where the heat was smothering."

It required six days for the steamboat to reach Cincinnati. Here the Swiss learned that their boat would go no farther, and so their contract was automatically cancelled. Their resources were almost depleted, but they managed to secure a more favorable rate to St. Louis, which they reached in five days. From this point they journeyed by steamboat to Galena, Illinois, and thence proceeded overland to their new homes in Wisconsin.[465]

Despite the fact that New Orleans was said to harbor the "worst people in the United States" the southern route had many proponents.[466] James Peck declared that those who resided within "convenient distance of a seaport" would find it both "safe and economical" to ship their surplus clothing, bedding, books, etc., by way of New Orleans, especially if they steered for the navigable waters of the Mississippi.[467]

John B. Newhall also advocated the southern route for emigrants to Missouri, Iowa, and southern Illinois, since the expense was much less and there were fewer difficulties to contend with than by any other route. Upon his arrival in New Orleans, Newhall pointed out, the immigrant could leave his family on board the ship until he secured steamboat passage up the Mississippi. A little blooded stock could also be carried by way of New Orleans.[468]

Prior to 1845 it required about two weeks for a steamboat to complete the journey from New Orleans to St. Louis. After that year fast boats plied between these ports in from six to eight days. Cabin fare from New Orleans to St. Louis was twenty-five dollars, while freight cost around sixty-two and one-half cents per hundred. Since most immigrants could not afford cabin passage they usually booked as deck passengers. Adults were carried for three or four dollars — children at half fare. Deck passengers had to provide their own food and assist the crew in wooding-up.[469]

A group of Hollanders paid $2.50 in 1846 per passage from New Orleans to St. Louis — children under nine going at half fare. Each person was allowed one hundred pounds of baggage — the remainder being transported at the rate of twenty-five cents per hundred pounds. It required nine days to make the trip.[470]

When John Regan, bound upstream by steamboat from New Orleans, saw several of his English companions "gnawing a huge piece of beef off a square biscuit" he inquired of one John Adams how he had obtained his share. Regan was informed that members of the crew, having more than they could consume, had given it to the Englishmen and "were much amused to see with what a good appetite the emigrants demolished the remains of their kit of beef, which they were in the habit of throwing overboard at the end of meals." [471]

Upon his arrival at an American port the immigrant was usually pounced upon by a pack of hotel and trans-

On the Trail of the Immigrants

portation runners. The "frauds and outrages" committed by these crafty and unscrupulous "wolves" was sufficient to "shock" even a hardened New York legislative committee. These runners were employed by the month or worked on a commission. As immigration increased, companies developed the plan of hiring foreigners to prey upon their own nationalities. The New York commission found "the German preying upon the German — the Irish upon the Irish — the English upon the English".[472]

Here and there a ray of sunshine brightens what might otherwise be a rather sordid tale. The efforts of Americans to solve the immigration problem at Ward's Island, New York, was highly praised by Fredrika Bremer. "Thousands who came clad in rags, and bowed down with sickness are brought hither, succored, clothed, fed, and then sent out westward to the states of the Mississippi, in case they have no friends or relations to receive them at a less remote distance. Separate buildings have been erected for the sick of typhus fever; for those afflicted with diseases of the eye; for sick children; for the convalescent; for lying-in women. Several new houses were in progress of erection. Upon those verdant, open hills, fanned by the soft sea-breezes, the sick must, if possible, regain health, and the weak become strong. We visited the sick; many hundreds were ill of typhus fever. We visited also the convalescent at their well-supplied dinner-table." [473]

John Murray Forbes believed in applying strict business principles to the immigration problem. Writing to Edward Everett Hale in 1852 Forbes declared : "I have long been of the opinion that the subject of Emigration opened the widest field of this *century* . . . I know of no *elements* that offer more inducement to the economist to bring them together than the strong hands and empty stomachs of Europe, and the rich *Dollar-an-acre* Prairies of the West. California is a cypher in comparison, a mere producer of the measure of value, not of value itself. The railroads which are at last checkering the West in all directions will give a new element of *certainty* to the transit of the Emigrant . . . Benevolence may point the way and law may and must help to regulate the abuses which have grown up; but when you are dealing with an Emigration of 400,000 people who, I will venture to say, are fleeced $10 each to bring them from their hovels in the old world to their houses in the new, here is a premium of four millions per annum for the Devil to fight with." [474]

The trek of the foreigners westward to the Upper Mississippi was filled with many unhappy incidents. On July 14, 1851, the Galena *Advertiser* complained bitterly that immigrants were "robbed, cheated, and manhandled" at Quebec, New York, and Philadelphia. Prospective immigrants were urged by this solicitous editor to take the New Orleans route. Their health by this route would be "just as good" and they could expect to be "nicely treated" by both New Orleans and St. Louis officials.

The travel-worn immigrants must have breathed a sigh of relief when they reached Chicago and were near their journey's end. But their sorrows were not yet over : unscrupulous runners frequently pounced upon them there.

On the Trail of the Immigrants

Under the caption "Strangers in a Strange Land" a Dubuque editor noted the arrival of two families of Norwegian immigrants who had been brought down the river from Prairie du Chien. "This was in consequence of erroneous directions given them by Chicago runners in the genuine Chicago spirit, which would rather send emigrants to Russian America or Nicaragua than have them contribute to the population and prosperity of Iowa. These Norwegians had farms purchased by money forwarded by them to their friends, at the places mentioned, but had not money enough with them to carry them to their journey's end after the contemptible imposition practiced upon them." Fortunately for them a local railroad gave them free passage as far as the road could carry them.[475]

Such incidents were not uncommon, and many letters were sent home warning friends and relatives to trust no one. One immigrant refused to surrender his baggage check to the steamboat clerk upon reaching Minnesota. So great was his determination and so deep-rooted his distrust that he was finally permitted to take his baggage and retain his check. The son of this immigrant, Captain E. W. Holstrom, later operated the ferry between Lake City, Minnesota, and Stockholm, Wisconsin.[476]

Filled with the hope and enthusiasm of the frontier the more sordid incidents of the migrations westward to the Mississippi were soon forgotten. Life was constantly before them; rich lands beckoned on every hand : all their experiences were simply refining fires. Aboard a throbbing

Steamboating on Upper Mississippi

Upper Mississippi steamboat the final lap in their journey was made in comparative comfort. Today the sons of these immigrants rule the destinies of a dozen Commonwealths of the Upper Mississippi Valley.

37

To the North Star State

THE HEYDAY of steamboating on the Upper Mississippi was ushered in with the creation of the Territory of Minnesota in 1849. Between 1850 and 1870 steamboats were jammed from stem to stern with a curious array of immigrants hailing from the four quarters of the Union and from two score foreign countries. Steamboat captains reaped a rich harvest throughout this period as packets churned back and forth between St. Louis and St. Paul transporting settlers to their new homes. The mad stampedes to California and Oregon are dwarfed into insignificance when compared with the huge waves of land-hungry pioneers that surged up the Mississippi.

The first spray of settlers was a Kentucky family on board the *Virginia* bound for the lead mines. During the next seven years the movement upstream was slow despite the advent of the steamboat. By 1830 the frontier line barely impinged on the Half-breed Tract in what is now Lee County, Iowa; and it was not until June 1, 1833, that settlers entered the Black Hawk Purchase. Indeed, when the original Territory of Wisconsin was established in 1836 the census revealed only 22,218 inhabitants in what is now Wisconsin, Iowa, and Minnesota; and most of these were squatters in the mineral region. Fourteen years later (in 1850) there were a half million souls in this same area.

Steamboating on Upper Mississippi

During the next twenty years the population of these three States soared to 2,688,396, or almost equal that of the thirteen colonies on the eve of the American Revolution. Minnesota — the North Star State — had acquired a far greater population in twenty years than had New York State in a century and a half. At the same time the 160,697 foreigners in Minnesota in 1870 equaled the total population of Georgia in 1800 after sixty-seven years of settlement.[477]

Before 1850 the majority of those who settled along the Mississippi River in Illinois, Missouri, and Iowa, came from Indiana, Ohio, Kentucky, and Tennessee, although the Atlantic and Gulf States were well represented. Only one-eighth of the population of Missouri, Illinois, and Iowa was foreign-born in 1850, the remainder being almost equally divided between those born within their borders and migrants from other States. By 1870 the 1,467,353 foreigners in the five States of the Upper Mississippi Valley was greater than the total population of Missouri, Iowa, Wisconsin, and Minnesota in 1850.[478]

In 1853 St. Louis, the point of departure for immigrants bound upstream, was surpassed only by New York and New Orleans in enrolled steam tonnage. New York enrolled 101,487 tons; New Orleans 57,174 tons; and St. Louis 48,557 tons, about one-seventh of which was engaged in transporting immigrants to the Upper Mississippi region. That year St. Louis had a greater steam tonnage than Wheeling, Cincinnati, Louisville, New Albany, Nashville, and Memphis combined. It had required less than a third of a century since the arrival of the steamboat for St. Louis to attain this prosperous commercial position.[479]

But the growth of steamboating on the Upper Mississippi was hardly less spectacular. Immigration was the principal factor in increasing the number of steamboat arrivals at St. Louis from the Upper Mississippi from 647 in 1848 to 1524 in 1860. Measured by the number of steamboat arrivals, the activity of Upper Mississippi craft almost equaled that of the Lower Mississippi, the Missouri, the Illinois, the Ohio, the Tennessee, the Cumberland, and the Arkansas rivers combined. Two years before (in 1858), St. Paul registered 1090 boats at her bustling wharves. The aggregate tonnage of the sixty-three boats which docked at St. Paul that year was 12,703, or about one-half the enrolled tonnage of Philadelphia. St. Louis and the Ohio River towns employed 7065 tons in the St. Paul trade, Galena, Dubuque, and Dunleith 3141 tons, Prairie du Chien 977 tons, the Minnesota River 1254 tons. Two craft totaling 266 tons hailed from no particular port. Immigration was the life of the St. Louis and St. Paul trade between 1850 and 1870.[480]

St. Paul could not claim all the tonnage employed on the Upper Mississippi above St. Louis, since many steamboats never reached that port. Three fairly equal sections of trade developed between the port of St. Louis and the Falls of St. Anthony. The first covered the 200 mile stretch between the mouth of the Missouri and Keokuk where the Lower Rapids presented a physical barrier to navigation. The second extended 225 miles above the

[335]

rapids to the lead district where the concentration of population attracted steam craft. The third and longest section embraced the 275 miles between the lead mines and the Falls of St. Anthony. Along this broad waterway thousands of immigrants were carried upstream for a period of fifty years. The steamboat was the principal means of transportation in the early development of each section.[481]

Not all steamboats bound upstream from St. Louis could be termed Upper Mississippi packets. The Missouri River craft left the Mississippi after an eighteen mile trip upstream. Alton, seven miles above the mouth of the Missouri, had from an early date a daily packet. The Illinois River boats ascended the Mississippi forty miles to Grafton, discharging what St. Louis freight and passengers they had aboard along the way. These were not true Upper Mississippi River packets. Although restricting their operations to the lower section of the river, the daily short lines from St. Louis to Quincy and Keokuk must be considered as Upper Mississippi steamboats.

The growth in population of the counties adjoining the Mississippi between St. Louis and St. Paul presents in miniature the astonishing development of the entire Upper Mississippi Valley. Ever since the voyage of the *Virginia*, settlers had been filtering into the country above St. Louis, choosing those locations which appeared most likely to prosper. Pike and Marion counties, Missouri, and Adams County, Illinois, attracted many immigrants. The latter, with Quincy as its metropolis, had by 1850 surpassed in population the more readily accessible Illinois counties as far south as St. Louis.[482]

The increase in population was not uniform, some counties quickly surpassing their neighbors. For example, Lewis and Clark counties, Missouri, were not self-sustaining in 1836, and by 1840 they were eclipsed by Lee and Des Moines counties in Iowa. Again, in 1850 Dubuque County had as large a population as Scott and Muscatine counties combined. By 1860 the population of the four principal lead mining counties was 110,000, or almost equal to the four most populous counties clustered about the Lower Rapids. Although situated at the head of navigation, Ramsey, Hennepin, and Washington counties in Minnesota could boast a greater population in 1860 than any other three counties located in Wisconsin and Minnesota as far south as the lead district. In the main, however, the entire country along the Upper Mississippi had enjoyed a substantial growth, only three counties below the lead district having less than 10,000 people in 1860. They were Calhoun and Henderson counties, Illinois, and Ralls County, Missouri.[483] No other single factor was so important as the steamboat in conveying settlers to the country immediately adjoining the Mississippi River.

The halcyon days of steamboating are best revealed by following in the wake of the immigrants steaming northward following the creation of the Territory of Minnesota. Native Americans formed the vanguard. Craftsmen of every trade came to St. Paul in 1849 to swell the tide; professions were crowded; and every building was requisitioned for temporary shelter. The erection of new structures was attested by the incessant pounding of hammers. Glowing accounts were carried eastward of a thriving metropolis at the head of navigation on the Upper Mississippi. One settler who arrived at St. Paul on the *Senator* in October was dumfounded to find a rough frontier village, whereas newspaper accounts had led him to picture a city surpassed only by New York.[484] Indeed, when some immigrants arrived on the *Highland Mary* in July they were greeted by the raucous whoops of Sioux warriors on one side of the river and welcomed by cheers from the white settlers on the other. Both were probably attracted by the gay music from the boat's brightly lighted cabin. A barge which was lashed to the side of the *Highland Mary* contained about one hundred cows belonging to the immigrants. Under the glare of the torch, the wild staring eyes of the cattle plainly indicated intense hunger.[485]

Thousands of immigrants from the Ohio and Lower Mississippi were carried upstream from St. Louis. Hundreds were left at ports below the lead district, but large numbers continued northward into Wisconsin and Minnesota where the abundance of cheap land offered a strong inducement to the poor. St. Louis had felt a tremendous increase as early as 1846 when Iowa was admitted into the Union. Charles Lanman arrived at St. Louis that year to find the "wharfing ground so completely crowded with merchandise of every possible variety, that travellers were actually compelled to walk from the steamboats to the hotels." [486]

To the North Star State

When Philip Hone arrived at St. Louis in 1847 he found it bustling with "boatmen, draymen, and laborers, white and black; French, Irish, and German, drinking, singing, and lounging on benches." He relates that "fifty large steamboats, at least, lie head on, taking in and discharging their cargoes; some constantly arriving from New Orleans and other ports on the Mississippi; Cincinnati, Louisville, etc., on the Ohio; from the great Missouri and its tributaries; the Illinois River, where we are bound, and the whole Western and Southern waters, which make this place their mart; whilst others are departing, full of passengers, and deeply laden with the multifarious products of this remarkable region. The whole levee is covered, as far as the eye can see, with merchandise landed or to be shipped; thousands of barrels of flour and bags of corn, hogsheads of tobacco and immense piles of lead (one of the great staples), while foreign merchandise and the products of the lower country are carried away to be lodged in the stores which form the front of the city." [487]

The same bustle and confusion were noted by Fredrika Bremer in 1850. St. Louis looked "as if it were besieged from the side of the river by a number of immense Mississippi beasts, resembling a sort of colossal white sea-bears. And so they were; they were those large, three-decked, white-painted steamers, which lined the shore, lying closely side by side to the number of above a hundred; their streamers, with names from all the countries on the face of the earth, fluttering in the wind above their chimneys, which seemed to me like immense nostrils, for every steamboat on the Mississippi has two such apparatus, which send forth huge volumes of smoke under the influence of 'high-pressure.' " Miss Bremer was told that immigration to St. Louis was increasing every year — "especially from Germany." The city doubled in population between 1845 and 1849.[488]

Scores of steamboats lay at the St. Louis levee awaiting the immigrants from New Orleans. A passenger aboard the *Excelsior* in June, 1851, described crowds of immigrants, cabin passengers, and the freight. "A number of Prussian emigrants of the better class, with their beards, good figures, & foreign customs, a party of Irishmen, said to be 'noble', a certain officer of the army undoubtedly 'royal'; who amused us & astonished us by his wit & extensive information, merchants from St. Louis & the east, & Wisconsin & every state in the Union, with Canada & Europe were found in the Cabin. On Deck were Germans and Irish, a filthy set, whose uncleanliness no doubt hastened the deaths which occurred among them & I was heartily glad when we landed the last at Dubuque." [489]

The coming of foreign groups is well illustrated by Nauvoo where only three Americans remained following the Mormon exodus. When Charles Lanman steamed by in 1846 he described Nauvoo as a city "capable of containing a hundred thousand souls. But its gloomy streets bring a most melancholy disappointment. Where lately resided no less than twenty-five thousand people, there are not to be seen more than above five hundred." [490] By 1851 Nauvoo had become a haven for a large Icarian community composed largely of three hundred and fifty French, with a scattering of other foreign immigrants.⁴⁹¹

Early in the spring of 1851 the *Minnesota* arrived at Galena with two hundred and fifty passengers. The *Wyoming* came up in July with a group of German immigrants (seemingly people of means) bound for Guttenberg. An editor urged that the New Orleans and St. Louis officials should teach such immigrants rules of health. On her next trip the *Wyoming* brought a sunburned group of immigrants from Mecklenburg who were planning to establish a socialist community at "El Kader" in North-eastern Iowa. Fall immigration was very heavy, the *Wisconsin* leaving ten families of sixty people at La Crosse alone.

A St. Paul paper declared that ten new large first class steamers were to be put on the Upper Mississippi should the Senate ratify the treaty of Traverse des Sioux. This plan was intended to accommodate the tremendous rush of immigrants to Minnesota. Another paper remarked that three boats a week would be necessary in 1852, and that a daily line would be imperative in 1853. As the season of 1851 drew to a close steamboats were unable to transport the huge cargoes of immigrants and freight; the *Lamartine* was offered three times as much as she could carry at Galena alone.⁴⁹²

Galena was then the metropolis of the lead region : it numbered almost seven thousand inhabitants. Pigs of lead were heaped along her wharves ready for exportation. Noisy and bustling at all times, Galena bore the brunt of

the traffic from Chicago until the completion of the railroads to Rock Island, Fulton, Dunleith, Prairie du Chien
and La Crosse robbed her of a considerable portion of her
trade and tended to distribute it along the river.
Mrs. Elizabeth F. Ellet recorded her astonishment at
Galena's activity in 1852. "It was a novel amusement in
the evenings to sit by the window and see rushing under
it, with the noise made by the Western high-pressure boats,
steamers so large as apparently to fill up the little river
that skirts the city, and is now shrunken by the drought
into half its accustomed limits. At night the appearance
of these boats, lighted up and filled with lively passengers,
is very picturesque. All that ascend or descend the Mississippi, stop at Galena. The 'fast boats' make the trip to
St. Paul and back in a little over three days, averaging two
a week; but we were counselled to wait and take a slow
boat in preference, that the scenery might be seen to better
advantage." [493]

The linking of the Atlantic with the Mississippi by railroad decreased the Ohio River traffic. But the early effect
was to increase the trade and fatten the receipts of Upper
Mississippi steamboat owners. Each train brought hundreds of immigrants from the East and dumped them on
the banks of the Mississippi. In 1853 the St. Paul wharf
boat master declared that "no one can judge of the large
amount of immigrants coming in, unless they watch the
landing closely. They land and are off to the country before our citizens are aware of their presence."

Early in June the *Dr. Franklin* and the *West Newton*

arrived at St. Paul with an unusually heavy load of immigrants. Sixteen boats, mainly Upper Mississippi craft, lay at the St. Louis levee. Those destined for the Upper Mississippi were crowded with immigrants, although the cargoes were not always heavy. A few days later six of these steamboats were discharging freight and passengers at St. Paul. Many immigrants, moreover, had been left along the way : the *Dr. Franklin* had left twenty or thirty families at Hastings alone.[494]

A veritable deluge of immigrants poured into the Upper Mississippi Valley during the mid-fifties. In 1854 Thurlow Weed of the Albany *Journal* found the St. Louis levee lined for more than a mile with steamboats which gave a highly commercial aspect to the city. "Steamers lay here with steam up and placarded for New-Orleans, Louisville, Cincinnati, Pittsburgh, Council Bluffs, Galena, St. Paul, &c., &c., while others from these places are discharging cargoes. The scene is as busy as that along South-st. in New York. Time is working a phenomena upon the Mississippi River. In a business point of view this river is beginning to run up stream! In other words, a large share of the products of the Valley of the Mississippi are soon to find a market up instead of down the river. There is a West growing with a rapidity that has no parallel, which will consume largely of the sugar, cotton, rice, &c., &c., of the South; while the railroads that are being constructed from Cincinnati, Toledo, Chicago, &c., to the Mississippi, are to take the corn, pork, beef, &c., &c., to a northern instead of southern markets." [495]

[343]

Steamboating on Upper Mississippi

"By railways and steamers", wrote the editor of the Keokuk *Whig*, "the flood of immigration continues pouring into the great West. The lake-shore roads are crowded to their utmost capacity; single trains of fourteen or fifteen cars, all full of men, women, and a large sprinkling of children, are almost daily arriving at Chicago. The Ohio River steamers are crowded in the same way. On Friday last, two steamers brought into St. Louis some 600 passengers; most of whom, being destined for the northwest, have already passed through this place. And 'still they come,' from Pennsylvania, from Ohio, Indiana, and other States, until, by the side of this exodus, that of the Israelites becomes an insignificant item, and the greater migrations of later times are scarcely to be mentioned."

Returned from a two weeks furlough another Keokuk editor observed : "No one can travel up and down the Mississippi without being astonished at the immigration constantly pouring into Iowa from all parts of the country; but especially from Indiana and Ohio." Burlington and Davenport were crowded with immigrants moving westward. Immigrants arrived hourly at Dubuque from Ohio, Kentucky, Indiana, and Illinois; while thousands came "from the hills and valleys of New England, bringing with them that same untiring, indomitable energy and perseverance, that have made their native States the admiration of the world." [496]

Most of the passenger trains arrived at Chicago with two locomotives. A Chicago editor noted that "*twelve thousand passengers* arrived from the East, by the Michigan

To the North Star State

Southern road, during the last week — a city in the short space of six days!" Twenty-five cars left Albany for Buffalo with thirteen hundred immigrants bound for Chicago and the Northwest, and another train load containing fifteen hundred more followed within twenty-four hours. There was a heavy influx of immigrants into Northern Iowa : in 1850 Lansing had but one log cabin, but in 1854 it boasted four hundred inhabitants. Likewise the population in Allamakee and Winneshiek counties was growing rapidly. Decorah was unable to accommodate those wanting to enter lands; beds upon the floor were at a premium; while good prices were paid for an opportunity to "lean against sign posts or hang on a hook." Many of those who landed at Lansing were intelligent, industrious, "well-to-do-Easterners" who bought improved farms at from $800 to $4000 each.[497]

Every road leading to the Northwest was thronged with immigrants in 1856. Nine thousand passed through Chicago in a single day. Every boat bound upstream was crowded : the *Galena* left Dunleith with over eight hundred passengers aboard, most of whom were destined for Minnesota. The *City Belle* arrived at the Winona levee with emigrants composing the Minnesota Settlement Company. These were warmly cheered by the citizens of Winona before setting off into the interior for some unknown settlement.[498]

Harriet Bishop was amazed at the throng that packed Upper Mississippi steamboats. "It is a strange medley, indeed, that which you meet aboard a Mississippi steamer.

Steamboating on Upper Mississippi

An Australian gold-hunter, just returned by way of England, from Melbourne; a merchant on a trip of pleasure; a professor in an eastern University, going out to invest in Minnesota; a St. Croix raftsman, returning from a trip down river, with a small fortune of logs; a New York doctor, with a pocket full of land warrants; an eastern man, who administers electro-chemical baths; a South Carolina boy, with one thousand dollars and a knowledge of double-entry; a sturdy frontierman, with a saw mill for the interior; an engineer, who escaped the Panama fever on the Isthmus railroad; a Yankee schoolmaster, who has become a small speculator in oats; and scores of others of doubtful character, who sport heavy moustaches, and keep their mouths shut. Verily, a strange medley do you find aboard a Mississippi steamer!" [499]

When Nathan H. Parker took passage on Captain Preston Lodwick's *Northern Belle* he found five hundred already aboard. According to Parker "State-rooms were entirely out of the question, and bunks upon the floor or seats at the table were at a premuim. Standing at the lower end of the cabin, and gazing upon the hundreds of persons whose beds covered almost every foot of the cabin floor, I intuitively exclaimed, 'This is going West.' I mused upon the various situations and climates and nations these peoples had left; the misfortunes that had befallen some, and the fortunes that had fallen to others, alike impelling them to seek the 'land of promise — the great West,' each individual having different plans and anticipations for the future, and each seeming to delight in being one of this hurly-burly, motley throng." Passenger traffic had already become so heavy on the Upper Mississippi that Parker felt that anyone who was fortunate enough to possess a stateroom and enjoy all the comforts and luxuries of the "floating palaces" must consider himself highly favored.[500]

The same activity prevailed at Dunleith when the Illinois Central reached the Mississippi. Incoming trains were met by agents and runners for the different boats who pounced upon the startled immigrants and travelers, pointing with pride to their own craft and disparaging the opposition boat. In 1856 a runner for the *Lucy Bertram* told C. C. Andrews "with great zeal and perfect impunity" that no other boat would leave for St. Paul within twenty-four hours when it was perfectly obvious that the mail boat would start that evening. The activity of such runners was often unnecessary, for usually there were more passengers than the boats could comfortably accommodate.

Andrews went aboard the *Lady Franklin* and was fortunate enough to secure a stateroom. "But what a scene is witnessed for the first two hours after the passengers begin to come aboard! The cabin is almost filled, and a dense crowd surrounds the clerk's office, just as the ticket office of a theatre is crowded on a benefit night. Of course, not more than half can get state-rooms and the rest must sleep on the cabin floor. Over two hundred cabin passengers came up on the Lady Franklin. The beds which are made on the floor are tolerably comfortable, as each boat is supplied with an extra number of single mattresses."[501]

Steamboating on Upper Mississippi

St. Paul presented the same activity. When the *North-ern Light* arrived early in May, 1857, the *Frank Steele*, the *Messenger*, the *Orb*, the *Golden State*, the *Equator*, the *Key Stone*, the *Saracen*, the *Sam Young*, the *Mansfield*, the *Ocean Wave*, the *Red Wing*, the *Golden Era*, the *Minnesota*, the *Conewago*, the *Kate French*, the *Time and Tide*, the *Hamburg*, the *Wave*, the *Excelsior*, and the *W. L. Ewing* lay diagonally with the levee. "Instead of presenting the appearance of a city of houses", a traveler observed, "the levee looked like a city of steamboats." In this flotilla were steamboats hailing from distant Cincinnati and Pittsburgh. Frozen Lake Pepin was responsible for so colorful an array at St. Paul.[502]

Sleeping accommodations were not always at their best. On April 16th the *Reveille* arrived at St. Paul with her decks thronged with people who had been delayed at the foot of the Lake. "Most of those who came in her", according to a contemporary account, "were obliged to be content, so far as sleeping arrangements were concerned, with a chance to lie two deep on the greasy cabin floor, with their carpet bags under their heads for pillows, whilst the wind whistled a lullaby through the broken and almost sashless windows of the vessel." In July of 1857 two hundred Norwegians destined for the "Dunkirk Precinct" in Goodhue County were landed at Red Wing by the *Metropolitan*. Six hundred more were to come in October to the same settlement.[503]

The following year a Red Wing dispatch read : "The Wednesday morning packet landed at our levee another

[348]

delegation of immigrants for the Norwegian settlement, who packed four heavy teams with their goods and passed back into the interior. Dunkirk will soon become about the most flourishing settlement in the State. More are yet to arrive." A short time later the *Northern Belle* came up with a colony of three hundred Swedes who expected to settle in the vicinity of Red Wing. Foreign immigrants were discharged at every port above St. Louis.[504] "We noticed on the Levee, the other day", declared a Dubuque newspaper, "a number of Bohemians, just arrived. The men were stout and able-bodied, and the women fat, stumpy and good-looking. They were dressed in the peculiar style of their country." [505]

As long as the railroads did not run parallel with the river this immense traffic continued. Clusters of foreigners, congregated at the various railway terminals along the river, anxiously awaited the arrival of the first steamboat bound for the rich lands above. A party of two hundred and fifty Norwegians arrived at Dunleith in June, 1866, and prepared to take passage on the *Jennie Baldwin*. Under the title, "Emigrants by the Car Load", the Dubuque *Herald* commented that "the Dunleith depot presents a picturesque appearance just at present. Twelve carloads of German emigrants came in Tuesday, bound for some point up the river, and being too late for the boats they were compelled to lie over. And *lie over* it is in a literal sense. From one end of the depot to the other they were scattered over the floor, dovetailing together in the most workmanlike manner possible while their huge trunks and bundles make an effective barricade against all intruders." A deckload of passengers bound for Minnesota departed on the *Key City* on June 23rd; and it was noted that six hundred emigrants were in Chicago awaiting the arrival of five thousand more from the mother country.[506]

The next year a party of two hundred Norwegians reached Dunleith on their way to Minnesota. Their trunks and bundles filled five freights. "Capt. Webb received them with open arms, as he was short of help, and pressing them in the ranks, loaded the *Itasca* with their ponderous chests, and five cars of miscellaneous freight besides, nearly cleaning out the Dunleith depot. The boat departed with a big trip for a dull season." [507]

Throughout the sixties steamboats continued to carry large numbers of passengers to Upper Mississippi ports. The *Davenport* arrived at Dubuque late in April, 1867, with seventy-five cabin and forty deck passengers. On May 21st she was recorded at Dubuque with 425 cabin passengers. On her next trip up, one hundred cots had to be placed on the floor to accommodate the crowded cabin. In mid-June the *Davenport* passed Dubuque with 600 passengers aboard, 300 of whom were raftsmen. An editor predicted that when navigation came to a close the *Davenport* would show the largest season's business. In both passengers and freight, it was said, the season of 1867 provided upstream boats with cargoes "equal to previous years." [508]

The season of 1868 was also profitable. A Dubuque editor expressed deep satisfaction because immigrants were showing a preference for Iowa rather than locating in the "wilds of Kansas, Nebraska or Colorado." [509]

On July 11, 1869, the steamboat *Muscatine* churned past Dubuque with a heavy load that included 300 cabin and 300 deck passengers. A week later the *Minneapolis* arrived at Dubuque with a heavy freight and over 700 passengers registered, most of whom were still on board. Staterooms on the *Minneapolis* commanded a premium : passengers "lucky enough to snooze in a chair" were considered fortunate. A short time later the *Tom Jasper*, jammed with passengers, put in her appearance at Dubuque. While rejoicing over the prosperous trip a Dubuque editor could not help lamenting that the cook on the *Tom Jasper* was the "black rascal that induced Mrs. Joe Howard to leave her husband last week and took her to St. Louis."

Throughout the season of 1869 the *Canada*, the *Dubuque*, the *Mollie McPike*, the *Northern Belle*, the *Minnesota*, the *Savanna*, and the *Sucker State* arrived at Dubuque "black" with passengers. "Travel on the river was never better than it is this summer", declared the Dubuque *Herald* of August 5, 1869. "Every up river boat is crowded beyond its capacity for comfort, and those passengers who are fortunate enough to secure a state room are indeed lucky. Even sleeping room in the cabin commands a premium." [510]

The seventies witnessed a precipitate decline in the passenger traffic as railroads had come to afford a speedier and more dependable means of year-round transportation. By the seventies, however, the grain trade had grown to immense proportions. Steamboat captains reaped a golden harvest towing barges of grain to Upper Mississippi railroad elevators as well as to St. Louis and distant New Orleans. It was the immigrants swarming upstream by steamboats as far as the North Star State that made the grain trade possible and staved off for almost a generation the decline and ultimate extinction of steamboating on the Upper Mississippi.

38

Life on the Deck and in the Cabin

RUNNERS, BLACKLEGS, and gamblers, explosions, tornadoes, and devastating fires, snags and sandbars, poor food and wretched accommodations, sickness, suffering, and death — these possibilities faced the bewildered immigrant as he embarked aboard an Upper Mississippi steamboat on his journey to the promised land. Cabin passengers enjoyed a certain degree of comfort, but life on the lower deck was sometimes insufferable.

The hardships of immigrants aboard steamboats was not restricted to the ordinary affairs of life. Epidemics of Asiatic cholera swept the country in the decades preceding the Civil War and steamboats often carried the disease from port to port. Sanitation was little known, and deaths were all too frequent among the immigrants. It was not an uncommon sight to see a steamboat land and the crew jump ashore and hastily dig a shallow grave for the latest victim.

The callous indifference of Americans to life on the steamboat frontier caused Captain Marryat to exclaim: "I hate the Mississippi, and as I look down upon its wild and filthy waters, boiling and eddying, and reflect how uncertain is travelling in this region of high-pressure, and disregard for social rights, I cannot help feeling a disgust at the idea of perishing in such a vile sewer, to be buried in mud, and perhaps to be rooted out again by some pig-nosed alligator." [511]

Immigrants were urged to be extremely careful in their diet and not run into excess of any kind. A little nutmeg or essence of peppermint and water added to some burnt cork poured in a teaspoonful of brandy and mashed with loaf sugar was considered a sure cure for cholera in 1824. Cholera victims during the forties probably breathed more freely on learning that four or five of Wright's Indian Vegetable Pills taken each night on retiring would quickly "rid the body of every description of suffering." [512]

In spite of these nostrums cholera took a heavy toll of lives during the late forties and early fifties. It appeared first on Lower Mississippi steamboats in December of 1848 and quickly spread to the Upper Mississippi boats. Six Trappist monks from Waterford, Ireland, bound for Dubuque aboard the steamboat *Constitution*, died of cholera near St. Louis in 1849. Two hundred and thirty-six cases existed in Quincy that year. Some immigrants aboard the *West Newton* in 1850 saw six dead bodies floating in the river — evidently poor passengers who had been thrown overboard "to save the trouble of burial and to escape quarantine regulations." [513]

A passenger aboard the *Excelsior* in 1851 wrote : "The first intimation I received of the presence of death in our midst was the tolling of the bell & the mooring of the boat at the foot of a high bluff on the Illinois shore. Soon some hands jumped ashore, a grave was speedily dug & as the last rays of the setting sun glided from the waters face, a bird sent up a joyful note over the grave of the infant which an hour before had breathed its last. We proceeded on our way an[d] 'ere two days had passed we had buried *five* deck passengers, I fear some of them victims of cholera no doubt aggravated or induced by filthiness, exposure, fatigue & improper diet." Nine cases, some of them fatal, broke out on the *Galena* while on her way upstream to St. Paul. One of the victims lay in a canoe on the St. Paul levee surrounded by some fellow passengers who vainly strove to revive him.[514]

The Upper Mississippi Valley was thrown into a panic in 1866 when the *Canada* arrived at Dubuque with several cases of cholera reported on board. Passengers declared that three bodies had been thrown overboard and several of the stricken victims put ashore. When the boat arrived at La Crosse a physician pronounced the malady "cholera morbus, brought on by eating green apples, and drinking whiskey and milk." One of the sufferers was robbed of two hundred dollars by some "heartless wretch". When the *Minnesota* arrived at Davenport a little later several passengers were reported ill. "Three deaths occurred yesterday afternoon, the victims being deck passengers. One was buried at 3 o'clock, one at 6 o'clock, and one at 9. We did not learn their names." Such laconic reports were read with extreme uneasiness.[515]

Charges were made at St. Louis that Dubuque was trying to harm the Northern Line by urging immigrants not to patronize its boats. This charge was stoutly refuted at Dubuque. Travelers were told not to shun the *Canada* and other Northern Line craft as they were among the cleanest on the river. When it was rumored at Dubuque that the *Sucker State* had twenty-five cases of cholera aboard and that ten had been buried on islands, the city council granted the wharfmaster power to hail and inspect boats bound upstream. The *Sucker State*, the *Minnesota*, and the *Lady Pike* were thoroughly examined and pronounced free of cholera. The unfortunate *Canada* also passed inspection, but was known ever after as the "pest boat" which lost her many a passenger.[516]

Cholera was more common among the deck passengers who lived in filth on the lower deck, ate coarse food, slept in the most convenient spot, and often drank to excess. Ole Munch Raeder, in commenting on his voyage on the *Red Wing* in 1847, said that "first class passengers occupy the cabins on top of the deck, where there is plenty of fresh air and the balcony enables one to take a little exercise without getting dirty. But if one ventures down on the deck he finds the most terrible filth, mud, stagnant water, and a most offensive odor everywhere".[517]

Another person noted that "cattle and horses, wagons and plows, and barrels of flour" had been taken aboard the *Senator* at Prairie du Chien and McGregor as the property of immigrants bound for Minnesota. Passengers took a keen delight in watching boats discharge their cargo of livestock. "The work was accomplished by the cattle being forcibly pushed over the gunwales, and each beast, as it fell, was submerged for the instant, then rose, and, expelling the water from its nostrils, made for the shore, a process so rude and novel that it brought every passenger to view the scene." [518]

Many travelers complained of the untidy washrooms. All the men aboard the *Red Wing* used a huge towel suspended over a wooden roller. "One must lay aside all instinct of cleanliness when one enters this place, which really ought to minister to the cause of cleanliness", Raeder laments. Such conditions were common. On one occasion when a complaint was made to the purser that the towel in the public washroom was filthy, the indignant officer replied : "Wal now, I reckon there's fifty passengers on board this boat, and they've all used that towel, and you're the first on 'em that's complained of it." [519]

A like condition existed in the ladies' cabin. Only a few of the staterooms on a miserable old low-water tub were supplied with "ewers and basins". The other cabin passengers, according to Mrs. Ellet, were expected "to perform their ablutions in a small wash-room, scantily supplied with water and towels, and allowed but a minute and a half for the duty, elbowed and grumbled at in the mean time by half a dozen impatient for the succession. This was uncomfortable enough for those who could be content with 'a wipe' over the prominent parts of the face, and an imperfect cleansing of the hands; but for us whom the habitual and plenteous use of the Croton had made absolutely dependent for life and comfort on a daily *bonâ fide* bath — the evil was intolerable. We had no resource but to brave the cabinmaid's frowns and a general stare, by seeking an introduction to the concealed water barrel, filling stolen or borrowed pitchers to the brim, carrying them resolutely to our staterooms, and fastening the door." She felt, however, that the poorest boats would be better provided with conveniences for washing were they required; but most immigrants seemed satisfied with limited facilities.[520]

Cabins were freely criticized. When Mrs. Ellet arrived at Keokuk "several runners on the bank set forth the merits of the rival boats — the St. Paul and the Kate Kearney — in voluble recommendation. 'Not a bug to be seen — will give the passage if you find one' — was music in our ears, after the direful experiences of the last three nights, when, driven from the staterooms by the 'native population' we had been constrained to take on the cabin floor such rest as could be obtained amid the voluble chattering of Irishwomen, who seemed to think they could not have their money's worth unless they murdered the sleep of every body else." [521]

The same condition was found by Charles Francis Adams and his son on a trip to St. Paul with William H. Seward in 1860. On returning they were forced to take the *Alhambra*, which was then used as a freight and immigrant boat. "Old and bad at the best", the *Alhambra* was crowded with passengers. The elder Adams declared the condition of the berths so "dubious that I deemed it most prudent not to risk the reception of vermin. Hence I was awake most of the night." His son was equally displeased. "The boat was in every respect a wretched one, — old, dirty and full of vermin." [522]

Life on the Deck and in the Cabin

The food of the deck passengers was hardly better than the "grub pile" of the crew. When Samuel Pond, a Sioux missionary, came to Minnesota in 1833 he cut expenses by going as a decker and "clubbing with other passengers of the same class the table expense." These meals were so coarse that Pond was obliged to go ashore at landings to secure better food.[523] In 1829, according to Caleb Atwater, the *Missouri* and *Red Rover* stopped at the frontier villages along the way to procure fresh supplies of ice, butter, eggs, and chickens.[524]

Some of the immigrants on the *Indian Queen* set out on a hunting expedition while the boat ascended the Lower Rapids. A herd of about thirty deer went "bounding" by, and one was bagged. Then, while the *Indian Queen* puffed upstream, the immigrants hurried to Nashville, Iowa, and "got together about half-a-dozen Indian corn cakes, shaped like cheeses, about 7 lbs. weight each, called, by way of eminence, 'Corn Dodgers;' several piles of buckwheat cakes, dough nuts, pancakes, wheaten bread in twenty various forms, and skim and buttermilk in four good sizeable water pails. We roasted our venison upon hazel switches and ate heartily. This noble repast, all of which we could not consume, cost us less than a picayune a piece." [525]

Although cabin fare was much better, Munch Raeder was not enthusiastic about the food placed before him on the *Red Wing*; and he was displeased with the lack of milk for his tea. Perhaps he was consoled by the hearty appetite of a woman passenger. "I have never before seen

[359]

a woman blessed with such an appetite! She is one of the first at the table and also one of the last, and when she finally does decide to leave she takes along some provisions — tea, bread and butter, ham or fish — so that she may not starve before the next meal." [526]

Cabin passengers were not slow in responding to the dinner gong. "We had three tables set", relates a passenger aboard the *Lady Franklin*, "and those who couldn't get a seat at the first or second tables sat at the third. There was a choice, you may believe, for such was the havoc made with the provisions at the first table that the second and third were not the most inviting. It was amusing to see gentlemen seat themselves in range of the plates as soon as they were laid, and an hour before the table was ready." [527]

Another person noted that "as the dinner hour drew near, the doors of the saloon were besieged very much as those of an opera-house are at a popular singer's benefit; and upon their being opened, a rush took place, succeeded by a hot contest for seats. This was a most disagreeable process, and one which was very apt to lead to unpleasant results; so we used generally to wait until two detachments of unshaven ruffians had dined, and then we came in for the scraps at a late hour in the afternoon." [528]

Competition tended to keep the meals served at a fairly high level. As population increased, boats had no difficulty in replenishing their larder with fresh vegetables, fruit, meats, fish, and game. Boat stores were located along the river and these took on a busy appearance as soon as navigation opened. Immigrants found Phil Pier's saloon at Dubuque always well stocked. Equally good food could be purchased at the other levee stores. Thus, Koehler & Brothers were well supplied with the choicest of meats, including beef, mutton, pork, veal, and lamb. In 1869 sirloins were selling at seventeen and one-half cents, veal and roasts at twelve and one-half cents and fifteen cents, corned beef and boiling pieces at ten cents, and mutton at ten and twelve and one-half cents. It is doubtful whether any passenger suffered from lack of food, though protests were frequently registered about the quality.[529]

A number of travelers and immigrants who took passage on steamboats which plied the Upper Mississippi recorded their contempt for the poor facilities afforded. In 1847 the *Red Wing* was likened to a "mere trading-vessel in a half civilized country" which continually boasted of her youth despite her age. "The walls, the ceiling, the beds, all are uniformly painted white. Even in the ladies' salon there are none of the chandeliers, the lamp globes, the gilded scrolls and arabesques, the pianos, the sofas, and the couches which made the Lakes steamships so pleasant. A few red tables and yellow chairs, that is the total — except that in the ladies' salon there are some of those rocking-chairs which seem to be a sort of *sine qua non* of feminine existence everywhere in America. The only sign of luxury in the men's parlor is that the tables and parts of the floor are left uncovered so that the men can indulge to their heart's content in their favorite pastime of 'unrelenting, merciless spitting,' of which Mrs.

Trollope speaks with such evident disgust. Their operations generally center about the two stoves, where they sit as silent as statues, each one chewing his tobacco. A further convenience for this occupation of theirs is found in a hole in the floor which is so large that a lady could easily get her foot caught in it; to prevent such a calamity, the carpet has been cut away around the hole so that everyone can see and avoid it ... A whole mess of wreaths and other decorations of colored paper have been hung from the ceiling of the cabin and whenever anyone opens one of the doors so there is a draft, there is a buzzing sound as if hundreds of women were whispering to their neighbors the important news that Mr. A. has entered the room or Mr. B. had gone out." [530]

But the *Red Wing* was not an old boat. Built at Cincinnati the previous year, she was 147 feet long, twenty-four feet beam, four and one-fourth feet hold, and measured 142 tons. Since she served a pioneer community it is not strange that the absence of filigrees was noted. The influx of immigrants, together with its attendant increase in passenger traffic, resulted in larger and better steamboats. Corporations made possible expensive craft, and such boats as the *Golden Era* and the *Saint Paul* were well over two hundred tons. When the *Ben Campbell* slid from the Pittsburgh ways in 1852, she boasted fifty large staterooms. Mrs. Ellet pointed out that she "rivalled in size and elegance of arrangement the Lake and Ohio steamers; the state-rooms were large, and generally furnished with double beds and wardrobes, and the fare was so excellent, that one was naturally at a loss to conceive how passengers could possibly be conveyed four hundred miles, lodged and fed sumptuously, and provided with attendance for four dollars each, less than one would have to pay at an ordinary hotel; at a time, too, when the *furore* of competition was over, the decline in the waters having stopped the running of many first-class boats." [531]

Destined to serve Upper Mississippi immigrants for sixteen years, the second *War Eagle* was launched at a cost of about $33,000 at Cincinnati in 1854. According to the Cincinnati *Times* "the cabins are furnished, with just enough of the gilt work to give them a cheerful appearance. All the modern steamboat improvements have been attached, and the barber shops, wash room, &c, are on a liberal scale. She will draw but 24 inches water, light, and only 5 feet when loaded to the guards. The carpets, of the finest velvet, are from Shilito & Co.'s; the furniture from S. J. Johns; mirrors from Wiswell's; and the machinery by David Griffey." Some fine views of the Upper Mississippi adorned her cabin. [532]

During the sixties such boats as the *Canada*, the *Hawkeye State*, the *Sucker State*, the *Dubuque*, and the *Phil Sheridan* averaged five times the tonnage of the boats which frequented the Upper Mississippi twenty years before. The *Phil Sheridan* alone measured 728.46 tons. Immigration was the prime factor in enlarging and beautifying Upper Mississippi craft. [533]

Grim tragedy sometimes stalked in the wake of steamboats. Hardly a trip was made without an accident of some kind. Immigrant deck passengers were frequently lost overboard, the yearly toll often reaching a staggering figure. When the *Sarah Ann* reached Hannibal in 1845, a sleeping immigrant rose, stepped off the bow, and was seen no more. His wife and child returned to friends. Two deck passengers were drowned in attempting to pass from the *Tempest* to her barge. Bound for Minnesota with his wife, child, and sister, Courtland Starr, an immigrant from Adams County, Illinois, was pulled in while attempting to draw a bucket of water for his horse. Another immigrant was butted over by his oxen and drowned. Near Wild Cat Bluff at the head of Coon Slough [below Brownsville, Minnesota] an immigrant fell in and failed to rise. Sixty dollars was raised among the cabin passengers for his bereaved wife and child. The loss of "David Lambert, Esq, of St. Paul" was chronicled as a "Melancholy Event". Intoxicated, Lambert fancied some people were about to arrest him and jumped overboard.[534]

Captains seldom turned back at the cry of "Man overboard!" This was not mere indifference, for it was generally conceded that the boat's wheel seldom missed its mark. But travelers sometimes had singular escapes. While the *War Eagle* was paddling upstream from La Crosse a young German deck passenger fell over just forward of the wheel. According to a contemporary account he "passed under it, was struck full in the forehead by one of the buckets and thrown senseless on the surface of the water, where he lay motionless until picked up", which was done immediately. On another occasion a passenger fell off the *Dr. Franklin* just below St. Paul and was given up as lost. His wife returned on the *Dr. Franklin*; but when the *West Newton* arrived at St. Paul the lost one was aboard. Alive and well, he had swum ashore with no other damage than a refreshing bath on a warm night. "The widow", concluded an observer, "will be somewhat surprised to meet him again, after passing the ordeal of her first weeks grief!"

Many instances of heroism brighten these otherwise sordid pictures. While the *Luella* lay at Galena a little girl fell overboard, and her father, who could not swim, plunged in after her. Both were rescued with difficulty. A German decker aboard the *Tishomingo* was not so fortunate in his effort to save an Irishman : both were sucked under the wheel. Unable to pay his passage above St. Paul, another German immigrant was attacked by three men while proceeding along the bank of the Minnesota River. The ruffians beat him and threw him into the river, but his faithful dog managed to hold him up until the steamboat *Globe* arrived.[535]

Explosions, collisions, snags, heavy winds, and fires were responsible for the loss of many lives. Bound upstream from St. Louis in 1837, the larboard boiler of the *Dubuque* burst with terrific force, throwing a torrent of scalding water and steam over the deck passengers. Twenty-two lives were lost in this explosion — one of the first and most appalling on the Upper Mississippi.[536]

Seven years later (1844) the *Potosi* burst a boiler near Quincy, killing three persons instantly and scalding twenty others. Three German deck passengers — a woman, a boy of fourteen, and a girl of eleven — were badly scalded when the *Red Wing* collapsed a flue a short distance above Rock Island in 1847 : a severe gust of wind had careened the boat until the leeward guard was submerged. But such explosions were neither so frequent nor so gruesome as those on the Ohio or Lower Mississippi.[537]

The light-draught, top-heavy steamboat was always an easy victim of the violent winds which held them at their mercy. Lake Pepin was a death-trap in a storm, and captains became wary of the weather upon approaching it. In 1845 the *Galena* ran into a gale which blew down her chimneys and threatened to tear off her cabin. When the *Otter* steamed by a short time later the *Galena* was lying up with the bedding out to dry. The hurricane left a track three miles wide on shore and lashed the waves of Lake Pepin ten feet high. The elements played havoc with steamboats all along the river. While landing at Port Louisa, a sudden gust of wind knocked down the *Michigan's* chimneys and capsized a wood boat she was towing. Thirty men — members of the crew and immigrants working their passage — were thrown into the river and four were drowned. Three others were blown from the *Michigan* and seen no more. The boat presented a sorry spectacle as she paddled upstream with her cabin demolished. The *Nominee*, known as the "pious boat", lost her whistle and fifteen feet of her chimney when blown against a tree. She was unable to blow "Old Hundred" at Galena the following Sunday.[538]

Life on the Deck and in the Cabin

Collisions were frequent. In 1842 a steamboat struck the *Indian Queen's* keelboat while descending the Lower Rapids. The *Dr. Franklin* stove in several feet of timber on the larboard side of the *Amaranth* near Clarksville, Missouri, in 1849. Eight or ten lives were lost in 1857 when the *Ben Coursin* rammed the *Key City* about six miles above La Crosse. Both the *Amaranth* and the *Ben Coursin* had violated the river navigation law.[539]

Next to explosions, perhaps, fires were feared most. Twenty-three steamboats were destroyed by fire at St. Louis in 1849 — the worst marine disaster on western waters. Seven of the lost craft were regular Upper Mississippi boats, while several others made transient visits.[540]

Two sister ships, the *War Eagle* and the *Galena*, met their fate by fire. Built at Cincinnati in 1854, the *Galena* was completely destroyed by fire at Red Wing. Her passengers, chiefly immigrants, were panic stricken. "Men, women, and children rushed down the gangway, and over board from all sides of the boat, many of them with nothing but their nightclothes about them. The rush was so great that the stages could not be launched; and but for the remarkable coolness and wise action on the part of the officers of the boat, more lives would have been lost." Only five were reported lost, but possibly many who were burned went unrecorded. In 1870 the *War Eagle* burned to the water's edge at La Crosse with a loss of six lives and a property damage of $215,000.[541]

Filled with the hope and enthusiasm of the frontier, immigrants probably gave little thought to such almost

[367]

daily occurrences. Life was constantly before them, and rich lands beckoned to them on every side. No doubt many came inspired by Charles A. Dana's account of the region in 1854. "There is no region, I think, which can sustain a larger population than that on both sides of the northern Mississippi. A rich soil, suited to every product of the temperate zone, and absolutely inviting the hand of the farmer; a climate genial but not enervating; frequent streams to afford water power and fuel abundant in the earth; the great river for a highway, and railroads which, in forty-eight hours, land the traveler on the Atlantic — with all these advantages the entire country must become the home of one of the freest, most intelligent, most powerful and most independent communities of the world." Many immigrants worked their passage up and back to seek out and stake a claim. The *Clarion* ran up the Blue Earth and laid over a full day in order to allow her hands to select choice lands.[542]

Besides discussing the merits of the new land, immigrants found time to ponder over and weigh the nation's problems. The leading topics of conversation on the river, according to the *Minnesota Pioneer* of May 6, 1852, were: "Minnesota, the treaties, California, the Maine Liquor Law. The telegraph and the newspapers, now make the same topics of discussion universal, at the same time, wherever the English language is spoken. The presidency and Kossuth, and Jenny Lind, are not now much talked of. Our people require a fresh topic every few days."

The arrival at a port was a signal for a dash to the guards

Life on the Deck and in the Cabin

and upper decks to watch the boat discharge and take on freight and passengers. A clever deck hand perched high on a swinging stage always attracted attention. The explicit directions of the mate also proved both entertaining and instructive. Fights around the levee occurred daily, and immigrants and passengers were often drawn into bloody riots. In 1857 the passengers and crew of the *Saracen* were attacked by the citizens of Fort Madison when they captured and severely beat a negro guilty of insubordination. The negro was tied to a stanchion where "severer punishment was to be inflicted." Several aboard the *Saracen* were wounded and one citizen of Fort Madison was killed in the pitched battle. In the same year drunken rafters, armed with stones, knives, and guns, made a vicious onslaught on the *Galena* at Reed's Landing. At Dubuque in 1858 an Irishman, who rejoiced in the sobriquet of "Rocky Ryan", led his hoodlum followers in an attack on the deck hands of the *Alhambra*.[543]

Those who worked their passage assisted in wooding up the boat. This was a novel sight at night. Charles Francis Adams, Jr., records that "as the hands, dressed in their red flannel shirts, hurried backward and forward, shipping the wood, the lurid flickerings from the steamer's 'beacon-lights' cast a strong glare over their forms and faces, lighting up steamer, flat-boat and river, and bringing every feature and garment out in strong relief." [544]

Steamboats frequently experienced an unexpected addition to the passenger list. An "interesting incident" occurred to an Irish woman aboard the *Northern Belle*

[369]

in 1856. Wrapped in flannel, the newly born infant weighed eleven pounds and was promptly christened "Preston Lodwick" McCormack in honor of the captain. A similar episode took place on board the *Golden Era* bound for St. Paul. A purse of $40 was raised for the benefit of the new parents. Since a physician was not always on board the duty of midwife once fell to the captain. Thus, a woman aboard the *Lady Pike* experienced "some peculiar symptoms, which soon resulted in bringing into this world of sin and sorrow, a bouncing boy. The officers of the boat were all attention, Cap't Bradford officiating as chief physician on the important occasion. It is stated that he performed his arduous duties in a workmanlike manner. At last accounts both mother and child were prospering finely." [545]

So life went on, in fair weather and foul, aboard the throbbing steamboats. The men and women who carved out their homes in the Upper Mississippi were not readily deterred by the vicissitudes of life about them. Their yoke had not been an easy one back home : here in the Upper Mississippi Valley they could hope for a better life. Fully aware of the impelling forces, but amazed at the mad rush to the Northwest the New York *Independent* declared that "probably not less than a quarter of a million of people will emigrate the present year to our frontier States and Territories. Never was there such excitement on the subject before. It pervades all classes, in every city, town, and village. Students in colleges, professional, businessmen — the most talented in all quarters — are taking possession of the soil, as surer foundation for permanent prosperity than can be found in any other vocation. What a glorious spectacle, and how promising the future!" [546]

This same bustling energy and spirit was exhibited by the polyglot passengers aboard Upper Mississippi steamboats. The more sordid events of life were quickly forgotten amid new friends and fresh scenes. Bound for Minnesota in 1849, E. S. Seymour, a traveler aboard the steamboat *Senator*, was delighted with the activity at Prairie du Chien and McGregor as the boat took on board "a large number of cattle and horses, wagons and plows, and barrels of flour" belonging to Minnesota immigrants and the Winnebago Indians at Crow Wing. As Seymour relates : "We had now a respectable cargo, and some eighty passengers, principally destined for St. Paul, the new and flourishing metropolis of Minnesota. Laboring men, enticed by the allurements of high wages, were wending their way hither. Doctors, lawyers, and divines were on board, seeking in this last of modern El Dorados a new field for professional labors. Invalids, desirous of recruiting their health by inhaling the bracing air of a northern clime, were pushing forward for a higher latitude, to enjoy that boon of nature — good health — without which all other enjoyments are imaginary and insipid; citizens of Minnesota, residing in different portions of that territory, who had been below for the transaction of business, were returning home on this boat. An interesting circle of intelligent travelers; a good boat, without a liquor bar to disturb its quietness, commanded by an obliging and sociable captain, assisted by polite and attentive officers and an orderly crew; the beautiful and novel scenery and fine weather, caused the hours to pass away in an agreeable manner. As the sun threw its first rays upon the hill-tops, we sprung from our berths to catch a glimpse of the fresh morning landscape; and as his last rays, at the close of day, were lingering on the declivities, new and interesting features of natural scenery still attracted our attention, and furnished themes for conversation and reflection." [547]

39

Cabin and Deck Passage

THE CREATION of the Territory of Minnesota in 1849 opened to settlement most of the country adjoining the Upper Mississippi. During the late forties the potato famine in Ireland and the revolutions on the continent were responsible for a tremendous influx of immigrants. The "Fashionable Tour" and the normal movement of people up and down the Mississippi added to the profits of steamboat captains. Just as lead dominated the period before 1850 so the passenger traffic exceeded in value that of any other single cargo between about 1850 and 1870. While it would be difficult to set a definite date at which one could say that passenger receipts became greater than those on freight, the turn of the half century seems to mark the transition.

During the thirties the rate of passage for immigrants did not differ greatly from that of a later date, although there was an appreciable difference in the safety, convenience, speed, and luxury of steamboats. Passenger fares were governed by the number of passengers, the number of boats in the trade, the season of the year, and the stage of the water.

In 1833 Samuel W. Pond, a Sioux missionary, advised his brother Gideon that cabin fare from Pittsburgh to St. Louis was twenty-four dollars and deck passage but eight dollars. Cabin fare from St. Louis to Galena was fifteen dollars, and deck passage could be procured for five dollars. Provisions could be "found" along the way; but Samuel warned against the "coarse fare" of the steerage and counseled that it would be better to "pay a little more than too little". He suggested bread as the principal diet. In purchasing a ticket Pond warned his brother not to get one "clear through", since captains often decided not to go the full distance and would not refund the money.[548]

The following year Reverend Robert Baird published a guide to the West. According to Baird it cost fifty-five dollars to travel by stage and steamboat from Philadelphia to St. Louis. By traveling as a deck hand and assisting the crew at landings, immigrants could reduce the fare from Pittsburgh to Galena to as low as ten dollars. Immigrants who preferred the New Orleans route had little difficulty in meeting the ordinary expenses to Galena. From New Orleans to St. Louis cabin passage could be secured for twenty-five dollars and from that point one could travel for six dollars to Beardstown or Quincy. The usual fare from St. Louis to Galena was twelve dollars. "Those who cannot afford to take what is called a *cabin passage* in a steam boat", Baird writes, "may be accommodated with what is called a *deck* passage. The *deck*, for the use of such passengers, is protected from the weather, but has no other convenience. Passengers on deck furnish their own beds and provisions. Many respectable emigrants find it to their advantage to travel in this way." [549]

Peck also spoke highly of the frugality and popularity

of a deck passage. "The *deck* for such passengers is usually in the midship, forward the engine, and is protected from the weather. Passengers furnish their own provisions and bedding. They often take their meals at the cabin table, with the boat hands, and pay 25 cents a meal. Thousands pass up and down the rivers as deck passengers, especially emigrating families, who have their bedding, provisions, and cooking utensils on board." [550]

An English family of seven, bound upstream from New Orleans to St. Louis in 1831, found traveling as deck passengers both enjoyable and cheap. "We had engaged to find our own provisions", the mother relates, "but on account of their cheapness, or partly because I acted the part of matron to such as needed my assistance, we were frequently presented with young fowls, coffee, rice, &c., so that our food cost us very little on the river." [551]

On July 16, 1836, Reverend Alfred Brunson arrived at Prairie du Chien from the headwaters of the Ohio. His mode of travel was frequently adopted by pioneer families. "He brought with him from Meadville, Pennsylvania, by canal, French creek and the Alleghany river to Pittsburgh, thence eighteen hundred miles by the Ohio and the Mississippi a keel-boat with four families, including his own, and a dwelling-house ready to be put together. The cost of towage from Pittsburg by steamboats was $650 of which $400 was the charge from St. Louis to Prairie du Chien." [552]

During the forties the rate from St. Louis to Galena remained around twelve dollars with deck passengers trav-

eling at half that figure. The fare from Galena to St.
Paul stood at about eight dollars when there was no competition. Boats operating on the Mississippi and its tributaries charged a proportionate sum. The following schedule for the Mississippi-Wisconsin rivers was posted at
Galena in 1845 by the *Maid of Iowa*:

GALENA TO	NUMBER OF MILES	PASSAGE
Dubuque	27	$1.00
Potosi	42	1.50
Cassville	57	2.00
Prairie du Chien	90	3.00
English Prairie	140	4.00
Helena	166	4.50
Sac Prairie	191	4.75
Fort Winnebago	220	5.00
Point Boss	350	8.50

Deck passengers were carried either way at half fare and
paid only twenty-five cents for meals. Freight charges
were twenty-five cents per hundred to Prairie du Chien,
fifty cents to English Prairie or Helena, seventy-five cents
to Fort Winnebago, and one dollar and a half to Point Boss.
The *Maid of Iowa* left Galena with a heavy load of freight
and passengers for Mississippi and Wisconsin river ports.[553]

Competition brought rates to a ruinous level, and captains were often barely able to pay the wood bill after a
trip. Captain Harris waged a bitter fight against the Minnesota Packet Company in 1852. Immigrants could travel
from Galena to St. Paul for from one to three dollars —
a rate which most persons felt ashamed to pay. A typical

Cabin and Deck Passage

news item for 1852 reads : "The West Newton and the Nominee, both crowded with passengers, arrived at St. Paul Tuesday night, at about the same minute, in a strife all the way up. The old Nominee tucked up her petticoats and the way she did leg it through, kept the West Newton at the top of her speed. We regret that this competition is reaching to such a pitch — or in fact that it should reach *any* pitch. Let the lines both live and work at fair prices, without any such strife." [554]

Fat years followed the lean ones, however, and in 1855 the Minnesota Packet Company declared dividends amounting to $100,000 for the season's business. Captain Harris cleared $44,000 with the *War Eagle*; while the *City Belle* made $30,000 in profits. [555]

The balance sheet of the steamboat *Milwaukee* for the year 1857 shows that the sum of $53,939.65 was taken in on passages, while the receipts on freight totaled only $22,809.65. The net profit at the close of the season was $20,333.05. The *Milwaukee* cost the Prairie du Chien, Hudson, and St. Paul Company $41,741.22 ı she was well on the way to paying for herself the first season. The following year the *Ocean Wave*, a boat which cost $19,500, earned $26,451.63 on passages and $9,373.13 on freight. Despite intense competition the *Milwaukee* took in $29,399.86 in passages and $9,779.44 in freight in 1859. [556] Deck passengers were carried from Dubuque to St. Paul for two dollars in 1859. [557] The Galena, Dubuque, Dunleith, and Minnesota Packet Company schedule for two successive years was as follows: [558]

[377]

Steamboating on Upper Mississippi

PLACE	FARE		FREIGHT	
	1858	1859	1858	1859
McGregor & Prairie du Chien	$3.00	$2.50	20	10
Lansing	3.50	2.75	22	15
La Crosse	4.50	3.50	25	15
Winona	5.00	4.00	27	15
Reed's Landing	6.00	5.00	30	15
Prescott & Hastings	7.50	5.75	33	20
St. Paul	8.00	6.00	33	20

In spite of the movement of troops and volunteers a temporary lull occurred during the early stages of the Civil War which tended toward a more equal division of freight and passenger receipts. The *Milwaukee* and *Itasca* received $26,775.45 and $25,973.61 respectively on passages, while their freight receipts amounted to $20,682.58 and $25,973.12.[559]

It would be difficult to estimate the exact earnings in the passenger trade throughout the period of immigration into the Upper Mississippi Valley. Rates were high in some seasons only to be knocked down when competition broke out. In 1866 the Northwestern Packet Company announced a rate of ten dollars for cabin passage between Dubuque and St. Paul. Deck passengers were carried for six dollars. Such rates would ensure a good return if there was any traffic on the river.[560]

When the balance sheet of the Northwestern Union Packet Company was struck for 1867, the *Phil Sheridan*, the *Milwaukee*, the *War Eagle*, the *Northern Belle*, the *Addie Johnston*, the *Itasca*, the *Key City*, the *Diamond Jo*, and the *Keokuk* each averaged almost $30,000 profits for the season. The *Northern Belle* alone cleared $36,675.18 in 1867.[561] Most of these boats were engaged in the passenger and freight business and did no bulk towing. The heavy trips in immigrants and ordinary passengers reported by these boats throughout a highly competitive season make $150,000 a fair estimate of their earnings from passages.

Beginning with the year 1868 the fight between Davidson's White Collar Line and the Northern Line of St. Louis developed into a death struggle for supremacy. Rates of passage from St. Louis to St. Paul might vary anywhere from five dollars to eighteen dollars. The rates might change several times during the course of a season as the two corporations came to an agreement, only to break it at the first opportunity.

The season of 1868 opened with a brisk rate war which was terminated by a mutual agreement in mid-June when the two contestants agreed to charge uniformly reasonable rates. "The time for cheap traveling and cheap shipping is over for this season", declared the *Dubuque Herald* on June 18, 1868. "Even rich companies and corporations 'cool down' when their pocket is affected by competition. Their 'mad' has played out". Cabin passage from St. Louis to Davenport was set at nine dollars, and eighteen was charged to St. Paul. The rates from Dubuque up were set as follows:

Dubuque to Cassville	$1.50
Dubuque to McGregor	3.00
Dubuque to Lansing	4.00

Steamboating on Upper Mississippi

| Dubuque to La Crosse | 4.75 |
| Dubuque to St. Paul | 9.00 |

The following month, however, competition broke out with renewed fury as the Northern Line instructed its agent at St. Paul not to "let a passenger slip out of his hands at any rate of passage." [562] Whole families and colonies of immigrants might be carried at ridiculously low rates on such occasions.

The influx of immigrants gave captains and owners their richest profits during the prosperous days of Upper Mississippi steamboating. In diverting immigrants northward steamboats shaped the political, economic, social, and religious structure of the Upper Mississippi Valley. Thousands of immigrants, both native and foreign, were led to the land of Canaan by letters from those who had gone before and were delighted with the facility of transportation as well as with the soil and climate.

A colorful drama was enacted on the decks of such boats as the *War Eagle*, the *Grey Eagle*, the *Canada*, the *Hawkeye State*, the *Sucker State*, the *Tom Jasper*, the *Milwaukee*, the *Davenport*, the *Phil Sheridan*, and the hundreds of craft which plied the Upper Mississippi during the heyday of steamboating. Such boats in landing their cosmopolitan passengers left their tribute of farmers, landseekers, tradesmen, soldiers, and others who helped to settle the Upper Mississippi Valley.

40

Many Cargoes and Strange

UPSTREAM CARGOES included all the personal possessions of immigrants together with the steadily mounting shipments of the manufactured goods from the East. Old bills of lading showed rakes, hoes, spades, axes, grindstones, and an ever increasing number of tools and farm machinery. A precious cargo of freight carried by the *Dr. Franklin* in 1853 listed three barrels of whiskey, one barrel of brandy, one barrel of Old Rye whiskey, one barrel of crackers, a ten gallon keg of gin, a keg of port wine, another of dark brandy, some St. Cruse rum, peach brandy, and Holland gin, together with an appropriate number of flasks, tumblers, and decanters in which to serve such refreshments.[563]

Fredrika Bremer, noted Swedish author, traveled on several Upper Mississippi steamboats during the course of her peregrinations in the Mississippi Valley. Both passengers and cargoes were carefully noted by this observative traveler. On one occasion, while aboard the steamboat *Belle Key* bound downstream for New Orleans, Miss Bremer expressed amazement at the livestock carried on the lower deck. "I call it Noah's Ark", she writes, "because it has more than a thousand animals on board, on the deck below us and above us. Immense oxen, really mammoth oxen, so fat that they can scarcely walk — cows, calves, horses, mules, sheep, pigs, whole herds of them,

[381]

send forth the sounds of their gruntings from the lower deck, and send up to us between times any thing but agreeable odors; and on the deck above us turkeys gobble — geese, ducks, hens, and cocks crow and fight, and little pigs go rushing wildly about, and among the poultry pens." [564]

Cargoes of livestock added profit as well as odor to steamboating. The earliest steamboats were too small to carry herds of cattle and hogs, and so these were generally driven overland. On May 11, 1836, the initial issue of the Du Buque *Visitor* notified drovers that five to six hundred head of cattle could be disposed of advantageously at that point. By 1850, with steamboats larger and barges coming into use, captains began to load their boats to the water's edge with livestock. In June, 1851, the *Excelsior* carried seventy-seven head of beef cattle northward for the Sioux who were negotiating the Treaty of Traverse des Sioux. A month later the *Nominee* brought farmers with cattle, horses, and agricultural implements — besides 150 head of cattle and sixty head of sheep for Coulter & Rogers, butchers.

A citizen of St. Paul was astounded at the fine stock brought upstream on the *Dr. Franklin* in 1853 — one "milch cow" alone weighing "upwards of sixteen hundred pounds". In 1857 the *City Belle*, the *W. H. Denny*, the *W. L. Nelson*, and the *W. L. Ewing* were jammed with horses, mules, cattle, sheep, and hogs from central Illinois. By that time northern Iowa was contributing livestock to Minnesota; a Dubuque editor saw twenty head of fine cattle driven aboard the *Northern Belle*. In 1858 the *Pembina* arrived at St. Paul with 216 cattle and 100 hogs.[565]

Sawmills, gristmills, and flourmills were transported aboard Upper Mississippi steamboats. On December 21, 1836, the Du Buque *Visitor* announced that a Philadelphian would bring a steam sawmill around to Dubuque immediately after the opening of navigation. In 1838 the steamboat *Palmyra* brought supplies and equipment to establish the first sawmill on the St. Croix River.[566] The *Red Wing* steamed proudly up to the St. Paul levee in May of 1857 with the machinery and equipment necessary to construct a sawmill at Kasota. A month later the *Hamburg* appeared with a sawmill which was shipped aboard the *Medora* to South Bend on the Minnesota River. At the same time the *Jacob Traber* was seen at the St. Paul levee with the engines and machinery for two sawmills to be installed at New Ulm on the Minnesota River.[567]

In 1844 a steamboat brought up the brick for the Dousman home at Prairie du Chien.[568] Eight years later the pious *Nominee* brought up a $600 organ for Rev. E. D. Neill's church at St. Paul. Although the Reverend Neill was not a Baptist, the organ had been accidentally immersed en route. It was hoped the damage could be repaired.[569]

In July of 1858 the steamboat *Tigress* arrived at Dubuque with a large cargo of the "celebrated Nauvoo stone" of the same quality that had been used in constructing the Mormon Temple at Nauvoo. The stones were "cut and shaped" for the new Custom House; but an editor declared that Dubuque limestone was just as good and that local labor and enterprise should be allowed to make the money.[570]

There was rejoicing among St. Paul firemen in 1858 over the arrival of the fire engine, *Hope Company No. 1.* This handsome "double deck" machine, which weighed 2800 pounds and cost $2400, was painted a "rich blue" and was "appropriately guilded". It was equipped with 500 feet of durable hose reeled on a tender and could throw five streams at once. Its arrival was marred by an unhappy note : the steamboat had charged $100 for transportation, which the city council paid under protest. The excessive charge was in retaliation for the high wharfage collected by the city. The fire-fighters promptly withdrew their patronage from the boat.[571]

Immense shipments of farm machinery were carried aboard steamboats. The development of agricultural implements is exhibited by the character of farming machinery transported upstream : tools were simple during the thirties and forties, as manifested by bills of lading, but each decade witnessed an advance. Seventeen plows and eight ox yokes were aboard the *Arizona* in 1857 when she arrived at St. Paul from Pittsburgh. A decade later (in 1866) steamboats were discharging reapers, mowers, plows, and miscellaneous assortments of tools and machinery at Upper Mississippi ports. Competitive trials were often held to determine the superiority of such agricultural implements as Ball's Ohio, the Dodge, the

Buckeye, the McCormick, the J. P. Manny, the Kirby, the Quaker Boy, and the Champion.[572]

The steamboat *Canada* passed Dubuque in May, 1867, with 264 reapers aboard. Throughout the season the *Canada*, the *Reserve*, and other craft landed farm implements at Dubuque and other ports. The following year the *Molly McPike*, the *Ida Fulton*, the *City of St. Paul*, and the *Hawkeye State* left their tribute of mowers, reapers, threshers, plows, and other agricultural implements. On July 24, 1869, the *Bannock City* arrived at Dubuque from Fulton with four barges loaded principally with agricultural implements. The *Bannock City* put off four threshers at Dubuque; and on the same day the *Sucker State* and the *Bill Henderson* were industriously discharging threshers and reapers.[573]

In the fall of each year steamboats carried heavy cargoes of fruit upstream. The *Henry Clay* left 200 barrels of apples at Dubuque in October, 1857. Thousands of barrels of apples were discharged at Dubuque and upriver ports in the fall of 1866: in a single trip the *Minnesota*, the *Muscatine*, and the *Pembina* were seen putting off from 200 to 500 barrels each. Early in November the *Pine Bluff* came up with 1000 barrels; and the *Sucker State* put in an appearance a few days later with 1100 more. The apple trade at Dubuque was described as enormous. In the fall of 1869 rousters on the *Canada*, the *City of St. Paul*, the *Dubuque*, and the *Lady Pike* rolled barrel after barrel down the gangplank — the *Tom Jasper* alone leaving over a thousand at Dubuque. For more than a generation the transportation of fresh fruits to river towns afforded steamboats a profitable seasonal employment.[574]

From distant Pittsburgh steamboats brought hundreds of tons of glassware, hardware, and other merchandise. Cincinnati, Louisville, and St. Louis added to the volume of manufactured goods passing upstream to a country not yet self-sufficient. Sometimes Upper Mississippi steamboats went to Pittsburgh to open their upriver season with a thumping cargo of from 300 to 700 tons of merchandise. On one trip in 1857 the *Cremona* discharged at Dubuque alone 1924 packages weighing over 111 tons! [575]

Wild boats in the Ohio River trade would frequently bring a cargo around to the Upper Mississippi. "The Delaware, an outside boat", notes the Dubuque *Herald* of May 12, 1866, "arrived yesterday from Pittsburgh, which place she left with 1,400 tons of iron, nails, glass, and drugs loaded on her deck and on three barges. After discharging about 35 tons here she pushed on up the river." Most of the time, however, Ohio River merchandise was transferred at St. Louis to an Upper Mississippi boat.[576]

The heavy cargoes of stoves carried from St. Louis and Ohio River ports each fall are suggestive of the great number of new hearth fires. Within the space of ten days in 1869, seven steamboats deposited nearly three hundred stoves on the Dubuque wharf boat. The *Ida Fulton* brought up forty-four stoves, the *Diamond Jo* sixty-seven, and the *Phil Sheridan* seventy-six. In addition each boat discharged a large amount of merchandise.[577]

Still another cargo originating in Pittsburgh was coal.

Many Cargoes and Strange

In 1855 the Dubuque Gas Company, after experimenting with Rock Island and La Salle coal, found neither satisfactory. The following spring a Dubuque editor expressed delight that coal could be brought all the way from Pittsburgh and cost "on delivery, 40 cents per bushel".[578] In 1857 the *Resolute* brought to Dubuque two barges and three flats with 6000 bushels of Illinois coal, 4000 bushels of Pittsburgh coal, and 2600 bushels of coke from the same port.

St. Paul was not so pleased with the charges on Pittsburgh coal. Late in May, 1857, the steamboat *La Crosse* arrived with 200 tons of coal which cost at the mine only three or four cents per bushel. After carrying it two thousand miles by water (over half the distance being upstream) the coal came to one dollar a bushel in St. Paul. The captain of the *La Crosse* estimated that it had cost him $600 to bring the coal over the Des Moines Rapids, and $150 to carry it over the Upper Rapids. A few days later the *Rocket* arrived at St. Paul with 4500 bushels of coal, 1500 kegs of nails, and a large quantity of iron and hardware. A St. Paul editor complained that the manifest of the *Rocket* was "three yards long"; though he had offered to print all manifests, he did not attempt this one.[579]

Downstream cargoes included the products of a raw frontier community. From Minnesota, steamboats towed ice downstream to take care of the needs of those living in southern climes. In 1860 a Minnesota paper noted that special barges for ice shipments had been built in Minne-

[387]

apolis by the firm of Eustis & Brackett. "They are each 120 feet in length, 22 feet wide, and contain 375 tons of ice", the editor remarked. "Ice in Minnesota is a pretty tolerable reliable crop, and being in good demand among the fire-eaters of the South, will, no doubt prove a profitable business in the future." [580]

Early in April, 1869, the *Lady Pike* took two barges of ice south. The *Bengal Tiger* also towed ice barges in 1869. Late in October she left the ice business and went after the "potato trade in a lively way". After a brief flurry in potatoes, the boat headed for New Orleans with three barges of pressed hay which her enterprising skipper planned to sell at the ports below. [581] Shipment of hay to New Orleans had been inaugurated as early as 1860 when the "mammoth hay boat" *Challenge* left Muscatine with 97,000 bundles of lath, 25,000 sacks of grain, and almost 2000 bales of hay. [582]

Minnesota cranberries were frequently observed aboard steamboats bound downstream : 2135 bushels were shipped from Minnesota as early as 1849. In 1851 the steamboat *Excelsior* left a barge at St. Paul to be filled with about eighty tons of "vitreous white sand" for a St. Louis manufacturer. An editor hoped that sand would soon be used in manufacturing at St. Paul. The growth of Minnesota in manufacturing is attested by the arrival of the *Minneapolis* at Dubuque from above with 651 sleigh shoes and 50 "cauldron kettles". [583]

Strange cargoes often found their way on board. The loungers on the levee at St. Louis in 1831 must have stared in open-mouthed amazement as a giant elephant complacently ambled off a boat from below.[584] A generation later Galenians awaited the arrival of Herr Dreisbach with his mammoth circus, including the elephant Hannibal (weighing 10,830 pounds), a rhinoceros, some lions, and other "varmints". The smaller pioneer communities often spoke wistfully of such traveling menageries and in 1851 the *Minnesota Pioneer* carried a Cincinnati item noting that Herr Dreisbach and his "celebrated Pet, the Brazilian Tiger, called Col. Alexander", had both registered in the clerk's book and taken passage on the *Julia Dean*. The other occupants of the cabin doubtless gave "Col. Alexander" a wide berth as he stalked silently through the cabin with his master.[585]

In 1853 the Territory of Minnesota sent a splendid buffalo as one of its contributions to the Crystal Palace Exhibition in New York. The patience of this rather surly beast was not improved by the irritating prods of the roustabouts on the *Ben Franklin*. After being roughly pushed from boat to boat, led through the streets of Cincinnati, and finally shipped by train to New York, the distracted beast gave vent to his feelings when the committee appeared to pass on his fitness as an exhibit : a furious charge sent the members scurrying for safety as they formulated their verdict. He was not accepted.[586]

In August, 1861, a La Crosse dispatch noted that the steamboat *Key City* collided with Dan Rice's circus steamboat nineteen miles below that point. Neither boat was damaged, but the cage containing the "trained Rhinoceros" was knocked overboard. First accounts indicated that "Mr. Rhinoceros", who was valued at $20,000, had been drowned. No "insurance on his life" was carried, so the loss would have been a heavy one. Happily for all, the rhinoceros appears to have been rescued; for, a few days later William E. Wellington, the genial clerk of the Minnesota Packet Company, found "Mr. Rhinoceros" making heroic efforts to extricate himself from the buoy chain of the wharf boat at Dubuque.[587]

The following June a Dubuque newspaper suggested: "All persons who have never seen a gorilla had better avail themselves of seeing the only one ever in the Western country. He is on exhibition at the Wharf Boat and is one of the rarest specimens of his species in America. He is owned by Barnum, in New York, who sent him to Iowa to pasture for a few weeks. He is to be shipped to St. Louis on the *Canada*, Tuesday morning." [588]

Such were the cargoes carried by Upper Mississippi steamboats in the balmy days of river transportation. From hold to texas, steamboats frequently constituted a veritable museum that for sheer novelty would have done credit to Phineas T. Barnum himself. But steamboats went Barnum one better : the unique cargoes ranging from apes to zebras added interest but little profit to steamboating. It was the steady flow of the bulk commodities of an ever expanding frontier that helped to sustain steamboating and bolster the receipts of captains and corporations.

41

Captain Joseph Throckmorton

PRIOR TO THE advent of the railroad no type of pioneer was more influential than the steamboat captain in expanding the frontier and building an empire in the West. Adventurous, hardy, ambitious, he brought his crude craft into waters frequented hitherto only by the transient visit of the keelboat. He offered a means of communication and transportation to the Indian Agent, the missionary, the fur trader, and the soldier, as well as to the pioneers who were straggling into the West with their families and few worldly possessions. He played an important rôle in the economic life of the Mississippi Valley.

Of all the pioneer river captains on the Upper Mississippi, none was better known than Joseph Throckmorton who over a period of twenty years commanded a dozen boats and had a financial interest in probably as many more. Efficient, prudent, and every inch a gentleman, he won the respect of those he served and established a high standard for steamboat transportation.

Little is known of the early life of this picturesque riverman. Born in Monmouth County, New Jersey, on June 16, 1800, he made his first venture in the business world as a youngster with a mercantile firm in New York City. But he soon tired of this work, and in 1828 moved to Pittsburgh where in company with several other young men he bought a part interest in the steamboat *Red Rover*. While plying between Pittsburgh and Zanesville, Ohio, the boat collided with another vessel and sank. After she was raised Throckmorton seems to have acquired a controlling interest; he then brought his boat around to St. Louis where he immediately engaged in the upriver trade.[589]

The *Red Rover* arrived at St. Louis late in the month of June, 1828, just five years after the *Virginia* had made the maiden steamboat trip above the Des Moines Rapids to Fort Snelling.[590] A few scattered villages were cropping up on both sides of the river below the Lower Rapids; and farmhouses were beginning to appear above the rapids on the Illinois shore. The western side was a wilderness broken only by an occasional Indian village or the rude hut of a half-breed. Except for the few military outposts and fur-trading establishments along the Mississippi and the lead mines huddled about Fever River, the country was still a virgin estate.

Scarcely two dozen steamboats had preceded the *Red Rover* in the five years that had elapsed since the trip of of the *Virginia*, and most of these were transient craft. Lead shipments had just reached a point where captains could look for a plentiful cargo, and Throckmorton was not slow in taking advantage of this opportunity. Occasionally a boatload of supplies or a detachment of troops afforded a profitable trip to Fort Crawford at Prairie du Chien or Fort Snelling at the mouth of the Minnesota. The transportation of Indian annuities and delegations also brought a tidy sum to this ever watchful steamboat captain. But the year of 1828 was rather unprofitable and Throckmorton was forced to make several trips to the Illinois and Missouri rivers. When winter shut him off from this trade he went around to the Ohio and engaged in the commerce of that river with the Lower Mississippi.[591]

Navigation opened early in 1829. The *Red Rover* was lying at the St. Louis levee on April 14th, having already completed one trip to Fever River.[592] Midsummer found the boat at the head of the Lower Rapids, unable to proceed downstream on account of low water and hopefully waiting for a cargo with which to return to the mines. Here Caleb Atwater, one of the three commissioners appointed by the government to treat with the Indians at Prairie du Chien, came upon the impatient Throckmorton. The low stage of the water had abruptly ended Atwater's voyage on the steamboat *Missouri* at the foot of the rapids. While making his way on foot along the river from Fort Edwards to the head of the rapids, he found many of the packages which he had forwarded several weeks before scattered along the banks and exposed to the elements. The sight of the *Red Rover* must have been as pleasing to Atwater as the prospects of a lucrative trip were to Throckmorton.[593]

By sunset most of the goods were on board and provision was made for the shipment of the remainder on the next trip. Darkness set in before the boat had gone many miles and orders were given to tie up for the night. It was not

[393]

until noon of the third day that Throckmorton was able to reach Rock Island. Low water and innumerable sandbars made steamboating extremely hazardous. In order to lighten the boat so that she might more easily twist and squirm her way to the head of the Upper Rapids all passengers were required to walk along the shore. Only Brigadier General John McNeil and the ladies on board were excepted. All afternoon was spent in bringing the boat to the head of the Rock Island or Upper Rapids where Captain Throckmorton tied up for the night.

Two days later the *Red Rover* reached the mouth of Fever River. After visiting the lead mines at both Galena and Dubuque, the boat proceeded to Prairie du Chien. Here the commissioners were landed. Then Throckmorton steamed down the river to pick up a cargo of lead and return with the remaining annuity goods which had been left at the head of the Lower Rapids. In the middle of August the *Red Rover* again carried to St. Louis all the commissioners except Atwater who returned overland to his home.[594]

In 1830 the first coöperative association of steamboat captains on the Upper Mississippi was formed by Throckmorton and Captain S. Shallcross. During the period of low water Captain Shallcross operated the *Chieftain* between St. Louis and the Lower Rapids, while the *Red Rover* plied the river above. To avoid delay in the transit of goods, keels were provided to transport freight over the rapids in the event of extreme low water. Previous to this agreement, about the first of August, Throckmorton had made six trips to the lead district and so had covered a distance of about six thousand miles. The new plan met with immediate success since both passengers and shippers were disposed to patronize the boat that could guarantee the completion of a trip.[595]

In 1831 Throckmorton bought the *Winnebago* and formed a similar combination with Captain James May of the *Enterprise*.[596] Late in the fall, however, he sold his interest in the *Winnebago* and went over on the Ohio River to build the steamboat *Warrior*. Subsequent events proved the fitness of this name.

The steamboat *Warrior* is one of the most celebrated of Upper Mississippi steamboats. Owned by Captain Throckmorton and William Hempstead of Galena, the *Warrior* and her safety barge were built at Pittsburgh during the winter of 1831-1832. She was 111 feet 5 inches long, had a 19-foot beam, a 5-foot hold, and measured 100 tons burden. She had one deck and no mast, a transom stern, a cabin above deck for officers and crew, and a figurehead. Power was furnished by a high pressure engine and three boilers.

The *Warrior* was one of the few steamboats to tow a safety barge on the Upper Mississippi. Such an innovation served both as a protection to the passengers from explosions and as a means of decreasing the draft of the boat to facilitate passing over the rapids in low water. The safety barge, was 111 feet 8 inches long, had a 16-foot beam, a 4-foot 8 inch hold, and measured 85 tons.[597] It was probably modeled after the pioneer of its kind which had been used on the Ohio River by the *Merchant* in 1826. This safety barge had fifty-two berths, three cabins, and drew but twenty inches of water.[598] Captain Throckmorton was the third man to bring this type of craft to the Upper Mississippi : Captain Shallcross of the steamboat *St. Louis and Galena Packet* had introduced one as early as 1827.[599]

Early in the spring of 1832 the rumblings of the approaching Black Hawk War were daily becoming more threatening, and when the storm finally broke the steamboats on the Upper Mississippi and Illinois rivers were soon busily engaged in transporting troops and supplies. Steamboating on these waters became so hazardous that it was necessary to barricade the cabins and pilot house against the fire of the Indians who frequently lay in ambush along the shore and fired upon the passing boats. It was midsummer before Throckmorton brought the *Warrior* and her barge to St. Louis, whence he immediately set out for the seat of war.[600]

The *Warrior* arrived at Prairie du Chien just as Black Hawk and his band were retreating toward the Mississippi. She was immediately pressed into service, and the captain was given orders to patrol the river above the fort to prevent the Indians from crossing. Lieutenants James W. Kingsbury and Reuben Holmes, together with a company of fifteen regulars and six volunteers, were sent aboard and a small six-pounder was placed in the bow of the boat.

Captain Throckmorton first steamed to Wabasha's village where about a hundred and fifty "friendly" Indians were enlisted to help patrol the river. Thence he proceeded

Captain Joseph Throckmorton

downstream and reached the spot where De Soto now stands just as Black Hawk and his warriors were pouring through the hills to the river. Although Throckmorton was not in command of the troops aboard the *Warrior*, he also participated in the fight. On August 3rd he penned a laconic account from Prairie du Chien :

"On our way down we met one of the Sioux band, who informed us that the Indians, our enemies, were on Bad Axe River to the number of four hundred. We stopped and cut some wood and prepared for action. About four o'clock on Wednesday afternoon [August 1st] we found the gentlemen where he stated he left them. As we neared them they raised a white flag and endeavored to decoy us; but we were a little too old for them, for instead of landing, we ordered them to send a boat on board, which they declined. After about fifteen minutes' delay, giving them time to remove a few of their women and children, we let slip a six-pounder loaded with canister, followed by a severe fire of musketry; and if ever you saw straight blankets, you would have seen them there. I fought them at anchor most of the time, and we were all very much exposed. I have a ball which came in close by where I was standing, and passed through the bulkhead of the wheel-room. We fought them for about an hour or more, until our wood began to fail, and night coming on, we left and went on to the Prairie. This little fight cost them twenty-three killed and, of course, a great many wounded. We never lost a man and had but one man wounded".[601]

While this brief skirmish was of no great significance

[397]

in itself it served to check the Indians sufficiently to allow the troops to come up and completely rout them at Bad Axe a short time later. After the battle of Bad Axe, Brigadier General Henry Atkinson took passage on the *Warrior* to Jefferson Barracks. A short time later the *Winnebago* brought down Black Hawk and eleven of his headmen as prisoners.[602]

It was not merely the vicissitudes of war which presented perils to steamboat captains. In 1833 an event occurred on board the *Warrior* which might have proved far more fatal. This elicited "a gentle caution" from Throckmorton which was published in the *Missouri Republican* at St. Louis.

"We have many hardships to encounter, and are exposed to many dangers, which of course we submit to without a murmur;" wrote the captain, "but we would respectfully request our friends not to heap upon us, through their *kindness*, more than we can conveniently endure. Now, *a short story at a woodpile.* On loading my boat at a place of this kind last trip, I discovered several black marks upon the deck, which, on examination, I found to be gunpowder, from a box which my men were about to store away as dry goods, which in part did contain dry goods, but in the middle concealed, was a considerable quantity of powder, so carelessly placed, that it was strewn throughout the package. Now, I have only to request, that whenever any of my customers have powder to ship, that they will not conceal it, and thereby endanger our lives, but inform us of it. I am not a little surprised that so respectable a concern should attempt a thing of this kind, particularly as the freight would not have been more upon the article of powder than any other. I should suppose that shippers would have taken the *hint* after what has recently occurred on our western waters. At any rate, it is high time that *we* should. It is not my wish to complain, but *it is* my wish to run my boat with as much safety as possible; and I trust this gentle caution will be attended to." [603]

This sharp but courteous letter reveals a man not afraid to lose his trade if an abuse might be corrected. The "hint" undoubtedly referred to the explosion which occurred in July of the previous year on board the *Phoenix* as she was making her way up the Mississippi from New Orleans. A fire broke out on the *Phoenix*, but the boat might have been saved by the strenuous efforts of the captain and crew if some gunpowder, secreted in packages, had not exploded. [604]

Throckmorton continued in command of the *Warrior* until the close of the season of 1835. The boat remained on the upper river in command of Captain E. H. Gleim throughout the season of 1836, but thereafter she disappeared from the record. [605] Five years of active service probably made the boat unfit for further use.

The 119-ton *St. Peters* (said to be the largest boat on the Upper Mississippi at the time) arrived at Galena in command of Captain Throckmorton on June 8, 1836. [606] On July 2nd she tied up at Fort Snelling with a cargo of supplies. Among the passengers were the French geographer

J. N. Nicollet, and several ladies from St. Louis who were on a pleasure excursion to the Falls of St. Anthony. Throckmorton continued in the upriver trade with the *St. Peters* until early fall, when he went back to Pittsburgh and built the *Ariel* [607] and the *Burlington*. Late in May, 1837, Throckmorton brought out the *Burlington* [608]— a boat that should be remembered if only for the many notable characters who graced her deck. By June 28, 1838, Throckmorton had completed his third trip to Fort Snelling, bringing with him one hundred and forty-six recruits of the Fifth Infantry. Prominent among the passengers carried that season were Colonel John Bliss, George Catlin, J. N. Nicollet, John C. Frèmont, Henry Atkinson, Franklin Steele, and the widow of Alexander Hamilton. [609]

At the beginning of the season of 1839 Throckmorton replaced the *Burlington* with the *Malta*, which was built in Pittsburgh at a cost of $18,000. [610] The usual business of carrying supplies and annuities to the forts on the Upper Mississippi occupied the first season. In the summer of 1840 the *Malta* was advertised in the Galena *Gazette* to make a pleasure excursion to the Falls of St. Anthony. [611] During the season of 1841 she made four trips to the lead district with five keels in tow, for which her total receipts were estimated to be $4000 on freight and $4000 on passengers. [612] Late in the fall of 1841, Throckmorton engaged the *Malta* in the Missouri River trade where she was snagged two miles above Laynesville, Missouri, at a point henceforth called Malta Bend. Within one minute she

Steamboat *Nominee* in the Galena basin in the early 1850's. This probably is the earliest photo in the *Petersen Collection* of almost 2,000 Upper Mississippi steamboats. Note the pigs of lead, weighing 70 pounds each, ready for shipment to St. Louis.

From Lewis's Das Illustrirte Mississippithal.

Dubuque was strategically located on the Mississippi and outstripped Galena in importance during the 1850's. Lead shipped from these two thriving ports was the dominant cargo until about 1850. The amount reaching St. Louis was double in value the Missouri River fur trade and the traffic on the Santa Fe Trail during the late 1840's.

JOSEPH THROCKMORTON
1800-1872

Joseph Throckmorton was one of the outstanding steamboatmen in the period from 1828 to 1848. He was a great favorite of Hercules Dousman and the American Fur Company. He commanded and owned, in whole or in part, a dozen different steamboats. After twenty years on the Upper Mississippi, Throckmorton entered the insurance business in St. Louis but in 1854 returned to steamboating, this time on the Missouri River. (See Chapter 41)

Risvold Collection

Russell Farnham, an employee of John Jacob Astor, traded in the Fort Edwards area until his death from cholera at St. Louis in 1832. His shipment of furs to the Chouteaus in 1829 is typical of the use made of steamboats.

In November of 1831 George Davenport and Russell Farnham testified that they had employed thirty clerks, traders, and boatmen in the Rock Island-Flint Hills area for seven years. They had brought out their American goods by means of steam, keel, or Mackinac boats. Their supplies consisted of horse bells and bridles, butcher knives, traps, tin, iron, and brass kettles, silver wrist bands, wampum, shot, ball, bar lead, powder, salt, rifles, guns, tobacco, and cotton. In addition, a wide variety of English goods was imported ranging from needles and thread to colored blankets and varied hued strouds.

View of steamboats lined up along Front Street in St. Louis in 1840.

St. Louis was the entrepot for steamboats hailing from the tributaries of the Mississippi.

The St. Louis levee in 1860—showing the Keokuk Packet Company wharfboat on the right.

Grain began to be carried downstream during the 1850's but the peak was reached in the period 1870-1890. Warehouses along the river, such as those shown above, and the bird's-eye view of Bellevue below, lined the Mississippi from St. Louis to St. Paul.

The importance of lumbering on Bellevue economy is depicted above.

Warehouses were frequently endangered by high water, as seen at East Dubuque.

The main cabin of the *Grand Republic*, rebuilt from the *Great Republic* in 1876, and measuring 350' x 56'8" x 10'6". She took 8,210 bales of cotton to New Orleans in 1876—a record to that date. The magnificent floating palace was short-lived, however, for on September 19, 1877, she caught fire at St. Louis and burned—a total loss. Contrast her palatial cabin with that of a more modest Upper Mississippi cabin of the Diamond Jo Line.

The above cabin would be typical of the cabins of steamboats of 500 tons and more that plied the Upper Mississippi in the period between 1860 and 1890. They did not have the "sumptuous" furnishings of Lower Mississippi boats, nor could they boast the deluxe menus rivaling those of the finest hotels and watering places in America. Although not as luxurious, Upper Mississippi craft won warm praise from the passengers who made the Grand Excursion of 1854. (See Chapter 32)

WILLIAM F. DAVIDSON
1825-1887

Commodore Wm. F. Davidson, whose steamboat career began in 1855 between La Crosse and St. Paul, crushed his competitors and ultimately absorbed all Upper Mississippi companies except the Diamond Jo Line. His boats carried white collars on their smokestacks and hence were known as the "White Collar Line."

(*Below*) Two views of the St. Louis levee showing barrels of apples still being shipped out in the 20th Century as they had been forwarded to Upper Mississippi ports since the 1850's.

Missouri Historical Society Photos.

Famous in song and story is the great race of the *Robert E. Lee* and the *Natchez* from New Orleans to St. Louis. The time of the winner—the *Robert E. Lee*—was 3 days, 18 hours, and 14 minutes for what was then given as 1,218 miles. The time may be compared with that of such Upper Mississippi race horses as the *Phil Sheridan*, the *Hawkeye State*, and the *Sucker State*.

On July 6, 1867, the *Dubuque Herald* noted that the *Phil Sheridan* and the *Hawkeye State* raced from St. Louis to Dubuque, the former winning in 40 hours and 45 minutes, making 17 landings enroute. The *Hawkeye State* continued upstream making a record run from St. Louis to St. Paul of 2 days, 21 hours, and 49 minutes. The following log was kept in the pilothouse of the *Hawkeye State*:

Wednesday—July 3		Thursday—July 4		Friday—July 5		Saturday—July 6	
Port	Hour	Port	Hour	Port	Hour	Port	Hour
St. Louis	4:30 P.M.	Louisiana	2:49 A.M.	Lyons	4:30 A.M.	Winona	2:31 A.M.
Alton	6:30 P.M.	Hannibal	5:35 A.M.	Dubuque	10:55 A.M.	Minneiska	4:18 A.M.
Grafton	7:58 P.M.	Quincy	7:23 A.M.	Guttenberg	2:40 P.M.	Red Wing	9:05 A.M.
		Keokuk	11:22 A.M.	Pr. du Chien	4:50 P.M.	Prescott	11:00 A.M.
		Burlington	3:45 P.M.	Lansing	7:40 P.M.	Hastings	11:15 A.M.
		Muscatine	8:46 P.M.	La Crosse	11:23 P.M.	St. Paul	1:52 P.M.
		Davenport	11:39 P.M.				

Steamboat	Date	Days	Hours	Minutes
Sucker State	June, 1861	3	16	57
Hawkeye State	June, 1861	3	6	20
Sucker State	June, 1867	2	23	48
Hawkeye State	July 3-6, 1867	2	21	49
Hawkeye State Round-trip Time	July 3-8, 1867	6	3	22

Leaving Clinton with two excursion barges in tow.

Diamond Jo steamboat *Josephine* with her excursion barge.

The raftboat *Musser* with Fourth of July excursionists.

The *Walk-in-the-Water* was the first steam craft to navigate the Upper Great Lakes. Launched at the Black Rock shipyards (now Buffalo, N.Y.) on May 28, 1818, she made her maiden trip in August and continued in service until wrecked off Buffalo in 1821. Thousands of immigrants crossed the Great Lakes to the Upper Mississippi. (See Chapter 36)

Fort Benton has generally been considered the head of navigation on the Missouri although a few boats might continue up to Great Falls. The story of the *Chippewa's* trip to Fort Benton is told in Chapter 48.

For two generations the Selkirk Colonists brought their furs and buffalo robes from Canada in huge two-wheel carts up the Red River of the North and down the Minnesota River to St. Paul to await the opening of navigation. (See Chapter 19)

FOR SAINT LOUIS!

The Regular Steam Packet

EAGLE!

THE undersigned, having chartered the above Steam-boat, for the purpose of accommodating all the citizens of ALTON, and the vicinity, who may wish to see the

Four Negroes Executed,

At St. Louis, on *FRIDAY NEXT*, would inform the public that the Boat will leave this place at SEVEN o'clock, A. M., and St. Louis at about FOUR, P. M., so as to reach home the same evening.

The Boat will be repaired and fitted up for the occasion; and every attention will be paid to the comfort of Passengers.

FARE FOR THE TRIP TO ST. LOUIS & BACK
ONLY $1 50 !!!

The Negroes are to be hung on the point of *Duncan's Island,* just below St. Louis. The Boat will drop alongside, so that ALL CAN SEE WITHOUT DIFFICULTY.

For Passage, apply to
W. A. Wentworth,
P. M. Pinckard.

ALTON, JULY 7, 1841

1888 Merry Christmas! 1888

STEAMBOAT EXCURSION!
TO

Fountain City!
On Tuesday, Dec. 25th.

STEAMER ROBERT HARRIS

And two barges will leave the levee at 2 o'clock in the afternoon for Fountain City with the Gate City Band aboard. All excursionists will please uniform in linen dusters and straw hats. Refreshments will be served on board, consisting of Minnesota Strawberries and Cream, Soda Water, Pop, Lemonade and Ice Cream.

FANS DISTRIBUTED FREE OF CHARGE

What is Home without a Mother? What is Winona without an

Excursion on Christmas Day?

Capt. Shorty will furnish Pop Corn to the boys and Boquets, Sweet Violets, Roses and Water Lillies to the Girls. O the Flowers that Bloom in the Spring, Tra La.

ROUND TRIP TICKETS ONLY 50 CENTS.

At Haesly's Cigar Store. For State Rooms apply to

W. C. PIERCE, Manager,   162 & 164 Walnut Street

Steamboat Bill and Skipper Bessie send their packet of Christmas cheer in the above reproduction of a historic hand bill.
MR. AND MRS. WILLIAM J. PETERSEN

Excursions of every variety have been held on Upper Mississippi steamboats.

The *Phil Sheridan,* the *Canada,* and the *Hawkeye State,* three of the finest Upper Mississippi steamboats, preparing to take on freight and passengers. Although normally not engaged in the excursion traffic, arrangements could be made in advance to charter one of these large boats on special occasions.

EMIGRATION

UP THE MISSISSIPPI RIVER.

The attention of Emigrants and the Public generally, is called to the now rapidly improving

TERRITORY OF MINNESOTA,

Containing a population of 150,000, and goes into the Union as a State during the present year. According to an act of Congress passed last February, the State is munificently endowed with Lands for Public Schools and State Universities, also granting five per cent. on all sales of U. S. Lands for Internal Improvements. On the 3d March, 1857, grants of Land from Congress was made to the leading Trunk Railroads in Minnesota, so that in a short time the trip from New Orleans to any part of the State will be made in from two and a half to three days. The

CITY OF NININGER,

Situated on the Mississippi River, 35 miles below St. Paul, is now a prominent point for a large Commercial Town, being backed by an extensive Agricultural, Grazing and Farming Country; has fine streams in the interior, well adapted for Milling in all its branches; and Manufacturing WATER POWER to any extent.

Mr. JOHN NININGER, (a Gentleman of large means, ideas and liberality, speaking the various languages) is the principal Proprietor of Nininger. He laid it out on such principle as to encourage all MECHANICS, Merchants, or Professions of all kinds, on the same equality and footing; the consequence is, the place has gone ahead with such rapidity that it is now an established City, and will annually double in population for years to come.

Persons arriving by Ship or otherwise, can be transferred without expense to Steamers going to Saint Louis; or stop at Cairo, and take Railroad to Dunleith (on the Mississippi). Steamboats leave Saint Louis and Dunleith daily for NININGER, and make the trip from Dunleith in 36 to 48 hours.

NOTICES.

1. All Railroads and Steamboats giving this card a conspicuous place, or *gratuitous insertion* in their cards, AIDS THE EMIGRANT and forwards their own interest.

2. For authentic documents, reliable information, and all particulars in regard to Occupations, Wages, Preëmpting Lands (in neighborhood), Lumber, Price of Lots, Expenses, &c., apply to
THOMAS B. WINSTON, 27 Camp street, New Orleans.
ROBERT CAMPBELL, St. Louis.
JOSEPH B. FORBES, Dunleith.

Ambitious townsite developers used every means to attract settlers to what came to be known as "Paper Towns." Pokeepsie, in north central Iowa, Rollingstone and Nininger, along the Mississippi in Minnesota, are but a few of such widely advertised townsites.

(*Middle*) The *Minnesota* was a 482-ton Northern Line packet built in Wheeling, West Virginia, in 1866. She was a regular in the Upper Mississippi trade to the North Star State for more than a decade.

(*Bottom*) The *Alex Mitchell* was a 512-ton North Western Union Packet Company boat built at La Crosse, Wisconsin, in 1870. Named for a prominent Wisconsin banker, railroad man, and congressman, she plied the Upper Mississippi until 1881 when she was dismantled and her engines placed in the *Gem City* while her cabin was put on to the *St. Paul*.

The *Hawkeye State* jammed with Iowa troops headed South.

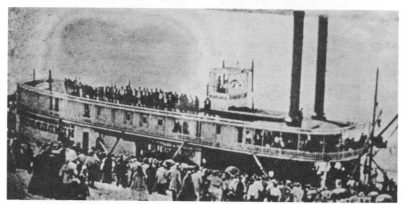

The *Bill Henderson* leaves Bellevue with Iowa Volunteers.

Harper's Weekly, May 25, 1861.

The Governor's Greys and Jackson Guards leaving Dubuque in 1861.

Harper's Weekly, February 1, 1862.

Departure of "Great Mississippi Expedition" downstream from Cairo.

Harper's Weekly, May 20, 1865.

Explosion of the Steamboat *Sultana,* April 27, 1865. The *Sultana,* with exchanged prisoners of war aboard, was destroyed on the Mississippi seven miles above Memphis. Fully 1,450 lives were lost, making it one of the five greatest marine disasters in history.

Bombardment and capture of Island Number Ten on April 7, 1862.

Hospital steamboat *Imperial* taking wounded to St. Louis after the battle of Pittsburgh Landing.

The Estes House at Keokuk (*upper center*) became a hospital for Union soldiers.

Harper's Weekly, August 1, 1863.

Capture of Vicksburg, July 4, 1863. Arrival of Admiral Porter's fleet.

Harper's Weekly, August 8, 1863.

The Opening of the Mississippi—Arrival of the Steamboat *Imperial* at New Orleans from St. Louis, July 16, 1863.

Missouri Historical Society.

One of the finest steamboat museums is maintained by the Missouri Historical Society in the Jefferson Memorial Building in Forest Park, St. Louis. The Upper Mississippi is well-represented in this outstanding display of river lore.

The Lee County Historical Society took a leading role in bringing the towboat *Geo. M. Verity* to Keokuk and developing her into a river museum.

S. Derward Hoag Collection.

The *Rhododendron*, formerly the *Omar*, was acquired by the Clinton Park Commission in 1965. She is being used as a showboat with a small Mississippi River museum.

sank in fifteen feet of water. Both the boat and the cargo of furs for the American Fur Company were a total loss.[613]

In 1842 Throckmorton brought the *General Brooke* into the Upper Mississippi trade.[614] Receipts for five trips to the mines that year amounted to $10,000, while in 1843 fifteen trips to the lead district produced $25,000.[615] During the same year the boat made seven trips between Galena and Fort Snelling, besides engaging for a while in the Missouri River trade. A card of thanks for the many favors extended on a trip to Galena early in 1843, signed by Henry Dodge and fourteen others, is eloquent testimony of the character and standing of Captain Throckmorton.[616]

The *General Brooke* started the season of 1845 as a regular St. Louis, Galena, and St. Peter's packet, but in midsummer Throckmorton sold her to Joseph La Barge for $12,000. This was the first boat La Barge owned, and he immediately entered her in the Missouri River trade. It was in the great fire of 1849 at St. Louis that the *General Brooke* met her fate, together with twenty-two other steamboats. She was being used at the time as a towboat by Captain A. J. Ringling, who estimated his loss at only $1500.[617]

After making a few trips on the *Nimrod*[618] (an American Fur Company boat) Throckmorton bought the *Cecilia*[619] and ran her in the St. Peter's trade for the remainder of the season of 1845. Once she poked up the St. Croix River as far as Stillwater. Throckmorton's old boat, the *Ariel*, had been the second to navigate that tributary in the fall of 1838.[620] When the Mexican War broke out in 1846, Throckmorton brought the dragoons stationed at Fort Crawford and Fort Atkinson down to St. Louis on the *Cecilia*. During the remainder of the season many volunteers crowded her deck.[621]

During the winter of 1845-1846 Throckmorton built the side-wheel steamboat *Cora* [622] at Rock Island — a significant index to the development of the country in which he had been a steamboating pioneer. Throckmorton took command of the *Cora* late in the fall of 1846. In the following year he was the first to reach Fort Snelling, battering his way through floating ice to reach that port on April 7th. The boat was advertised in the Galena newspaper for the St. Peter's trade as early as the twenty-sixth of February. Throughout the season of 1848 Throckmorton continued to command the *Cora*, but in March, 1849, he sold her to Captain Robert A. Reilly who took her into the Missouri trade.[623]

When Throckmorton disposed of the *Cora* he ended his career as an active captain on the Upper Mississippi. For a few years he was agent for the Tennessee Insurance Company at St. Louis, but the urge of a pulsing steamboat overpowered him and he returned to his former occupation on the Missouri River. For three years he commanded the *Genoa* which he built in 1854. In 1857 he built the *Florence* and in 1864 the *Montana*. Four years later he purchased the *Columbia* and employed her in the trade between St. Louis and Fort Benton. After several trips on the Illinois River he sold her to the Arkansas River Packet Company.

Captain Joseph Throckmorton

Captain Throckmorton spent the last two years of his life as a United States engineer under Colonel John N. Macomb in the improvement of the Upper Mississippi. He died in St. Louis in December, 1872, after having engaged in river work for almost fifty years. It is said that he accumulated several fortunes during his colorful career as a river captain, but he finally died a poor man.[624]

Joseph Throckmorton showed himself to be a conservative steamboat captain during his twenty years of service on the Upper Mississippi. Unlike Daniel Smith Harris, who was continually seeking to establish new speed records or exploring hitherto unnavigated streams, Throckmorton was ambitious to establish a reliable and remunerative business. This could not be accomplished with a "nigger" hanging on the safety valve. His enterprising spirit was evidenced by his formation of the first coöperative agreement between steamboat captains on the Upper Mississippi, and again shortly afterward when he used the safety barge as a further means of gaining business.

Chief Keokuk was so impressed with the personality and character of Throckmorton that it is said he offered him the site of "Flint Hills", where Burlington now stands, as a token of friendship. Hercules L. Dousman, agent of the American Fur Company at Prairie du Chien, recommended Throckmorton's boats in preference to those of rival captains. His steamboats were indeed among the finest then afloat. Their popularity was attested by the type of passengers he carried. Cabin passengers rarely failed to subscribe a title to their names, so that the register became a galaxy of generals, majors, doctors, and judges. If nothing better was available an "Esquire" was appended to lend dignity to a signature.

Throckmorton's cargoes varied widely. On April 10, 1830, for example, the *Red Rover* arrived at Galena with five hundred and thirty-seven packages, bales, and barrels in addition to a thousand feet of plank. Four hundred and sixty-three packages had been unloaded at various towns on the way. In addition to the freight the boat had brought up nineteen cabin passengers and a hundred and twenty-five deck passengers. Pigs of lead constituted the main cargo downstream.[625]

Amusements on board these boats were as varied as human ingenuity could devise. A landing at a town or fort was always an interesting event. Indian villages were often visited, and the red men could usually be prevailed upon to perform their dances and sing their songs for a nominal sum. Dancing and games were popular among the cabin passengers. During the presidential years innumerable straw votes were cast.

It was the captain's duty to pass among his cabin passengers and minister to their wants in a kindly and courteous manner. At the end of the trip the cabin passengers would often meet informally and select a committee to draw up resolutions commending the captain and his officers for their many courteous and gentlemanly qualities. These resolutions with the names of the passengers subscribed were then printed in a newspaper. Indeed, this practice became so common that one English traveler

Captain Joseph Throckmorton

humorously wrote that Mississippi steamboat captains must be an exceptionally polite and cultured class. Among the deck passengers games of chance, coarse jokes, fishing, and often drunkenness prevailed. Robberies were frequent. In 1833 some thieves carried away almost every piece of wearing apparel they could find belonging to the passengers on the *Winnebago*.[626]

Captain Throckmorton witnessed a remarkable change in the country he helped to develop. In 1828 there were few settlements above the head of the Lower Rapids. Eight years later Galena and Dubuque newspapers advertised the sale of lots at Port Byron, New York, Oquawka, Rockingham, Paris, Platteville, Pauquette, Van Buren, Bloomington, Parkhurst, Illinois City, Burlington, New Rochester, Keithsburg, and Rockport — towns that in many instances are probably unknown even to the oldest inhabitants of the region.[627]

Within this broad valley today there dwell many people descendants of the pioneers who were carried on the decks of the *Red Rover*, the *Winnebago*, the *Warrior*, the *St. Peters*, the *Ariel*, the *Burlington*, the *Malta*, the *General Brooke*, the *Nimrod*, the *Cecilia*, and the *Cora*.

42

Daniel Smith Harris: A Fighting Skipper

ST. PAUL WAS in a pandemonium. Whistles blew, cannon boomed, and the crowd roared an enthusiastic welcome as the trim and speedy *Grey Eagle* (Daniel Smith Harris commanding) swished up to the levee to open the season of navigation on March 25, 1858. It was an epoch in steamboating, marking the earliest recorded arrival at the chief port of call on the Upper Mississippi. It also marked the seventh time in fifteen years that the gallant and enterprising Harris had braved the dangers of ice-locked Lake Pepin to reach St. Paul first. The steam in the *Grey Eagle's* boilers had scarcely subsided before Captain Harris was informed that a banquet would be held in his honor, attended by the newly elected Governor and the leading citizens.[628]

It was fitting that Henry Sibley, the first chief executive of the North Star State, should be chosen to preside at the banquet. At the conclusion of a sumptuous repast, Governor Sibley eulogized the resourceful and energetic Harris for his splendid work in developing Minnesota and the Upper Mississippi Valley. He hailed him as the senior commander and acknowledged peer of the hundred captains then plying the river between St. Louis and St. Paul. It was scarcely necessary to speak of one whose name was a byword wherever steamboats docked. His matchless

Daniel Smith Harris : A Fighting Skipper

courage as a commander, his skill and cunning as a pilot, his love of fast boats and record-breaking runs, his venturesome forays up hitherto unnavigated streams, his coolness in the face of danger had been often displayed. But it was his work as the pioneer navigator of almost every tributary above the Des Moines Rapids that particularly impressed Governor Sibley, and so he emphasized the importance of the discovery of the head of navigation of streams in Minnesota and the other Commonwealths along the Upper Mississippi.[629]

Prior to the Civil War no steamboat captain was better known or more highly respected than Daniel Smith Harris. His father, James Harris, was born in Connecticut in 1777 of an old Massachusetts family that extended back to the Pilgrims who landed at Plymouth Rock on the *Mayflower*. As a young man James Harris had emigrated to New York State where he married Abigail Bathrick, a resident of Kortright, Delaware County. The first child of this union was Daniel Smith Harris, born at Kortright on July 24, 1808.

After residing in New York for several years the wanderlust again seized James Harris and he moved with his family to Cincinnati. Here he remained until financial difficulties beset him when he decided to join the Moses Meeker colony to the Fever River mines in 1823. At this time Daniel was a robust lad of fifteen; accordingly he was withdrawn from school to join the expedition. Three younger brothers (Robert Scribe, Martin Keeler, and James Meeker) were left behind with their mother until a suitable home could be provided for them. A fifth son, Jackson, was born to James and Abigail Harris at Galena in 1828.[630]

The trip to the lead mines on the keelboat *Colonel Bomford* must have seemed the merriest kind of lark to the vigilant and inquiring lad of fifteen. Daniel saw the boat carried swiftly down the Ohio. But when the Mississippi was reached the sluggish keelboat appeared in sharp contrast to the steamboat *Virginia* as it churned proudly by the *Colonel Bomford* on her way to St. Louis. "Smith" Harris, for so he became generally known, quickly observed the archaic mode by which he was traveling. Did a new field of endeavor lay open to him?[631]

The voyage of the *Virginia* inspired in the youthful Harris a strong desire to own and captain a steamboat. But to own such a craft a large outlay of capital was required; and so, during the year 1823, he roamed the hills of the mining district with an Indian boy prospecting for lead — a task which at first he pursued with indifferent success. The year after James Harris and his eldest son arrived at Galena, the three younger boys came west to the lead mines to assist their father on his new farm in Jo Daviess County. The produce of the Harris farm found a ready market in a community devoted almost entirely to mining. The returns on their labor must have been as great as that reaped by many of the miners themselves. Even as late as 1836 the need for farmers and farm products provoked considerable comment in the lead district.

In 1824 Smith Harris and his brother Scribe prospected

together. One Sunday, Smith struck an old deserted shaft in West Galena. By working it he discovered one of the richest leads ever found in the region. West Diggings, as his mine was called, soon made him one of the most prosperous miners in the Fever River district. The two boys took 35,000 pounds of mineral from the first pocket, and ultimately 4,000,000 pounds from the mine. They successfully fought off the claim-jumpers who attempted to deprive them of their find and continued in the mining business all their lives. Whenever misfortune befell them in steamboating they relied on their mines to recoup the losses.

The year 1829 was noteworthy for Daniel Smith Harris. His aggressive character and success had attracted the attention of Captain David G. Bates, one of the best-known steamboat captains on the Upper Mississippi. Heavy lead shipments were being made to St. Louis, and when a vacancy occurred in the pilot house of the steamboat *Galena* Captain Bates offered Smith Harris an appointment as cub pilot — a position which he accepted without hesitation. A little later, when an assistant engineer was needed, Scribe Harris was assigned to the berth. The training which the two boys received under Captain Bates laid the foundation for their future skill and daring in steamboating.[632]

The Black Hawk War brought a lull in river transportation. Only six steamboats dared to enter the lead district in 1832. Stillman's Run threw the entire Upper Mississippi Valley into panic; and Galena, gripped by fear, soon became an armed camp under martial law. Smith Harris enlisted as a lieutenant in Captain James W. Stephenson's regiment and was active throughout the war, participating in the decisive battle of Wisconsin Heights. Following this struggle, he heard the Indians sue for peace.

"About daybreak the next morning", he relates, "the camp was alarmed by the clarion voice of the Prophet, from a hill nearly a mile away. At first, we thought it was an alarm, but soon found that the Prophet wanted peace. Although he was so far distant, I could distinctly hear every word, and I understood enough to know he did not want to fight. The interpreter reported that the Prophet said 'they had their squaws and children with them, and that they were starving, that they did not want to fight any more, and would do no more harm if they were allowed to cross the Mississippi in peace.' " The brutal massacre of women and children at Bad Axe a short time later is a dark page in the military annals of the United States. In 1893, two weeks before his death, Captain Harris received a pension for his services during the Black Hawk War.[633]

At the conclusion of the war, Harris decided to build a steamboat of his own. His experience under Captain Bates, his love for the river and the pulsing deck of a steamboat, a fairly substantial income from his mines, and the scarcity of boats in the trade probably induced him to return to steamboating. The sight of the hull of the keelboat *Colonel Bomford* near West Diggings, it is said, prompted him to construct a boat. Scribe was dispatched to Cincinnati to purchase an engine and machinery, while Smith busied himself with putting the hull of the keel in shape and fitting it out with a cabin. Scribe discovered an old engine on a scrap-heap on the Cincinnati levee, drove a sharp bargain, and returned in triumph with his prize to their boat at the Portage, three miles below Galena and about halfway to the mouth of the Fever River. In later years Harris built a canal across this narrow neck of land large enough for the biggest packets to go through. Harris Slough, as this canal is marked today on government charts, is a fitting memorial to the industry and activity of Daniel Smith Harris.[634]

To be the builder and master of a steamboat at the age of twenty-five was no mean accomplishment, and young Harris could well be excused for viewing complacently the newly launched craft. All Galena rejoiced in the honor brought by her enterprising young citizen, for it was the first steamboat built in the lead district and probably the first constructed on the Upper Mississippi above Alton. The boat was named the *Jo Daviess* in honor of the county. According to her enrollment at the Port of St. Louis, the *Jo Daviess* was 90 feet 5 inches long, 15 feet 3 inches beam, had a 2-foot hold, and measured 26 tons. She had a transom stern, a cabin above deck, and no figure-head. Her flywheel was made of lead, the metal most accessible to Harris. Of the twenty-two steamboats docked at St. Louis in 1835 the *Jo Daviess* was the smallest — insignificant beside the *Great Mogul* which had a capacity of 700 tons.[635]

Steamboating on Upper Mississippi

Almost as soon as Captain Harris had guided his craft out into the Mississippi he exhibited the audacity which characterized him to the end. In July, 1834, the *Jo Daviess*, loaded to the guards with troops and military stores, ascended the Wisconsin River to Fort Winnebago at present-day Portage; and during the course of the summer she made two more trips to that point. Late that fall Captain Harris took a shipment of lead to St. Louis where he disposed of both cargo and craft and set out for Cincinnati to superintend the construction of a new boat.[636]

Even before the country along the banks of the Mississippi was partially occupied, restless pioneers were beginning to push their way up the tributary streams. Town sites began to appear, and settlers and speculators were anxiously waiting for steamboats. Shallow water, an unknown and deceptive channel, together with sparse settlement, all served to deter most captains from navigating unknown streams. But such obstacles were mere trifles to Captain Harris; and in 1836, two years after the voyage of the *Jo Daviess* up the Wisconsin, he piloted the *Frontier* up the Rock River as far as Dixon's Ferry.[637] This feat was hailed with delight throughout the Upper Mississippi Valley and Captain Harris was granted a lot at each town site along the Rock River by grateful settlers and owners. In 1850 he piloted the *Dr. Franklin No. 2* up the Chippewa River to the mouth of the Menominee, carrying goods for the Knapp and Wilson lumber camp on that stream. This was the first steamboat to go so far up the Chippewa.

Daniel Smith Harris : A Fighting Skipper

Captain Harris received one hundred dollars for making the trip.[638]

The first steamboat to enter the Minnesota River had been the *Rufus Putnam* in 1825, with Captain David G. Bates in command; but Harris's old master had ascended only one mile up that stream. In 1850 four excursions were made up the Minnesota River; and Martin Keeler Harris, a younger brother of Captain Smith Harris, gained the distinction of reaching what is now Judson in Blue Earth County. The people about St. Paul and in the Minnesota Valley hoped that a steamboat would penetrate still farther.

The opportunity came in 1853 when Captain Smith Harris's *West Newton* was selected to carry troops and government stores to the new post which later was named Fort Ridgely. "Of great strength and power, and in the hands of skillful men", observed an editor aboard the *West Newton*, "it was felt that if there were dangers and difficulties in the way of reaching the destined point, she would be better able to brave them than any other craft known in these waters". Two smaller boats, the *Tiger* and the *Clarion*, were sent ahead, but were quickly overtaken and passed by the *West Newton*. "Soldiers and soldiers' baggage — soldiers' wives and soldiers' children — soldiers' stores and soldiers' equipment — soldiers' cattle and soldiers' dogs" were strewn about the *West Newton* from stem to stern. She also shoved a heavily loaded barge. The Minnesota River was at flood stage so the *West Newton* experienced little difficulty in ascending the snaky channel.

Steamboating on Upper Mississippi

A week was required to make the round trip and Captain Harris was warmly praised for the success of the voyage. "His careful, quick, discerning eye, saw everything at a glance, and made all his calculations with a lightning velocity of thought; so that we struck no snags, collapsed no flue, and burst no boiler; though we did tear off the guards, throw down the pipes, and leave the cabin maid's-washing of linen 'high and dry' on a tree, which bent down to receive the line." "This trip alone", wrote Harriet E. Bishop, an author who was aboard the *West Newton*, "would entitle Captain Harris to a wreath of fame".[639]

After the sale of his first boat (the *Jo Daviess*) Smith Harris acquired the *Hermione*, ran her throughout the season of 1835, and then disposed of her. For the next quarter century Captain Harris commanded almost a score of vessels : he probably had a financial interest in as many more. This does not include the craft he became interested in as a member of the Minnesota Packet Company. In quick succession he captained, sometimes for a season, sometimes for only a trip or two, such boats as the *Frontier*, the *Smelter*, the *Pizarro*, the *Pre-emption*, the *Relief*, the *Sutler*, the *Otter*, the *War Eagle* (first), the *Time*, the *Lightfoot*, the *Senator*, the *Dr. Franklin No. 2*, the *New St. Paul*, the *West Newton*, the *War Eagle* (second), and the *Grey Eagle*. His restless energy was exhibited by his impatience with most of the steamboats he built or purchased. Only five seem to have been satisfactory enough for him to run them two or more seasons, although he ran the historic *Otter* for five years and sold the first and second *War Eagle* and the *Dr. Franklin No. 2* at the close of three seasons. The *West Newton* was snagged at the end of her second year. The *Grey Eagle*, the pride of the Upper Mississippi, served the gallant skipper from 1857 to 1861.[640]

To Smith Harris, the *sine qua non* in any steamboat was speed. The sight of a long, lean craft as sleek and fast as a greyhound delighted him. In July, 1836, he ran the *Frontier* from St. Louis to Galena in three days and six hours, having stopped between twenty and thirty hours on the way up. The following year he astonished the mining district by making the trip between Dubuque and Cincinnati in the *Smelter* in five days. The return trip was made in exactly the same time.[641]

It was not until 1845, however, that he brought out a boat which easily outraced all rivals. This was the first *War Eagle* — perhaps the swiftest boat to navigate the Upper Mississippi before 1850. She was built at Cincinnati in 1845 and was 152 feet long, with a 24-foot beam, a 4 foot 6 inch hold, and measured 155 tons. Competition being exceedingly keen during 1845, the *War Eagle* steamed back and forth between St. Louis and Galena at a terrific rate of speed, lowering her time each trip. The *St. Croix*, a trim and speedy craft, snapped at the *War Eagle's* heels for a time but gave up when the *War Eagle* ran from St. Louis to Galena in forty-three hours and fifty-two minutes, a record which stood for many years.[642]

In the years that followed, Smith Harris and steamboat

racing became synonymous. His race with the *West Newton* against the *Die Vernon* in 1853, his brilliant run against time and the *Itasca* in 1858, and his thrilling contest with the *Hannibal City* in 1861 were the talk of the Upper Mississippi Valley. In the whole gamut of Upper Mississippi steamboating no other captain could match these exploits of Smith Harris. Each deserves a separate chapter in the annals of steamboating.

The daring skipper won laurels in other ways. Between 1844 and 1861 Daniel Smith Harris habitually opened the season of navigation by bringing his boats into port first. He achieved the same distinction by braving the dangers of a frozen river in order to transport belated passengers and freight to their destination at the close of navigation. Most captains had already placed their boats in winter quarters when Smith Harris was starting out on his last trip of the season. Such qualities were bound to win the respect and admiration of his fellowmen.

Known and beloved for his skill and daring throughout the Upper Mississippi Valley, Captain Harris seldom let his enthusiasm interfere with the stern reality of steamboating. His boats were steady and dependable, and pioneers placed the utmost faith and reliance in his work. "Last night we came upon a shoal but we didn't stick", wrote a belated traveler aboard the *Dr. Franklin No. 2* in November, 1849. "The boat walked right over on stilts. The chandeliers rattled as though we were stumbling over the hump of an earthquake. Woke at 6 and found the Franklin in bed with the Yankee under a lee bluff. The

Daniel Smith Harris : A Fighting Skipper

Franklin was discharging upon the Yankee a few bbls of pork . . . The Franklin pays her wood bills in pork".[643]

In 1841 the *Otter* made fifteen trips from Galena to St. Louis, towing nine keelboats up the river during the season. At its close, the receipts were found to be $15,000 from freight and $7000 from passengers. Her small size and light draught enabled the *Otter* to ply the Mississippi at all seasons of the year, so that when navigation closed she had cleared an amount equal to over four times her value.

During 1842 Captain Harris made eleven trips with the *Otter*, towed six keelboats, and cleared $13,000 on freight and passengers. During 1843 a rate war developed and freight was carried for less than half the price of former years. Nineteen times during the season, the *Otter* forced her way out of Fever River with her keels and lower deck creaking under the heavy lead freight and with passengers crowding the upper decks. When the boat was laid up for the winter in the slough near Galena, her profits for the season were found to be only $6000 on freight and $4000 on passengers. Had the rates of 1841 been in force, Captain Harris would have cleared close to $30,000; while a profit of almost $45,000 would have resulted from the low water rate of 1839.[644]

When the lead traffic waned, Captain Harris sought other sources of revenue. No other form of diversion brought more enjoyment and better returns than a trip to the Falls of St. Anthony, designated by George Catlin as the "Fashionable Tour". Early in May, 1837, Harris informed citizens of Galena, Dubuque, and Belmont, that he would make a trip to the Falls of St. Anthony in the *Smelter* if a sufficient number of passengers presented themselves. Realizing that tourists would patronize only those boats which offered the best facilities, Harris had built private staterooms in the *Smelter* — a speedy side-wheeler launched at Cincinnati in the spring of 1837. The boat was described as the fastest, most luxurious, and largest craft on the Upper Mississippi, and the colorful skipper "greatly delighted" in her speed. Each new boat had some innovations. Thus, the *Pizarro*, built in 1839, at a cost of $16,000, boasted a fire engine and hose attached to her main engine.[645]

Increasing competition in the excursion trade forced captains to offer more inducements to passengers each year. Captain Harris realized the necessity of allowing sufficient time at historic spots. He apprised the citizens of Dubuque of an excursion to the Falls of St. Anthony by telling them that "the War Eagle is a new and Splendid Boat, and will be two weeks making the trip. Capt. Harris intends to make a pleasure excursion in *reality*, and will stop at all places of curiosity or amusement as long as the passengers may desire."[646]

His activity in the lead traffic and excursion trips, together with the profits derived from the transportation of Indians, missionaries, fur traders, and soldiers, gave Harris a preëminent position among his fellow steamboat-men. By 1840 he and his brother Scribe were sole owners of the *Otter* and at the same time held a large interest in the *Pre-emption* which Scribe commanded. The firm of Glasgow, Shaw, & Larkins of St. Louis, and Block and McCune of Louisiana, Missouri, shared with the Harris brothers in the earnings of the *Pre-emption*.[647] Supported by such well-known mercantile houses, Captain Harris had little to fear when competition threatened.

It was not long, however, before Captain Harris gained the enmity (and also the wholesome respect) of Hercules L. Dousman, the agent for the American Fur Company at Prairie du Chien. Fearful of Harris's aggressive character, Dousman often wrote Henry Sibley, his associate at Mendota, urging him to trade with such captains as Joseph Throckmorton or John Atchison. When the steamboat *Lynx* sank in 1844, Captain Harris expressed a desire to acquire a share in her when raised. "I believe it is the best thing we can do", wrote the cautious Dousman to Sibley, "provided he comes in on the *same terms* as we do & makes up our share of the loss — that is the amt we will be deficient on the Boat to be added to what she will sell for at auction & each party take half — say Harris half, Steele & you one sixth — Brisbois same & me the same".

Such a plan evidently did not appeal to Captain Harris for he remained outside the circle and continued to ply in the St. Peter's trade in opposition to the American Fur Company boats. When Throckmorton proposed that a line be formed between St. Louis and Mendota, Dousman wrote Sibley : "I am in favor of it & shall encourage him to do so, as it will be a benefit to the Outfit & hurt the Harris's which I desire very much." [648]

Steamboating on Upper Mississippi

The sinking of the *Argo* in the fall of 1847 had led to the formation of the Minnesota Packet Company. During the following winter Captain M. W. Lodwick went to Cincinnati, Ohio, with clerk Russell Blakeley and purchased the *Dr. Franklin*. Built at Wheeling, Virginia, in 1847, the new boat was 156 feet long, had a 24-foot beam, a 4 foot 2 inch hold, and measured 149 tons. Her original owners were Orrin Smith and B. H. Campbell (of the firm of Campbell and Smith), Henry Corwith, M. W. Lodwick, and Russell Blakeley; H. L. Dousman, Brisbois, Rice, and H. H. Sibley acquired shares in her a little later. From this humble beginning there gradually evolved through a series of kaleidoscopic changes the Northwestern Union Packet Company, the greatest monopoly on the Upper Mississippi.[649]

Meanwhile Captain Harris had been running his boats on the Upper Mississippi and its tributaries. The heavy lead traffic between Galena and St. Louis engaged most of his time; but when lead was scarce he often plied on the Mississippi and its tributaries as far north as St. Peter's and Stillwater. When Harris withdrew from the lead traffic in the spring of 1848 to enter the St. Peter's trade, the Packet Company insisted that he continue between Galena and St. Louis. Highly incensed, Harris took up arms against the new group, running the *Senator* in opposition to the *Dr. Franklin*. After a spirited contest, in which business was "lively, if not profitable", Harris agreed to sell the *Senator* to the Packet Company and remain in the lead trade during 1849.

Daniel Smith Harris : A Fighting Skipper

The creation of the Territory of Minnesota on March 3, 1849, and its attendant influx of immigrants lent a new aspect to the situation and Captain Harris determined to return to the St. Paul trade. The ink on the new bill had hardly dried when Captain Harris appeared at the Galena levee with the *Dr. Franklin No. 2*. She was built at Wheeling in 1848 and was 173 feet long, with a 26 foot 6 inch beam, a 4 foot 4 inch hold, and measured 189 tons. She was a finer, better, and speedier boat than either the old *Dr. Franklin* or the *Senator*. Captain Harris always took a special delight in tormenting and annoying his opponents. Upon leaving a port he would run alongside his rival, allowing passengers and crew to fling taunts at those aboard the slower craft. As the next port hove in sight he would dash ahead and pick up the lion's share of the freight and passengers offered. Since the *Senator* was an exceptionally slow boat she lost much trade, the fickle public generally preferring the faster craft.[650]

The "Old Doctor", however, was almost a match for the *Dr. Franklin No. 2*, and so Captain Harris had to keep his new steamboat in fine trim in order to hold his advantage. Once, in May of 1851, while these two boats were engaged in tearing up the river bed in a port to port race to St. Paul, Captain Harris found himself hard pressed to maintain his lead. Indeed, when no freight or passengers were offered he was several times obliged to swing out the stage and discharge a willing and nimble passenger while his boat was moving under a slow bell.

Noting that his rival's boat lacked her usual speed, Cap-

[421]

tain M. W. Lodwick rang for a full head of steam and momentarily threatened to pass the *Dr. Franklin No. 2*. Captain Harris frustrated these attempts at first by swinging the stern of his craft across the path of the "Old Doctor", forcing her to reverse to avoid a collision. Once the two boats almost crashed, skillful piloting and full speed astern on the part of the "Old Doctor" alone preventing a castastrophe. Incensed by these persistent and well-nigh successful attempts to wrest the lead from him, Captain Harris sprang from the pilot house to the hurricane deck brandishing a rifle, forced the pilot of the "Old Doctor" to back into the brush, and threatened to shoot if another attempt was made. This rash act and his refusal to give way was bitterly denounced in the St. Paul press in a statement signed by those aboard the "Old Doctor".[651]

For three years this bitter, ruinous struggle between the Minnesota Packet Company and Captain Harris continued. Both sides had loyal friends, and so the fight was not confined to the participants : merchants and settlers from Galena to St. Paul joined in the fray. Rates were reduced to a ridiculous figure, travelers often paying fifty cents for passage from Galena to St. Paul. "The boats continue to come loaded with passengers", declared the Minnesota *Pioneer* of July 22, 1852, "many of them seeking only recreation. Boats are crowded down and up. Some travel for the sake of economy and save the expense of tavern bills at home. Who that is idle would be caged up between walls of burning brick and mortar; in dog-days, down the

river, if at less daily expense, he could be hurried through
the valley of the Mississippi, its shores studded with towns
and farms, flying by islands, prairies, woodlands, bluffs —
an ever varied scene of beauty, away up into the lands of
the wild Dakota, and of cascades and pine forests, and
cooling breezes?" [652]

Both sides finally saw that there was plenty of business
and that hundreds were enjoying transportation for fifty
cents a trip when eight dollars would have offered a fair
return, and that continuance of the competition would
result in utter ruin. Fully aware of the value of Captain
Harris's coöperation, the Minnesota Packet Company invited him to join them. Shortly afterward, the name of
Daniel Smith Harris was listed as a director. Had the
fighting skipper failed in this struggle he would have been
forced out of the St. Paul trade and ultimately been driven
from the Upper Mississippi. Luckily, a steady income
from his lead mines tided him through several bad seasons. [653]

Despite his affiliation with the Minnesota Packet Company Captain Harris continued to manifest his pronounced
individuality. In 1856 a rate war arose between the Packet
Company and the large number of "wild boats" which
plied the Upper Mississippi. As usual a number of cities
and individuals promptly joined in the struggle, Winona
being particularly vigorous in its opposition to the monopoly. The *Tishomingo* was purchased to run between
Dunleith and Winona. In the hope that his popularity
would soothe any ill-feelings arising out of the competi-

tion, Captain Harris was chosen to run his *War Eagle* against the *Tishomingo*. A test soon came.

One day the *War Eagle* came over from Dubuque to Dunleith and in landing tore away a portion of the guard of the *Tishomingo* which lay taking on freight and passengers. Standing on the hurricane deck unmoved by the incident, Captain Harris calmly announced that passage to Winona aboard his boat would cost but fifty cents. These two acts drew a storm of protest, La Crosse and Dubuque joining with Winona against the Galena monopoly. "Don't travel on the Galena boats unless you make a positive bargain before hand, and to avoid being swindled don't travel with them at all", declared a paper, after three men had been charged four dollars each for passage between La Crosse and Winona. About the same time the *War Eagle* landed one hundred barrels of flour on the Winona levee and Captain Harris instructed his agents to "sell it if they could, and if they could not dispose of it, to start a Bakery!" "The offer to carry freight on board the foul bird of prey War Eagle for a trifle was promptly refused by our business men, stating to the runner that they would give all their trade to the Tishomingo", observed the Winona *Republican* of May 20, 1856. "The opposition", it continued, "is not alone against our boat, but is against the merchants — our best class of men, who have for years been building up a trade — and now that they are commencing to reap the fruits of their labors, Galena comes in Eagle-eyed for a large share of what is justly the due of our dealers."

Daniel Smith Harris : A Fighting Skipper

It was generally felt that the "*Noble Tish*" could not be driven away by the *War Eagle*, even by offers to carry goods at ten cents per hundred. Despite Winona's slogan that the *War Eagle* "shall and will not be patronized", despite the fact that twenty-five barrels of flour which the *War Eagle* landed at the levee were destroyed and fifty others rolled in the river and damaged, Captain Harris retained his old time popularity.[654]

It was not merely while in the pursuit of business that Captain Harris exhibited a pugnacious spirit. Hailed by the press for their gentlemanly deportment, one might readily assume that steamboat captains had acquired their cultural training at the Court of St. James before applying for their license. Such an assumption would be quite erroneous. As chief architect and builder of an empire in the Middle Border, the steamboat captain was a component part of the frontier where men were men first, and sometimes, though perhaps not always, gentlemen afterwards. In the ordinary civilities of his profession, Captain Harris was doubtless equal to any other man on the Upper Mississippi; but he had a fiery temper, and he was especially vindictive to those who persisted in attacking him.

During 1857 the editor of the St. Paul *Daily Pioneer and Democrat* had made bitter recriminations against the Packet Company. One hot day in July, W. A. Croffut, the assistant editor of the St. Paul *Daily Times* (a paper friendly to Harris and the Packet Company) boarded the *Grey Eagle* to write a letter. Mistaking Croffut for the editor of the unfriendly paper, Captain Harris approached, called him a scoundrel, and "swearing great, round oaths, that he didn't want him to come aboard his boat" ordered him off. Astonished at such violent language, Croffut demanded an explanation and inquired if the *Grey Eagle* was not public to all who chose to come aboard. This was too much. Seizing Croffut by the collar, the captain dragged him to the stairway and kicked him down to the lower deck. Following immediately he took another hold, and "swearing most profanely all the time, dragged him out upon the wharf, and there left him and returned to his boat". Unable to offer any resistance, the unfortunate Croffut was "bruised considerably, but had no bones broken". Harris was arrested and brought before a magistrate. Acknowledging the assault, he was fined "*ten dollars and costs*". The incident was a matter of deep regret to Captain Harris; but no apology could placate the "bruised" pride of Mr. Croffut.[655]

On the other hand, Captain Harris often demonstrated a touching generosity to his fellowmen. He was ever willing to aid the poor and distressed. An old man, driven from his daughter's home at Fort Madison, sought and received passage to Louisville, Kentucky, aboard the *Smelter*. The thought of a lonely life in Kentucky broke the old man's heart and he died a short distance below Alton. Captain Harris had him decently interred. No charge was made on the cabin register. Again, in 1852 the *West Newton* picked up two ministers of the gospel at Rollingstone, Minnesota. Both were astonished at the terrific speed of the boat. "She fairly danced with us like a Nymph upon the waves", wrote one, "Everything about the boat in general, and the table in particular, was in perfect '*apple-pie order*'. When we called at the Clerk's office to pay our fare, on learning our profession, he very gentlemanly remarked, 'Nothing to pay Sir!' to which, of course, we did not object; but for the favor were *truly thankful*. May other clergymen be equally favored." [656]

Captain Harris's sentimental attachment· to his boat elicited the following comment from the *Daily Minnesotian* : "The Grey Eagle and her Commander, Capt. Harris, both sustained a sad and irreparable loss on Thursday evening, while between Hastings and this place. The boat took a slue on the Pilot, and ran into the bank, breaking off and losing her jack staff. Now, jack-staffs themselves are not so valuable, because, in this country where pine lumber is so plentiful, the boat's Carpenter could have repaired the loss in a few hours. But at its top there fluttered, conscious of the proud position it occupied, a gilt chicken cock, which, like the eagles of Napoleon, that soared over all his battle fields through many years, and long wars — had pointed the way with its glistening beak on every boat sailed by the old Commodore for many years, and seemed as if always leading him on to victory, inseparably associated with the success of whatever boat he has commanded. Of course the Captain is inconsolable for the loss of his chicken-cock, and says he would rather have lost $500. He is endeavoring to find it, and probably it may yet soar at the head of his jack staff, years after the Grey Eagle is rotten and used up " [657]

Strange to say the "chicken cock" was recovered and the prophecy fulfilled.

Late in the afternoon of May 9, 1861, the *Grey Eagle* crashed into the Rock Island bridge and sank almost immediately in twenty feet of water. Six or seven people were drowned including an insane man who had been chained to the lower deck. Captain Harris was found wandering about the upper deck in a dazed condition, picking up little odds and ends of no consequence compared with the $60,000 craft he had just lost. Broken hearted over the loss of his *Grey Eagle*, he retired from active river life, retaining only a few shares of stock in the Packet Company.[658]

Among the odds and ends which he recovered from the wreck was the much loved "chicken cock". The historic bird had been carved from a single block of solid oak at the boat yards at Cincinnati, had been hoisted for the first time on the *War Eagle* in 1845, and had been passed on to the *Senator*, the *Dr. Franklin No. 2*, the *West Newton*, the second *War Eagle*, and finally the *Grey Eagle*. Harris took it to Galena where it roosted quietly in his barn for thirty years when it was brushed up and placed on top of the arch surmounting the entrance to Grant Park in Galena. Replaced by a brilliant electric light, the "chicken cock" again went into temporary retirement at the home of Captain Harris's daughter (Mrs. Irene Gillette) where Captain Walter A. Blair found it and placed it in the cabin of the *Helen Blair*. After selling his boat, Captain Blair presented it to the Davenport Public Museum.[659]

Daniel Smith Harris : A Fighting Skipper

When Daniel Smith Harris died in 1893 it was said he was the oldest settler in Galena and of the State of Illinois. Coming to the lead mines in 1823 (the same year that the steamboat *Virginia* navigated the Mississippi to Fort Snelling), Captain Harris participated in the halcyon days of steamboating on the Upper Mississippi prior to the Civil War. He lived to see the corporation of which he was once a heavy stockholder pass into oblivion in the late eighties. At his death the Diamond Jo Line was the lone survivor of many years of bitter competition on the Upper Mississippi.[660]

Captain Harris was twice married. His first wife, whom he married in 1833, was Sarah M. Langworthy, a sister of the Langworthy brothers, well-known figures in the history of northeastern Iowa. She died in 1850. In 1851 he married Sarah Coates, who died in 1886. Captain Harris was survived by ten children — eight daughters and two sons.

On several occasions Captain Harris was accompanied by his wife on boat trips. John P. Owens describes the second Mrs. Harris as "a proficient in and enthusiastic admirer of the natural sciences, which promises to be of advantage to us in our researches among the soils, rocks and plants of the Upper Minnesota." He added, "She has as her guest a well-known St. Paul lady, whose enthusiasm for pioneering, and being the first white woman to set foot upon this and that remote, out-of-the-way place is proverbial." This guest was Harriet E. Bishop, author of *Floral Home; or, First Years of Minnesota.*[661]

Steamboating on Upper Mississippi

The character of Captain Harris was a composite of the strongest and best traits of men. Deprived of a liberal education, he overcame this handicap by making good use of an exceptionally alert and vigorous mind. His remarkable memory stood him in good stead, and in later years he was looked upon as an authority on matters relating to the early history of Galena. As a captain his personality always made a deep impression on his passengers. While traveling in western Pennsylvania in 1890 a citizen of Galena met an old lady who had traveled widely in her youth. Upon learning the residence of the traveler she spoke at some length of her trip on the Upper Mississippi in a boat commanded by a Captain Harris during the cholera years. Forty years had failed to efface from her memory the genial personality and indomitable character of this famous pioneer.

No other captain who engaged in steamboating on the Upper Mississippi prior to the Civil War could approach the record of Daniel Smith Harris. "In enterprise, activity, liberality, in constructive talent, in the ability to meet a great requirement in transportation in the early development of the Northwest, the fame of this courageous and efficient man is secure." To him, more than to any other single pioneer captain, was due the startling growth in the use of steamboats on the Upper Mississippi, the rapid expansion of their use on tributary streams, and their constant development in speed, comfort, and efficiency, so necessary for the quick transportation of the vast waves of immigrants moving northward.[662]

43

The Race of the Grey Eagle
A Message from Queen Victoria

ON AUGUST 6, 1857, the U. S. S. *Niagara* and the H. M. S. *Agamemnon* set out from the west coast of Ireland and commenced laying a cable across the Atlantic Ocean. The ships had been "suitably equipped" for this work and loaned to Cyrus W. Field and his associates by the governments of Great Britain and the United States. As they proceeded slowly westward the cable which was being paid out from the *Niagara* suddenly snapped and the end was lost. Unable to continue, the *Niagara* and the *Agamemnon* accordingly returned to Plymouth and the remainder of the cable was carefully stored away.

Undaunted by this initial failure, Field raised additional capital and constructed seven hundred miles of new cable. A fresh start was made early in 1858, but misfortune again stalked the venture as a double break resulted in the loss of 144 miles of cable. By July 17th, however, the *Niagara* and the *Agamemnon* were ready for a third attempt. Proceeding to mid-ocean the ends of their respective cables were carefully spliced and on July 29, 1858, the two ships separated. The *Niagara* proceeded slowly toward Newfoundland while the *Agamemnon* steamed cautiously to the Irish coast. Should the vessels succeed in their undertaking news in Europe and America would become the common and instantaneous property of both hemispheres. Breathlessly people on both sides of the Atlantic awaited the outcome.[663]

In the United States great strides had been made in telegraph construction since the first message had been flashed between Washington and Baltimore in 1844. The Atlantic seaboard had been linked with the Mississippi at a number of points between St. Louis and Dubuque as early as 1848. A decade later every important river town as far north as Prairie du Chien could boast a connection with the East. Citizens of Keokuk, Fort Madison, Burlington, Muscatine, Davenport, and Dubuque would learn of the successful laying of the Atlantic cable the instant the work was consummated. But St. Paul and the river towns in Minnesota must still rely on the steamboat to bring them this important news.[664]

For a week before the cable was actually laid the *Daily Pioneer and Democrat* at St. Paul had amused its readers with imaginary messages between Queen Victoria and President James Buchanan. But the complete isolation of the North Star State weighed heavily upon the editor for well he knew that such towns as Dubuque, Galena, and Prairie du Chien would chide St. Paul for her backwardness. Still unaware that the Atlantic cable had already been laid, the editor urged his readers on August 18th to give financial assistance to the company already chartered to build a telegraph line between Prairie du Chien and St. Paul. Only $40,000, or $150 per mile, was needed to perform the work. He considered it a "shame" that every

The Race of the *Grey Eagle*

State save Minnesota should be connected with the Atlantic seaboard by telegraph. Because of her isolation Minnesota was "way behind" and must "sit apart" from the rest of the world until local pride saw to it that the telegraph line was built. Minnesota, he concluded, was farther from Prairie du Chien in 1858 than Prairie du Chien was from London or Constantinople.[665]

Almost simultaneously with the penning of these words the first message flashed across the Atlantic. "Europe and America are united by telegraph. Glory to God in the highest, on earth peace, and good-will to men." Other messages followed and none more notable than Queen Victoria's to President James Buchanan.[666]

Since Dubuque lay sixty-five miles below Prairie du Chien and since the Packet Company had boats scheduled to leave both these ports on their regular run at exactly the same time it was generally conceded that the Prairie du Chien boat would reach St. Paul first. But Captain Daniel Smith Harris of the speedy *Grey Eagle* determined that it should be otherwise. And it was the *Grey Eagle* that was scheduled to leave Dubuque at nine o'clock Tuesday morning, the same hour the *Itasca* was leaving Prairie du Chien.

News of the laying of the Atlantic telegraph, together with Queen Victoria's message, reached Dubuque on the evening of August 16th and was printed in a special edition by the local press. While Dubuque was rejoicing over this epochal event, Captain Harris determined to celebrate the occasion by beating Captain David Whitten into St.

[433]

Paul with the news. In order to do this it would be necessary to run the *Grey Eagle* 265 miles while the *Itasca* was traveling 200 miles. This was not an easy task, since the *Itasca* was a boat that had been hanging up records for fast time.[667]

The *Grey Eagle* left Dunleith at 8:30 A. M. on August 17, 1858, carrying copies of the Dubuque and Galena papers containing the Queen's message:

"The Queen desires to congratulate the President upon the successful completion of this great international work, in which the Queen has taken the deepest interest.

"The Queen is convinced that the President will join with her in fervently hoping that the Electric Cable which now connects Great Britain with the United States will prove an additional link between the nations whose friendship is founded upon their common interest and reciprocal esteem.

"The Queen has much pleasure in thus communicating with the President, and renewing to him her wishes for the prosperity of the United States." [668]

Every bit of combustible material — pitch, butter, and grease — that could be obtained was aboard the *Grey Eagle* when she started up the Mississippi. The boat responded nobly to the extra fuel, sped swiftly up Maquoketa Chute, past Cassville, Guttenberg, Prairie du Chien, La Crosse, and reached Winona, one hundred and fifty miles above Dunleith, at about 9:30 P. M. The *Itasca* had arrived just three and one-half hours before, so that her nine hour lead had been reduced by almost two-thirds despite the fact that the *Grey Eagle* had towed a wood flat for twenty miles. After a twenty minute delay at Winona the *Grey* Eagle continued upstream, so far ahead of schedule that Captain Harris ordered a deck hand to stand on the stage and heave the mail to the bank at each landing as the boat went by at half speed. Freight was discharged only where necessary and many of the passengers, induced by a generous offer of free meals and berth and moved by a desire to be a party to what already promised to be a record-breaking run, agreed to remain on board.[669]

At 4 A. M. the next day, the *Grey Eagle* came snorting up to the Red Wing levee, sixty-five miles above Winona and only fifty miles from St. Paul. The *Itasca* had not stopped at Red Wing, thereby gaining several precious minutes on Captain Harris's boat. Fire brands streamed from the funnels of the *Grey Eagle* as she continued upstream, past Cannon River, Vermilion Slough, Sturgeon Lake, Diamond Bluff, and on to Prescott, at the mouth of the St. Croix. The *Itasca* blew for Hastings, just two and one-half miles away, as the *Grey Eagle* came up to the Prescott levee. Mail and freight were dumped pell mell on the levee, and the *Grey Eagle* whisked by Point Douglas and over to Hastings in time to see the smoke of the *Itasca* disappear around the bend of the river about two miles upstream.[670]

When Captain Whitten discerned the smoke of a racing boat hard astern it did not take that shrewd Yankee long to guess the reason for this haste. He promptly ordered the engineer to crowd on every pound of steam possible. Just below Pine Bend the astonished master of the *Itasca* saw the *Grey Eagle* poke her nose around a curve a mile away, running almost ten hours ahead of her regular schedule. At Merrimac Island the distance was reduced to three-quarters of a mile, at Newport a half mile intervened, Red Rock found the *Grey Eagle* a hundred yards closer. Kaposia, Pig's Eye, Dayton Bluff — and a boat's length separated the two boats. One mile further and they would be in St. Paul.

The frenzied passengers and crew of the *Grey Eagle* cheered madly as the gap slowly closed and the bow of their boat drew abreast of the *Itasca's* stern. But the latter had the inside track and in the next quarter of a mile it was clear that Captain Harris could not hope to reach the levee first. In the succeeding minute, the two boats drew almost neck to neck, with whistles blowing and cannon booming, but the *Itasca* nosed into the wharf first. While her crew was busy putting out the stage, the *Grey Eagle* glided alongside with a deck hand perched on the swinging stage, a number of papers fastened into the notch of an arrow of wood. The next instant they were cast into the arms of Harris's agent on the dock.

Captain Harris had made the run from Dunleith to St. Paul in twenty-four hours and forty minutes, making twenty-three landings, and taking on thirty-five cords of wood en route. His average speed, counting all stops, was a fraction over eleven miles an hour upstream, but the *Grey Eagle* probably ran thirteen miles an hour while under way. This was the fastest time ever made by a steamboat; it eclipsed the *Die Vernon's* record of 1853 by over three hours.[671]

The race of the *Grey Eagle* against time and the *Itasca* is without a parallel in Upper Mississippi steamboating. The fast time of such boats as the *War Eagle* (first), the *Die Vernon*, and the *West Newton* pale beside this colorful exploit. For sheer drama it equals the heated contest between the *Robert E. Lee* and the *Natchez* in 1870. Only a venturesome skipper like Daniel Smith Harris would have conceived a plan so daring. Only a sleek boat like the *Grey Eagle* could have carried such a plan to a victorious conclusion.

44
When Captains Ruled Like Kings

MARK TWAIN has sung the praises of Lower Mississippi pilots — their skill and daring, their professional clannishness, and their prestige. But the Mississippi that Mark Twain knew in the late fifties had already grown to steamboat maturity. Hannibal, the boyhood home of Mark Twain, was unborn when Daniel Smith Harris skimmed by in the keelboat *Colonel Bomford* in 1823. In fact Smith Harris had been steamboating on the Mississippi for six years before Samuel Langhorne Clemens was born at Florida, Missouri, in 1835. Clemens was not so much as one year old when Harris piloted the *Frontier* up the Rock River as far as Dixon's Ferry. In a word, Daniel Smith Harris had come to be recognized as a veteran river captain and pilot when Mark Twain was still in his infancy.

Harris was at the full tide of his glorious career when in 1857 the youthful Clemens quit writing letters to the Keokuk *Post* to begin his brief steamboat career. By that time Harris had already owned or commanded a score of boats, and was just bringing out his beautiful *Grey Eagle*. Indeed the four and one-half years that Samuel Clemens (for so his name is written on his first and only pilot's license issued at St. Louis on April 9, 1859) spent on the Mississippi coincides exactly with Harris's career as captain of the *Grey Eagle*. The outbreak of the Civil War abrupt-

ly ended Mark Twain's river career on the Lower Mississippi; while Daniel Smith Harris brought his thirty-three
years of steamboating to a dramatic close when he dashed
the *Grey Eagle* to pieces on a jutting pier of the Rock
Island bridge on May 9, 1861.[672]

In character and ability, in courage and resourcefulness,
Upper Mississippi steamboat captains were unexcelled.
Skippers like Daniel Smith Harris were held in even greater esteem than Lower River pilots. For it must be remembered that the typical Upper Mississippi steamboat captain
before the Civil War was himself a pilot. There were many
captains like Daniel Smith Harris who took their regular
turn at the wheel despite the press of other duties.

Among these versatile commanders there were pilots
whose skill and ability could match the adroit Mr. Bixby
under whom Mark Twain served as cub. Indeed Mr. Bixby is dwarfed by comparison with Harris for that fiery
skipper had seen almost as many years of steamboating as
Mr. Bixby could count birthdays when Samuel Clemens
was studying the mysteries of an ever changing channel
under him. Mr. Bixby might know the Mississippi from
St. Louis to New Orleans, but Harris had piloted the western waters between St. Paul and Pittsburgh and had blazed
a trail on many tributaries. In addition to this Harris invariably piloted his boats over both the Lower Rapids and
Upper Rapids — a feat which was generally reserved for
skilled rapids pilots who knew every inch of the twisted,
tortuous channel. There were few steamboat pilots who
could perform this feat in a good stage of water. Fur-

thermore Harris always ran the dangerous cross-currents of that Nemesis of the steamboats — the Rock Island bridge. For five consecutive years he piloted the *Grey Eagle* through this dangerous obstruction, always relieving the pilot on duty in order to assume the responsibility himself. Mark Twain, Mr. Bixby, and the other Lower Mississippi pilots before the Civil War had no bridges to run in the whole course of the river from St. Louis to New Orleans.[673]

But piloting was a small part of the work of the Upper Mississippi steamboat captain. His duties were far more onerous. A steamboat captain had to be a real leader — one who could command respect. He must be capable of making quick and accurate decisions. He must be a good judge of human nature for upon him fell the duty of choosing pilots, engineers, firemen, clerks, stewards, mates, deck hands, and roustabouts. He had to demonstrate sufficient business talent to show a profit at the end of a season.

Meeting people in every walk of life, the steamboat captain must so impress his passengers with his own ability and "gentlemanly deportment" that they would be inclined to choose his boat in preference to another in the future. In a day when a wide difference existed in the speed and luxury of river crafts the personality of the captain was often the determining factor in influencing a traveler's choice of the half dozen boats in port. The same was true with regard to freight : a popular captain would have little difficulty in securing a generous share of the merchandise and produce along the way.

Still other responsibilities faced Upper Mississippi steamboat captains. The danger of snags and sandbars, the threat of fires and explosions, the hazards of running the rapids, the fury of wind-swept Lake Pepin, all these must be encountered many times during the course of a season. Riots, bloodshed, drunken brawls, the presence of blacklegs and gamblers, the scourge of cholera, these too formed a part of the captain's life. In a word, while the pilot's work began and ended at the wheel, the captain must oversee the affairs of his craft from stem to stern, from texas to hold, from cabin to engine-room, and from the clerk's office to the pantry.[674]

Although their work was hard and frequently dangerous, steamboat captains usually displayed rare qualities of industry and resourcefulness in its performance. Sometimes the returns of a single trip were fabulous, actually paying the original cost of the steamboat. On the other hand, cut-throat competition frequently left a captain virtually bankrupt after a season of hard work. Perhaps it was this very element of uncertainty which served as a magnet to many an enterprising riverman. At any rate a picturesque group of men were lured by the throbbing, pulsing deck of a steamboat.[675]

Boldly written in the annals of steamboating are the names of Joseph Throckmorton and Daniel Smith Harris. Prior to the Civil War these men ranked as outstanding figures during the period of individual ownership. But there were many others whose names ought to be recorded. Thus, while Throckmorton was one of the earliest to ply the Upper Mississippi such men as James Clark, Alvah

Culver, and David G. Bates preceded him. Little is known about the career of many of these men : their presence is recorded chiefly by their arrivals at the Port of St. Louis and the Galena lead mines.

Take for example the career of David G. Bates, who might well be called the dean of Upper Mississippi steamboat captains. Bates captained a crew of French keelboatmen to the lead mines of Galena as early as 1819. The intrepid skipper began his steamboat career when he purchased the *Rufus Putnam* and brought a cargo of supplies to Fort Snelling in 1825. It was Bates who started Smith Harris on his steamboat career by taking him aboard the *Galena* as a cub pilot in 1829.

It was Captain Bates, too, who employed the surly Patrick O'Connor as a deck hand aboard the *Galena*. O'Connor later had the dubious honor of being the first man tried, condemned, and executed in Iowa. Captain Bates had taken pity on this dissolute Irishman in Galena when others reviled him. When the Dubuque lead miners tried O'Connor for murder he chose Captain Bates for his counsel. The resourceful steamboat captain made a forceful plea in O'Connor's defense, but to no avail, for O'Connor was hanged at Dubuque on June 20, 1834. Captain Bates was always identified with steamboating and lead mining. He died at Galena on November 22, 1850. His initiation of Daniel Smith Harris into the mysteries of piloting aboard the steamboat *Galena* alone entitles him to a place in steamboat history.[676]

The entire Harris family seems to have been inoculated

with the steamboat phobia. Robert Scribe, Martin Keeler, James Meeker, and even young Jackson Harris, all saw active service on the Upper Mississippi. Indeed steamboating appeared to intrigue whole families. The Atchison brothers (George W., Mark, and John Atchison) plied the Upper Mississippi during this period. Then there was D. B. Morehouse and his brother Le Grand Morehouse. Preston Lodwick and his brother, Kennedy Lodwick, also should not be forgotten. Such men as Hiram Bersie, W. H. Hooper, A. C. Montfort, Robert A. Reilly, E. H. Gleim, James Lafferty, Orrin Smith, and Russell Blakeley, were likewise prominent captains before the Civil War.[677]

A distinguishing characteristic of Upper Mississippi steamboat captains was their stubborn courage and perseverance. In 1857 Captain George H. Wilson of Onalaska, Wisconsin, brought out the powerful stern-wheel towboat *G. H. Wilson*. Built at Brownsville, Pennsylvania, this 159-ton craft was capable of showing a foaming wake to most of the race horses on the Upper Mississippi. After running somewhat irregularly in the St. Paul trade during the year 1857, Captain Wilson entered her in the Des Moines River trade. It was while engaged in this traffic that Captain Wilson demonstrated a "resoluteness in the face of difficulties" which is typical of the steamboat captain.

It appears that the Des Moines River was obstructed with numerous dams thrown across its course by mill owners. It was the practice of steamboatmen to take a run at these makeshift obstructions and force the boat through or over them. Sometimes a boat was hung up on the crest of the dam without being able to run either forward or back.

A story is told of the indomitable Captain Wilson wrestling with the dam at Keosauqua. The *G. H. Wilson* stuck several times in attempting to pass the dam and had to fall back and try it over again. "Getting desperate", eyewitnesses relate, "the captain ordered the engineer to get up a big pressure of steam, open the throttle valves wide, and shouted his commands so that they could be heard half a mile : 'Send her over — or blow her to hell!' The boat went over amid the cheers of the spectators. The engineer said afterwards that he rather expected the other alternative." [678]

Steamboat captains were kind of heart. Once, when a baby became ill aboard his steamboat, Captain Russell Blakeley landed at an "out-of-the-way point" and sent a boy up the bluff to get a pitcher of fresh milk for the sick child. On another occasion Captain William H. Gabbert held his boat over several hours for a woman whose child was born during the interval. [679]

In 1850 Benjamin Eaton hastened from St. Paul to Beetown, Wisconsin, to get his family out of the cholera region. While he was gone his home burned, leaving the family without shelter. When Captain Orrin Smith of the *Nominee* learned of this misfortune he refunded the fare of the entire Eaton family upon their arrival in St. Paul. It was this same Captain Smith who refused to allow his boat to turn a wheel on Sunday and conducted religious services himself when no minister was on board.⁶⁸⁰ In 1857 Captain Jones Worden allowed passengers to sleep on board the *Key City* during a cloudburst and while waiting for a train. This was against the rules of the company; but where human comfort was concerned steamboat captains often made their own rules.⁶⁸¹

In 1850 a card signed by forty persons appeared in a Galena newspaper thanking Captain John Atchison and his officers "for the uniform kindness and attention" on a recent trip from Stillwater to Galena aboard the *Highland Mary No. 2*. But Captain Atchison was unable to respond : the same issue carried the news of his death. He had been stricken suddenly with the cholera upon his arrival at that port. His passing was a distinct loss to Upper Mississippi steamboating for he had demonstrated enterprise and a fine business talent that was warmly tempered by a frank, generous, and amiable personality.

Nor were such characters as John Atchison readily forgotten by the river folk whom he had often befriended. Ten months after his death a St. Paul editor mourned: "Poor Old John Atchison, of the Highland Mary, always first to greet us in the Spring, is now no more; we miss him with his little brass band, whose music echoed upon our waters, whenever that figure head of Mary, the Highland lassie, showed its face around the bend at Pig's Eye." ⁶⁸²

Steamboat captains were frequently upbraided by the press for their failure to turn back when a passenger fell overboard. The courage of Captain William H. Laughton was, however, frequently demonstrated : during his forty or more years of service the fearless skipper plunged overboard nine times at the risk of his own life and rescued passengers from a watery grave. On one such occasion, while he was serving as mate on the *Nominee*, passengers presented Laughton with an "engrossed set of resolutions, and a silver loving cup made by Tiffany" for saving the life of a little girl who had fallen over the rail.[683]

Once the pulsing throb of a steamboat entered their veins steamboat captains found it difficult to forsake the river. Throckmorton forsook the Upper Mississippi in 1848 only to return to his first love. Those captains who did succeed in leaving the river demonstrated the same capacity for leadership in business and politics. Take, for example, the career of James May, who was born in Cape Girardeau, Missouri, in 1804 and commenced flat-boating on the Ohio in 1822. Five years later (1827) Captain May took the *Shamrock* from Pittsburgh to Galena on what has been described as "the first *business* trip ever made on the Upper Mississippi" by a steamboat. Later he commanded the *Enterprise* (first) and the *Dove*. In 1834, however, he retired from steamboating to enter the grocery and commission business at Pittsburgh. He also superintended the building of over fifty steamboats and more than twice as many barges and other craft. He was one of the original proprietors of Davenport but did not become a resident of that city until 1847. Later he became one of Davenport's wealthiest citizens.

Then there was W. H. Hooper who married Electa Har-

[446]

ris, a sister of the Harris brothers. Hooper was identified with such boats as the *Otter*, the *Time and Tide*, and the *Alexander Hamilton*. In 1848 he went to Salt Lake City and allied himself with the Mormons. His general ability was soon recognized and he was sent to Congress several times as a Territorial Delegate.[684]

Business ability was an important element of a steamboat captain's character. Louis Robert, a descendant of French settlers of Kaskaskia, was born at Carondelet, Missouri, on January 21, 1811. After spending his early life on the Missouri, Robert moved to Prairie du Chien in 1838. He became permanently identified with St. Paul in 1847 as one of the original proprietors of that town. Impulsive and loquacious, generous and warm-hearted, Robert was nevertheless a far-seeing business man. In 1853 he became interested in steamboating and at different times owned as many as five steamboats. He also engaged in the Indian trade. When he died in 1874 his estate was valued at $400,000.

Louis Robert was particularly gallant to the lady passengers. Of the *Time and Tide* he was wont to say that she would wait for no man; but "Louie Robair" would wait "fifteen minutes for one woman". This incident is said to be a "true leaf" from her log book : for once the *Time and Tide* swung idly from her mooring for half an hour while a lady "primped, painted and had a reef taken in her corsets." Meanwhile the one hundred fifty other passengers are said to have "dyed the ambient air a cerulian blue with curses not loud but deep." [685]

Steamboating on Upper Mississippi

Few captains exhibited a greater versatility than did Captain Asa Barlow Green. This versatile skipper was also known as a lawyer, a sheriff, a probate judge, a missionary, a minister, and an army chaplain. Born in Vermont in 1826, Green received a common school education, studied law, and was admitted to the bar in Wisconsin and Minnesota. Variously described as a Methodist and a Calvinist Baptist, Green's religious exhortations apparently satisfied the rough cravings of the lumberjacks. On at least one occasion his contact with these rude characters stood him in good stead.

On May 26, 1859, Captain Green started up Lake St. Croix for Stillwater with an excursion party of over three hundred men, women, and children from Hastings and Prescott. All were in a merry mood when suddenly a tornado struck the *Equator*, with terrific force, crippling her in an instant. Caught in the billowing troughs of the windswept lake, with waves sweeping over the main deck and down the open hatches, the whole upper works "threatened to go overboard." Captain Green held his post on the upper deck, bellowing instructions and endeavoring to calm the frightened women and children.

Suddenly a new element confronted the courageous captain. A rich sawmill owner of Prescott, a man over seventy years of age, who "ought to have been ready and willing to pass in his checks, crept up the companionway to the roof, and creeping on his hands and knees, got hold of the captain's legs and besought him to save him — 'Save me, Captain, Save me. I will give you a thousand dollars if you will save me!' " For perhaps the first and only time, Reverend Asa Barlow Green had a lapse from grace. "Let go of me and get below, you d — d cowardly old ——— ——— ———," roared the irate Captain as he kicked him off the roof and down the stairway.[686]

When Captain E. H. Gleim died at Galena in 1856 his loss was deeply mourned. Gleim had begun his career as first clerk aboard the steamboat *Warrior* in 1832. For more than a score of years he was identified with such boats as the *Warrior*, the *Wisconsin*, the *Monona*, the *Royal Arch*, the *Pawnee*, the *Highlander*, and the *Ocean Wave*. He was described as a "fit representative of a class of men, who, in the peaceful pursuits of commerce", had given "proof of every element of manhood" in a "difficult, laborious and hazardous occupation". A Galena editor asserted that such men as Gleim had been as "often tested" as Stephen Decatur or any other national hero. They had stood these tests "like steel" and had given a "high character to our river commerce".[687]

Many of the steamboat captains, whose careers may be traced back to the period of individual ownership, later became identified with the great packet companies that flourished in the golden days of steamboating. The lives of such men as Joseph Throckmorton, Daniel Smith Harris, William F. Davidson, and Joseph Reynolds portray graphically the profound changes which occurred in steamboating. The study of such corporations as the Keokuk Packet Company, the Minnesota Packet Company, the Northern Line, the White Collar Line, and the Diamond Jo Line present in miniature the transition which took place within the nation itself. These constitute, however, separate and complete chapters in the history of Upper Mississippi steamboating.[688]

45

The Opening of Navigation

THE OPENING OF navigation at St. Paul in 1849 was peculiarly dramatic. Fettered for nearly five months by ice-locked Lake Pepin, the tiny settlement anxiously awaited the arrival of the first steamboat. During the winter, mail had been brought up irregularly by dog or horse train, but the newspapers were several months old. It was not until late in January that word was received of the election of Zachary Taylor. Everyone hoped that the first steamboat would bring news of the creation of the Territory of Minnesota. The afternoon of April 9, 1849, was pleasant; the river was clear of ice, and yet no steamboat had appeared at the St. Paul wharf.

But Captain Daniel Smith Harris was nearing St. Paul with the *Dr. Franklin No. 2* loaded with immigrants who watched with awe a violent thunder storm that had begun at dusk. As the steamboat rounded the bend a vivid flash of lightning revealed her presence to those ashore. "In an instant the welcome news flashed like electricity, throughout the town. All were on the *qui vive*, and regardless of the pelting rain, the raging wind, and the pealing thunder, almost the entire male population rushed to the landing — hundreds clustered on the shore unmindful of the storm as the fine steamboat *Dr. Franklin No. 2* dashed gallantly up to the landing."

Steamboating on Upper Mississippi

The moment the boat's stage touched the shore the news-hungry "boarders" scrambled up, brushing aside the deck hands and immigrants about to come ashore. Captain Harris and his officers were the men of the hour. "The barkeeper had need of the arms of Briareus, the eyes of Argus, and the tongues of Rumor, to satisfy the demands, made upon him. — At length the news was known and one glad shout resounding through the boat, taken up on shore, and echoed from our beetling bluffs and rolling hills, proclaimed that the Bill for the organization of Minnesota Territory had become a law." [689]

The arrival of the first steamboat each spring was a big event in the life of every river town. Isolated through the long winter months and with only fragmentary news dispatches trickling in from the outside world, each embryonic frontier community hailed with enthusiasm that captain who opened the season of navigation. The first steamboat arrival was a memorable event and remained the topic of conversation for weeks. Later, in the fifties and sixties, some river towns, especially those above Lake Pepin, granted free wharfage during the ensuing year to the first boat — not a small item when the total disbursements for the season were counted. Furthermore, the captain who gained this much desired laurel was always certain of added popularity.

St. Louis was not greatly concerned over the opening of navigation. Ice closed the Mississippi at St. Louis on an average of twenty-nine days yearly between 1865 and 1882. Four times during this period the river was open

The Opening of Navigation

the year round : once (during the winter of 1880-1881) the Mississippi was closed for seventy-eight days.[690]

As steamboats ascended the Mississippi above the mouth of the Missouri, the opening of navigation became more important. Between Keokuk and Dubuque the river was ice-locked on an average of from 75 to 105 days each year. St. Paul, on the other hand, was "frozen in" on an average of almost five months yearly. Thus, the season of navigation for the port of St. Paul averaged only 222 days between the years 1849 and 1866, or a little more than seven months. The polar barrier erected by Lake Pepin deprived St. Paul of commerce with ports below for an average of 143 days during this period compared with twenty-nine days for St. Louis. Ports at the foot of Lake Pepin could usually depend on a month more of navigation than could St. Paul.[691]

Prior to 1850 the mineral region and the river towns below Galena and Dubuque were the chief ports of call for steamboats. Damaging floods preceded the opening of navigation at Galena in 1836. By mid-March the Fever River rose to the highest point since 1828 : Main Street was flooded and much property lost. The ice had hardly slipped out when navigation opened : the *Olive Branch* churned up the Fever River with her guards dripping on April 1st. On the following day the *Wisconsin* arrived from St. Louis. Hard in her wake came the *Galenian*, having first left a heavy tribute of freight and passengers at Dubuque. On April 3rd the *Dubuque*, the *Cavalier*, and the *Warrior* were discharging freight and passengers at the

Galena levee. The opening of navigation brought many new faces to Galena and Dubuque, so that the levees of these enterprising mining communities fairly bustled with activity.[692]

Although Dubuque and Galena continued to welcome steamboats, the completion of the telegraph to such points as St. Louis, Keokuk, Burlington, and Dubuque in 1848 made these towns no longer dependent on steamboats as messengers of news. And the construction of the railroads to the Mississippi during the fifties made most of the ports between St. Louis and La Crosse virtually independent of the steamboat. The admission of Wisconsin as a State in 1848 and the creation of the Territory of Minnesota in 1849 focused attention on ports situated above the mineral region.[693]

The *ultima thule* of spring navigation was St. Paul, at the head of navigation on the Upper Mississippi. Each spring the mad dash of steamboats for this port was chronicled by the press all the way up from St. Louis. The records hung up by Captain Harris illustrate graphically the intense human interest in gaining the honor of bringing in the first boat.

Between 1844 and 1861 inclusive, Captain Harris battered his way through ice-choked Lake Pepin seven times to win the much sought laurel. Sometimes a score of steamboats lay marshaled at the foot of Lake Pepin waiting for the ice to move so that competition was extremely keen. But no other captain could match the brilliant feats of Daniel Smith Harris in gaining St. Paul first.

[454]

The Opening of Navigation

In 1844 Harris reached St. Paul with the *Otter* on April 6th — the first arrival of the season. He repeated this performance in 1845 with the same boat, and, curiously enough, on the same date. In 1848 the *Senator* was first, arriving on April 7th. The following year the *Dr. Franklin No. 2* arrived on April 9th; while in 1853 the *West Newton* led the way to St. Paul with a considerable number of passengers and a large freight cargo. Two years later (1855) the *War Eagle* dashed into port with colors flying and cannons roaring while all St. Paul turned out to greet the gallant skipper. In his last victory, in 1858, the *Grey Eagle* came screeching past Pig's Eye on the 25th of March — the earliest arrival on record. His nearest rivals at this wild sport of playing checkers with frozen ice-cakes were Orrin Smith and John Atchison, both of whom managed to gain the laurel twice during this period, a record which pales before the seven victories of Captain Harris.[604]

"The arrival of the first steamer of the season is a great day for St. Paul", declared Harriet Bishop in 1853. "Anxiety has long run high; eyes are strained in anxious expectation, and when finally it rounds the bend, hundreds of citizens gathered at the river, send forth a prolonged shout of welcome, and the bluffs echo the general joy."

On at least one occasion, Miss Bishop recalls, the passengers actually chopped a lane through Lake Pepin. Early in 1850, the *Highland Mary* (John Atchison commanding) found the lake frozen solid. For days the boat lay at the foot of the lake, unable to proceed northward. Several of the passengers finally returned downstream in despair. In desperation the remainder of the passengers and crew volunteered their services and actually chopped a path through the ice. They received, as they well merited, "hearty shouts of congratulations from the people of St. Paul." [695]

Other passengers found it easier to walk around Lake Pepin. On April 14, 1856, William W. Pendergast, a Minnesota pioneer, reached Read's Landing only to find Lake Pepin frozen over. After waiting two days for the ice to break up, Pendergast and his companions walked the thirty miles round Lake Pepin over a muddy road to Wacouta. Here they found Captain Louis Robert's *Time and Tide* with "steam up" ready to set out for St. Paul. "This steaming up", Pendergast declared, "was only a trick to make us buy a ticket at once. It was played several times before the boat finally started." Pendergast did not reach St. Paul until the 17th. The following day the *Lady Franklin* came swooshing up to the levee, the first to batter her way through to St. Paul. [696]

It was not merely St. Paul that depended on the arrival of the first steamboat in the spring. Lake Pepin blocked off the St. Croix Valley, the Minnesota Valley, and the region above the Falls of St. Anthony. As spring approached the settlers in these areas waited impatiently for the arrival of fresh supplies. The opening of navigation in 1857 illustrates the dependence of St. Paul and the towns on the Minnesota River upon the steamboat.

Navigation on the Minnesota River was usually possible

several weeks before the first steamboat arrived at St. Paul from below because of the length of time required for Lake Pepin to open. Since each spring only a small quantity of freight from the previous winter remained in St. Paul, the trade of the Minnesota River was rather light until new supplies came from below. The winter of 1856-1857 was unusually severe, and the Minnesota River was open for navigation three weeks before Lake Pepin relinquished its grip on the Upper Mississippi. Ten boats lay at the foot of the lake several days before it opened, and a number of others were docked three miles below at Wabasha. In this colorful flotilla were steamboats hailing from distant Cincinnati and Pittsburgh. On April 29th twenty-two craft, crowded with passengers, impatiently awaited the moving out of the ice. The more venturesome captains had for several days butted the prows of their boats against the unbreakable wall in vain attempts to crash through.[697]

Fifteen hundred passengers fumed at the delay of the twenty-two stranded craft at the foot of Lake Pepin. Hundreds of others, exasperated at the obdurate tenacity of the lake, set out on foot for Red Wing, willing to endure the greatest hardships and inconvenience in order to reach St. Paul earlier than was possible if they remained aboard their boats. At Red Wing they were met by the Minnesota River packets, which flourished on this early season business made up of passengers who cared little what facilities were provided so long as they could reach their destination. On April 16th the *Reveille* arrived at

St. Paul from Red Wing, her decks thronged with people.[698]

Since Lake Pepin did not open until April 30th in 1857 the owners of the *Reveille* and the *Time and Tide* were able to amass snug fortunes before their season actually began on the Minnesota. Before daylight on April 17th the *Time and Tide* came into St. Paul with a full load of passengers and the Red Wing band. At the prevailing rates for passage the fares of the 246 cabin and 197 deck passengers netted the owner of the boat $1821 for a single trip. This amount was almost equal to her total passenger receipts for the first five trips on the Minnesota in 1857. On April 24th of that year the *Time and Tide* brought 196 cabin passengers and 145 "deckers" from Red Wing; three days later the same craft churned up to the St. Paul levee with 368 passengers perched precariously about her decks from stem to stern and occupying all available space from engine room to texas.

Such trips brought a broad grin to the face of Louis Robert, the jovial and picturesque captain of the *Time and Tide*. It was only five years since Captain Robert had purchased the little steamboat *Black Hawk* for six thousand dollars to run regularly on the Minnesota River. At the time the boat was the subject of lively newspaper comment, for it was the first steamboat owned entirely in St. Paul. In 1857 the *Time and Tide* alone earned enough in the spring trade between St. Paul and Red Wing to pay the original cost of the historic *Black Hawk*.[699]

A final yawn of the seemingly bottomless old Lake

The Opening of Navigation

Pepin split and ripped its winter coat wide open and produced a narrow but dangerous lane for steamboat captains to venture through. And venture they did. Battering their way through giant blocks of shifting, crumbling ice, the *War Eagle* and the *Galena* started up the ice-choked lake, risking all to gain the coveted laurel that went to the first steamboat to reach St. Paul. Hard in their frozen wake followed such boats as the *Rescue*, the *Henry Clay*, the *Hamburg*, the *Atlanta*, the *Conewago*, the *Sam Young*, the *Golden State*, and a dozen others. Just below St. Paul, when victory was almost in the *War Eagle's* grasp, a deck hand fell overboard and a yawl put out to rescue the unfortunate man. It was a humane but costly act : on May 2, 1857, the *Pioneer and Democrat* noted that Captain W. H. Laughton brought his *Galena* into port at 2:00 A. M. on May 1st and that the *War Eagle* landed fifteen minutes later.

And then the deluge! Twenty-five hundred tons of freight were dumped pell-mell upon the St. Paul levee in forty-eight hours by the score of boats that followed the *Galena* and the *War Eagle*. The St. Paul levee was the "only place of attraction" on those bustling first two days of May, 1857. And on May 3rd an additional two thousand tons were discharged, which kept every dray and wagon in St. Paul busy throughout the day and far into the night.[700]

From Dubuque and Galena, St. Louis and New Orleans, Cincinnati and Pittsburgh came the goods that formed the principal cargoes for steamboats running above the Falls

Steamboating on Upper Mississippi

or to the swiftly growing valley towns of the Minnesota
River. And from Chaska, Shakopee, Carver, Henderson,
St. Peter, Mankato, and still smaller entrepôts, the Big
Woods country was supplied through the medium of the
steamboats that made possible the rapid growth and devel-
opment of the region.

Steamboatmen and merchants in the various ports below
Lake Pepin were exasperated at the tenacity with which the
lake clung to her icy cloak. In 1857 the river was open at
Dubuque on March 25th; Winona was free of ice on April
1st; but St. Paul could not greet the steamboat until May
1st. Naturally such conditions elicited bitter editorials in
the various newspapers. In the spring of 1859 the Mississippi was described as a "National Highway" by D. H.
Dolterer, who urged it was to the best interests of Dubuque
to break through Lake Pepin when the river was open to
that point. Dolterer suggested that his "specially constructed" icebreaker, which opened Lake Cayuga for
steamboats during the winter of 1849-1850, could slash a
channel through Lake Pepin in one day. The novel invention broke ice a foot thick with ease by lifting the ice rather
than exerting a downward pressure. The icebreaker was
attached to a boat 120 feet long and could be removed
when not in use, thereby permitting the craft to be employed as a ferry or towboat.[701]

Dolterer's suggestion apparently went unheeded. Meanwhile, a Dubuque editor announced with pardonable pride
that the *Key City* reached St. Paul first in 1859. Captain
Jones Worden had started bucking the ice with the *Key*

City on the Minnesota side on April 19th. When but two miles below Lake City he was forced to cross through a crevass to the Wisconsin side. Worming his boat upstream two miles, Captain Worden found another gaping fissure and succeeded in recrossing to Lake City where the entire population greeted the plucky captain. The following morning at eight o'clock the citizens of St. Paul saw the smoke from an approaching steamboat. A grand rush for the levee ensued and there were "wild conjectures" as to what boat was approaching. By the time the *Key City* turned the bend a "stream of humanity" had poured down Jackson and Robert streets so that two thousand were on hand to greet the gallant craft as she made fast to the dock. The ferryboat and the Rotary Mills whistled a shrill welcome to the *Key City* and a cannon was discharged in honor of the occasion. Captain Worden and his officers were cheered to the echo by the assembled throng.[702]

In attempting to break through the ice barrier steamboat captains sometimes endangered the lives of passengers as well as the cargo. In 1857 reports drifted down to Dubuque that both the *Galena* and the *War Eagle* had suffered serious damages and that some boats had run aground or were proceeding with their holds filled with water. It was also rumored that St. Paul had increased the prize to $3000 cash, besides offering a set of colors for the boat and $300 for the pilot. These reports were later branded as untrue; but for over a week following the opening of Lake Pepin newspapers carried accounts of the great excitement at St. Paul and the ports below. And well might the Upper Mississippi Valley be excited, for Lake Pepin had blocked navigation to St. Paul until May 1st, the latest date on record between 1844 and 1884.[703]

The eccentricity of the weather and Lake Pepin was demonstrated when the *Grey Eagle* arrived at St. Paul on March 25, 1858. This was the earliest date on record between 1844 and 1884. The average date of arrival for this period of forty-one years was April 13th. Only three steamboats, besides the *Grey Eagle*, were able to batter their their way through Lake Pepin before April 1st : the *Annie* whisked up to the St. Paul levee on March 25, 1878, to tie the record of the *Grey Eagle*.[704]

Citizens in every port along the Mississippi anxiously studied the river each spring and looked forward with keen anticipation for the first boat of the season. For days in advance the newspapers chronicled the condition of the ice at the various ports above and below. Thus, on February 28, 1868, the Dubuque *Herald* recorded that navigation was open to Quincy — which was sooner than most old-timers could remember. The first appearance of the regular "River News" column occurred on March 10th with the observation that large crowds had gathered on the river to watch the ice. The Mississippi actually split its icy mantle a few times that day, but each time it quickly closed up. It was believed, however, that the river would soon be free of ice. Five days later the *Herald* announced that the Northern Line steamboat *Davenport* would leave St. Louis for points upstream. On March 19th it reported the river was open to La Crosse and chronicled the departure of the *Sterling* from Galena with 115 kegs of beer. The following day the *Lady Pike* arrived at the Dubuque levee to open the season. On March 21st the *Diamond Jo* arrived at Winona to initiate the season to that port. The *Diamond Jo* was headed for the foot of Lake Pepin which was still frozen. It was not until April 4, 1868, that the *Phil Sheridan* was able to smash her way through to St. Paul.[705]

The coming of the railroad to St. Paul proved the death-knell for steamboating. Its effect was quickly reflected in the passenger and freight receipts and in the general indifference to the opening of navigation. "Before St. Paul had railroad communication with the east", an editor observed in 1873, "the first steamboat arrival in the spring was an event of much greater importance than now. There was quite a celebration, ending with a dance on the boat — and the steamer was given the freedom of the city, that is, was allowed to use the levee free of wharfage all the season."

The effect of the coming of the "Robber Barons" was mournfully recorded when the steamboat *Northwestern* arrived in the spring of 1873. "One silent indication that causes were at work to rob the noble stream of its early glory was visible to all spectators, last evening — the omnibusses returned from the levee empty; and the first trip of the Northwestern was made remunerative by freight only, of which she made a very respectable showing." [706]

46

Closing of Navigation

A DUBUQUE EDITOR marvelled at the power of the ice
gnomes over the Mississippi River. In a frigid blast
throughout the Upper Mississippi Valley on December 13,
1859, the mercury fell from eight to thirteen degrees below zero in a "couple of hours". Numbed fingers set type
which vividly pictured the unequal struggle between King
Winter and the Mississippi. "It took a firm hold on the
Father of Waters — laying a giant's hand upon him, and
arresting his course, as easily as a boy does that of his toy-
wagon. In other words the weather commenced a few days
since bridging the river — it rafted down at first the
sleepers, and yesterday it put down the planking, and if
nothing hinders, the work to-day or to-morrow at farthest, will be finished in a style at once elegant and substantial." [707]

Fortunately Dubuque was no longer dependent on the
steamboat in 1859 : the railroads had already reached that
port. A decade before, however, the premature closing
of navigation would have been viewed with mingled regret and alarm. For, despite the large number of steamboat arrivals during the regular season of navigation, river
towns frequently found themselves with insufficient supplies to face the rigors of a long winter siege.

Small wonder that anxious river towns joyfully welcomed those steamboat captains who risked the dangers of floating ice to bring last minute supplies before navigation closed. "Steamboats continue to arrive at our wharves, laden with merchandize and passengers", a St. Paul editor asserted late in 1849. "Within the past week, the Senator, the Yankee, the [Dr.] Franklin No. 2 and the [Dr.] Franklin No. 1, have all paid us a visit."

Although winter was fast approaching, the arrival of another boat was hopefully anticipated. Everyone breathed a "sigh of relief" as the *Yankee* poked her nose around the bend before daylight on November 19th. Late in November the *Enterprise* dashed up to the Red Wing levee, and after discharging all her freight and passengers hastened back through Lake Pepin. An irate St. Paul editor upbraided the captain for not continuing upstream and wondered if the *Enterprise* had lived up to her name.[708]

Late season trips were scarcely pleasant, either for crew or passengers. As one belated traveler in 1853 records: "We have just emerged from the exciting pleasures of a six day's trip on board the steamer Blackhawk, from Galena to a point on Lake St. Croix opposite Hudson. The officers and crew did all in their power to render their passengers happy and comfortable but the boat and the river were against them. The Hawk is a worthless old tub, and the Mississippi is turned bottom up. We can safely say that navigation is closed for the season."

But the river at St. Paul was not yet closed : the *Clarion* arrived a week later with news of the Crimean War and the New York election — "just what people wanted to hear about". And the following week, on November 26th, the *Jenny Lind* was recorded. Her welcome was hardly a kindly one for the sheriff boarded her with bills for $200 and had her "in limbo" for two hours "when she performed the usual trick of transient boats of cutting her cable and departing." [709]

A capricious climate often caused editors to forecast the close of navigation several weeks before it actually occurred. On November 11, 1854, a St. Paul newspaper records : "The *Galena* yesterday took down what few still lingered of the visitors to Minnesota during the past season, and our city has assumed her wonted appearance. During the summer thousands of strangers crowded our streets, and it was almost impossible to distinguish the citizen from the stranger. But winter comes, and we are left alone to mingle with ourselves and form those re-unions which we have heretofore so much enjoyed."

And yet navigation continued for almost a month. Five steamboats (the *Alice*, the *Minnesota Belle*, the *Henrietta*, the *Excelsior*, and the *Luella*) discharged freight and passengers at the St. Paul levee the very next day. Many of those who came apparently planned to test the "rigors" of the North Star State. The *Navigator*, the *Clarion*, and the *Alhambra* followed within a week — the latter bringing one of the largest freights she ever carried and charging twelve dollars for cabin passage downstream. On November 20th the *Lady Franklin* dropped off her passengers at Point Douglas, and on the following day the *Minnesota Belle* made the journey as far as Prescott.

Closing of Navigation

On November 23, 1854, just as St. Paul was again ready to "settle down" for a long winter, the shrill whistle of a steamboat was heard and citizens rushed to the levee to find the *Navigator* back again with a huge cargo of freight and passengers. It was her best trip of the season. Prospective passengers and shippers were warned that the boat would leave immediately for winter quarters below. The captain of the *Navigator* was commended for taking the mails free.

Two weeks had passed since the newspaper had forecast the close of navigation; and yet the Mississippi remained open. A few days later the river was full of ice; but on November 30th there was very little ice and the editor, vexed no doubt at his failure as a weather prophet, observed that citizens were "anxious for winter". He declared it was "provoking" that the Mississippi did not close. Finally, on December 5, 1854, it was announced that the Mississippi was "Closed at Last" to the "delight" of all St. Paul citizens who were ready to enjoy their winter sports.[710]

Steamboat captains charged high rates on both freight and passengers for late season trips. The St. Paul levee hummed with activity during the first two weeks of November in 1857. The *Henry Clay* left on the 5th with an "unusually large number of cabin passengers" who planned to spend the winter in the South or East. In addition the *Henry Clay* carried downstream copies of the *Pioneer and Democrat* of November 5, 1857, upbraiding the Pittsburgh *Post* of October 29th for asserting that ice was already floating in the river at St. Paul when the only ice to be found was in buckets. "From this time until the close of navigation", the editor concluded, "the boats will reap a rich harvest in the passenger business. The rates of fare have been raised, in accordance with the established custom of the Packet Company, just before the Close of Navigation." [711]

Many captains profited by the high tariffs prevailing late in 1857. Six steamboats docked at St. Paul on November 8th; the levee was jammed with boxes, barrels, and sacks until late at night. Two days later steamboat cargoes were dumped in mud three inches deep and a newspaper hoped that the levee might be paved in 1858 to avoid the recurrence of such "terrible " conditions. The *Milwaukee* put in her appearance at St. Paul on November 12th, followed by the *Minnesota*, the *Alhambra*, and the *Fanny Harris*. All encountered heavy ice flows between St. Paul and Lake Pepin. When the *Northern Light* reported the river nearly closed on the 13th, the *Pioneer and Democrat* lamented : "We are, from this time forward, for five months forced to the use of slow coaches to give us our news, and our visitors." [712]

Such last minute trips were profitable, but also dangerous. On November 23, 1857, John Saunders, pilot of the steamboat *Minnesota*, arrived in Dubuque with news that the *Minnesota*, after cutting her way through three miles of solid ice, had been "frozen in" opposite McGregor. Saunders reported that the *Envoy* and the *Flora* were also frozen in at Prairie du Chien. The river was closed. [713]

Closing of Navigation

If St. Paul fretted at the barrier which Lake Pepin presented, Winona smugly rejoiced at her rival's discomfiture. On November 27, 1855, the Winona *Republican* in chronicling the arrival of the *Ben Coursin* slyly observed that the Mississippi below was still free of ice. "Thus", chortled the editor, "while the calm and sluggish waters of Lake Pepin, present a Polar barrier to any river communication with any points above it, Winona is of easy access still, and the present prospect is favorable for a much longer continuance of open waters."

The *Ben Coursin* again reached Winona with a good freight on the night of December 3rd. She returned immediately to Dunleith. The *Kate Cassel* arrived the same day; and on December 8th that indefatigable craft again hustled up to the Winona levee. Her captain endeavored to reach St. Paul, but ice blocked his way eighteen miles below Lake Pepin. A week later it was noted that St. Paul had had 563 steamboat arrivals during 1855 while Winona could boast 583. Twenty steamboats, it was pointed out, had reached Winona since Lake Pepin closed.[714]

The following December (1856) the *Kate Cassel* managed to reach Hastings with an enormous load of freight. The activity on the Upper Mississippi at this season is revealed by the log of the steamboat *Flora* printed in the Dubuque *Express and Herald* of December 3, 1856: "Left Dunleith the 21st with nearly 400 passengers and a heavy freight; met Golden State below Guttenberg; Envoy passed down; met Northern Belle the 22d; met Fannie

Harris at Coon Slough; met Kate Cassel below La Crosse, evening 22d; met Gossamer at La Crosse; snowed all night; met Alhambra below Fountain City; got aground on Beef Slough and remained there Sunday night; went through Lake Pepin the 24th; reached Red Wing at 11 p. m.; snowing like great guns; reached Hastings morning of 25th; river gorged with ice for seven miles above and weather cold; left Hastings Tuesday; met Resolute Wednesday morning below Beef Slough; Progress there and could not get over; she returned to Winona and discharged her cargo; met J.[acob] Traber at Winona and Ben Coursin below La Crosse . . . The *Flora* brought down 250 passengers and went into winter quarters at the upper landing, Dubuque."

Galena, like St. Paul, was also handicapped in her location since the Fever River usually froze over before the Mississippi which gave a decided advantage to Dubuque. Thus in 1836 the season closed for Galena on November 15th, but the *Gipsey* was able to get to Dubuque as late as December 1st.[715]

The weather prophets of the Galena press were as inaccurate as their fellow-editors farther upstream. Ice was already forming when the *Danube* and the *Dubuque* with two barges in tow, came "whistling up" to the Galena levee on November 10, 1851, with one of the heaviest cargoes of the season. But the ice gnomes retreated, and on November 26th the arrival of the *Oswego* and the *Martha No. 2* was recorded.

Once more a film of ice formed on Fever River, but not

before the *Uncle Toby* put in at Galena shoving a barge of coal for Dubuque. A few days later news flashed to Galena that the *Wyoming* left St. Louis on November 26th and that the *Danube* had set out from the same port the following day. A local editor doubted that either craft would be able to reach Galena; but on Sunday evening, November 30th, the *Wyoming* arrived with the *Danube* trailing in only an hour behind her. Despite cold and blustering weather the *Shenandoah* managed to creep up to the Galena levee on December 3rd. Her hasty departure marked the close of navigation.[716]

In addition to floating ice ahead, captains had to run the risk of being caught in the vise-like jaws of a freezing river. Should this take place the boat must be left behind, and the men return overland. This left the cargo of the boat open to plunder and to possible destruction by an ice gorge in the following spring. None but the most venturesome would risk a late season trip.

Captain Daniel Smith Harris exhibited his usual skill and daring at this novel gamble with winter. On November 15th, 1836, he steamed out of Fever River with the *Science*, the last boat to depart that year. In 1840 the *Otter* left Galena on November 25th, and the following year the same little craft buffeted her way out of frozen Fever River on November 22nd. This feat, together with her arrival first at the St. Paul levee in 1844 and 1845, gives the *Otter* and her daring master a singularly unique record.[717]

In 1845 Captain Harris lost an exciting race with the

ice and was forced to run the first *War Eagle* into winter quarters near Rock Island.[718] Three years later Lake Pepin almost caught the *Senator*. "Ten years ago, the eleventh of this month", relates the Glencoe *Register* of November 24, 1848, in commenting on this incident, "navigation closed on the Mississippi above the foot of Lake Pepin. Franklin Steele, Esq., who at that time supplied most of the then Territory of Minnesota with goods and provisions, had a whole cargo frozen up on the 9th at the head of Lake Pepin, in the old steamer Senator, Capt. Harris. It was with the utmost difficulty that the Senator worked her way through the Lake on the 10th." [719]

The last trip of the season presented many dangers and hardships. It was difficult to secure a full crew to make the trip, and fabulous wages were often paid because the extremely rigorous climate and the possibility of returning on foot through a desolate, Indian infested, snow-covered country deterred all but the adventurous. But merchants and travelers were usually glad to pay double and triple the usual rates on the last trip of the season, and captains often made an extra profit.

On one occasion the Minnesota Packet Company learned that a large amount of freight still remained on the upper river and sent Captain Harris to get it. Although he was ready to put the *War Eagle* into winter quarters and was incensed because some other captain had not been dispatched, Harris steamed out of Fever River and proceeded up the Mississippi in the face of a biting wind. He refused to be governed by the prevailing tariff rates, however.

Closing of Navigation

"Now you keep your hands off", he declared to the Packet officials on departing, "and I'll make some money this trip."

Captain Harris succeeded in reaching Hastings, Minnesota, where an ice-locked river ahead and rapidly freezing river below forced him to turn back. Freight and passengers were found in abundance at almost every port. The hoarse whistle of the *War Eagle* on the cold, frosty air sounded a cheerful note to belated passengers and shippers. Four days after her departure the *War Eagle* came shivering up the Fever River. Upon boarding the boat to extend their congratulations, the Packet officials found Captain Harris gloomy and disconsolate. Inquiry finally revealed that Harris had set out to make $10,000 on the trip and had "cleaned up only $9,700". It was his failure to reach his goal and establish a record and not the loss of a few hundred dollars that wounded the pride of the ambitious captain.[720]

Despite the fact that he had bitterly denounced Captain Harris and the Minnesota Packet Company, a hostile editor could not refrain from paying a tribute to the popular skipper. "The steamer War Eagle", notes the Winona *Republican* of November 24, 1858, "came up as far as La Crosse on last Friday morning, having on board a large quantity of goods, and a considerable number of passengers, for Winona, and towns in the interior, but her captain (A. T. Kingman) being somewhat afraid of the floating ice, would not proceed any further. Her cargo was accordingly discharged at La Crosse. If the War

Eagle had been in command of the resolute Captain Harris, the ice of last Friday morning would not have prevented *him* from making this port".

The opening of navigation provided river towns with an opportunity for gala celebrations. The closing of navigation left them in dreary isolation. Both events afforded steamboat captains an opportunity to test their skill and daring in the face of a rigorous nature. Not even a fast record could surpass in importance the achievements of those hardy souls whose names were linked with the opening and closing of navigation.

47

Ice Gorges and Winter Quarters

SPRING NAVIGATION was a period of great travail for the Upper Mississippi River. Giant blocks of shifting, crumbling ice grated and jarred against one another night and day as the mighty waterway sought to shake loose its icy chains. Death and destruction often rode the crest of the devastating avalanche that was hurtled downstream.

Early in 1874 the ice on the Mississippi at Muscatine broke up and closed again within the space of twenty-four hours. "The movement of the ice", according to a Muscatine editor, "left it in jagged, irregular masses, or hummocks, not unlike the surface of a frozen Polar sea . . . The sleet covered trees on the opposite bank glistened beautifully in the sunlight, adding lustre to the scenery. In the evening the bright moon-light intensified and lent a weird-like effect to the scene, and the deep roaring of the crushing ice at a point above the city where the river was still open added majesty to the spectacle in the mind of the beholder." [721]

Rivermen lived in constant fear lest steamboats, wharf-boats, and ferries be destroyed by the innumerable ice gorges formed when the ice broke up. The impact of tons of floating ice frequently crushed and sunk steamboats at their moorings or swept them downstream. Accordingly steamboats were quartered each winter in a sheltered lagoon or slough, or in a small tributary of the Mississippi. A watchman was usually left on guard, and frequently a small force remained aboard to overhaul and repair the craft for the next season. As early as 1829 Captain Joseph Throckmorton put the *Red Rover* in winter quarters near the mouth of the Platte River a few miles north of Dubuque.[722]

One of the earliest and most noted ice gorges occurred at present-day Keokuk in 1832. The winter had been unusually severe, and when the river rose suddenly it shattered ice thirty-four inches thick and piled it so high that the trees on the opposite bluff were invisible. Five thousand pigs of lead buried in the mud by the weight of the ice were not recovered until the following June. Four hundred cords of wood were carried away; the keelboat *Ophelia* was lifted to an angle of forty-five degrees; and a large elm was sheared in half by the ice. The water rose fourteen feet in an hour; houses along the levee suffered many damages. Ten years later another ice gorge at Keokuk piled the ice thirty feet high, broke the steamboat *Otter* from her moorings, and "played all sorts of fantastic tricks with the boats and houses that came in its way." Eye-witnesses declared that the "force and weight of the ice were irresistible and terrible to behold." [723]

The destructive nature of the ice gorges which formed on the Upper Mississippi was quickly recognized by the pioneer steamboat captains. At the close of the season of 1835 both the *Warrior* and the *Galenian* were taken around to Pittsburgh to go into winter quarters.[724]

Ice Gorges and Winter Quarters

During the heyday of steamboating the number of safe winter quarters was limited. Upper Mississippi boats could be found as far south as St. Louis where the west bank in the vicinity of Arsenal Island was for many years "considered one of the safest winter-harbors on the river." [725] An additional advantage accrued from the number of skilled artisans and boat builders at St. Louis.

Despite the short winter season, the St. Louis waterfront was sometimes gouged by the tons of ice that choked the channel at that point. On December 16, 1865, and again on January 12 and 13, 1866, ice gorges at St. Louis caused damage amounting to nearly a million dollars. A score of steamboats were sunk, ranging in value from $10,000 for the *Sioux City* to $85,000 for the *Belle of Memphis*. A number of others were greatly damaged. [726]

Ten years later, on December 13, 1876, another ice gorge at St. Louis destroyed the *Jennie Baldwin*, the *Bayard*, the *Rock Island*, and the *Davenport*, and damaged the *Centennial*, the *Alex Mitchell*, the *War Eagle*, and the *Andy Johnson*. Not one of these boats was insured. Three small steamboats (the *Fannie Keener*, the *South Shore*, and the *Southern Belle*) were likewise sunk. Fortunately these captains carried insurance on their craft. [727]

The problem of retaining secure winter quarters at St. Louis was recognized by the United States Engineers in 1877 when the effect of closing the chute was pointed out: "The experience of the last winter from natural causes affords an illustration of what will be the yearly experience when the chute is closed by a dam. There will then

[477]

be no place within convenient distance of Saint Louis where boats can lie during the winter with reasonable safety. The tonnage employed on the upper rivers will be compelled to retire to Alton Slough betimes, and that of the lower river, of which a considerable part cannot pass under the bridge, will have no refuge, and must remain away from Saint Louis, or incur the risk of being lost should a sudden intense cold find them there. As the inevitable result of closing the chute will be to deprive the tonnage of Saint Louis of its only ice-harbor, it seems necessary to call attention to the danger, and to suggest a remedy; for the interests of commerce demand that there should be a winter harbor of refuge in the immediate vicinity of Saint Louis." [728]

St. Louis could well look to her laurels as winter quarters for steamboats. By 1873 the steamboat *Northwestern* and a dozen other boats of the Keokuk Northern Line were making their winter quarters in Alton Slough. [729]

Although no other point above St. Louis suffered such colossal marine disasters, the aggregate of damages was very high. Late in November, 1845, the *Iron City* and the *War Eagle* lost their race with the ice gnomes and were ice bound a short distance below the Upper Rapids. The following February a sudden return of warm weather allowed the two boats to escape to St. Louis. Late in December, 1848, the *Iron City* struck an ice gorge while on her way to the Illinois River and sank. Several of her crew were drowned. [730]

Early in April, 1866, the *Northern Light* was sunk by

[478]

ice in fifteen feet of water in Coon Slough. Her chimneys and upper works were battered by ice and carried away. On this occasion some valuable property was saved by a deck hand aboard the *Northern Light* who was "lowered by his heels" into the icy water through a hole cut in the upper deck. By previous arrangement "a kick was the signal for him to be hauled out when he could stand it no longer for want of breath." He won the "grateful remembrance" of the bar-keeper by recovering seventy-five dollars worth of valuable property.[731]

It was not alone while in winter quarters that steamboats were threatened by ice gorges. Sometimes captains started out too early in the spring and ran afoul of dangerous gorges that jammed the Mississippi. Witness, for example, the progress of the *Northwestern* upstream in the spring of 1874 : "Above New Boston she encountered her first ice gorge — and there she lay all Saturday night. On Sunday morning she was forced to 'butt' her way through the ice to Muscatine, and arrived there at 4½ o'clock Sunday afternoon. She remained there half an hour, discharging her cargo, and left for the North. Then came her trial. She met a gorge between Drury's and Fairport that she could not walk over — and she hugged the shore all night. Yesterday morning she put into a slough and came out near Andalusia, where she met another gorge. She was several hours in circumventing this icy barrier — but she did it at last and came out victorious — steaming then to Davenport." [732]

Steamboats in winter quarters sometimes escaped destruction as if by miracle. The uncanny escapade of the *Sucker State* at the Fort Madison ice gorge in the spring of 1867 was widely heralded by rivermen. It appears that the *Sucker State* and several other boats had gone into winter quarters the previous fall behind an island opposite Fort Madison. When the river broke up "with a crash" these craft "barely escaped destruction by the immense masses of ice that bore down upon them." The steamboat *Reserve* suffered "considerable damage"; the ferryboat *Niota* and the *Sucker State* were carried away. Authorities at Keokuk were telegraphed to be on the look-out should the boats stay afloat to that point.

When the *Sucker State* hove in sight "floating lazily along" in the ice-flow, the *Little Eagle* steamed boldly out into the ice-choked current and succeeded in landing her amid the shouts of joy from every one on hand. A Keokuk dispatch reads : "It seems almost miraculous that a large boat like the Sucker State should float 25 miles, without a soul to guide her, and not be destroyed. About the only damage she received was the breaking of her cross hog chains, the smashing of several stanchions on the starboard side, and the disfiguring of her cabin by a spar being driven through her in the vicinity of the wheel house. On her way down she made a landing at Sandusky, where she remained for an hour or so, and then swung round with as much grace as though an experienced pilot was guiding her, and continued 'on her way rejoicing' till overhauled by the Little Eagle." [733]

Ever jealous of the slightest advantage of other river

towns, Dubuque sought to secure a fair share of the spoils that accrued from repairing the steamboats that wintered along the Upper Mississippi. In 1861 an editor declared that Dubuque needed three things : (1) a drydock for the repair of steamboats and other river craft; (2) an ice harbor where steamboats could stay during winters; (3) the removal of the bar in front of the lower levee and inner slough. The nearest place where boats could be docked and repaired was Le Claire. It was shown that at slight expense Lake Peosta could be made into an ice harbor. The *War Eagle*, the *Ocean Wave*, the *Franz Siegel*, the *Durant*, and the *Pearl* passed the winter of 1863-1864 "in the slough".

Four years later (1868) Dubuque was still complaining because it lacked proper winter quarters : not a single boat of the Northern Line or the White Collar Line would winter at Dubuque and repairs were being done elsewhere. It was pointed out that the wharf boats of these companies were safely moored in the slough at Dubuque each winter. Ultimately the harbor at Dubuque gave the "Key City" of Iowa a distinct advantage over most river towns and provided a site for boat construction that has continued to function down to the steel barge era.[704]

No single port along the Mississippi could afford shelter for all the steamboats plying between St. Louis and St. Paul. Consequently strategic locations were selected by captains who would run their boats into winter quarters at these points. Cities brought pressure to bear upon the United States Engineers to make the sloughs in their vicinity safe winter quarters, thereby assuring employment for boatmen and carpenters during the winter months. "The Boats in our Harbor are preparing for Spring", observed the Dubuque *Herald* of February 13, 1861. "The Metropolitan is being caulked and having new guards put on her. She is to be painted and repaired generally, and will come out in the spring as good as new." The ferryboat was also being repaired, and the wharf boat was getting "two new aprons."

The closing of navigation in 1872 was chronicled by the Davenport *Democrat* of November 21st: "The Savanna immediately goes into winter quarters in Rockingham Slough, four miles below the city. This will be the last Northern Line boat which will divide the waters of the Mississippi this season. The Muscatine and Minneapolis both were expected down yet, but the former has gone on the ways at Le Claire, and the latter will winter at Savanna. The steamer Red Wing, which passed this point on Sunday evening, has laid up until spring in New Boston Bay. And thus suddenly and unexpectedly the navigation season of 1872 closes, and the grim reign of ice and frost over our rivers and bays will be undisturbed until the warm breezes of spring blow upon us again."

48

Namesakes of the Ojibway

FAR FLUNG AND powerful were the Ojibway warriors who ranged the land of the sky blue waters. Equally colorful were the steamboat namesakes of this mighty woodland tribe. Three boats bore the proud name of *Chippewa* on the waters of the Mississippi and its tributaries. Another was named *Chippewa Falls*, and still another, *Chippewa Valley*. The voyages of these boats carried them from Pittsburgh in Pennsylvania to Fort Benton in Montana, and from St. Paul in Minnesota to Vicksburg in Mississippi.[735]

The first boat to bear the name *Chippewa* was built at Pittsburgh in 1840 and was owned by Joseph Throckmorton and Hercules L. Dousman. Not long after her first appearance she was purchased by Captain Thomas H. Griffith and plied industriously in the lead trade for three seasons. Then she mysteriously disappeared from the record.[736]

In 1857 the second *Chippewa* and the *Chippewa Falls* appeared. The *Chippewa Falls* was a 93-ton stern-wheel passenger packet built at Monongahela City, Pennsylvania.[737] She appeared in the Chippewa River trade in 1858, running regularly for several seasons between Read's Landing and Eau Claire. In 1864 she was one of a fleet of eight steamboats that transported General Alfred Sully's expedition up the Missouri. After this episode the *Chippewa Falls* also vanished from the record.[738]

A rapidly expanding steamboat frontier is attested by the construction at Eau Claire, Wisconsin, of the 101-ton stern-wheel passenger boat *Chippewa Valley* — said to have been captured by the Confederates at Vicksburg.

A third *Chippewa* was built at La Crosse in 1866. She was a small 74-ton craft that plied for five seasons as a tri-weekly packet between La Crosse and Eau Claire. She was the first arrival of the season at Eau Claire in 1866, 1868, and 1870. The coming of the railroad in July, 1870, forced the *Chippewa* into the rafting trade. She burned to the water's edge in 1871 while in winter quarters at Rumsey's Landing on the Chippewa.[739]

But greatest of all the steamboats named after the Ojibway was the second *Chippewa*. This light draught stern-wheel craft arrived at St. Paul from Pittsburgh in the spring of 1857. She was in the Chippewa River trade in 1858 and also did effective work carrying passengers and freight to St. Paul during low water. In the spring of 1859 she made one trip to St. Paul from St. Louis and appeared destined to continue in this rather prosaic employment. But a far different destiny awaited her : she was chartered by the American Fur Company to join the *Spread Eagle* in transporting a cargo of supplies to Fort Benton.

Up to that time (1859) no steamboat had ascended the Missouri River as far as Fort Benton. The initial attempt was regarded as a hazardous and well-nigh impossible undertaking. Both boats carried a heavy cargo of freight. Low water and the dangers of navigation induced the captain of the *Chippewa* to throw up his contract at Fort Union and sell his boat to the Fur Company for little more than the value of the contract. The entire cargo of the *Spread Eagle* was then transferred to the *Chippewa*.

Panting under her heavy load the *Chippewa* continued upstream, reaching Brulé Bottom within fifteen miles of Fort Benton on July 17, 1859. Here a rapidly falling river forced her to discharge her cargo and hasten downstream. "This noteworthy event", Captain Hiram W. Chittenden declares, "must be classed as one of the celebrated feats in steamboat navigation. The *Chippewa* had reached a point further from the sea by a continuous water course than any other boat had ever been. She was now 3560 miles from, and 2565 feet above, the ocean, and the whole distance had been made by steam on a river unimproved by artificial works."

On July 2, 1860, the steamboats *Chippewa* and *Key West* made the whole trip to Fort Benton and tied fast to the bank. The following year, as the *Chippewa* was again churning up the turgid Missouri, misfortune suddenly overtook her. Members of the crew were enjoying their evening meal when the boat was discovered to be on fire. She was run ashore and then set adrift to avoid the danger of the explosion of gunpowder in her hold. The crippled *Chippewa* had floated downstream about a mile when the explosion occurred, blowing the boat to pieces and hurling fragments great distances. The fire was accidentally caused by deck hands who had gone into the hold to steal liquor.

The voyages of the second *Chippewa* were enacted on a stage whose boundaries were circumscribed by the Alleghenies in the East, the Falls of St. Anthony in the North, and the Rockies in the West. Powerful indeed were the Chippewa Indians and far flung the Valley to which they gave a name. No less dramatic were the exploits of the steamboats which carried an advancing civilization to the wilderness on such craft as the diminutive *Chippewa*.[740]

Notes and References

[1] Hodge's *Handbook of American Indians* (Bureau of American Ethnology Bulletin 30), Pt. 1, pp. 277-281.

[2] The first part of the name, missi, means great, being akin to the modern Chippewa word, Kitchi, and the Gitche of the poet Longfellow. The second part, sippi, otherwise spelled sipi, or sebe, or zibi, is the common Algonquian or Ojibway word for river. — Upham's *Minnesota Geographic Names* in *Minnesota Historical Collections*, Vol. XVII, pp. 4-6; Shankle's *State Names, Flags, Seals, Songs, Birds, Flowers, and other Symbols*, p. 76.

[3] Upham's *Minnesota Geographic Names* in *Minnesota Historical Collections*, Vol. XVII, pp. 4-6; Paullin's *Atlas of the Historical Geography of the United States*, Plates 23-A, 23-B, and 24; Brower's *Itasca State Park* in *Minnesota Historical Collections*, Vol. XI, pp. 273, 274.

[4] Schoolcraft's *Narrative of an Expedition through the Upper Mississippi to Itasca Lake, in 1832* (New York, 1834), pp. iii, 7-14; Brower's *The Mississippi River and its Source* in *Minnesota Historical Collections*, Vol. VII, pp. 142-151; *Dictionary of American Biography*, Vol. XVI, pp. 456, 457; Coues' *The Expeditions of Zebulon Montgomery Pike*, Vol. I, pp. 149-151. For an account of the expedition of 1820 see Schoolcraft's *Narrative Journal of Travels . . . to the Sources of the Mississippi River in the Year 1820* (Albany, 1821).

[5] Schoolcraft's *Narrative of an Expedition through the Upper Mississippi to Itasca Lake, in 1832*, pp. iv, v, 15-62.

[6] Nicollet's *Report Intended to Illustrate A Map of the Hydrographical Basin of the Upper Mississippi River* in *Senate Documents*, 26th Congress 2nd Session, Document 237, pp. 51-59; Baker's *The Sources of the Mississippi* in *Minnesota Historical Collections*, Vol. VI, p. 5.

[7] Brower's *Itasca State Park* in *Minnesota Historical Collections*, Vol. XI, pp. 252-278; Upham's *Minnesota Geographic Names* in *Minnesota Historical Collections*, Vol. XVII, pp. 126-134, 252, 253; Gale's *The Legend of Lake Itasca* and Hart's *The Origin and Meaning of the Name "Itasca"* in *Minnesota History*, Vol. XII, pp. 215-229; Blegen's *That Name "Itasca"* in *Minnesota History*, Vol. XIII, pp. 163-174.

[8] Van Koughnet's *The State Historical Convention of 1932* in *Minnesota History*, Vol. XIII, pp. 277-294.

[9] Blegen's *That Name "Itasca"* in *Minnesota History*, Vol. XIII, pp. 172-174.

[10] *The Galenian*, August 22, 1832. See also the edited letter quoted in *Niles' Register*, Vol. XLIII, p. 227. A file of *The Galenian* is in the library of the Chicago Historical Society.

[11] Brower's *Itasca State Park* in *Minnesota Historical Collections*, Vol. XI, pp. 94-99. The distances on the Mississippi, unless otherwise noted, are taken from the *Light List Mississippi and Ohio Rivers and Tributaries*, 1936.

[12] Thomas's *Basic Factors in Flood Frequency in the Lower Mississippi River* and Williams's *The Geography of the Mississippi Valley* in *The Annals of the American Academy of Political and Social Science*, Vol. CXXXV, pp. 1-11.

[13] Williams's *The Geography of the Mississippi Valley* in *The Annals of the American Academy of Political and Social Science*, Vol. CXXXV, pp. 7-11; *Editor's Table* in *Harper's New Monthly Magazine*, Vol. XXVI, pp. 413-418 (February 1863); *World Atlas*, 1933, p. 31.

[14] Bourne's *Spain in America* (The American Nation Series, Vol. III), pp. 162-167.

[15] Kellogg's *Early Narratives of the Northwest 1634-1691* in *Original Narratives of Early American History*, pp. 12, 15, 16.

[16] Kellogg's *Early Narratives of the Northwest 1634-1691*, p. 132; *Voyages of Peter Esprit Radisson*, edited by Gideon D. Scull, pp. 167, 168.

Notes and References

[17] Thwaites's *The Jesuit Relations*, Vol. LIX, pp. 87-163.

[18] Parish's *Michel Aco — Squaw-Man* in *The Palimpsest*, Vol. II, pp. 161-177.

[19] Petersen's *Perrot's Mines* in *The Palimpsest*, Vol. XII, pp. 405-413.

[20] Briggs's *Two Connecticut Yankees* in *The Palimpsest*, Vol. VII, pp. 15-29; Petersen's *Historical Setting of the Mound Region in Northeastern Iowa* in *The Iowa Journal of History and Politics*, Vol. XXXI, pp. 57-63; Upham's *Minnesota Geographic Names* in *Minnesota Historical Collections*, Vol. XVII, pp. 80-85, 443, 444; Carver's *Travels Through the Interior Parts of North American, in the Years 1766, 1767, and 1768.*

[21] *Journal of Peter Pond* in the *Wisconsin Historical Collections*, Vol. XVIII, pp. 314-354.

[22] Wilson's *Tesson's Apple Orchard* in *The Palimpsest*, Vol. IV, pp. 121-131; Petersen's *Julien Dubuque* in *The Palimpsest*, Vol. XII, pp. 421-433; Quigley's *The Giard Tract* in *The Palimpsest*, Vol. XII, pp. 1-6.

[23] Thwaites's *Original Journals of the Lewis and Clark Expedition*, Vol. I, pp. xxx-xxxvii, 16; Mott's *The Lewis and Clark Expedition in its Relation to Iowa History and Geography* in the *Annals of Iowa* (Third Series), Vol. XIII, pp. 99-125, 163-192; Coues' *The Expeditions of Zebulon Montgomery Pike*, Vol. I, pp. viii, ix, 1, 2.

[24] Coues' *The Expeditions of Zebulon Montgomery Pike*, Vol. I, pp. 149-151, 213-215; Thwaites's *Original Journals of the Lewis and Clark Expedition*, Vol. IV, pp. 337-340.

[25] Sutcliffe's *Robert Fulton*, pp. 138-141; Thurston's *Robert Fulton*, p. 130.

[26] Thurston's *Robert Fulton*, pp. 126, 129; Preble's *A Chronological History of the Origin and Development of Steam Navigation*, pp, 52-54, 57. Descriptions and measurements of the *Clermont* vary because changes were frequently made.

Steamboating on Upper Mississippi

[27] Sutcliffe's *Robert Fulton*, pp. 143, 144, 146, 147.

[28] Dunbar's *A History of Travel in America*, Vol. II, pp. 344, 345; Preble's *History of Steam Navigation*, pp. 53-58; Sutcliffe's *Robert Fulton*, pp. 142-152.

[29] Fulton had known Barlow for many years. The same year the *Clermont* was built Barlow published *The Columbiad* and dedicated it to Fulton who had made twelve illustrations for the book.

[30] Colden's *The Life of Robert Fulton*, pp. 175, 176.

[31] *Naval Chronicle*, Vol. XIX, p. 188 (1808), quoted in Dickinson's *Robert Fulton Engineer and Artist*, pp. 219-221. The letter is supposed to have been written by the Dean of Ripon Cathedral, an English guest aboard the boat.

[32] Sutcliffe's *Robert Fulton*, pp. 136, 137, 146, 147, 149, 152.

[33] Preble's *History of Steam Navigation*, p. 52; *Dictionary of American Biography*, Vol. XI, p. 324.

[34] Sutcliffe's *Robert Fulton*, p. 144; *The New International Encyclopedia* (1920), Vol. XXI, p. 480. The entrance of the British steamers *Sirius* and *Great Western* into the North Atlantic trade in 1838 is usually regarded as the beginning of practical steam service. For an interesting account see Cartwright's *The Tale of our Merchant Ships*, pp. 165-182.

[35] *Jefferson's Works*, Vol. IV, p. 431.

[36] Petersen's *Iowa in Louisiana* in *The Palimpsest*, Vol. XIII, p. 33.

[37] Cist's *Cincinnati in 1851*, p. 45; Scharf's *History of Saint Louis*, Vol. I, p. 309.

[38] Dunbar's *A History of Travel in America*, Vol. II, pp. 386-389; Paullin's *Atlas of the Historical Geography of the United States*, Plates 61-G, 76-D.

[39] Sutcliffe's *Robert Fulton*, pp. 174-176. On the Upper Mississippi, Benjamin Howard was Governor of Louisiana Territory and Ninian Edwards served in a similar capacity for Illinois Territory.

Notes and References

[40] Martin's *The History of Louisiana*, pp. 349, 354.

[41] Dunbar's *A History of Travel in America*, Vol. I, pp. 275-289.

[42] Gould's *Fifty Years on the Mississippi*, pp. 532-543.

[43] *Dictionary of American Biography*, Vol. XVI, pp. 133, 134, Vol. XVII, pp. 614-616; Turnbull's *John Stevens*, pp. 133-138; Latrobe's *A Lost Chapter in the History of the Steamboat*, pp. 15-23, 32, 33; Latrobe's *The First Steamboat Voyage on the Western Waters*, pp. 5-7. The Latrobe references appear in the *Fund Publications* of the Maryland Historical Society, Nos. 5 and 6.

[44] Cramer's *The Navigator* (Seventh Edition), pp. 33-40; Dunbar's *A History of Travel in America*, Vol. I, pp. 268-270, 290-292. Michaux's *Travels to the Westward of the Allegheny Mountains . . . in the Year 1802*, pp. 29-34, contains an excellent description of Pittsburgh as an entrepôt and shipbuilding center. Thanks are due Dr. Leland D. Baldwin of the University of Pittsburgh for his many helpful suggestions and criticisms on keelboats and flatboats. See his *Shipbuilding on the Western Waters, 1793-1817*, in *The Mississippi Valley Historical Review*, Vol. XX, pp. 29-44.

[45] Dunbar's *A History of Travel in America*, Vol. I, pp. 280, 281; Hulbert's *Historic Highways of America*, Vol. IX, pp. 102-106.

[46] Hulbert's *Historic Highways of America*, Vol. IX, pp. 113-128, 161; Dunbar's *A History of Travel in America*, Vol. I, pp. 272, 284-286.

[47] Wilkeson's *Recollections of the West and the First Building of Buffalo Harbor* in the *Publications of the Buffalo Historical Society*, Vol. V, pp. 178-181; Hulbert's *Historic Highways of America*, Vol. IX, pp. 107-112; Dunbar's *A History of Travel in America*, Vol. I, pp. 281, 282. Mohawk and Schenectady boats were still other forms of keelboats.

[48] Latrobe's *The First Steamboat Voyage on the Western Waters*, pp. 7-9, 14.

[49] *Niles' Register*, Vol. I, p. 10.

[50] Rothert's *The Outlaws of Cave-in-Rock*, p. 13; Latrobe's *The First Steamboat Voyage on the Western Waters*, pp. 8-11.

[51] Blair and Meine's *Mike Fink: King of Mississippi Keelboatmen*, pp. 105, 106.

[52] Blair and Meine's *Mike Fink*, p. 56.

[53] Latrobe's *The First Steamboat Voyage on the Western Waters*, pp. 7, 8.

[54] Hulbert's *The Romance of American Rivers* in *National Waterways*, Vol. VI, p. 24. In addition to Livingston, Fulton, and Roosevelt, the names of Daniel D. Tompkins and De Witt Clinton appear among the incorporators.

[55] Latrobe's *The First Steamboat Voyage on the Western Waters*, pp. 9-14. The remainder of this chapter, unless otherwise noted, is based on this same source, pp. 14-32. Some confusion exists concerning the name, measurements, and general construction of the boat. The writer is indebted to Dr. E. Douglas Branch of the University of Pittsburgh for source material generously placed at his disposal.

[56] Cramer's *The Navigator* (Seventh Edition), pp. 31, 32. Cramer gives the measurement at 138 feet keel and from 300 to 400 tons burden. *The Pittsburgh Gazette*, October 18, 1811, gives the measurements "150 feet keel, 450 tons burthen." Melish's *Travels through the United States* (1816) says the boat was 148½ feet by 32½ beam by 12 feet hold.

[57] *Louisiana Gazette and Advertiser* (New Orleans), February 12, 1812. A good brief account of the voyage is in Charles J. Latrobe's *The Rambler in North America* (London, 1835), Vol. I, pp. 104-109.

[58] Hulbert's *The Romance of American Rivers* in *National Waterways*, Vol. VI, p. 24.

[59] *Louisville Chronicle*, November 15, 1811, quoted in *Niles' Register*, Vol. I, p. 272.

Notes and References

[60] *Niles' Register*, Vol. I, p. 272.

[61] Cist's *Cincinnati Miscellany*, February, 1845; reminiscence of P. S. Bush, quoted by Hulbert in *National Waterways*, Vol. VI, p. 24.

[62] Sampson's *The New Madrid and other Earthquakes in Missouri* in the *Proceedings of the Mississippi Valley Historical Association*, Vol. VI, pp. 218-238.

[63] Bradbury's *Travels in the Interior of America* in Thwaites's *Early Western Travels*, Vol. V, pp. 211, 212.

[64] *Louisiana Gazette and Advertiser* (New Orleans), January 13, 1812; Martin's *The History of Louisiana*, p. 354. The entry in the New Orleans wharf register is January 12th, and Bradbury puts the date as January 13th.

[65] *Pittsburgh Mercury*, August 24, 1814; Flugel's *Pages from a Voyage down the Mississippi to New Orleans in 1817* in the *Louisiana Historical Quarterly*, Vol. VII, pp. 433, 434.

[66] Hulbert's *A Centennial of Western Steamboat Navigation* in the *Proceedings of the Mississippi Valley Historical Association*, Vol. IV, pp. 61, 62.

[67] Cist's *Cincinnati in 1851*, p. 45; Paullin's *Atlas of the Historical Geography of the United States*, Plate 61-G; *The World Almanac*, 1936, p. 240.

[68] Pfaff's *Henry Miller Shreve: A Biography* in *The Louisiana Historical Quarterly*, Vol. X, pp. 194-198.

[69] Lloyd's *Steamboat Directory*, pp. 41-44; Scharf's *History of Saint Louis*, Vol. II, pp. 1094-1096; Pfaff's *Henry Miller Shreve: A Biography* in *The Louisiana Historical Quarterly*, Vol. X, pp. 198-202, 215-218.

[70] *Niles' Register*, Vol. VIII, pp. 320, 404; Pfaff's *Henry Miller Shreve: A Biography* in *The Louisiana Historical Quarterly*, Vol. X, pp. 212-219.

[71] *Niles' Register*, Vol. X, pp. 348, 349; Lloyd's *Steamboat Direc-*

tory, pp. 44, 45; Pfaff's *Henry Miller Shreve: A Biography* in *The Louisiana Historical Quarterly,* Vol. X, pp. 203, 212-219.

[72] Hardin's *An Outline of Shreveport and Caddo Parish History* in *The Louisiana Historical Quarterly,* Vol. XVIII, pp. 822-829; Pfaff's *Henry Miller Shreve: A Biography* in *The Louisiana Historical Quarterly,* Vol. X, pp. 217-220; Gibbons *v.* Ogden, 9 Wheaton 1.

[73] Lloyd's *Steamboat Directory,* pp. 44, 45; Pfaff's *Henry Miller Shreve: A Biography* in *The Louisiana Historical Quarterly,* Vol. X, pp. 206, 212-214, 220-234; Gould's *Fifty Years on the Mississippi,* pp. 111, 112.

[74] Lionberger's *The Annals of St. Louis,* pp. 5-10; Scharf's *History of Saint Louis,* Vol. I, pp. 902, 903; Robeson's *Manuel Lisa* in *The Palimpsest,* Vol. VI, pp. 1-13; Shoemaker's *Herculaneum Shot Tower* in *The Missouri Historical Review,* Vol. XX, pp. 214-216.

[75] *Niles' Register,* Vol. XXXVIII, p. 97; Paullin's *Atlas of the Historical Geography of the United States,* Plate 76-E.

[76] *Missouri Gazette* (St. Louis), July 14, August 2, 1817, quoted in Scharf's *History of Saint Louis,* Vol. II, p. 1096; Peck's *Annals of the West,* p. 761.

[77] Scharf's *History of Saint Louis,* Vol. II, pp. 1096, 1097. A list of the first fifty-one boats built and documented on western waters, with the tonnage and the place and date of building of each, was furnished to Captain Fred A. Bill of St. Paul by the United States Department of Commerce, in 1923. It was published in the *Burlington Post,* May 12, 1923.

[78] *De Bow's Review,* quoted in Scharf's *History of Saint Louis,* Vol. II, pp. 1097-1099, 1109; *Niles' Register,* Vol. XXV, pp. 94, 95, Vol. XXXIII, p. 181, Vol. XXXVIII, p. 97; Birkbeck's *Notes on a Journey in America,* p. 174.

[79] Scharf's *History of Saint Louis,* Vol. II, pp. 1097-1100.

[80] *Missouri Gazette* (St. Louis), May 19, 1819, quoted in Scharf's *History of Saint Louis,* Vol. II, p. 1100.

Notes and References

⁸¹ Bryan's *Daniel Boone* in *The Missouri Historical Review*, Vol. III, pp. 89-98.

⁸² Rader's *The Location of the Permanent Seat of Government* and Thomas's *Missouri Valley Settlements — St. Louis to Independence* in *The Missouri Historical Review*, Vol. XXI, pp. 9-40; Paullin's *Atlas of the Historical Geography of the United States*, Plate 76-E. See James's *Account of an Expedition from Pittsburgh to the Rocky Mountains, performed in the Years 1819, 1820 . . . under the command of Maj. S. H. Long*, in Thwaites's *Early Western Travels*, Vol. XIV, p. 146. Information was also kindly furnished by Floyd C. Shoemaker, Secretary of the State Historical Society of Missouri.

⁸³ *Missouri Intelligencer* (St. Louis), May 21, 28, June 4, 1819, quoted in *The Missouri Historical Review*, Vol. I, pp. 309, 310; Scharf's *History of Saint Louis*, Vol. II, p. 1100; Peck's *Annals of the West*, p. 777.

⁸⁴ *American State Papers, Military Affairs*, Vol. II, pp. 68, 69, 324, 325; contract for transportation made by James Johnson with Brigadier General Thomas S. Jesup in December, 1819 — a manuscript in possession of the Minnesota Historical Society; Wesley's *Diary of James Kennerly 1823-1826* in *Missouri Historical Society Collections*, Vol. VI, pp. 41-44. See also *Documents in Relation to the Claim of James Johnson for Transportation on the Missouri and Mississippi Rivers* printed in *House Executive Documents*, 16th Congress, 2nd Session, Document 110 (Serial No. 55).

⁸⁵ *Pittsburgh Gazette*, March 30, 1819. For an account of the first steamboats built and operated on the Allegheny River see Kussart's *The First Steamboats on the Allegheny River* in *The Waterways Journal* (St. Louis), Vol. XLI (December 22, 1928), p. 6; *Niles' Register*, Vol. XVI, p. 368; Flint's *Letters from America* in Thwaites's *Early Western Travels*, Vol. IX, pp. 164, 165; James's *Account of an Expedition from Pittsburgh to the Rocky Mountains, performed in the Years 1819, 1820 . . . under the command of Maj. S. H. Long*, in Thwaites's *Early Western Travels*, Vol. XIV, pp. 39-108.

[86] Flint's *Letters from America* in Thwaites's *Early Western Travels*, Vol. IX,. pp. 164, 165; James's *Account of an Expedition from Pittsburgh to the Rocky Mountains* in Thwaites's *Early Western Travels*, Vol. XIV, pp. 108-221; Scharf's *History of Saint Louis*, Vol. II, pp. 1100, 1101.

[87] *American State Papers, Military Affairs*, Vol. II, pp. 68, 69, 324, 325.

[88] James's *Account of an Expedition from Pittsburgh to the Rocky Mountains* in Thwaites's *Early Western Travels*, Vol. XV, pp. 188-190, Vol. XVII, p. 97.

[89] Forsyth's *Fort Snelling: Col. Leavenworth's Expedition to Establish It, in 1819*, in *Minnesota Historical Collections*, Vol. III, p. 140. A manuscript copy of the Johnson contract is in the possession of the Minnesota Historical Society.

[90] Report of S. H. Long to John C. Calhoun, dated January 20, 1821, in Thwaites's *Early Western Travels*, Vol. XVII, pp. 117-119.

[91] Porter's *Journal of Stephen Watts Kearny* in *Missouri Historical Society Collections*, Vol. III, pp. 127-129. For an account of this journey see Petersen's *Trailmaking on the Frontier* in *The Palimpsest*, Vol. XII, pp. 298-314.

[92] This chapter was read on June 13, 1928, at the Fort Ripley session of the Seventh State Historical Convention under the auspices of the Minnesota Historical Society. It appeared in *Minnesota History*, Vol. IX, pp. 347-362. It was revised and enlarged to its present form and published in *The Palimpsest*, Vol. XIII, pp. 297-317.

[93] Beltrami's *A Pilgrimage in Europe and America*, Vol. II, pp. 126-128. The remainder of this article, unless otherwise noted, is based on Beltrami's description, pp. 126-200.

[94] *Niles' Register*, Vol. XXV, pp. 94, 95; *Burlington Post*, May 12, 1923. Further information concerning the *Virginia's* measurements and owners was obtained from Permanent Enrolment No. 92, December 21, 1822, Collector of Customs Office at New Orleans.

Notes and References

[95] Hill's *Constantine Beltrami* in *Minnesota Historical Collections*, Vol. II, p. 191.

[96] Meeker's *Early History of the Lead Region in Wisconsin* in *Wisconsin Historical Collections*, Vol. VI, p. 277.

[97] Wilkie's *Davenport Past and Present*, p. 157.

[98] Keating's *Narrative of an Expedition to the Sources of the St. Peter's River* (London, 1825), Vol. I, p. 283.

[99] Beltrami's *A Pilgrimage in Europe and America*, Vol. II, pp. 198-200.

[100] *Army and Navy Chronicle* (New Series), Vols. II and III, p. 104, quoted from the *Allegemeine Zeitung*.

[101] Blakeley's *History of the Discovery of the Mississippi and the Advent of Commerce in Minnesota* in *Minnesota Historical Collections*, Vol. VIII, p. 385.

[102] Bishop's *Floral Home; or, First Years of Minnesota*, pp. 60, 61.

[103] Blakeley's *History of the Discovery of the Mississippi and the Advent of Commerce in Minnesota* in *Minnesota Historical Collections*, Vol. VIII, pp. 385, 386.

[104] Baird's *Indian Customs and Early Recollections* in *Wisconsin Historical Collections*, Vol. IX, pp. 323-326. For relation of this incident to lead mining see Petersen's *Regulating the Lead Miners* in *The Palimpsest*, Vol. XVII, pp. 185-187.

[105] Lindley's *William Clark — The Indian Agent* in the *Proceedings of the Mississippi Valley Historical Association*, Vol. II, pp. 63-75.

[106] *Miner's Journal* (Galena), July 3, 24, 31, 1830; Kappler's *Indian Affairs, Laws and Treaties*, Vol. II (Treaties), pp. 305-310; Mahan's *Old Fort Crawford and the Frontier*, pp. 152-155; *Book of Accounts for expenditures for emigrating Indians . . . from 1828 to 1836, St. Louis Superintendency*, p. 74, in the *Clark Manuscripts*, Kansas Historical Society Library, Topeka, Kansas.

Steamboating on Upper Mississippi

[107] For example, treaties were negotiated at Fort Crawford in 1825, 1829, and 1830, and at Fort Armstrong in 1822, 1832, and 1836. — Kappler's *Indian Affairs, Laws and Treaties*, Vol. II (Treaties), pp. 202, 250-255, 297-303, 305, 345, 349, 474, 476, 546, 588, 591.

[108] Atwater's *Western Antiquities*, pp. 171, 224-234; *Missouri Republican* (St. Louis), July 14, 1829.

[109] Atwater's *Western Antiquities*, pp. 237-239.

[110] *Miner's Journal* (Galena), October 10, 1829, February 20, 1830; Kappler's *Indian Affairs, Laws and Treaties*, Vol. II (Treaties), pp. 297-303; Atwater's *Western Antiquities*, pp. 241-243; *Missouri Republican* (St. Louis), August 25, 1829.

[111] *Iowa News* (Dubuque), July 1, 15, 22, August 5, 12, 1837; Neill's *Occurrences in and around Fort Snelling, From 1819 to 1840*, in *Minnesota Historical Collections*, Vol. II, pp. 132-135; Kappler's *Indian Affairs, Laws and Treaties*, Vol. II (Treaties), p. 491.

[112] *Galena Daily Advertiser*, July 9, 11, 29, August 2, 13, 1851; Hughes's *The Treaty of Traverse des Sioux in 1851* in *Minnesota Historical Collections*, Vol. X, Pt. I, p. 103; Kappler's *Indian Affairs, Laws and Treaties*, Vol. II (Treaties), p. 588; Hughes's *Old Traverse des Sioux*, pp. 33-73. The material in the Hughes volume is from the original notes of James Goodhue written for the *Minnesota Pioneer*.

[113] An excellent description of the sufferings of the Sioux is given by Chief Walking Thunder in Hughes's *Old Traverse des Sioux*, pp. 47, 48.

[114] *Indian Office Files, Letters Received*, 1824 (manuscript in Pension Building, Washington).

[115] Neill's *Occurrences in and around Fort Snelling, From 1819 to 1840*, in *Minnesota Historical Collections*, Vol. II, p. 109.

[116] *Missouri Republican* (St. Louis), June 7, 1831.

[117] *Life of Black Hawk* (published by the State Historical Society of Iowa, 1932), pp. 137, 138.

Notes and References

[118] *Missouri Republican* (St. Louis), September 11, 1832.

[119] Stevens's *The Black Hawk War*, pp. 259-267; *Life of Black Hawk*, pp. 140, 141.

[120] *Northwestern Gazette and Galena Advertiser*, August 26, 1837; *Iowa News* (Dubuque), August 26, 1837; Neill's *Occurrences in and around Fort Snelling, From 1819 to 1840*, in *Minnesota Historical Collections*, Vol. II, pp. 132, 133; Kappler's *Indian Affairs, Laws and Treaties*, Vol. II (Treaties), pp. 493, 494.

[121] *Northwestern Gazette and Galena Advertiser*, November 11, 1837.

[122] From a manuscript receipt, dated November 10, 1837, in possession of the Minnesota Historical Society.

[123] Kappler's *Indian Affairs, Laws and Treaties*, Vol. II (Treaties), pp. 495, 498; Petersen's *The Second Purchase* in *The Palimpsest*, Vol. XVIII, pp. 88-97.

[124] Folsom's *Fifty Years in the Northwest*, pp. 92, 98; Kappler's *Indian Affairs, Laws and Treaties*, Vol. II (Treaties), pp. 491-493; *Burlington Post*, February 16, 1918.

[125] *Taliaferro Journal*, No. II, May 28, 29, 1821 (Manuscript in possession of the Minnesota Historical Society). For the year ending June 30, 1821, the Sioux and Chippewa received $2,227.74 in presents. These consisted of tobacco, powder, bar lead, Chinese vermilion, verdigris, gun flints, shot guns, blankets, blue and red stroudings, Selempores calico, thread, needles, brass kettles, garden hoes, fine combs, box wood fire steels, scissors, butcher knives, looking glasses, gartering, ribbon, finger rings, Madras handkerchiefs, shirts, arm bands, wrist bands, and other trinkets. See also Kappler's *Indian Affairs, Laws and Treaties*, Vol. II (Treaties), pp. 202, 207, 208, 250, *et seq.*

[126] Kappler's *Indian Affairs, Laws and Treaties*, Vol. II (Treaties), pp. 207, 208, 209, 301, 346, 349, 492. Indian treaties usually provided for land cessions. The Sioux treaty of 1851 stipulated that the upper and lower bands should receive a total of $3,075,000. The upper bands

were to receive $1,665,000 to be paid as follows: money for agricultural purposes, $30,000; $1,360,000 to be held in trust by the government and five per cent interest paid the Indians annually for a period of fifty years commencing on July 1, 1852. This interest amounted to $68,000 a year and was applied as follows: agriculture, $12,000; education, $6,000; goods and provisions, $10,000; money, $40,000. The lower tribes were to receive $1,410,000 which was divided in much the same way as that of the upper tribes. — Hughes's *Old Traverse des Sioux*, pp. 175-177; Hughes's *The Treaty of Traverse des Sioux in 1851* in *Minnesota Historical Collections*, Vol. X, Pt. 1, pp. 112-115.

127 Atwater's *Western Antiquities*, p. 220.

128 *Iowa Sun and Davenport and Rock Island News*, November 13, 1839.

129 *Senate Documents*, 28th Congress, 1st Session, Document 242, p. 3 (Serial No. 434).

130 *The Minnesotian* (St. Paul), November 20, 1852.

131 *The Minnesotian* (St. Paul), April 2, 1853.

132 *The Daily Pioneer and Democrat* (St. Paul), April 30, 1857.

133 Bell's *Early Steamboating on the Minnesota and Red Rivers* in *Minnesota Historical Collections*, Vol. X, Pt. 1, pp. 92, 93.

134 *The Daily Pioneer and Democrat* (St. Paul), April 30, May 6, 26, 1857.

135 *Niles' Register*, Vol. XLIII, pp. 210, 226, 267; *Army and Navy Chronicle* (New Series), Vol. II & III, p. 70.

136 *Northwestern Gazette and Galena Advertiser*, May 23, June 7, 9, 29, July 4, 12, August 1, 1848; *Weekly Northwestern Gazette* (Galena), October 5, 1849; Blakeley's *History of the Discovery of the Mississippi and the Advent of Commerce in Minnesota* in *Minnesota Historical Collections*, Vol. VIII, pp. 382-386.

137 *Northwestern Gazette and Galena Advertiser*, July 12, 1848.

Notes and References

[138] *Weekly Northwestern Gazette* (Galena), October 5, 1849, May 14, June 4, 1850. In defense of Governor Ramsey and Henry W. Rice it was pointed out that only those Indians were to be transported "who never have been removed, or who after having been removed have returned with the design of not going back to their new country."

[139] The writer interviewed Captain John Killeen of Dubuque, Iowa, for the incidents relating to the removal of the Sioux on the *Flora* in 1862. Captain Killeen was then mate on the *Flora*. See also the *Burlington Post*, April 17, 1915.

[140] *Annual Report of the Commissioner of Indian Affairs*, 1866, pp. 46, 47, 212, 213.

[141] *St. Paul Press*, quoted in *The Weekly Gate City* (Keokuk), May 27, 1863.

[142] *The Weekly Gate City* (Keokuk), June 3, 1863.

[143] A paper read at the annual meeting of the Mississippi Valley Historical Association at Lincoln, Nebraska, April 28, 1932. The bulk of this chapter, together with most of Chapter 19, was published in *Minnesota History*, Vol. XIII, pp. 221-243.

[144] Beltrami's *A Pilgrimage in Europe and America*, Vol. II, p. 127; *Niles' Register*, Vol. XXIII, p. 53.

[145] Letter from Thomas Forsyth to John C. Calhoun, October 11, 1824, and to William Clark, December 13, 1824, in Thwaites's *The Fur-Trade in Wisconsin, 1812-1825*, in *Wisconsin Historical Collections*, Vol. XX, pp. 356-358, 363-365.

[146] Letter from Taliaferro to Colonel Josiah Snelling, February 8, 1826, in *Taliaferro Letter Book, A*. These letter books are in the possession of the Minnesota Historical Society.

[147] Beltrami's *A Pilgrimage in Europe and America*, Vol. II, pp. 127-137, 149-195; Atwater's *Western Antiquities*, pp. 210-240; Bremer's *The Homes of the New World*, Vol. II, pp. 3-84; Marryat's *A Diary in America*, pp. 110-126.

Steamboating on Upper Mississippi

[148] Thwaites's *The Fur-Trade in Wisconsin, 1812-1825*, in *Wisconsin Historical Collections*, Vol. XX, p. 304. In 1936 the Dousman home was reconstructed into its old French style and presented to the city of Prairie du Chien with the restored title "Villa Louis".

[149] Williams's *Henry Hastings Sibley: A Memoir* in *Minnesota Historical Collections*, Vol. VI, pp. 262-267.

[150] Neill's *Occurrences in and around Fort Snelling, from 1819 to 1840*, in *Minnesota Historical Collections*, Vol. II, p. 110; *Taliaferro Journal*, March 31, 1826. Captain Bates received $107.50 from Indian Agent Lawrence Taliaferro for each trip in 1825. In addition Taliaferro paid him $75 for 150 lbs. of lead and $82 for 1 barrel of whiskey, 4 barrels of flour, and 2 barrels of pork. See *Book of Accounts of Lawrence Taliaferro*, No. 23, September 30, 1822, to September 30, 1834, pp. 7, 8, 13. The Taliaferro manuscripts are in the possession of the Minnesota Historical Society.

The boat, which was built in 1822 by Caleb Beston at Marietta, Ohio, for the firm of Green and Dodge, was a side-wheeler of 108 tons with high pressure engines. It ran on the Muskingum River for a year or two and was the first boat to ascend that stream to Zanesville, Ohio. Captain Bates bought it in the spring of 1825 and ran it in the Upper Mississippi trade until 1826, when it was snagged near Port Chicot. — *Burlington Post*, July 20, 1918; Hall's *The West: Its Commerce and Navigation*, p. 160.

[151] Atwater's *Western Antiquities*, p. 219.

[152] Letters from Dousman to Crooks, October 22, 1835, July 21, 1838, in *American Fur Company Papers*; some bills of lading in the possession of the writer. The *American Fur Company Papers* are in the possession of the New York Historical Society; the Minnesota Historical Society has photostatic copies of all letters cited in this book.

[153] An invoice of merchandise shipped by the American Fur Company on the steamboat *Belleview* to Sibley "for acct. and Risk of Sioux," is in the *Sibley Papers* for 1836. These papers are in the possession of the Minnesota Historical Society.

Notes and References

[154] List of charges on goods imported from England in 1835, in the *Sibley Papers*.

[155] An analysis of some bills of lading in the possession of the writer and bills of lading owned by Captain Fred A. Bill of St. Paul warrants this conclusion.

[156] An invoice of goods shipped by the steamboat *Warrior* bound for St. Peter's and consigned to Sibley for account of the Sioux Outfit, in the *Sibley Papers*, 1835.

[157] *Taliaferro Journal*, March 31, April 6, 14, 15, 17, 21, 26, May 2, 1826.

[158] A list of captains and steamboats between 1823 and 1860 has been compiled by the writer from the St. Paul, Winona, McGregor, Galena, Dubuque, Davenport, Muscatine, Burlington, Keokuk, and St. Louis newspapers. Blakeley gives a fairly complete list of boats and captains for the period from 1836 to the Civil War in *Minnesota Historical Collections*, Vol. VIII, pp. 375-412.

[159] *Pioneer and Democrat* (St. Paul), November 18, 1858; letter from Dousman to Sibley, June 29, 1840, in the *Sibley Papers*; Fonda's *Early Reminiscences of Wisconsin* in *Wisconsin Historical Collections*, Vol. V, p. 240.

[160] Riggs's *Mary and I: Forty Years with the Sioux*, pp. 32-37.

[161] *Weekly Northwestern Gazette* (Galena), June 4, 1850. A file of this paper is in the *Galena Gazette* office at Galena, Illinois. See Petersen's *Captain Joseph Throckmorton* in *The Palimpsest*, Vol. X, pp. 129-144; Petersen's *Captain Daniel Smith Harris* in *The Iowa Journal of History and Politics*, Vol. XXVIII, pp. 505-542.

[162] Letter from Dousman to Sibley, November 20, 1838, in the *Sibley Papers*.

[163] The official records of these boats are found in the following manuscripts: *Enrolment of Vessels*, Collector of Customs Office, Pittsburgh, Vol. III, 1835-1839. The *Ariel* was 125 feet long, with a 17½-

foot beam and a 4½-foot hold, and measured only 95 tons — Enrolment 24, March 13, 1837. The *Burlington* was 150 feet long, had a 23½-foot beam, a 6-foot hold, and a double rudder stern, and measured 200 tons — Enrolment 54, May 27, 1837. The *Malta* was 140 feet long, had a 22-foot beam, was 5 feet deep, and measured 114 tons — Enrolment 73, April 30, 1839. Every new boat had to be officially enrolled before it was allowed to proceed on a trip. A change of ownership or construction required a boat's reënrollment. The document on which the record was spread was designated "Enrolment, in conformity to an Act of the Congress of the United States of America, entitled 'An Act for enrolling and licensing ships or vessels, to be employed in the Coasting Trade and Fisheries, and for regulating same'." The captain usually enrolled his boat and was required to swear that he and the owners were citizens of the United States. A description of the boat and her measurements also was given.

[164] The records of the boats noted are as follows: The *Chippewa*, Enrolment 40, March 10, 1840, in *Enrolment of Vessels*, Vol. V, 1839-1841; the *Cecilia*, Enrolment 32, October 26, 1841, and the *General Brooke*, Enrolment 81, March 25, 1842, in Vol. VI, 1841-1845, all in the Collector of Customs Office, Pittsburgh. The *Lynx*, Enrolment 40, April 15, 1844; the *Nimrod*, Enrolment 42, April 22, 1844; and the *Cecilia*, Enrolment 95, August 8, 1845, in the Collector of Customs Office at St. Louis. The *Lynx*, Enrolment 25, March 25, 1844, the *Cora*, Enrolment 101, September 29, 1846, and the *Nominee*, Enrolment 37, March 14, 1850, in the Collector of Customs Office at Cincinnati.

[165] "H. L. Dousman amt. Stock subscribed in the Prairie du Chien, Hudson & St. Paul Packet Compy," December 24, 1857, in the *Dousman Papers*, in the possession of the Minnesota Historical Society.

[166] Letter from Dousman to Crooks, December 14, 1839, in the *American Fur Company Papers*.

[167] Letter from Dousman to Sibley, May 9, 1845, in the *Sibley Papers*.

Notes and References

[168] Letter from Dousman to Sibley, March 30, 1845, in the *Sibley Papers*.

[169] Letter from Dousman to Sibley, April 20, 1838, April 5, 16, 1839, in the *Sibley Papers*. On April 16, 1839, Dousman wrote: "The Ariel came in last night and is [I] was much disappointed in not recev^g. by her our Spring supplies of Provisions, Groceries, &c from S^t. Louis. She brot. up only what remained in her all winter at the Rapids — but as I know you were badly off I prevailed on the Capt. [Lyon] to go up by giving him our Chippewa freight which the Pavilion brot up a few days since. I also send Brown, Robinson & Farribaults Goods. You will find with this Memor^a & Bill Lading of all I have been able to put on board for you, by the next Boat I shall probably be able to send the bal^n of your Provisions. The goods from N. York marked S, also those from S^t. Louis S&S are on board as you will see by Bill Lading. The Boats which were stopped by the Ice last fall, have had a good deal of their freight pilfered &c Boxes opened & goods taken out — also a good many packages missing — so that you must be very particular in your examination of the two Lots mentioned above, as they have not been landed here and the Capt. tells me that he knows of several articles missing."

[170] Letter from Dousman to Sibley, June 18, 1838, in the *Sibley Papers*.
"I recd. yours pr. Burlington, together with the Packs, Feathers, &c all in good order. The Ariel arrived this morning with the Goods for the Suttler Store and as the freight was not sufficient to justify her going up, they were all Landed & stored here. news has just arrived that 150 recruits are on the way from the Bay for your place, & we have prevailed on the Qr. Master to promise to transpt^a to the Ariel & she now goes up merely to take up your things & be back in time for the Recruits. I have paid the frt. on the Goods from St Louis to this place at 87½ pr. c say $95.38. Send down in the Ariel all your Packs as we are waiting for them to start the Boats for Fort Winnebago. The Clerk of the Burlington tells me that you told him after closing your Letter that the Flour by that Boat came out correct — there were on board as I wrote to you 35 Bbl^s for Sioux O [utfit] & how much for

S. & S. I know not as I did not see the Bill Lading, the shipment having been made to you direct. The 10 Bbl^a Pork which you mentioned as not being in the Bill Lading belong here & were taken up in the Boat with the understanding that they should be brot back as they were not handy when they went up. I regret they were left as we are in want of them, but I suppose you may as well keep them. they were ordered for Retail here & are what is called *clear mess* & cost $5 more than the other kind."

[171] Letter from S. W. McMaster to Franklin Steele, March 22, 1844, and letter from Dousman to Sibley, March 23, April 12, 1844, in the *Sibley Papers*. "I give you a Statement of the ranges of prices. Coon 37½ to 80 cents Red fox 1^{00} to 1^{50} Fisher 2$ to 350 & 4 for large size Wolf 37½ to 62½ Otter is not so much sought after but is worth (Prime) 5$."

Dousman was at the foot of Lake Pepin when news arrived of the invasion of his domain. He wrote to Sibley:

"You had better send and secure all the Furs you can in the hands of the Traders on the St Croix and about your place before the Steam Boats get up as there will be a number of buyers and speculators up & if they can be disappointed this year they will not be apt to return. even if we make nothing on the purchases I think it is a great object to prevent the Furs getting in other hands. I would have sent this by express to you but was afraid to creat[e] suspicion and as the mail leaves here in two days you will have time by moving promptly to do all that is to be done before a Steam Boat can get through the Lake. The [General] Brooke came to the Prairie on the 12th Inst. & there has no doubt been several other Boats there before this. The Lynx will be at Galena about 10 or 15 April."

A few weeks later Dousman wrote:

"There is a Fur buyer on board the Otter [Mr. Frost] who buys for Smith Brothers & Co St. Louis. look sharp after him. he appears to be a very Gentlemanly man & offers good prices."

[172] Some bills of lading scattered through the *Sibley Papers*; others in the possession of the writer and Captain Fred A. Bill of St. Paul.

Notes and References

[173] Letter from Dousman to Sibley, November 19, 1845, January 14, April 30, May 24, 1846, in the *Sibley Papers*.

[174] Wood's *The Red River Colony* in the *Chronicles of Canada*, Vol. XXI, pp. 15-34; Folwell's *A History of Minnesota*, Vol. I, pp. 213-217.

[175] Bill's *Steamboating on the Red River of the North* in the *North Dakota Historical Quarterly*, Vol. II, pp. 100, 101.

[176] *Missouri Republican* (St. Louis), September 3, 1823; *The Mercury* (Pittsburgh), October 21, 1823. A file of *The Mercury* is in the Carnegie Library at Pittsburgh.

[177] *Bloomington* (Muscatine) *Herald*, September 4, 1847.

[178] *Pioneer and Democrat* (St. Paul), March 26, 1857; *Galena Daily Advertiser*, November 22, 1848; *Northwestern Gazette and Galena Advertiser*, July 18, 1848; *Weekly Northwestern Gazette* (Galena), September 18, 1849. Files of the last three papers are in the office of the *Galena Gazette*.

[179] *The Minnesotian* (St. Paul), July 23, 1853.

[180] *Minnesota Democrat* (St. Paul), July 15, 22, 29, August 12, 1851; *Galena Daily Advertiser*, July 22, 25, 1851; Bill's *Steamboating on the Red River of the North* in the *North Dakota Historical Quarterly*, Vol. II, pp. 101-110.

[181] *The Herald* (Dubuque), April 22, May 11, 1866. A file of this paper is in the public library at Dubuque.

[182] *The Grant County Herald*, quoted in the *Northwestern Gazette and Galena Advertiser*, July 5, 1844; *History of Grant County, Wisconsin*, p. 476.

[183] See Wesley's *Guarding the Frontier: A Study of Frontier Defense from 1815-1825*, pp. 118-165; Beers's *The Western Military Frontier: 1815-1846*, pp. 27-53.

[184] *Northwestern Gazette and Galena Advertiser*, July 5, 1844; Hansen's *Old Fort Snelling*, pp. 18-30; Mahan's *Old Fort Crawford*

Steamboating on Upper Mississippi

and the Frontier, pp. 65-88, 120-139; Tanner's History of Fort Ripley, 1849 to 1859, in Minnesota Historical Collections, Vol. X, Pt. 1, pp. 179-202; American State Papers, Indian Affairs, Vol. II, p. 265; Van der Zee's Forts in the Iowa Country in The Iowa Journal of History and Politics, Vol. XII, pp. 163-204.

[185] Missouri Republican (St. Louis), May 24, 1824; Forsyth's Fort Snelling: Col. Leavenworth's Expedition to Establish It, in 1819, in Minnesota Historical Collections, Vol. III, p. 140; Bishop's Floral Home; or, First Years of Minnesota (New York, 1857), p. 32; Neill's Occurrences in and around Fort Snelling, From 1819 to 1840, in Minnesota Historical Collections, Vol. II, pp. 102-116.

[186] American State Papers, Military Affairs, Vol. II, p. 69.

[187] See references in Chapter XI, "The Story of the Western Engineer".

[188] Schoolcraft's Narrative Journal of Travels . . . to the sources of the Mississippi River; Schoolcraft's Narrative of an Expedition through the Upper Mississippi to Itasca Lake, in 1832; Keating's Narrative of an Expedition to the Source of the St. Peter's River (London, 1825); Drumm's Robert E. Lee and the Improvement of the Mississippi River in Missouri Historical Collections, Vol. VI, p. 161; Wilson's The Des Moines Rapids Canal in The Palimpsest, Vol. V, pp. 117-132.

[189] Dubuque Tribune, quoted in the Iowa Republican (Iowa City), April 14, 1852, and reprinted in the Annals of Iowa (Third Series), Vol. XII, p. 345.

[190] Explorations and Surveys for a Railroad Route from the Mississippi River to the Pacific Ocean (Washington, 1860), Vol. XII, Book 1, p. 35.

[191] Missouri Republican (St. Louis), April 5, 1824, September 27, 1831; St. Louis Enquirer, May 24, 1824; Neill's Occurrences in and around Fort Snelling, From 1819 to 1840, in Minnesota Historical Collections, Vol. II, p. 108.

[192] Miner's Journal (Galena), July 3, 1830; Northwestern Gazette

Notes and References

and Galena Advertiser, May 23, June 7, 9, 29, 1848; *Galena Daily Advertiser*, July 9, 1851; *Annual Report of the Commissioner of Indian Affairs*, 1866, pp. 46, 47, 212, 213. An account of the incidents of the trip down the Minnesota River was given the writer by Captain John Killeen of Dubuque.

[193] *Missouri Republican* (St. Louis), July 19, 26, 1827, May 31, 1831; *Missouri Observer* (St. Louis), September 5, 1827, quoted in *Niles' Register*, Vol. XXXIII, p. 68.

[194] *Missouri Republican* (St. Louis), April 10, 17, May 8, 22, 1832.

[195] *Missouri Republican* (St. Louis), May 29, 1832. This issue alone carried news dispatches brought by the *Caroline, Souvenir*, and *Winnebago*.

[196] *Missouri Republican* (St. Louis), June 5, 1832.

[197] *Enrolment of Vessels*, Collector of Customs Office, Pittsburgh, Vol. II, 1831-1835. Enrolments 30 and 31, June 2, 1832, reveal the measurements and ownership of the *Warrior* and her safety barge. The *Warrior* was owned by Joseph Throckmorton and William Hempstead of Galena. She was 111 feet 5 inches long, with a 19-foot beam and a 5-foot hold, and measured 100 tons burden. She had one deck and no mast, a transom stern, a cabin above deck for officers and crew, and a figurehead. Power was furnished by a high pressure engine and three boilers. Her safety barge was 111 feet 8 inches long, with a 16-foot beam, and a 4 foot 8 inch hold, and measured 55 tons. According to Edward Jones, the Surveyor at Pittsburgh, the safety barge had a square stern, a cabin above deck, and a plain figure. The *Warrior* was one of the few steamboats to tow a safety barge on the Upper Mississippi.

[198] *Missouri Republican* (St. Louis), July 10, 1832; *Niles' Register*, Vol. XLIII, pp. 5, 12, 13, 51, 78, 79.

[199] *Missouri Republican* (St. Louis), May 29, June 5, 26, July 10, August 14, 21, 28, September 11, 1832; *Niles' Register*, Vol. XLIII, p. 26.

Steamboating on Upper Mississippi

[200] *Northwestern Gazette and Galena Advertiser*, May 15, 19, 1846, April 6, 1847.

[201] *Northwestern Gazette and Galena Advertiser*, June 26, July 3, 1846, February 2, April 6, 20, 1847; *Bloomington* (Muscatine) *Herald*, June 26, 1846.

[202] *The Dubuque Herald*, January 30, February 7, 1861.

[203] *The Dubuque Herald*, April 27, 1861.

[204] *The Dubuque Herald*, April 28, June 1, 3, 6, 13, 1861.

[205] *Daily Democrat and News* (Davenport), May 4, 1861.

[206] *Daily Express and Herald* (Dubuque), August 18, 1861.

[207] *Goodhue County Republican* (Red Wing), November 22, 1861.

[208] *Gate City* (Keokuk), December 19, 1921.

[209] Smith's *History of the Seventh Iowa Veteran Volunteer Infantry During the Civil War*, p. 5.

[210] *Daily Democrat and News* (Davenport), April 2, 8, 27, May 1, 2, 3, 1861.

[211] *Missouri Republican* (St. Louis), March 25, 1861; *Des Moines Valley Whig* (Keokuk), May 6, 1861; *The Dubuque Herald*, July 17, 1861; *Daily Democrat and News* (Davenport), March 30, 1861.

[212] Briggs's *The Enlistment of Iowa Troops During the Civil War* in *The Iowa Journal of History and Politics*, Vol. XV, pp. 373-375.

[213] *Gate City* (Keokuk), December 19, 1921.

[214] *The Weekly Gate City* (Keokuk), April 8, 1863.

[215] *The Weekly Gate City* (Keokuk), March 25, 1863.

[216] Porter's *The Naval History of the Civil War*, p. 352.

[217] *Gate City* (Keokuk), December 19, 1921.

[218] *Taliaferro Journal*, No. II, p. 24.

Notes and References

[219] *Taliaferro Journal*, No. II, pp. 60-62; *St. Louis Enquirer*, May 24, 1824.

[220] *Niles' Register*, Vol. XXVII, pp. 149, 150.

[221] *St. Louis Herald*, November 8, 1826, quoted in *Niles' Register*, Vol. XXXI, p. 226; *Missouri Republican* (St. Louis), July 19, 26, 1827.

[222] *American State Papers, Military Affairs*, Vol. III, pp. 655, 656.

[223] *Missouri Republican* (St. Louis), April 29, 1828; *American State Papers, Military Affairs*, Vol. III, pp. 624, 625, Vol. IV, p. 9.

[224] *Missouri Republican* (St. Louis), May 31, 1837, quoted in the *Northwestern Gazette and Galena Advertiser*, June 10, 1837.

[225] *Northwestern Gazette and Galena Advertiser*, September 3, 21, 1839.

[226] *Northwestern Gazette and Galena Advertiser*, April 30, 1842; Gould's *Fifty Years on the Mississippi*, p. 437.

[227] *The Dubuque Herald*, July 24, 1860.

[228] Since the government appears to have usually paid a higher tariff than did ordinary passengers, the round trip fare has been placed somewhat above the regular rate. There is a possibility, of course, that the amount might exceed even this sum, particularly if there were any more James Johnsons among steamboat captains with friends in Congress.

[229] *Missouri Republican* (St. Louis), August 6, 1823, August 26, 1824, July 26, 1827; *St. Louis Enquirer*, October 18, 1824.

[230] *Missouri Republican* (St. Louis), August 6, 1823.

[231] *Missouri Republican* (St. Louis), August 9, 1824.

[232] *Taliaferro Journal*, No. III, May 17, 26, 27, June 1, 1826.

[233] Bliss's *Reminiscences of Fort Snelling* in *Minnesota Historical Collections*, Vol. VI, pp. 335-342.

Steamboating on Upper Mississippi

[234] *Senate Documents*, 27th Congress 1st Session, Document 242, pp. 1, 2 (Serial No. 434).

[235] *Weekly Northwestern Gazette* (Galena), May 21, 1850; *The Minnesotian* (St. Paul), May 21, 1853; *Daily Pioneer and Democrat* (St. Paul), August 2, 1857; Van der Zee's *Forts in the Iowa Country* in *The Iowa Journal of History and Politics*, Vol. XII, pp. 197, 198.

[236] *The Minnesotian* (St. Paul), April 2, 1853.

[237] Thwaites's *Notes on Early Lead Mining in the Fever (or Galena) River Region* in *Wisconsin Historical Collections*, Vol. XIII, p. 271; Schafer's *The Wisconsin Lead Region*, pp. 1-20. In 1840, when the aggregate production of lead in the United States was given as 31,240,000 pounds, the Territory of Wisconsin was credited in the census with 15,130,000. At the same time Illinois produced 8,755,000 and Missouri 5,295,000 pounds.

[238] Petersen's *The Mines of Spain* in *The Palimpsest*, Vol. XII, pp. 405-413, 421-433.

[239] Petersen's *Regulating the Lead Miners* in *The Palimpsest*, Vol. XVII, pp. 185-192; Thwaites's *Notes on Early Lead Mining in the Fever (or Galena) River Region* in *Wisconsin Historical Collections*, Vol. XIII, pp. 283-289.

[240] Kappler's *Indian Affairs, Laws and Treaties*, Vol. II (Treaties), pp. 132, 133, 292, 293, 297-302, 349-351; *Niles' Register*, Vol. XXXVII, p. 19, Vol. XLIV, p. 179; Thwaites's *Notes on Early Lead Mining* in *Wisconsin Historical Collections*, Vol. XIII, pp. 288-292.

[241] *Northwestern Gazette and Galena Advertiser*, March 12, 1842; Petersen's *Regulating the Lead Miners* in *The Palimpsest*, Vol. XVII, pp. 185-200; Thwaites's *Notes on Early Lead Mining* in *Wisconsin Historical Collections*, Vol. XIII, pp. 290-292; *Niles' Register*, Vol. XXXVII, p. 131, Vol. XLI, p. 340, Vol. LXIII, p. 388.

[242] *Northwestern Gazette and Galena Advertiser*, February 26, 1841; *Niles' Register*, XXXVIII, p. 204; *Senate Documents*, 28th Congress,

Notes and References

1st Session, Document 242, p. 5; *The Merchants' Magazine and Commercial Review*, Vol. XVIII, p. 292.

²⁴³ Bowen's *American Almanac of Useful Knowledge*, p. 134; *Lead Book* (manuscript volume in the possession of the writer).

²⁴⁴ Bowen's *American Almanac of Useful Knowledge*, p. 134; *Northwestern Gazette and Galena Advertiser*, February 26, 1841, March 12, 1842; *Merchants' Magazine*, Vol. XVIII, pp. 103, 285-292.

²⁴⁵ *Galena Gazette*, March 17, 1893; Meeker's *Early History of Lead Region of Wisconsin* in *Wisconsin Historical Collections*, Vol. VI, pp. 276-279; Wilkeson's *Recollections of the West and the First Building of Buffalo Harbor* in *Buffalo Historical Collections*, Vol. V, pp. 176-181; *Burlington Post*, February 9, 1918.

²⁴⁶ Beltrami's *A Pilgrimage in Europe and America*, Vol. II, pp. 60-197; *Galena Gazette*, March 17, 1893; Meeker's *Early History of Lead Region of Wisconsin* in *Wisconsin Historical Collections*, Vol. VI, pp. 277-279.

²⁴⁷ *History of Jo Daviess County, Illinois* (1878), pp. 233-242.

²⁴⁸ The *Mandan* and the *Indiana* visited Fever River in 1824; the *Rufus Putnam*, the *Lawrence*, and the *Gen. Neville* were there in 1825; and the *Lawrence*, the *Sciota*, the *Mexico*, and the *Eclipse* appeared in 1826. The arrivals and departures of steamboats for the Upper Mississippi were taken by the writer from the files of the *Missouri Republican* (St. Louis).

²⁴⁹ *History of Jo Daviess County, Illinois* (1878), pp. 227, 228, 246, 251.

²⁵⁰ *Missouri Republican* (St. Louis), March 15, April 19, 1827; *History of Jo Daviess County, Illinois* (1878), p. 247.

²⁵¹ *Missouri Republican* (St. Louis), April 19, 1827. The boats were seldom advertised for the posts above, but rather for the Fever River lead mines. The *Indiana* had completed five trips to the lead region before June 30, 1827.

Steamboating on Upper Mississippi

252 Scott's *Newspapers and Periodicals of Illinois: 1814-1879*, pp. 52, 182. This reference incorrectly gives the date of establishment of the *Miner's Journal* as 1826. The writer has worked over all the issues of Vol. I in the possession of the Wisconsin Historical Society at Madison. See also *History of Jo Daviess County, Illinois* (1878), p. 254. The writer is in possession of a photographic copy of Vol. I, No. 1 of the *Chicago Democrat* dated November 26, 1833.

253 *Niles' Register*, Vol. XXXV, p. 120.

254 From a manuscript in the *Connolly Collection* in the Minnesota Historical Society Library. The letter, dated March 27, 1828, expressed hope that when the boundary line was drawn for the new Territory of Wisconsin, the lead district would be found within its borders.

255 According to a count made by the writer in the *Missouri Republican* (St. Louis) from June 9 to July 9, 1828, there had been fifteen arrivals from and thirteen departures for the mines. — *Niles' Register*, Vol. XXXVI, p. 130.

256 A count of the number of steamboat arrivals and departures was kept while working through the files of the *Missouri Republican* (St. Louis). The Galena newspapers also served as a valuable index to the different boats which visited the mines. A list of boats for each year is the result. Chandler's *Map of the United States Lead Mines on the Upper Mississippi River* (1829), printed in *Wisconsin Historical Collections*, Vol. XI, opposite p. 400, is authority for the arrival of 99 steamboats and 74 keelboats in 1828.

257 *Northwestern Gazette and Galena Advertiser*, November 29, December 13, 1834. The files for these dates give the specific figures, while the estimates are a result of the compilation in the possession of the writer.

258 *Northwestern Gazette and Galena Advertiser*, July 25, December 5, 1835.

259 *Northwestern Gazette and Galena Advertiser*, March 12, 1842.

Notes and References

[260] *Northwestern Gazette and Galena Advertiser*, July 1, 1847; *Merchants' Magazine*, Vol. XX, p. 449.

[261] *Bloomington* (Muscatine) *Herald*, May 8, 1846. A list of arrivals and departures for the months of May and June enabled the writer to reach these conclusions.

[262] These figures are the result of a record kept of the number of different boats together with the total yearly arrivals. The writer has a list of 345 different steamboats as a result of his research in the St. Louis, Galena, Dubuque, Muscatine, and Keokuk newspaper files, but in view of the fact that the papers would doubtless miss some of the boats he has added a score to his own list. It is believed that this is within five per cent of the correct number.

[263] "List of the First Steamboats Built and Documented on Western Waters", published in the *Burlington Post*, May 12, 1923, and in the *Wabasha County Herald*, June 26, 1924.

[264] *Senate Documents*, 28th Congress, 1st Session, Document 242, p. 8.

[265] *Merchants' Magazine*, Vol. XX, p. 448.

[266] *Missouri Republican* (St. Louis), May 4 and 11, 1826, March 4 and July 23, 1828. The departure of steamboats, as well as an occasional keelboat, is chronicled in a *Lead Book*, 1828-1830, a manuscript volume in the possession of the writer.

[267] *Missouri Republican* (St. Louis), February 1, June 7, 1827.

[268] *Missouri Republican* (St. Louis), October 25, 1827.

[269] *Missouri Republican* (St. Louis), March 4, 1828.

[270] *Missouri Republican* (St. Louis), May 5, 1832; *Enrolment of Vessels*, Collector of Customs Office, Pittsburgh, Vol. II, 1831-1835, Enrolments 30 and 31, June 2, 1832.

[271] *Northwestern Gazette and Galena Advertiser*, November 25, 1842.

[272] *Northwestern Gazette and Galena Advertiser*, July 21, 1846.

[273] *Northwestern Gazette and Galena Advertiser*, April 21, 1848.

[274] *Northwestern Gazette and Galena Advertiser*, November 16, 1839.

[275] *Northwestern Gazette and Galena Advertiser*, June 7, 1848.

[276] Ellet's *Summer Rambles in the West*, pp. 47, 48.

[277] Petersen's *The Illinois Central Comes* in *The Palimpsest*, Vol. XIV, pp. 363-378, and *The North Western Comes* in *The Palimpsest*, Vol. XIV, pp. 317-333.

[278] *Express & Herald* (Dubuque), April 17, 22, May 30, 1858.

[279] *The Dubuque Herald*, July 29, August 25, 1860.

[280] Bale's *Galena's Century Milestone*, pp. 8-19.

[281] Marryat's *A Diary in America*, Vol. II, pp. 156, 157.

[282] *Burlington Post*, December 29, 1917.

[283] *Senate Documents*, 28th Congress, 1st Session, Document 242, p. 9.

[284] Quoted in *Northwestern Gazette and Galena Advertiser*, May 31, 1844.

[285] *Senate Documents*, 28th Congress, 1st Session, Document 242, p. 9.

[286] *Northwestern Gazette and Galena Advertiser*, October 3, 10, and 17, 1843. The arguments filled several columns in three successive issues.

[287] *Senate Documents*, 28th Congress, 1st Session, Document 242, p. 9; *Northwestern Gazette and Galena Advertiser*, September 8, 28, October 29, 1839.

[288] *Bloomington* (Muscatine) *Herald*, May 4, 1847.

[289] *Bloomington* (Muscatine) *Herald*, July 10, 1846.

Notes and References

[290] *Senate Documents*, 28th Congress, 1st Session, Document 242, p. 9; *Northwestern Gazette and Galena Advertiser*, October 29, 1839. The editor complained of the high prices charged in spite of a fine stage of water. Captains were demanding $2 per 100 pounds upstream and $1 per 100 pounds downstream.

[291] *Northwestern Gazette and Galena Advertiser*, November 24, 1841.

[292] *Northwestern Gazette and Galena Advertiser*, November 24, 1845.

[293] *American State Papers, Public Lands*, Vol. IV, p. 523.

[294] The total is derived from a knowledge of the rate for some of the years and a comparison of averages for the years immediately following 1843, when complete figures are available.

[295] Figures compiled from data, given in *Senate Documents*, 28th Congress, 1st Session, Document 242, pp. 6-9.

[296] *Northwestern Gazette and Galena Advertiser*, April 18, 1835.

[297] *Northwestern Gazette and Galena Advertiser*, November 16, 1839.

[298] *Northwestern Gazette and Galena Advertiser*, May 5, 1843.

[299] Figures compiled from data given in *Senate Documents*, 28th Congress, 1st Session, Document 242, p. 8.

[300] *Senate Documents*, 28th Congress, 1st Session, Document 242, p. 8.

[301] *Senate Documents*, 28th Congress, 1st Session, Document 242, p. 8. See also the *Iowa News* (Dubuque), June 3, 10, 1837, and the *Miner's Journal* (Galena), June 19, 26, July 3, 24, 1830.

[302] A compilation of steamboats made by the writer for the various years indicated, from the files of the Galena newspapers.

[303] *Northwestern Gazette and Galena Advertiser*, April 16 and May 14, 1844; Gould's *Fifty Years on the Mississippi*, pp. 536-542.

Steamboating on Upper Mississippi

[304] *Northwestern Gazette and Galena Advertiser*, July 9, 1836, October 19, 1840, June 4, 19, and July 3, 1841, May 13, 1845.

[305] *Northwestern Gazette and Galena Advertiser*, March 28, April 25, May 30, 1845.

[306] *Northwestern Gazette and Galena Advertiser*, May 16, 1843; *Galena Daily Advertiser*, May 18, 1849.

[307] *Niles' Register*, Vol. XXIII, p. 96.

[308] *American State Papers, Public Lands*, Vol. IV, p. 801; Drumm's *Robert E. Lee and the Mississippi* in *Missouri Historical Society Collections*, Vol. VI, p. 161. The fact that surveys were made from time to time is indicative of the fact that the rapids constituted a serious problem. Furthermore, while money was expended lavishly it was not until the completion of the Des Moines Canal (1867-1877) and the Le Claire Canal many years later that the problem was solved.

[309] *Miner's Journal* (Galena), quoted in *Niles' Register*, Vol. XXXVII, pp. 51, 52.

[310] *Miner's Journal* (Galena), quoted in *Niles' Register*, Vol. XXXVII, pp. 51, 52.

[311] Libby's *Chronicle of the Helena Shot-Tower* in *Wisconsin Historical Collections*, Vol. XIII, pp. 338, 339, *et passim*.

[312] *Milwaukee Courier*, quoted in *Miners' Express* (Dubuque), September 4, 1841. For a further discussion see the *Iowa Standard* (Iowa City), January 29, 1841.

[313] *Chicago American*, quoted in the *Northwestern Gazette and Galena Advertiser*, January 16, 1836.

[314] *Wisconsin Herald* (Lancaster), September 26, 1846, quoted in Libby's *Significance of the Lead and Shot Trade in Early Wisconsin History* in *Wisconsin Historical Collections*, Vol. XIII, p. 300.

[315] *Merchants' Magazine*, Vol. XX, p. 449.

[316] Libby's *Significance of the Lead and Shot Trade in Early Wis-*

Notes and References

consin History in *Wisconsin Historical Collections*, Vol. XIII, p. 318 *et passim; Buffalo Advertiser,* quoted in *Niles' Register,* Vol. LXVIII, p. 102.

[317] A comparison of the amount of lead received both at St. Louis and New Orleans with the total production of the Upper Mississippi warrants this statement.

[318] *Dictionary of American Biography,* Vol. III, pp. 574, 575.

[319] Catlin's *North American Indians,* Vol. II, pp. 129, 130; Hennepin's *A New Discovery of a Vast Country in America* (Chicago, 1903), Vol. I, p. 223.

[320] Beltrami's *A Pilgrimage in Europe and America,* Vol. II, pp. 204, 205.

[321] *Taliaferro Journal,* No. III, May 2, 1826, p. 85.

[322] *Weekly Northwestern Gazette* (Galena), June 5, 28, 1850; *The Minnesota Pioneer* (St. Paul), May 9, July 1, 1850; *Burlington Post,* January 17, 1914.

[323] *The Minnesota Pioneer* (St. Paul), July 1, 1850; *Chicago Daily Tribune,* June 16, 1854.

[324] Murray's *Travels in North America During the Years 1834, 1835, 1836,* Vol. II, p. 111.

[325] Bliss's *Reminiscences of Fort Snelling* in *Minnesota Historical Collections,* Vol. VI, pp. 340, 341.

[326] Neill's *Occurrences in and around Fort Snelling, From 1819 to 1840,* in *Minnesota Historical Collections,* Vol. II, pp. 126, 127.

[327] Catlin's *North American Indians,* Vol. II, pp. 132, 135, 136.

[328] *Miners' Express* (Dubuque), June 25, 1845. Contemporary sources disagree as to the time intervening between the arrival of steamboats. Catlin declares it was a week in 1835 while Stephen R. Riggs was told that several weeks separated the departure of boats from St. Louis to Fort Snelling in 1837. An analysis of the files of the *North-*

Steamboating on Upper Mississippi

western Gazette and Galena Advertiser indicates extreme irregularity. Sometimes several craft arrived within the space of a week's time while as often two or three weeks might elapse between boats.

³²⁹ Catlin's *North American Indians*, Vol. II, pp. 135-145; Neill's *Occurrences in and around Fort Snelling, From 1819 to 1840*, in Minne-. sota *Historical Collections*, Vol. II, pp. 126, 127.

³³⁰ *Northwestern Gazette and Galena Advertiser*, June 11, 18, July 2, 30, August 13, 1836; *Enrolment* of *Vessels*, Collector of Customs Office, Pittsburgh, Vol. III, 1835, 1839, Enrolment 34, May 3, 1836.

³³¹ *Northwestern Gazette and Galena Advertiser*, May 13, 20, 1837. An item in the issue of May 13th noted similar advertisements in the *Du Buque Visitor* and the *Belmont* (Wisconsin) *Gazette*.

³³² *Iowa News* (Dubuque), August 5, 1837.

³³³ *Northwestern Gazette and Galena Advertiser*, June 10, 17, 24, September 30, 1837; *Iowa News* (Dubuque), June 17, 1837; Neill's *Occurrences in and around Fort Snelling, From 1819 to 1840*, in Minnesota *Historical Collections*, Vol. II, pp. 126, 127; Catlin's *North American Indians*, Vol. II, pp. 129, 130; Marryat's *An English Officer's Description of Wisconsin in 1837* in *Wisconsin Historical Collections*, Vol. XIV, pp. 137-154.

³³⁴ Stanchfield's *History of Pioneer Lumbering on the Upper Mississippi and its Tributaries* in *Minnesota Historical Collections*, Vol. IX, pp. 326, 327.

³³⁵ *Northwestern Gazette and Galena Advertiser*, May 29, June 14, 19, 1840; *Enrolment of Vessels*, Collector of Customs Office, Pittsburgh, Vol. V, 1839-1841, Enrolment 34, February 27, 1840.

³³⁶ Stanchfield's *History of Pioneer Lumbering on the Upper Mississippi and its Tributaries* in *Minnesota Historical Collections*, Vol. IX, pp. 326, 327.

³³⁷ The writer has excursion advertisements for various years from Keokuk, Bloomington (Muscatine), Galena, and Dubuque newspapers.

Notes and References

[338] *Iowa News* (Dubuque), May 19, June 16, 1838.

[339] *Northwestern Gazette and Galena Advertiser*, May 15, June 25, July 2, 13, 1839, May 29, June 5, 1840, June 13, 27, July 1, 3, 8, 1845.

[340] Palmer's *Western Wisconsin in 1836* in *Wisconsin Historical Collections*, Vol. VI, p. 305.

[341] Rodolf's *Pioneering in the Wisconsin Lead Region* in *Wisconsin Historical Collections*, Vol. XV, pp. 339, 340.

[342] *Northwestern Gazette and Galena Advertiser*, April 22, May 13, 1837; Folsom's *Fifty Years in the Northwest*, p. 689; *Burlington Post*, September 28, 1918.

[343] *Northwestern Gazette and Galena Advertiser*, April 22, 1839; *Enrolment of Vessels*, Collector of Customs Office, Cincinnati, Enrolment (Temporary), March 27, 1839.

[344] *Northwestern Gazette and Galena Advertiser*, April 7, 1838, September 25, 1841; *Burlington Post*, January 10, 1914; *Enrolment of Vessels*, Collector of Customs Office, St. Louis, Enrolment 88, August 22, 1844.

[345] *Northwestern Gazette and Galena Advertiser*, June 8, 1839; *Enrolment of Vessels*, Collector of Customs Office, Pittsburgh, Vol. III, 1835-1839, Enrolment 73, April 30, 1839; *Burlington Post*, April 21, 1917.

[346] *Northwestern Gazette and Galena Advertiser*, October 17, 1845; *Enrolment of Vessels*, Collector of Customs Office, St. Louis, Enrolment 125, October 16, 1845.

[347] *The Minnesota Pioneer* (St. Paul), May 6, 1852.

[348] *Northwestern Gazette and Galena Advertiser*, June 13, 1845; Paulding's *The Mississippi* in *Graham's Magazine*, Vol. XXII, pp. 219, 220; Rodolf's *Pioneering in the Wisconsin Lead Region* in *Wisconsin Historical Collections*, Vol. XV, p. 340.

[349] *Miners' Express* (Dubuque), June 25, 1845.

Steamboating on Upper Mississippi

350 *Weekly Northwestern Gazette* (Galena), July 24, 1849; *The Minnesota Democrat* (St. Paul), June 10, July 22, 1851; *The Minnesotian* (St. Paul), June 11, July 23, 1853; *Daily Pioneer and Democrat* (St. Paul), June 21, July 23, 1857; *Daily Express and Herald* (Dubuque), August 24, 1857.

351 Blakeley's *History of the Discovery of the Mississippi and the Advent of Commerce in Minnesota* in *Minnesota Historical Collections*, Vol. VIII, pp. 381-389.

352 *The Minnesota Pioneer* (St. Paul), July 22, 1852.

353 *The Minnesota Pioneer* (St. Paul), June 3, 1852; Blakeley's *History of the Discovery of the Mississippi and the Advent of Commerce in Minnesota* in *Minnesota Historical Collections*, Vol. VIII, pp. 389-393.

354 *Burlington Post*, August 15, 1914. Merrick follows his description of the *Die Vernon* by a full and interesting account of the race given by Captain John O. Roberts of Clarksville, Missouri. It was originally printed in an issue of the *Minneapolis Journal* for 1910. The exact measurements of the *Die Vernon* are taken from *Enrolment of Vessels*, Collector of Customs Office, St. Louis, Enrolment 30, March 13, 1852.

355 *Burlington Post*, August 22, 1914.

356 *The Minnesotian* (St. Paul), June 18, 1853; *Burlington Post*, August 22, 1914. Merrick views the race from the standpoint of an Upper Mississippi steamboatman. — *Burlington Post*, August 15, 1914. John O. Roberts, on the contrary, leans in his sympathy towards the *Die Vernon*.

357 *Burlington Post*, August 15, 22, 1914; *The Minnesotian* (St. Paul), June 18, 25, July 2, 1853. For the exact distance the writer has used the official mileage given in the *Light List Upper Mississippi River and Tributaries* (Thirteenth District), Washington, 1930.

358 *Burlington Post*, August 15, 22, 1914.

Notes and References

[359] Blakeley's *History of the Discovery of the Mississippi and the Advent of Commerce in Minnesota* in *Minnesota Historical Collections*, Vol. VIII, pp. 393-395.

[360] For an extended account of the excursion of 1854, see Farnam's *Memoir of Henry Farnam*, pp. 69-89 (New Haven, 1889). See also the *New York Semi-Weekly Tribune*, June 20, 1854, and Leonard's *A Famous Rock Island Trip* in the *Rock Island Magazine*, Vol. XXII, p. 9.

[361] *Daily Tribune* (Chicago), June 1, 1854; *Daily Minnesota Pioneer* (St. Paul), June 9, 1854; *The Minnesotian* (St. Paul), June 9, 1854.

[362] *The Minnesotian* (St. Paul), June 9, 1854.

[363] *Daily Tribune* (Chicago), June 5, 6, 7, 1854; *New York Tribune*, June 9, 13, 1854.

[364] *Daily Tribune* (Chicago), June 8, 9, 1854; *New York Tribune*, June 13, 1854. Authorities vary as to the number of additional boats chartered by the Minnesota Packet Company, but most sources indicate that one or two were added to the original five. Dana asserts that one was added; Flint notes the *Jenny Lind* and the *Black Warrior*, probably the *Black Hawk*. Miss Sedgwick recorded seven steamboats in the flotilla which left Rock Island.

[365] *Daily Tribune* (Chicago), June 7, 8, 1854; Sedgwick's *The Great Excursion to the Falls of St. Anthony* in *Putnam's Monthly Magazine*, Vol. IV, p. 322; *The Minnesotian* (St. Paul), June 9, 1854.

[366] *Daily Tribune* (Chicago), June 8, 1854.

[367] Sedgwick's *The Great Excursion to the Falls of St. Anthony* in *Putnam's Monthly Magazine*, Vol. IV, p. 320; *New York Tribune*, June 20, 1854.

[368] *New York Tribune*, June 20, 1854; *Daily Tribune* (Chicago), June 8, 1854.

[369] *New York Tribune*, June 20, 1854.

Steamboating on Upper Mississippi

370 Sedgwick's *The Great Excursion to the Falls of St. Anthony* in *Putnam's Monthly Magazine*, Vol. IV, p. 323; Bill's *When Rock Island Road Reached River, The Famous Excursion Train of 1854*, in the *Burlington Post*, September 23, 1922; Paulding's *The Mississippi* in *Graham's Magazine*, Vol. XXII, p. 219.

371 Sedgwick's *The Great Excursion to the Falls of St. Anthony* in *Putnam's Monthly Magazine*, Vol. IV, p. 323; *New York Tribune*, June 6, 20, 1854.

372 Sedgwick's *The Great Excursion to the Falls of St. Anthony* in *Putnam's Monthly Magazine*, Vol. IV, p. 323; *New York Tribune*, June 20, 1854; *Daily Tribune* (Chicago), June 13, 1854.

373 *Daily Tribune* (Chicago), June 13, 1854; *New York Tribune*, June 20, 1854.

374 *The Minnesotian* (St. Paul), June 9, 1854.

375 *New York Tribune*, June 20, 1854.

376 *Galena Jeffersonian*, quoted in the *Daily Tribune* (Chicago), June 16, 1854; *Daily Tribune* (Chicago), June 13, 1854.

377 *The Minnesotian* (St. Paul), June 9, 1854; *New York Tribune*, June 20, 1854.

378 *Minnesota Pioneer*, June 10, 19, 30, 1854; *Daily Tribune* (Chicago), June 13, 16, 1854; *New York Tribune*, June 20, 1854.

379 Farnam's *Memoir of Henry Farnam*, p. 88.

380 Sedgwick's *The Great Excursion to the Falls of St. Anthony* in *Putnam's Monthly Magazine*, Vol. IV, p. 323; *New York Tribune*, June 20, 1854.

381 Bill's *When Rock Island Road Reached River, The Famous Excursion Train of 1854*, in the *Burlington Post*, September 23, 1922; *New York Tribune*, June 20, 1854; Sedgwick's *The Great Excursion to the Falls of St. Anthony* in *Putnam's Monthly Magazine*, Vol. IV, p. 320; Farnam's *Memoir of Henry Farnam*, pp. 86, 87. For an inter-

esting account of the steward's duties, see Merrick's *Old Times on the Upper Mississippi*, pp. 126-129.

382 Sedgwick's *The Great Excursion to the Falls of St. Anthony* in *Putnam's Monthly Magazine*, Vol. IV, p. 323.

383 *New York Tribune*, June 20, 1854.

384 *Daily Tribune* (Chicago), June 13, 1854; *New York Tribune*, June 20, 1854.

385 Sedgwick's *The Great Excursion to the Falls of St. Anthony* in *Putnam's Monthly Magazine*, Vol. IV, p. 322; *New York Tribune*, June 23, 1854.

386 *The Minnesotian* (St. Paul), October 12, 14, 18, 1858; *The Dubuque Herald*, July 24, 31, 1860, July 14, 17, 1866; Bill's *William H. Seward's Visit to Minnesota in 1860* in the *Burlington Post*, November 25, 1922; Blegen's *Campaigning with Seward in 1860* in *Minnesota History*, Vol. VIII, pp. 150-171.

387 Sutcliffe's *Robert Fulton*, p. 138; Scharf's *History of Saint Louis*, Vol. II, p. 1094.

388 *Missouri Gazette* (St. Louis), June 9, 1819, quoted in Gould's *Fifty Years on the Mississippi*, p. 116.

389 *The History of Jo Daviess County, Illinois* (1878), pp. 254, 255; *The History of Dubuque County, Iowa* (1880), p. 336. Military expeditions observed the Fourth of July previous to this date, viz., Kearny in 1820. The American flag was also raised at Fort Madison and by military expeditions such as that of Zebulon M. Pike.

390 *Northwestern Gazette and Galena Advertiser*, June 29, 1839.

391 *Northwestern Gazette and Galena Advertiser*, June 10, 1849.

392 *The Winona Republican*, June 24, July 8, 1856.

393 *The Dubuque Herald*, July 3, 6, 7, 11, 1860.

391 *The Herald* (Dubuque), July 4, 1866, July 4, 1867; *Weekly Gate City* (Keokuk), May 20, 1874.

Steamboating on Upper Mississippi

[395] A manuscript in the possession of the Missouri Historical Society, Jefferson Memorial Library, St. Louis, Missouri.

[396] Price's *The Execution of Patrick O'Connor* in *The Palimpsest*, Vol. I, p. 94.

[397] *Daily Express and Herald* (Dubuque), September 3, 7, 1858; *The Herald* (Dubuque), September 30, 1869.

[398] *The Herald* (Dubuque), July 4, 1867, September 29, 30, October 4, 5, 1868.

[399] *The Herald* (Dubuque), June 16, July 3, 4, August 6, 1861, July 30, 1867, August 28, 1868.

[400] *Daily Express and Herald* (Dubuque), August 10, 24, 27, 1858; *The Dubuque Herald*, May 22, 23, 31, 1860.

[401] Paullin's *Atlas of the Historical Geography of the United States*, Plates 76-D, E, F, G, and 77-A, B, C.

[402] Van der Zee's *The Roads and Highways of Territorial Iowa* in *The Iowa Journal of History and Politics*, Vol. III, pp. 181-191; Bill's *Ferry Boats on the Upper Mississippi* in the *Burlington Post*, July 12, 19, 26, 1924; Johnson's *Crossing the Mississippi* in *The Palimpsest*, Vol. I, pp. 169-182.

[403] Channing and Lansing's *The Story of the Great Lakes*, pp. 237, 238, 254. The same authors declare that until 1858 the Erie Canal was "the all-important transportation route between the Great Lakes and the Atlantic. Even the coming of the railroad did not take away its trade, and as late as 1862 the ton-mileage of canal traffic was more than double the combined ton-mileage of the New York Central and the Erie railroads." See pp. 263, 264.

[404] *Niles' Register*, Vol. LXXII, p. 263.

[405] Cole's *The Era of the Civil War 1848-1870* (Centennial History of Illinois, Vol. III), pp. 20-30.

[406] Petersen's *Population Advance to the Mississippi* in *The Iowa Journal of History and Politics*, Vol. XXXII, pp. 312-353.

Notes and References

407 Petersen's *The Rock Island Comes* in *The Palimpsest*, Vol. XIV, pp. 285-300.

408 Petersen's *The Burlington Comes* in *The Palimpsest*, Vol. XIV, pp. 381-395.

409 Petersen's *The North Western Comes* in *The Palimpsest*, Vol. XIV, pp. 317-333; Petersen's *The Illinois Central Comes* in *The Palimpsest*, Vol. XIV, pp. 363-378.

410 Petersen's *The Burlington Comes* in *The Palimpsest*, Vol. XIV, p. 394.

411 Petersen's *The Milwaukee Comes* in *The Palimpsest*, Vol. XIV, pp. 413-428.

412 Raney's *The Building of Wisconsin Railroads* in *The Wisconsin Magazine of History*, Vol. XIX, p. 392.

413 Paullin's *Atlas of the Historical Geography of the United States*, Plate 139-B.

414 Raney's *The Building of Wisconsin Railroads* in *The Wisconsin Magazine of History*, Vol. XIX, p. 393.

415 *Census of the United States*, 1860, Mortality and Miscellaneous Statistics, p. xx; Paullin's *Atlas of the Historical Geography of the United States*, Plates 62 B, 64-A, 76-F, 77-B, 138-K, 138-L, 139-A, 139-B.

416 Murray's *Travels in North America during the Years 1834, 1835, & 1836*, Vol. I, p. 148.

417 Marryat's *A Diary in America*, Vol. I, pp. 142, 143.

418 Hall's *Travels in the United States*, Vol. I, pp. 146, 147.

419 *Niles' Register*, Vol. LXVIII, p. 247.

420 Paulding's *The Mississippi* in *Graham's Magazine*, Vol. XXII, p. 218.

[421] *Chicago Democrat*, November 26, 1833; *The Chicago Daily News Almanac and Year-Book*, 1927, pp. 270, 271.

[422] Quoted in the *Chicago Democrat*, November 26, 1833.

[428] *Greeen River Advocate* (Hopkinsville, Kentucky), quoted in the *Chicago Democrat*, November 26, 1833; Lindley's *Indiana as Seen by Early Travelers* in *Indiana Historical Collections*, Vol. I, p. 523.

[424] Marryat's *A Diary in America*, Vol. II, pp. 207, 208.

[425] Quoted in Baird's *View of the Valley of the Mississippi, or the Emigrant's and Traveller's Guide to the West*, pp. 359, 360.

[426] Hall's *The West: Its Commerce and Navigation*, pp. 146-148; Baird's *View of the Valley of the Mississippi, or the Emigrant's and Traveller's Guide to the West*, p. 352.

[427] Flagg's *The Far West: or, A Tour Beyond the Mountains*, Vol. I, pp. 54, 55.

[428] Quoted in Parker's *Iowa as It Is in 1857*, p. 63.

[429] From the *Iowa City Reporter*, quoted in Parker's *Iowa as It Is in 1857*, p. 55.

[430] *Rock Island News*, May 26, 1855, quoted in the *Muscatine Journal*, May 30, 1855.

[431] *Niles' Register*, Vol. LXXI, p. 281.

[432] From the *Burlington Telegraph*, quoted in the *Muscatine Journal*, October 11, 1854.

[433] Quoted in Parker's *Iowa as It Is in 1857*, p. 57.

[434] *Muscatine Journal*, October 27, 1855.

[435] Quoted in Parker's *Iowa as It Is in 1857*, pp. 56, 57.

[436] *Rock Island News*, May 26, 1855, quoted in the *Muscatine Journal*, May 30, 1855.

[437] Quoted in Parker's *Iowa as It Is in 1857*, p. 57.

Notes and References

438 Parker's *Iowa as It Is in 1857*, pp. 57-59.

439 *Des Moines Valley Whig* (Keokuk), May 15, 1851.

440 Quoted in Parker's *Iowa as It Is in 1857*, p. 56.

441 Quoted in the *Des Moines Valley Whig* (Keokuk), October 30, 1851.

442 *Muscatine Journal*, March 3, 1854.

443 *Muscatine Democratic Enquirer*, July 19, 1851.

444 Regan's *The Western Wilds of America*, pp. 401-404.

445 *Census of the United States*, 1860, Mortality and Miscellaneous Statistics, p. li.

446 Marryat's *A Diary in America*, Vol. I, pp. 123, 124; Murray's *Travels in North America during the Years 1834, 1835, & 1836*, Vol. I, p. 197.

447 *Census of the United States*, 1860, Mortality and Miscellaneous Statistics, pp. li-lviii; Marryat's *A Diary in America*, Vol. I, p. 17.

448 *Census of the United States*, 1860, Mortality and Miscellaneous Statistics, p. li; Bremer's *The Homes of the New World*, Vol. I, pp. 554, 555. Miss Bremer's letters covered the years 1849-1853. Her book appeared in 1853.

449 *Census of the United States*, 1860, Mortality and Miscellaneous Statistics, p. li.

450 Mann's *The Emigrant's Complete Guide to Port Stephens, Van Dieman's Land, New Zealand; The Cape of Good Hope and Natal; Canada, New Brunswick, and Nova Scotia*, pp. 61-68 (Canadian section).

451 *Niles' Register*, Vol. LXXIII, pp. 78, 80; Willcox's *International Migrations*, Vol. I, p. 360.

452 *Niles' Register*, Vol. LXXII, p. 370.

Steamboating on Upper Mississippi

[453] From the *Buffalo Courier*, quoted in *Niles' Register*, Vol. LXXII, p. 263; Mann's *The Emigrant's Guide to Port Stephens*, etc., p. 68 (Canadian section); Willcox's *International Migrations*, Vol. I, p. 360.

[454] Raeder's *America in the Forties*, pp. 1, 2; Baird's *View of the Valley of the Mississippi, or the Emigrant's and Traveller's Guide to the West*, pp. 349-352; Steele's *Western Guide Book, and Emigrant's Directory*, pp. 5-11; Regan's *The Western Wilds of America*, pp. 403, 404; Newhall's *The British Emigrant's "Hand Book"*, p. 96.

[455] Rynning's *True Account of America*, pp. 98, 99.

[456] Oliphant's *Minnesota and the Far West*, pp. 102-104.

[457] For a vivid description of such a trip, see Raeder's *America in the Forties*, pp. 3, 4.

[458] See Marryat's *A Diary in America*, Vol. I, pp. 172, 173, Vol. II, pp. 40, 41.

[459] Bremer's *The Homes of the New World*, Vol. I, p. 597.

[460] Ferguson's *America: By River and Rail*, p. 434.

[461] *Niles' Register*, Vol. LXXII, p. 281.

[462] Ambler's *Transportation in the Ohio Valley*, p. 147; Hulbert's *The Great American Canals* (Historic Highways of America, Vol. XIII), pp. 169-215.

[463] *Niles' Register*, Vol. LXXIII, p. 48.

[464] Janson's *The Background of Swedish Immigration, 1840-1930*, p. 129; Flom's *The Early Swedish Immigration to Iowa* in *The Iowa Journal of History and Politics*, Vol. III, pp. 602-604.

[465] For accounts of the Swiss immigration, see Duerst's *Diary of one of the Original Colonists of New Glarus, 1845*, in *Wisconsin Historical Collections*, Vol. XV, pp. 310-325; Luchsinger's *The Swiss Colony of New Glarus* in *Wisconsin Historical Collections*, Vol. VIII, pp. 416-418.

Notes and References

[466] Regan's *The Western Wilds of America*, pp. 401-404.

[467] Peck's *A New Guide for Emigrants to the West*, p. 365.

[468] Newhall's *The British Emigrant's "Hand Book"*, pp. 95, 96.

[469] Rauschenbusch's *Einige Anweisungen für Auswanderer* (Elberfeld, 1848), p. 50; Kargan's *St. Louis in früheren Jahren. Ein Gedenkbuch für das Deutschthum*, p. 311; Baird's *View of the Valley of the Mississippi*, pp. 358, 363, 364; Regan's *The Western Wilds of America*, pp. 401-404; Williams' *Appleton's Southern and Western Travellers' Guide*, pp. 136-138.

[470] Letter of Hendrick Barendregt to Henry P. Scholte, dated St. Louis, December, 1846, quoted in Van der Zee's *The Hollanders of Iowa*, pp. 339-343.

[471] Regan's *The Western Wilds of America*, p. 25.

[472] Mann's *The Emigrant's Complete Guide to the United States*, pp. 56, 57; Raeder's *America in the Forties*, pp. 2, 3; *The British Mechanic's and Labourer's Hand Book, and True Guide to the United States*, pp. 41-46; Kapp's *Immigration and the Commissioners of Emigration of the State of New York*, pp. 62-64.

[473] Bremer's *The Homes of the New World*, Vol. I, pp. 68, 69.

[474] Pearson's *An American Railroad Builder: John Murray Forbes*, pp. 67-69.

[475] *The Herald* (Dubuque), June 16, 1867.

[476] This story was told to the writer by Captain Holstrom while he was making a stormy and thrilling trip across Lake Pepin in 1928.

[477] Petersen's *To the Land of Black Hawk* in *The Palimpsest*, Vol. XIV, pp. 53-68; Paullin's *Atlas of the Historical Geography of the United States*, Plates 76-F, 76-G, 77-A; *The World Almanac*, 1932, p. 386; Quaife's *Wisconsin: Its History and Its People 1634-1924*, Vol. I, p. 442.

[478] *Census of the United States*, 1850, pp. XXXVI-XXXVIII, 663,

717, 925, 948, 996, 1870, p. 299; Parker's *Iowa as It Is in 1855*, pp. 52-61; *Illinois State Gazette and Business Directory, For the Years 1864-65*, pp. 52-54.

[479] Scharf's *History of Saint Louis*, Vol. II, p. 1128; Peck's *Annals of the West*, p. 761.

[480] *The Daily Pioneer and Democrat* (St. Paul), November 18, 20, 1858; Scharf's *History of Saint Louis*, Vol. II, pp. 1126, 1129; Blakeley's *History of the Discovery of the Mississippi and the Advent of Commerce in Minnesota* in *Minnesota Historical Collections*, Vol. VIII, p. 406.

[481] The short line packet remained a favorite type and was used extensively by the principal corporations in connection with their through trade. In addition to these lines between St. Louis and Keokuk, runs were made between such ports as Fort Madison and Davenport, Davenport and Dubuque, Savanna and Dubuque, Dubuque and St. Paul, Prairie du Chien and St. Paul, and La Crosse and St. Paul. Some lines had even shorter runs.

[482] Scharf's *History of Saint Louis*, Vol. II, pp. 1115-1123; *The Daily Gate City* (Keokuk), March 8, 1856; *The Dubuque Herald*, March 16, 1860, March 23, 1861.

[483] *Census of the United States*, 1870, Vol. I, pp. 23, 27, 28, 40, 43, 44, 73.

[484] Bishop's *Floral Home; or, First Years of Minnesota*, p. 125; Johnson's *Fort Snelling from its Foundation to the Present Time* in *Minnesota Historical Collections*, Vol. VIII, p. 431.

[485] *The Minnesota Pioneer* (St. Paul), July 26, 1849.

[486] Lanman's *A Summer in the Wilderness*, p. 13.

[487] *The Diary of Philip Hone, 1828-1851*, Vol. II, p. 809.

[488] Bremer's *The Homes of the New World*, Vol. II, pp. 84, 88.

[489] *Memoranda &c. Journey from Baltim[or]e to St. Paul's Minne-*

Notes and References

sota, May 7 to June 20, 1851. This manuscript is in possession of the Minnesota Historical Society.

[490] Lanman's *A Summer in the Wilderness*, p. 30.

[491] *Galena Daily Advertiser*, July 19, 1851; Gallaher's *Icaria and the Icarians* in *The Palimpsest*, Vol. II, pp. 97-112.

[492] *Weekly Northwestern Gazette* (Galena), March 24, 1851; *Galena Daily Advertiser*, July 9, 18, 29, September 13, October 28, 1851; *The Minnesota Democrat* (St Paul), August 12, 19, 1851.

[493] Ellet's *Summer Rambles in the West*, pp. 47, 48.

[494] *The Minnesotian* (St. Paul), May 14, June 11, 18, 25, 1853; Scharf's *History of Saint Louis*, Vol. II, p. 1128.

[495] *New York Semi-Weekly Tribune*, June 20, 1854.

[496] Parker's *Iowa as It Is in 1855*, pp. 52-61.

[497] *The Daily Tribune* (Chicago), June 2, 1854; *Daily Express and Herald* (Dubuque), November 29, 1855; *The Daily Minnesota Pioneer* (St. Paul), May 27, 30, 1854; Parker's *Iowa as It Is in 1855*, pp. 52-61.

[498] *The Winona Republican*, May 6, 1856.

[499] Bishop's *Floral Home; or, First Years of Minnesota*, pp. 174, 175.

[500] Parker's *Minnesota Handbook for 1856-7*, pp. 9, 10.

[501] Andrews' *Minnesota and Dacotah* (1857), pp. 29, 30.

[502] *Daily Express and Herald* (Dubuque), May 8, 1857.

[503] *The Daily Pioneer and Democrat* (St. Paul), April 17, July 8, 1857.

[504] *Red Wing Republican*, August 13, September 3, 1858.

[505] *Daily Express and Herald* (Dubuque), August 5, 1858.

[506] *The Herald* (Dubuque), June 20, 21, 23, 27, 1866.

[507] *The Herald* (Dubuque), July 31, 1867.

Steamboating on Upper Mississippi

[508] *The Herald* (Dubuque), April 28, May 21, June 2, 15, 19, 1867.

[509] *The Herald* (Dubuque), June 20, 24, 1868.

[510] *The Herald* (Dubuque), July 11, 17, 20, 24, 25, August 3, 4, 5, 7, 8, 10, 11, 12, 19, 25, 1869.

[511] Marryat's *A Diary in America*, Vol. II, p. 143.

[512] *Galena Daily Advertiser*, April 2, 3, 1849; *Missouri Republican* (St. Louis), September 20, 1824; *Northwestern Gazette and Galena Advertiser*, August 24, 1847; Peck's *Annals of the West*, p. 808.

[513] *Weekly Northwestern Gazette* (Galena), September 7, December 11, 1849, July 9, 16, 1850.

[514] *Memoranda &c. Journey from Baltimore to St. Paul's Minnesota*, May 7 to June 20th, 1851 (manuscript in possession of the Minnesota Historical Society); *The Daily Minnesota Pioneer* (St. Paul), June 17, 1854.

[515] *The Herald* (Dubuque), August 14, 15, 16, 17, 19, 1866.

[516] *The Herald* (Dubuque), August 19, 26, 30, 1866.

[517] Raeder's *America in the Forties*, p. 120.

[518] Seymour's *Sketches of Minnesota*, p. 69; Coolbaugh's *Reminiscences of the Early Days of Minnesota, 1851 to 1861*, in *Minnesota Historical Collections*, Vol. XV, p. 483.

[519] Raeder's *America in the Forties*, p. 121; Oliphant's *Minnesota and the Far West*, p. 295.

[520] Ellet's *Summer Rambles in the West*, pp. 170, 171.

[521] Ellet's *Summer Rambles in the West*, p. 170.

[522] Blegen's *Campaigning with Seward in 1860* in *Minnesota History*, Vol. VIII, pp. 150-171. Copies of the original diaries are in the possession of the Minnesota Historical Society.

[523] Pond's *Two Volunteer Missionaries Among the Dakotas*, pp. 14

Notes and References

et passim; Pond Manuscript, 1833-1839 (in possession of the Minnesota Historical Society).

[524] Atwater's *Western Antiquities,* p. 228.

[525] Regan's *The Western Wilds of America,* pp. 31, 32.

[526] Raeder's *America in the Forties,* pp. 122, 123.

[527] Andrews' *Minnesota and Dacotah,* pp. 30, 31.

[528] Oliphant's *Minnesota and the Far West,* p. 294.

[529] *The Herald* (Dubuque), February 19, 1869, March 31, 1870.

[530] Raeder's *America in the Forties,* pp. 121, 122.

[531] *Enrolment of Vessels,* Collector of Customs Office, St. Louis, Enrolment 46, May 16, 1846, Enrolment 33, March 23, 1852, Enrolment 36, April 9, 1852; Ellet's *Summer Rambles in the West,* pp. 59, 60; *The Minnesota Pioneer* (St. Paul), June 17, 1852.

[532] *The Minnesotian* (St. Paul), April 15, 1854.

[533] *Proceedings of the Seventeenth Annual Meeting of the Board of Supervising Inspectors* (Washington, 1869), pp. 171-189; *Burlington Post,* October 25, November 1, 1919.

[534] *Northwestern Gazette and Galena Advertiser,* September 5, 1845, May 8, 1846; *Weekly Northwestern Gazette* (Galena), June 10, 1851; *Galena Daily Advertiser,* September 25, 1851; *The Minnesota Democrat* (St. Paul), June 10, 1851; *The Winona Republican,* April 29, 1856; *The Minnesota Pioneer* (St. Paul), November 8, 1849, June 12, 1851.

[535] *The Daily Minnesota Pioneer* (St. Paul), August 5, 1854, April 10, 1855; *The Minnesotian* (St. Paul), June 25, 1853, October 8, 1853; *The Winona Republican,* June 17, 1856.

[536] *Iowa News* (Dubuque), August 19, 26, 1837; *Northwestern Gazette and Galena Advertiser,* August 19, 26, 1837.

Steamboating on Upper Mississippi

[537] *Northwestern Gazette and Galena Advertiser*, October 11, 1844, June 4, 1847.

[538] *Muscatine Journal*, quoted in *The Minnesotian* (St. Paul), July 2, 1853; *The Minnesota Pioneer* (St. Paul), October 17, 1850; *Northwestern Gazette and Galena Advertiser*, June 10, 13, 1845.

[539] Regan's *The Western Wilds of America*, pp. 33, 34; *Galena Daily Advertiser*, March 26, 29, 1849; *The Daily Pioneer and Democrat* (St. Paul), October 6, 1857; *Dubuque Daily Times*, October 8, 1857.

[540] *Galena Daily Advertiser*, May 19, 1849; Scharf's *History of Saint Louis*, Vol. II, pp. 1110, 1111.

[541] *Burlington Post*, June 12, 1915, October 25, November 1, 1919; *Daily Express and Herald* (Dubuque), July 3, 1858.

[542] *The New York Semi-Weekly Tribune*, June 20, 1854; *The Minnesotian* (St. Paul), May 21, 1853.

[543] *Daily Express and Herald* (Dubuque), June 5, August 2, 20, 1857, September 15, 19, 1857, March 17, 1858.

[544] Blegen's *Campaigning with Seward in 1860* in *Minnesota History*, Vol. VIII, p. 167.

[545] *Galena Daily Advertiser*, quoted in *The Henderson Democrat*, June 10, 1856; *The Daily Pioneer and Democrat* (St. Paul), April 30, 1857; *The Herald* (Dubuque), May 7, 1867.

[546] Quoted in Parker's *Minnesota Handbook*, pp. 108, 109.

[547] Seymour's *Sketches of Minnesota*, p. 69.

[548] *Pond Manuscript, 1833-1839*, pp. 3, 4.

[549] Baird's *View of the Valley of the Mississippi, or the Emigrant's and Traveller's Guide to the West*, pp. 363-365.

[550] Peck's *A New Guide for Emigrants*, pp. 372, 373.

[551] *A True Picture of Emigration* (G. Berger, London, 1848), p. 17.

Notes and References

[552] Davidson's *In Unnamed Wisconsin*, p. 185.

[553] *Northwestern Gazette and Galena Advertiser*, July 3, 1845.

[554] *The Minnesota Pioneer* (St. Paul), July 3, 22, 1852.

[555] Williams' *A History of the City of St. Paul, and of the County of Ramsey, Minnesota*, in *Minnesota Historical Collections*, Vol. IV, p. 360.

[556] Balance sheet of the *Milwaukee* dated November 19, 1857, and November 1, 1859; balance sheet of the *Ocean Wave* dated September 30, 1858; statement of the Prairie du Chien, Hudson, & St. Paul Packet Company affairs up to December 19, 1857. Photostats of these papers are in possession of the writer from originals in the *Dousman Papers*, Minnesota Historical Society Library at St. Paul.

[557] *Daily Express and Herald* (Dubuque), February 17, June 12, 1859.

[558] *Daily Express and Herald* (Dubuque), April 7, 1858, February 17, 1859.

[559] The writer has a photostat of the original which is among the *Dousman Papers* in possession of the Minnesota Historical Society Library.

[560] *The Herald* (Dubuque), March 15, 1866.

[561] Photostat of the balance sheet of the Northwestern Union Packet Company, January, 1858, from the original in the *Dousman Papers*, Minnesota Historical Society Library.

[562] *The Herald* (Dubuque), June 18, July 12, 1868.

[563] Some bills of lading in the possession of the writer.

[564] Bremer's *Homes of the New World*, Vol. II, pp. 172, 173.

[565] *The Minnesota Democrat* (St. Paul), June 17, July 22, 1851; *The Minnesotian* (St. Paul), October 1, 1853; *The Daily Pioneer and Democrat* (St. Paul), May 16, 21, 1857; *Express & Herald* (Dubuque), May 19, 28, 1857, September 7, 1858.

Steamboating on Upper Mississippi

[566] Folsom's *Fifty Years in the Northwest*, pp. 92-98.

[567] *Daily Pioneer and Democrat* (St. Paul), May 7, June 2, 1857.

[568] Charles Minney has furnished the writer with this information from a manuscript bill of lading in the Dousman Home at Prairie du Chien.

[569] *The Minnesota Pioneer* (St. Paul), September 9, 1852.

[570] *Daily Express and Herald* (Dubuque), July 16, 17, 1858.

[571] *Daily Minnesotian* (St. Paul), October 25, November 19, 1858.

[572] *Daily Pioneer and Democrat* (St. Paul), May 13, 1857; *The Herald* (Dubuque), June 19, 26, 27, 1866.

[573] *The Herald* (Dubuque), May 26, June 16, July 11, 14, 24, 1867, July 24, 1869.

[574] *Daily Express and Herald* (Dubuque) October 24, 1857; *The Herald* (Dubuque), September 11, 19, 25, November 6, 10, 14, 1866, August 25, 31, September 1, 7, 8, 14, 25, 28, October 5, 13, 28, 30, November 2, 12, 1869; *Daily Times* (Dubuque), November 3, 8, 16, 1871.

[575] *Daily Express and Herald* (Dubuque), August 11, 1857. The issue for April 31, 1857, contains an excellent example of receipts at the "Port of Dubuque" from St. Louis and Cincinnati. The *Orb* brought tobacco, snuff, salt, boots and shoes, glazed sash, bureaus, plows, stoneware, coffee, bed cords, and a miscellaneous array of merchandise from St. Louis. From the same port the *Minnesota Belle* brought hams, liquors, an engine and boiler. The *Northern Light* transported from Cincinnati office chairs, bedsteads, springs, rockers, nurse rockers, walnut stands, center tables, children's chairs, willow and stuffed chairs, sofas, divans, mattresses, ottomans, brooms, soap, currants, dried apples, sugar, rice, coffee, carpets, oilcloth, codfish, cheese, herring, tea, soda, whiskey, beans, peaches, fish, mustard, sweet potatoes, lemons, and drugs, stoves, bedsteads, washstands, office tables, looking glass, trunks (both empty and filled), chests, corks, pumice stone,

Notes and References

trundle beds, bookcases, wagons, glassware, hogs and dogs, cows and calves.

[576] The manifest of the steamboat *Rosalie* illustrates the large number of ports a steamboat called on during the course of her journey from St. Louis to St. Paul. After visiting most of the ports between St. Louis and Dubuque and discharging 40 tons at the latter port, the *Rosalie* sank on a pile of rocks at Dunleith. An examination of her manifest shows that she still contained goods for Clayton City, McGregor's Landing, Lansing, La Crosse, Winona, Fountain City, Minneiska, Lake City, Red Wing, Prescott, Hastings, St. Paul, Minneapolis, and St. Anthony. Among the hundreds of items listed were stoves, wagons, buggies, boilers, glassware, corn, whiskey, salt, fish, pickles, bedsteads, furniture, and a piano. See *Daily Express and Herald* (Dubuque), July 7, 1857.

[577] *The Herald* (Dubuque), September 28, October 1, 3, 5, 6, 1869.

[578] *Daily Express and Herald* (Dubuque), May 13, 1856, June 3, 1857.

[579] *The Daily Pioneer and Democrat* (St. Paul), May 24, 26, 1857.

[580] *The Winona Republican*, quoted in the *Goodhue County Republican* (Red Wing), May 25, 1860.

[581] *The Herald* (Dubuque), April 1, August 29, October 23, 1869.

[582] *Muscatine Journal*, quoted in *The Dubuque Herald*, July 12, 1860.

[583] *Northwestern Gazette and Galena Advertiser*, October 9, 1849; *The Minnesota Democrat* (St. Paul), June 17, 1851; *The Herald* (Dubuque), October 21, 1869.

[584] *Missouri Republican* (St. Louis), March 8, 1831.

[585] *Northwestern Gazette and Galena Advertiser*, July 16, 23, 1851, and the *Minnesota Pioneer* (St. Paul), April 24, 1851, quoting a dispatch from the Cincinnati *Commercial Advertiser*.

Steamboating on Upper Mississippi

[586] Le Duc's *Minnesota at the Crystal Palace Exhibition, New York, 1853*, in the *Minnesota History Bulletin*, Vol. I, pp. 351-368.

[587] *The Dubuque Herald*, August 21, 29, 1861.

[588] *The Dubuque Herald*, June 8, 1862.

[589] Gould's *Fifty Years on the Mississippi*, pp. 604, 605; Blakeley's *History of the Discovery of the Mississippi and the Advent of Commerce in Minnesota* in *Minnesota Historical Collections*, Vol. VIII, pp. 415, 416.

[590] *Missouri Republican* (St. Louis), July 1, 1828, *Miner's Journal* (Galena), July 22, 1828; *Burlington Post*, June 1, 1918.

[591] *Missouri Republican* (St. Louis), July 1, 1828. The activity of the *Red Rover* and other boats is chronicled in the column of daily arrivals and departures.

[592] *Missouri Republican* (St. Louis), April 14, 1829.

[593] Atwater's *Western Antiquities*, pp. 229-237.

[594] Atwater's *Western Antiquities*, pp. 238, 239; *Miner's Journal* (Galena), October 10, 1829. The *Red Rover* was still plying in the lead trade in late October. — *Miner's Journal* (Galena), November 3, 1829.

[595] *Missouri Republican* (St. Louis), July 27, 1830.

[596] *Missouri Republican* (St. Louis), August 9, 1831; *Enrolment of Vessels*, Collector of Customs Office, Pittsburgh, Vol. II, 1831-1835, Temporary Enrolment 6, February 16, 1833. The *Winnebago* was built at Pittsburgh in 1831. She was 111 feet 7 inches long, 17 feet 10 inches beam, 4 feet 10 inches hold, and measured 91 tons.

[597] *Enrolment of Vessels*, Collector of Customs Office, Pittsburgh, Vol. II, 1831-1835. Enrolments 30 and 31, on June 2, 1832, reveal the measurements and ownership of the *Warrior* and her barge. According to Edward Jones, the Surveyor at Pittsburgh, the safety barge had a square stern, a cabin above deck, and a plain figure.

Notes and References

[598] *Niles' Register*, Vol. XXXI, p. 304.

[599] *Missouri Republican* (St. Louis), October 25, 1827. Her safety barge was named the *Lady Washington*. According to the *Missouri Republican* of March 4, 1828, the *Missouri* also towed a safety barge.

[600] *Niles' Register*, Vol. XLIII, pp. 12, 13; *Missouri Republican* (St. Louis), May 29, June 26, July 10, August 14, 1832.

[601] *Niles' Register*, Vol. XLIII, pp. 12, 13, 51; *Missouri Republican* (St. Louis), August 14, 1832; Stevens' *The Black Hawk War*, p. 227.

[602] *Missouri Republican* (St. Louis), September 11, 1832.

[603] *Missouri Republican* (St. Louis), July 12, 1833.

[604] *Niles' Register*, Vol. XLIII, p. 4.

[605] *Northwestern Gazette and Galena Advertiser*, May 14, 1836; *Du Buque Visitor*, May 11, 18, 1836.

[606] *Northwestern Gazette and Galena Advertiser*, June 11, 1836; *Du Buque Visitor*, June 8, 1836; *Enrolment of Vessels*, Collector of Customs Office, Pittsburgh, Vol. III, 1835-1839, Enrolment 34, May 3, 1836. The *St. Peters* was built at Pittsburgh in 1836 and was owned by Joseph Throckmorton and the firm of Hempstead and Beebe, all of St. Louis. She was 139 feet long, 18 feet 8 inches beam, 5 feet 9 inches hold, and measured 119 tons. Merrick is in error in his data on the *St. Peters* in the *Burlington Post*, August 10, 1918.

[607] The *Ariel* appeared first and seems to have been commanded by at least three of her owners the first season: Throckmorton, McNeal, and Waggoner. — *Enrolment of Vessels*, Collector of Customs Office, Pittsburgh, Vol. III, 1835-1839, Enrolment 24, March 13, 1837. The *Ariel* was launched at Pittsburgh in the spring of 1837. She was captained by George McNeal, an owner. The others were Throckmorton, Hempstead, Chouteau, and Isaac Newton Waggoner of Illinois. The *Ariel* was 125 feet long, 17½ feet beam, 4½ feet in the hold, and measured 95 tons.

[608] *Enrolment of Vessels*, Collector of Customs Office, Pittsburgh,

Steamboating on Upper Mississippi

Vol. III, 1835-1839, Enrolment 54, May 27, 1837. The *Burlington* was built at Pittsburgh in 1837 and was owned by Joseph Throckmorton, Pierre Chouteau, Jr., and the firm of Hempstead and Beebe, all of St. Louis. She was 150 feet long, 23½ feet in width, with a 6-foot hold, and measured 200 tons. She had a double rudder stern.

[609] *Iowa News* (Dubuque), June 3, 10, 17, 24, 1837; *Northwestern Gazette and Galena Advertiser*, September 30, 1837; Neill's *Occurrences in and around Fort Snelling, From 1819 to 1840*, in *Minnesota Historical Collections*, Vol. II, pp. 133, 134.

[610] *Enrolment of Vessels*, Collector of Customs Office, Pittsburgh, Vol. III, 1835-1839, Enrolment 73, April 30, 1839. The *Malta* was built at Pittsburgh in 1839. She was 140 feet long, had a 22-foot beam, and a 5-foot hold, and measured 114 tons. She was owned by Throckmorton and Pierre Chouteau, Jr., of St. Louis.

[611] *Northwestern Gazette and Galena Advertiser*, June 5, 1840.

[612] *Senate Documents*, 28th Congress, 1st Session, Document 242, p. 8.

[613] *Burlington Post*, April 21, 1917.

[614] *Enrolment of Vessels*, Collector of Customs Office, Pittsburgh, Vol. VI, 1841-1845, Enrolment 81, March 25, 1842. The *General Brooke* was built at Pittsburgh in 1842. She was 144 feet long, 20 feet in breadth, 5 feet 2 inches hold, and measured 143 tons. She was owned by Joseph Throckmorton, John Sanford, John B. Sarpy, Kenneth Mackenzie, all of St. Louis, and Hercules L. Dousman of Prairie du Chien.

[615] *Senate Documents*, 28th Congress, 1st Session, Document 242, p. 8.

[616] *Miners' Express* (Dubuque), May 12, 1843; *Burlington Post*, July 10, 1915.

[617] *Burlington Post*, July 10, 1915.

[618] *Enrolment of Vessels*, Collector of Customs Office, St. Louis,

Notes and References

Enrolment 43, January 29, 1845. The *Nimrod* was built at St. Louis in 1844 and was owned by Joseph Throckmorton, Pierre Chouteau, Jr., and John B. Sarpy. She was 156 feet long, 25 feet 10 inches broad, 5½ feet in depth, and measured 210 tons.

[619] *Enrolment of Vessels*, Collector of Customs Office, St. Louis, Enrolment 95, August 8, 1845. The *Cecilia* was built at Pittsburgh in 1841 and was owned solely by Joseph Throckmorton. She was 140 feet long, 20 feet 9 inches in breadth, 4 feet 5 inches in depth, and measured 111 tons.

[620] Neill's *Occurrences in and around Fort Snelling, From 1819 to 1840*, in *Minnesota Historical Collections*, Vol. II, p. 136; *Burlington Post*, November 1, 1913.

[621] *Northwestern Gazette and Galena Advertiser*, June 26, July 3, 1846.

[622] *Enrolment of Vessels*, Collector of Customs Office, St. Louis, Enrolment 101, September 29, 1846. Built at Rock Island in 1846, the *Cora* was 139 feet 8 inches long, 23 feet beam, 4 feet 9 inches hold, measured 144 tons, and was owned solely by Throckmorton.

[623] *Northwestern Gazette and Galena Advertiser*, October 9, 1846; *Burlington Hawk-Eye*, April 20, 1884; *Burlington Post*, May 30, 1914.

[624] Blakeley's *History of the Discovery of the Mississippi and the Advent of Commerce in Minnesota* in *Minnesota Historical Collections*, Vol. VIII, pp. 415, 416.

[625] *Miner's Journal* (Galena), April 10, 1830.

[626] *Missouri Republican* (St. Louis), April 30, 1833.

[627] *Northwestern Gazette and Galena Advertiser*, March 3, May 14, 1836; *Du Buque Visitor*, May 25, August 3, September 7, 1836; *Iowa News* (Dubuque), June 17, July 1, 8, August 5, 1837.

[628] *Red Wing Republican*, March 26, 1858.

[629] *Daily Express and Herald* (Dubuque), April 2, 1858.

Steamboating on Upper Mississippi

[630] *Galena Gazette*, March 17, 1893; *Burlington Post*, February 9, 1918.

[631] Meeker's *Early History of Lead Region of Wisconsin* in *Wisconsin Historical Collections*, Vol. VI, pp. 277-279.

[632] *Miner's Journal* (Galena), October 3, 1829; *Niles' Register*, Vol. LXIII, p. 388; *Burlington Post*, June 5, 1915, February 9, 1918; *Galena Gazette*, March 17, 1893; *History of Jo Daviess County, Illinois*, (1878), pp. 240, 241.

[633] *The History of Lee County, Iowa* (1879), pp. 342-344; *Galena Gazette*, March 17, 1893.

[634] *Burlington Post*, September 9, 1916; *Map of the Mississippi River from the Falls of St. Anthony to the Junction of the Missouri River*.

[635] *Enrolment of Vessels*, Collector of Customs Office, St. Louis, Enrolment 21, July 7, 1835; *Galena Gazette*, March 17, 1893; *Missouri Republican* (St. Louis), May 23, 1835, quoted in *Niles' Register*, Vol. XLVIII, p. 250. Merrick declares the *Jo Daviess* was a side-wheeler.

[636] *Burlington Post*, September 9, 1916; *Galena Gazette*, March 17, 1893.

[637] *Miner's Journal* (Galena), July 3, 1830; *Northwestern Gazette and Galena Advertiser*, May 21, 1836.

[638] *Minnesota Pioneer* (St. Paul), April 25, 1850.

[639] *The Minnesotian* (St. Paul), May 7, 1853; Petersen's *Early History of Steamboating on the Minnesota River* in *Minnesota History*, Vol. XI, pp. 123-144; Bishop's *Floral Home: or, First Years of Minnesota*, pp. 298, 299.

[640] Compilation of Upper Mississippi steamboats prepared by the writer. Merrick's *Steamboats and Steamboatmen of the Upper Mississippi* in the *Burlington Post*, September 13, 1913, to December 6, 1919, is the most complete compilation accessible to the student.

[641] *Northwestern Gazette and Galena Advertiser*, July 9, 1836; *Iowa News* (Dubuque), June 10, July 15, 1837.

Notes and References

[642] *Northwestern Gazette and Galena Advertiser*, March 28, April 25, May 30, 1845; *Enrolment of Vessels*, Collector of Customs Office, St. Louis, Enrolment 14, March 5, 1845.

[643] *Minnesota Pioneer* (St. Paul), November 8, 15, 1849.

[644] *Senate Documents*, 28th Congress, 1st Session, Document 242, p. 8.

[645] *Northwestern Gazette and Galena Advertiser*, April 22, May 13, 1837, April 22, 1839; Folsom's *Fifty Years in the Northwest* (St. Paul, 1888), p. 689; *Enrolment of Vessels*, Collector of Customs Office, Cincinnati, Enrolment 20, March 27, 1839.

[646] *Miners' Express* (Dubuque), June 25, 1845.

[647] *Enrolment of Vessels*, Collector of Customs Office, Cincinnati, Enrolments 14 and 16, March 10, 17, 1844; *Enrolment of Vessels*, Collector of Customs Office, St. Louis, Enrolment 25, March 17, 1844.

[648] Letters from Hercules L. Dousman to Henry Hastings Sibley, May 3, November 20, 1844, March 30, May 9, 1845, in the *Sibley Papers*.

[649] *Enrolment of Vessels*, Collector of Customs Office, St. Louis, Enrolment 33, March 16, 1848; Blakeley's *History of the Discovery of the Mississippi and the Advent of Commerce in Minnesota* in *Minnesota Historical Collections*, Vol. VIII, pp. 381-388.

[650] *Enrolment of Vessels*, Collector of Customs Office, St. Louis, Enrolment 44, April 4, 1849; Blakeley's *History of the Discovery of the Mississippi and the Advent of Commerce in Minnesota* in *Minnesota Historical Collections*, Vol. VIII, pp. 381, 382; *Minnesota Pioneer* (St. Paul), May 2, August 1, 15, 1850.

[651] *Minnesota Democrat* (St. Paul), May 27, 1851.

[652] *Minnesota Pioneer* (St. Paul), July 1, 22, 29, 1852; Blakeley's *History of the Discovery of the Mississippi and the Advent of Commerce in Minnesota* in *Minnesota Historical Collections*, Vol. VIII, pp. 388, 389.

⁶⁵³ *Daily Express and Herald* (Dubuque), January 15, 1859; Blakeley's *History of the Discovery of the Mississippi and the Advent of Commerce in Minnesota* in *Minnesota Historical Collections*, Vol. VIII, pp. 388, 389.

⁶⁵⁴ *The Winona Republican*, May 20, 27, June 3, 10, 17, 1856; *Shakopee Independent*, June 18, 1856.

⁶⁵⁵ *Daily Pioneer and Democrat* (St. Paul), July 15, 1857.

⁶⁵⁶ *Northwestern Gazette and Galena Advertiser*, July 15, 1837; *Minnesota Pioneer* (St. Paul), July 29, 1852.

⁶⁵⁷ *The Daily Minnesotian* (St. Paul), October 9, 1858.

⁶⁵⁸ *The Dubuque Herald*, May 10, 14, 22, 1861; *Rock Island Argus*, May 10, 1861; *Des Moines Valley Whig* (Keokuk), May 13, 1861; *Daily Democrat and News* (Davenport), May 10, 1861.

⁶⁵⁹ *Burlington Post*, October 30, 1915.

⁶⁶⁰ *Galena Gazette*, March 17, 1893.

⁶⁶¹ *Galena Gazette*, March 17, 1893; *The Minnesotian* (St. Paul), May 7, 1853.

⁶⁶² *Galena Gazette*, March 17, 20, 1893; *Burlington Post*, May 31, 1919.

⁶⁶³ Field's *History of the Atlantic Telegraph* (1867), pp. 131-245; Briggs's *The Story of the Telegraph, and a History of the Great Atlantic Cable* (1858), pp. 92-194.

⁶⁶⁴ Wilson's *Telegraph Pioneering* in *The Palimpsest*, Vol. VI, pp. 373-393.

⁶⁶⁵ *Daily Pioneer and Democrat* (St. Paul), August 18, 1858.

⁶⁶⁶ *The New International Encyclopedia* (1921), Vol. II, pp. 322, 323.

⁶⁶⁷ *Daily Express and Herald* (Dubuque), August 17, 1858; *Light List Upper Mississippi and Tributaries*, Thirteenth District, Washington,

Notes and References

1930. The Queen's message of August 16th contained only the first paragraph but early on the morning of August 17th the complete message was forwarded.

[668] Briggs's *The Story of the Telegraph*, pp. 187-188; *Daily Minnesotian* (St. Paul), August 20, 1858.

[669] *Daily Express and Herald* (Dubuque), August 17, 20, 21, 1858; *The Dubuque Daily Times*, August 21, 1858; *National Democrat* (La Crosse), August 24, 1858; *The Winona Republican*, August 25, 1858. The Winona editor pointed out that his extra containing the Queen's message actually appeared fifteen hours before St. Paul papers notified their readers and upbraided St. Paul editors for their claims.

[670] *Red Wing Republican*, August 20, 1858; *Transcript* (Prescott, Wisconsin), August 21, 1858.

[671] *Daily Minnesotian* (St. Paul), August 19, 20, 1858; *St. Paul Daily Times*, August 19, 1858.

[672] Twain's *Life on the Mississippi* (1883), pp. 70-131, 152-192; De Voto's *Mark Twain's America*, pp. 26, 100-114. The writer discovered Mark Twain's pilot's license at St. Louis during the summer of 1927 and has a letter of congratulation from a descendant of Mark Twain's — Cyril Clemens of California.

[673] In defense of Mr. Bixby it may be suggested that it is doubtful if another captain on western waters packed more thrilling episodes into a career of thirty-three years than did Daniel Smith Harris.

[674] A good description of the work of the steamboat captain may be found in Merrick's *Old Times on the Upper Mississippi*, pp. 71-77.

[675] *Senate Documents*, 28th Congress, 1st Session, Document 242, p. 8.

[676] Blakeley's *History of the Discovery of the Mississippi and the Advent of Commerce in Minnesota* in *Minnesota Historical Collections*, Vol. VIII, p. 415; Merrick and Tibbals' *Genesis of Steam Navigation on Western Rivers* in *Proceedings of the State Historical Society of Wisconsin*, 1911, p. 116 (also reprinted with the title, *Genesis of Steamboating on Western rivers; with a Register of Officers on the*

Steamboating on Upper Mississippi

Upper Mississippi 1823-1870); Price's *The Execution of O'Connor* in *The Palimpsest*, Vol. I, pp. 90, 91; *Burlington Post*, June 5, 1915.

[677] Blakeley and Merrick have both compiled excellent lists of steamboat captains for the period before the Civil War. To this the writer can add in number and supplement in amount of material about each, largely as a result of his researches in the various newspaper files.

[678] Hussey's *History of Steamboating on the Des Moines River, From 1837 to 1862*, in *Annals of Iowa* (Third Series), Vol. IV, p. 365; *Burlington Post*, May 29, 1915.

[679] Merrick and Tibbals' *Genesis of Steam Navigation on Western Rivers* in *Proceedings of the State Historical Society of Wisconsin*, 1911, p. 114.

[680] *Minnesota Pioneer* (St. Paul), September 26, 1850.

[681] *Express and Herald* (Dubuque), October 2, 1857.

[682] *Weekly North Western Gazette* (Galena), June 4, 1850; *Minnesota Pioneer* (St. Paul), April 10, 1851.

[683] Merrick and Tibbals' *Genesis of Steam Navigation on Western Rivers* in *Proceedings of the State Historical Society of Wisconsin*, 1911, pp. 114, 134. Laughton was born in London in 1823 and settled at Platteville, Wisconsin, in 1844. After serving as a seaman on the Great Lakes for two seasons, he began his river life in 1852 as a mate aboard the *Nominee*. He was mate on the *Galena* for two seasons and then commanded such boats as the *City Belle*, the *Galena*, the *Golden Era*, the *Northern Belle*, the *Milwaukee*, the *Alex Mitchell*, and the *Lucy Bertram*. He died at Platteville in 1883.

[684] Merrick and Tibbals' *Genesis of Steam Navigation on Western Rivers* in *Proceedings of the State Historical Society of Wisconsin*, 1911, pp. 131, 137; Wilkie's *Davenport Past and Present*, pp. 193-196.

[685] Folsom's *Fifty Years in the Northwest*, pp. 561, 562; *Burlington Post*, December 14, 1918.

[686] *Burlington Post*, January 30, 1915.

[687] *Galena Advertiser*, quoted in the *Daily Express and Herald* (Dubuque), May 21, 1856; Merrick and Tibbals' *Genesis of Steam*

Notes and References

Navigation on Western Rivers in *Proceedings of the State Historical Society of Wisconsin*, 1911, pp. 126, 127.

[688] Men like "Diamond Jo" Reynolds and William F. Davidson had many and divergent interests. Each man contributed much to steamboating and each is worthy of a volume by himself.

[689] *Minnesota Pioneer* (St. Paul), April 28, 1849. Blakeley, basing his statement on data received from Philander Prescott, the Indian interpreter at Fort Snelling, says the *Highland Mary* arrived first in 1849, but the *Minnesota Pioneer* of April 28, 1849, credits the *Dr. Franklin No. 2* with the victory.

[690] Scharf's *History of St. Louis*, Vol. II, p. 1003.

[691] Data compiled from the newspapers of the period by the writer together with information furnished by the U. S. Engineers' Office at St. Paul, Rock Island, and St. Louis warrant these conclusions.

[692] *Northwestern Gazette and Galena Advertiser*, March 19, April 9, 1836.

[693] Wilson's *Telegraph Pioneering* and *By Wire* in *The Palimpsest*, Vol. VI, pp. 373-393, Vol. VII, pp. 233-260. See the writer's series of articles on the coming of the railroads to Iowa in the August, September, October, November, and December, 1933, issues of *The Palimpsest*.

[694] *Daily Pioneer and Democrat* (St. Paul), November 18, 1858; Blakeley's *History of the Discovery of the Mississippi and the Advent of Commerce in Minnesota* in *Minnesota Historical Collections*, Vol. VIII, p. 413; *The Herald* (Dubuque), December 21, 1866.

[695] Bishop's *Floral Home; or, First Years of Minnesota*, p. 178.

[696] Pendergast's *Sketches of the History of Hutchinson* in *Minnesota Historical Collections*, Vol. X, Pt. 1, p. 75.

[697] *Daily Pioneer and Democrat* (St. Paul), April 28, 29, 30, 1857; *Express and Herald* (Dubuque), May 1, 2, 5, 8, 1857.

[698] *Daily Pioneer and Democrat* (St. Paul), April 17, 29, 1857.

[699] *Minnesota Pioneer* (St. Paul), July 8, 1852; *Daily Pioneer and*

Democrat (St. Paul), April 18, 25, 28, 1857; manuscript register of the *Time and Tide*, on deposit with the Minnesota Historical Society.

[700] *Daily Pioneer and Democrat* (St. Paul), May 2, 3, 5, 6, 1857.

[701] *Express and Herald* (Dubuque), April 16, 1859.

[702] *Express and Herald* (Dubuque), April 23, 24, 1859.

[703] *Express and Herald* (Dubuque), May 1, 2, 5, 8, 1857; *The Burlington Hawk-Eye*, April 20, 1884.

[704] *Red Wing Republican*, March 26, 1858; *Burlington Hawk-Eye*, April 20, 1884.

[705] *The Herald* (Dubuque), February 28, March 10, 15, 19, 20, 26, 1868; *Burlington Hawk-Eye*, April 20, 1884.

[706] Quoted in *The Gate City Weekly* (Keokuk), April 30, 1873.

[707] *The Dubuque Herald*, December 14, 1859.

[708] *Minnesota Pioneer* (St. Paul), November 15, 21, 28, 1850.

[709] *The Minnesotian* (St. Paul), November 12, 19, 26, 1853.

[710] *Daily Minnesota Pioneer* (St. Paul), November 11, 13, 14, 15, 17, 20, 21, 22, 24, 27, 30, December 5, 1854.

[711] *Daily Pioneer and Democrat* (St. Paul), November 5, 1857.

[712] *Daily Pioneer and Democrat* (St. Paul), November 8, 10, 11, 13, 14, 1857.

[713] *Express and Herald* (Dubuque) November 24, 1857.

[714] *The Winona Republican*, November 27, December 4, 11, 1855.

[715] *Northwestern Gazette and Galena Advertiser*, December 3, 17, 1836.

[716] *Northwestern Gazette and Galena Advertiser*, November 11, 26, 29, December 2, 4, 1851.

[717] *Northwestern Gazette and Galena Advertiser*, December 3, 1836, November 24, 1841, February 17, 1846.

[718] *Northwestern Gazette and Galena Advertiser*, February 17, 1846.

Notes and References

[719] Quoted in the *Winona Republican*, November 24, 1858. Minnesota Territory was not legally created until March, 1849.

[720] *Burlington Post*, November 1, 1919.

[721] *Muscatine Journal*, quoted in *The Weekly Gate City* (Keokuk), January 14, 1874.

[722] *Miner's Journal* (Galena), March 13, 1830.

[723] *History of Lee County, Iowa* (1879), pp. 663, 664.

[724] *Northwestern Gazette and Galena Advertiser*, November 7, 1835.

[725] *Annual Report of the Chief of Engineers to the Secretary of War*, 1877, Pt. 1, pp. 81, 505, 506.

[726] Scharf's *History of Saint Louis*, Vol. II, p. 1112.

[727] Scharf's *History of Saint Louis*, Vol. II, p. 1113.

[728] *Report of the Chief of Engineers*, 1877, Pt. 1, pp. 505, 506.

[729] *Weekly Gate City* (Keokuk), November 12, 1873.

[730] *Northwestern Gazette and Galena Advertiser*, November 24, 1845, February 17, 1846; *Galena Daily Advertiser*, January 9, 1849.

[731] *The Herald* (Dubuque), April 12, 14, 17, 1866.

[732] *The Weekly Gate City* (Keokuk), March 25, 1874.

[733] *The Herald* (Dubuque), March 6, 1867.

[734] *The Herald* (Dubuque), November 28, 1868; Oldt's *History of Dubuque County, Iowa*, pp. 209, 211, 223, 234, 235.

[735] *Burlington Post*, March 28, April 4, 1914.

[736] *Enrolment of Vessels*, Collector of Customs Office, Pittsburgh, Enrolment 40, March 10, 1840. The first *Chippewa* was 127 feet long, had a 19-foot beam, a 4-foot 8-inch hold, and measured 107 tons. — *Senate Documents*, 28th Congress, 1st Session, Document 242, p. 8; *Burlington Post*, March 28, 1914.

[737] *Enrolment of Vessels*, Collector of Customs Office, St. Louis. According to her enrolment, dated December 3, 1858, the *Chippewa*

Steamboating on Upper Mississippi

Falls was owned by Captain W. R. Van Pelt together with John McFarland and James Francis, all of Oquawka, Illinois. She was 120 feet long, had a 24-foot beam, a 3½-foot hold, and measured 93 tons. Another steamboat *Chippewa Falls*, said to have been built at Pittsburgh in 1861 and measuring 142 tons, is recorded in the *Proceedings of the Seventeenth Annual Meeting of the Board of Supervising Inspectors of Steam Vessels* (1869), p. 183.

[788] *Burlington Post*, April 4, 1914.

[789] *Proceedings of the Seventeenth Annual Meeting of the Board of Supervising Inspectors of Steam Vessels* (1869), p. 182; *Burlington Post*, March 28, April 4, 1914.

[740] Chittenden's *History of Early Steamboat Navigation on the Missouri River*, Vol. I, pp. 218-221; McDonald's *The Missouri River and Its Victims* in *The Missouri Historical Review*, Vol. XXI, p. 234; *Burlington Post*, March 28, 1914.

In addition to those mentioned in the footnotes, the writer is indebted to scores of others: to Captains John Killeen, Fred Bill, George Merrick, and Walter Blair; to J. P. Higgins and Major General T. Q. Ashburn; to Steamboat Inspectors George B. Knapp and Harry Suiter; to Solon J. Buck, Theodore C. Blegen, Joseph Schafer, and Paul Angle. He is especially grateful to Louis Pelzer for critical and friendly advice and counsel.

Index

Index

tion of, 344, 432; site of, 403; activities at, 454
Burlington, 156, 157, 159, 227, 257, 400, 405
Burlington Railroad, 299
Burlington *Telegraph*, comment in, 309
Bushwhacking, 212
Butler, Captain, 172

Cabin passage, 328, 353-380, 374
Cabin passengers, food of, 358-360; names of, 403, 404
Cairo (Ill.), Charles Dickens at, 26; mention of, 179, 300
Calhoun, John C., 83
Calhoun, 86
California, population of, 301; reference to, 330; trips to, 333
Camp Kearny, 140
Camp McClellan, Sioux at, 140
Campbell, B. H., 420
Canada, 140-142, 181, 184, 194, 293, 351, 355, 356, 363, 380, 385, 390
Cannon River, 105, 435
Canoe, cost of, 50
Cantonment Jesup, 172
Cap au Gris, 24, 92
Cape à l'Ail Sauvage (Capoli Bluff), 101
Cape Girardeau, 87
Cape Winebegos, 101
Capoli Bluff, 24, 101, 255
Captains, status of, 153, 176; earnings of, 228, 373; activities of, 438-450
Cargoes, discussion of, 381-390, 538-539
Carver, Jonathan, use of "Mississippi" by, 12; explorations of, 32, 33; book by, 33; land granted to, 33; Carver's Cave in honor of, 33
Carver's Cave, 33, 105
Cass, Lewis, 13, 14, 299
Cass Lake, 13, 15, 22
Casse-Fusils, naming of, 102, 103
Cassville (Wis.), 217, 220, 237, 288, 290, 291, 376, 379
Catfish Creek, Fox village at, 111; Catlin at, 256; excursionists at, 288
Catholic Institute of Dubuque, 293
Catlin, George, data on, 248; paintings of, 248, 254, 255; scenes described by, 249, 250; mention of, 253, 257, 261, 400; Indian performance before, 254, 255; comment by, 417, 418
Catlin, Mrs. George., 253, 257

Cattle, 196, 197, 356, 381, 382
Cavalier, operation of, 453
Cavileer, Charles, office of, 164
Cecilia, captain of, 155; mention of, 157, 160; troops on, 179; purchase of, 401; service of, 402; passage on, 405
Centennial, destruction of, 477
Chain of Rocks channel, 91
Challenge, cargo of, 388
"Channel of the Foxes", 93
Chariton (Mo.), 81, 85
Chateau Brilliante, 146
Cheyenne American Fur Company, 145
Chicago (Ill.), mention of, 216, 271, 303, 304, 316, 318, 322, 330, 344; canal at, 244, 245, 246; newspaper editors of, 273, 303; railroad connection of, 298; steamboat at, 321
Chicago and Rock Island Railroad, 271
Chicago Convention, 295
Chickasaw Bluffs, De Soto at, 28
Chickasaw Indians, 63
Chieftain, service of, 175, 178, 394
Chippewa, 157, 160, 483, 484, 485, 486
Chippewa Falls, 483, 484
Chippewa Indians, 116, 119, 126, 127, 128, 130, 206, 254, 255, 486
Chippewa River, 14, 24, 33, 104, 144, 145, 412, 483
Chippewa Valley, 483, 484, 486
Chittenden, Hiram W., comment by, 485
Choctaw Indians, removal of, 134
Cholera, spread of, 353, 354, 355, 356, 444, 445
Chouteau, E. F., 149
Chouteau, Pierre, Jr., boats owned by, 157
Cincinnati (O.) population of, 42, 53, 318; *New Orleans* at, 60; description of, 121, 122; mention of, 210, 287, 334, 386, 415, 420, 437, 439; immigrants at, 327, 339; boats built at, 363, 367; Scribe Harris at, 411
Cincinnati *Gazette*, 272
Circus, shipment of, by boat, 389
City Belle, 345, 377, 382
City of Memphis, soldiers on, 185
City of St. Paul, cargo of, 385
Civil War, service of steamboats in, 174, 179-189, 378; effect of, on steamboat business, 180-189; refugees of, 181, 182; mention of, 203, 438, 439, 441
Clark, George Rogers, victory of, 34

Index

Index

369, 432; supplies from, 202; ice near, 480

Fort Osage, 85

Fort Randall (Neb.), 140

Fort Ridgely, 168, 195, 413

Fort Ripley, 168, 195

Fort St. Anthony, mention of, 90, 190; *Virginia* at, 105; name of, 171, 172

Fort Snelling, Schoolcraft at, 20; expeditions to, 83, 251, 253, 392, 400, 401, 402, 429; site of, 87, 168, 169, 195; naming of, 90, 171, 172; incident at, 107; councils at, 113, 116, 124, 126; Indians removed to, 138; fur trade at, 145, 147, 254; mention of, 152, 153, 159, 160, 193, 200, 250, 254, 280, 442; steamboats at, 153, 154, 399; Red River Valley trade at, 163; supplies for, 197, 199, 201, 202; mail to, 201; description of, 201; Indian Agency at, 254; painting of, 255

Fort Winnebago, 14, 148, 168, 201, 202, 243, 249, 376, 412

Fortress Monroe, Black Hawk at, 122

Fortune, keelboats with, 223

Fourth of July, excursions on, 287, 288

Fowle, John, 199

Fox Indians, mention of, 11, 96, 119, 129, 130, 134, 144, 145, 167, 174, 175; village of, 98, 100; massacre of, 111; treaty with, 113; delegation of, at Washington, 124; lead mines of, 205

Fox River, 14, 30, 148, 161, 192, 243

Frank Steele, 348

Franklin (Mo.), 80, 81, 82, 85

Franz Siegel, winter quarters of, 481

Free Trader, 321

Freight barge, 46

Freight rates, on steamboats, 159, 160, 228-233; on overland routes, 244

Frémont, John C., 257, 400

French, Daniel, *Comet* launched by, 69

French, explorations of, 28-32; immigration of, 318

Frontier, record of, 240; officers of, 412, 414, 438

Fuller, Hiram, writings of, 272

Fulton, Robert, mention of, 25, 35; plan of, for Mississippi navigation, 36, 39, 40, 43-47; description of, 37; comment of, on *Clermont*, 37, 38; letter by, on steamboat monopoly, 44; steamboat company formed by, 57

Fulton, 199

Fulton-Livingston monopoly, formation of, 41-47; breaking of, 68-74

"Fulton's Folly", 36 (see also *Clermont*)

Fur trade, profits of, to steamboats, 144, 148, 159, 160, 161; centers of, 147; comment of Atwater on, 147; routes of, 147-149; in Red River Colony, 163-166; characters of, 204; value of, 209

Fur trading posts, 144, 145, 146

Furs, transportation of, 68, 144-161, 505

G. H. Wilson, 443, 444

G. W. Spar-Hawk, 273, 278

Gabbert, William H., 444

Galena (Ill.), mention of, 14, 32, 112, 156, 159, 160, 178, 180, 200, 249, 266, 454; Black Hawk at, 121; steamboats at, 123, 215-220, 225, 237, 335, 343, 399, 401, 404, 411, 453, 470, 471; trade at, 131, 149, 163, 243, 442, 459; lead mines at, 205; government mineral agent at, 205; land sold at, 207; population of, 207, 215, 225, 226, 327, 341, 342, 395, 408, 422; telegraph line to, 178; soldiers from, 179; naming of, 214, 225; position of, as port, 215-226; description of, 216, 224, 225; newspaper of, 216, 405; railroad at, 225; decline of, 225, 226; home of Grant at, 225; visit of Jenny Lind at, 225; hot weather at, 228; excursions at, 259, 260, 275, 287, 288, 294, 417, 445; accident at, 365; transportation to, 374, 375, 376, 420; visit to, 417, 445; history of, 430

Galena, accident on, 194, 366, 367, 369; mention of, 273, 459, 461, 466; arrival of, 345; pilot of, 442; race with, 459

Galena, Dubuque, Dunleith, and Minnesota Packet Company, schedule of, 377, 378

Galena *Advertiser*, comment in, 313, 330

Galena & Chicago Union Railroad, 299 (see also North Western Railroad)

Galena *Gazette*, 400

Galena River (see Fever River)

Galenian, 217, 453, 476

Gautier, Antoine, fur trade of, 145

Gear, H. H., 215

General Brooke, 155, 157, 158, 401, 405

Index

Index

Index

rates on, 159, 160; mention of, 260; description of, 262; passage on, 400, 405

Mandan, mention of, 147, 199; captain of, 171, 172, 198; time made by, 190, 191

Mankato (Minn.), Indians removed from, 138, 139

Mann, Alice, comment by, 321

Manny, J. P., farm machinery of, 384, 385

Mansfield, 348

Manufactured goods, shipment of, 386

Marais d'Ogé (Marais Dosier Slough), 98

Marais Dosier Slough, 98

Marcpee (Indian), incident of, 119, 120

Mark Twain, early home of, 23, 211; mention of, 89; writings of, 438 (see also Clemens, Samuel)

Marquette, Pierre, 23, 30, 31

Marryat, Frederick, mention of, 145, 257, 317; travels of, 227; comments by, 227, 228, 302, 305, 323, 353

Marsh, J. W., 251, 252

Marshall, John, decision of, 73

Martha No. 2, arrival of, 470

Mascouten Indians, village of, 30

Mason, Mr., 291

Massachusetts, emigrant company in, 314; resident of, 407

May, James, career of, 174, 395, 446

Mayer, Frank B., painting by, 117

Mayflower, passage on, 407

Mechanic, lead cargo on, 215

Medora, cargo of, 383

Meeker, James, service of, 443

Meeker, Moses, colony of, 210, 212, 407

Memphis (Tenn.), 134, 300, 334

Menard, Pierre, commission of, 113-115

Mendota (Minn.), treaty at, 113; mention of, 116, 164; fur trade at, 146

Menominee Indians, 100, 119, 120

Merchandise, shipment of, 386

Merchant, operation of, 396

Merrick, George, characterization of, 204

Merrimac Island, 436

"Meschasipi" (Mississippi), 12

Messenger, 348

Metropolitan, excursion of, 292; passengers on, 348

Mexico, lead cargo of, 215

Mexican War, service of steamboats in, 174, 178, 179, 203, 401, 402

Miami Indians, 30, 32, 205

Michigan canal, transportation on, 324

Mico (Mississippi) River, 12

Middleton, W., 126, 127

Military posts, erection of, 168; dependence of, on steamboats, 168, 169; inspection tours of, 171, 172; troops and supplies transported to, 190-203

Military supplies, transport of, by steamboat, 83, 196-203; value of, 201, 202

Miller, Reuben, Jr., 258

Milwaukee (Wis.), trade route to, 244, 245, 316; railroad to, 299; immigrants at, 318

Milwaukee, reference to, 286, 293; profits made by, 377, 378; passage on, 378, 380; operation of, 468

Milwaukee and La Crosse Railroad, completion of, to Mississippi, 286

Miner's Journal (Galena), first issue of, 216

Minneapolis, arrival of, 351; cargo of, 388; winter quarters of, 482

Minnehaha Falls, excursions to, 253, 254, 259, 280

Minneiska, excursion to, 289

Minnesota, mention of, 22, 162; Carver land grant in, 33; forts in, 168; comment on, 280; population of, 301, 302, 333, 334, 337; route to, 316; immigrants in, 319, 331, 333, 338, 341, 350, 356, 359, 371; trip to, 333-352; livestock shipped to, 382; Governor of, 406; conditions in, 432, 433; resident of, 448; visitors to, 466

Minnesota, Territory of, 153, 333, 337, 373, 389, 421, 451, 452, 454

Minnesota, 341, 348, 351, 355, 356, 385, 468

Minnesota, First Years of, 429

Minnesota Belle, operation of, 466

Minnesota Historical Society, celebration of, at Itasca, 19

Minnesota Packet Company, contract of, to remove Indians, 138; organization of, 158, 266, 420; D. S. Harris with, 267; steamboats of, 271; excursion of, 270, 286; activities of, 376, 377; clerk of, 390; member of, 414; operation of, 422, 423, 472, 473; mention of, 449

Minnesota Pioneer, comment in, 368, 389

Minnesota River, mention of, 11, 24, 139, 140, 148, 152, 153, 163; first

[565]

Index

Neill, E. D., 383
Neutral Ground, 125, 135
New Albany, tonnage at, 334
New Boston Bay, winter quarters at, 482
New Brazil, mention of, 194; tonnage of, 221; keelboats with, 223; description of, 262
New England, residents of, 302, 317; emigrants from, 307, 312; immigrants in, 321
New Madrid (Mo.), mention of, 26; earthquake at, 63; *New Orleans* at, 63, 64
New Orleans (La.), mention of, 33, 149, 246, 439, 440; significance of, 41; population of, 42; *New Orleans* at, 65; barge service to, 68; battle of, 70; post at, 196, 316; steamboats from, 219; immigrants at, 322, 328, 330, 339, 374; conditions at, 327; shipments from, 334, 459; shipment to, 352; cargoes at, 381, 382
New Orleans, construction of, 57; naming of, 57; launching of, 57, 69; voyage of, 57-67; description of, 58, 60, 61; comments on, 59-62; Indian pursuit of, 63; fire on, 63; regular run of, 65; snagging of, 65; replica of, 65, 66; excursions of, 287
New Orleans (second), 65, 69, 72
"New Orleans", 50 (see also Flatboat)
New Orleans Crescent, suit against, 185
New St. Paul, excursion of, 265
New Sweden, founding of, 325
New York, editors from, 272; mention of, 302; immigrants in, 304, 312, 321, 322, 330; farmers in, 314; port at, 316; population of, 317, 334, 338; shipments from, 334; Joseph Throckmorton in, 391
New Ulm (Minn.), massacre at, 172
Newhall, Horatio, 215
Newhall, John B., opinion of, 327
Newman, John, 223
Niagara, post at, 196; mention of, 250
Niagara, work of, 431
Nicolet, Jean, exploration by, 29
Nicollet, J. N., exploration by, 17; tribute of, to Schoolcraft, 17; treaty signed by, 116; mention of, 257, 400
Niles' Register, comment in, 320
Nimrod, captain of, 155; reference to, 157; use of, 401; passage on, 405

Niota, damage to, 480
Nominee, Indians on, 116; mention of, 157, 266; expedition on, 171; race of, 270; accident on, 366; passage on, 377, 446; cargo of, 382, 383
North Western Railroad, 299
Northern Belle, excursion on, 265; mention of, 286, 369, 370; passage on, 346, 351; arrival of, 349; profits of, 378, 379; cargo of, 383; operation of, 469
Northern Light, reference to, 202, 286; excursion on, 290, 291; arrival at, 348; operation of, 468; sinking of, 478, 479
Northern Line Packet Company, contract of, for removal of Indians, 140; troops transported by, 181; business decline of, 182, 183; operation of, 355, 356, 449, 481; competition of, 379
Northern Oufitt, 158, 159
Northup, Anson, 165
Northwest, Old, States of, 301; immigrants in, 318
Northwestern, operation of, 463, 479; winter quarters of, 478
Northwestern Gazette and Galena Advertiser, quotation from, 218, 219
Northwestern Packet Company, rates of, 378
Northwestern Union Packet Company, profits of, 378; property of, 420
Norway, emigrants from, 318, 331, 348, 349, 350

Ocean Wave, operation of, 348, 377, 449, 481
O'Connell, 217
O'Connor, Patrick, execution of, 292, 442
Ohio, population of, 301, 304; emigrants from, 311, 312, 314, 316, 334
Ohio River, early boats on, 26, 49, 54, 57-67, 70, 149, 219, 221, 258, 298, 301, 305, 306, 307, 316, 335, 338, 339, 342, 344, 386, 393, 396; villages on, 211
Ohio Steamboat Navigation Company, incorporation of, 57, 69
Ojibway Indians, land of, 11; namesakes of, 483; Mississippi named by, 487
Oliphant, Lawrence, comment by, 322
Olive Branch, operation of, 154, 217, 453
Omaha (Nebr.), steamboat at, 80

Index

Index

of, in fur trade, 146; mention of, 159, 171, 180, 202, 252, 348; position of, in Red River Valley trade, 163-166; government trade at, 203; description of, 279; Grand Excursion to, 279, 280; comment on, 280; railroad to, 300; crossing at, 309; boats at, 333, 335, 462, 466, 467, 483, 484; immigrants at, 335, 341, 342; population of, 337, 338; fare to, 377, 378, 379, 380; livestock to, 383; cargo sent to, 384; transportation to, 406, 453; residents of, 413, 422, 447; telegraph line to, 432; trips to, 436, 444, 456; navigation to, 451

St. Paul, condition of, 358; size of, 362

St. Paul Chamber of Commerce, interest of, in steamboat, 165

St. Paul *Daily Pioneer and Democrat*, editor of, 425; reference to, 432; comment in, 459, 467, 468

St. Paul *Daily Times*, 425

St. Peter's (Minn.), mention of, 148, 149, 151, 156, 160, 170, 190, 196, 197, 217, 253, 264, 401, 402; steamboats at, 154; soldiers from, 179; military post at, 196; scenes around, 249

St. Peter's, mention of, 237; excursion of, 256; size of, 399, 400; passage on, 405

St. Peter's River, *Virginia* on, 105, 106; mention of, 144, 170, 249; fort at, 168

St. Vrain, Mrs. Felix, 253

Sam Gaty, attack on, 186, 187

Sam Young, 265, 348, 459

Sandbars, danger from, 76, 88, 89; delays caused by, 198

Sandy Lake, trading post at, 145

Sangamo Journal, quotation from, 304

Sanitation, lack of, 353

Santa Fé trade, characters in, 204, 209

Saracen, 348, 369

Sarah Ann, accident on, 364

Sargent, Epes, writings of, 272, 277

Saucy Jack (keelboat), 190

Sauk Indians, mention of, 95, 97, 112, 119, 129, 130, 134, 144, 145, 167, 174, 175; treaty with, 113; delegation of, at Washington, 124

Saukenuk, 96

Sault Ste. Marie, Schoolcraft at, 16;

mention of, 250; immigrants at, 322

Saunders, John, service of, 468

Savanna (Ill.), soldiers from, 179; mention of, 230, 293; excursion to, 291

Savanna, passage on, 351

Savannah, Atlantic crossed by, 41, 79

Schoolcraft, Henry Rowe, explorations of, 13-17, 170; biographical data on, 14; island named for, 16; book by, 16, 17, 18; "Itasca" coined by, 18, 20, 21; quotation from, 20; letter of, 20, 21

Schoolcraft Island, discovery of, 16

Schouler, William, work of, 272, 278

Schuyler, soldiers on, 186

Scientific expeditions, 170, 171, 203

Scioto, mention of, 199; lead cargo on, 215

Scotch, settlement of, 162, 318

Scott, Dred, owner of, 116

Scott, Winfield, tour of inspection by, 171, 172; Fort Snelling named by, 171, 172; mention of, 178

Scribe, Robert, service of, 443

Sea-Horse (ocean steamer), 79

Second Purchase, 124

Sedgwick, Catherine M., meeting with, 272; mention of, 275, 282; quotations from, 276

Selkirk, Earl of, 162

Selkirk Colony (see Red River Colony)

Seminole Indians, removal of, 134

Senator, removal of Indians on, 138; captain of, 155, 414; mention of, 164, 237, 338; cargo of, 356, 472; passage on, 371, 428; operation of, 420, 421, 455, 465

Seventh Iowa Volunteer Infantry, first casualty for, 184

Seward, William H., 286, 358

Seymour, E. S., comment by, 371

Shallcross, S., 223, 394, 396

Shamrock, lead on, 215; operation of, 446

Sheffield and Farnam, firm of, 271

Shenandoah, operation of, 471

Shilito & Co., purchases from, 363

Shot tower, erection of, on Wisconsin River, 243; location of, at Herculaneum (Mo.), 244

Shreve, Henry Miller, steamboat monopoly broken by, 68, 72; biographical data on, 68; Shreveport named for, 68, 74; barge service of, 68; profits

Index

[573]

Index

winter quarters of, 86; distinction of, 170

Wharf boat, exhibition at, 390

Wheeling (W. Va.), boat yard at, 49; Black Hawk at, 122; emigrants at, 307; tonnage at, 334

Whiskey, shipment of, 381

White Beaver, 121

White Collar Line, operation of, 449, 481

Whitney, Daniel, shot tower of, 243

Whitten, David, race with, 433

Wilcox, Joseph B., 138, 139

"Wild boats", 228, 229

Wild Life Refuge, features of, 101

Wilkins, William, 201

William Wallace, 178, 217

Wilson, George H., service of, 443, 444

Winnebago, Black Hawk on, 120, 121, 177; mention of, 178, 217; operation of, 395; passage on, 398, 405

Winnebago Chief, 243

Winnebago Indians, reference to, 29, 100, 109, 130, 144, 145, 156, 167, 174, 206; delegation of, 112; treaty with, 115, 116; lands ceded by, 124, 125; annuities for, 129; removal of, 134, 135-138, 140; description of, 140, 142; activities of, 141, 142; military visit to, 174; war service of, 177

Winnebagoshish Lake, 22

Winneshiek Bottoms, features of, 101

Winona (Minn.), scenery around, 103; *Virginia* at, 103, 104; mention of, 123; excursion from, 289; crossing at, 309; fare to, 378, 424; transportation to, 423; steamboat at, 463, 469

Winona *Republican*, comment in, 424, 469, 473

Winter quarters, 476, 480

Wiota, description of, 263; owners of, 263

Wisconsin, Carver land grant in, 33; fort in, 168; lead in, 204; immigrants in, 327, 338, 341; population of, 333, 337; resident of, 448

Wisconsin, mention of, 217; captain of, 234; cargo of, 234; operation of, 449, 453

Wisconsin Heights, battle of, 410

Wisconsin Herald, 245

Wisconsin River, mention of, 14, 24, 100, 144, 192, 206; fur trade on, 147, 148, 161; fort at, 168; expedition on, 170; route by way of, 243; shot tower on, 243; transportation on, 376, 412

Wood, B. F., 160

Wood, John, 211

Wood, William, 133

Wood, shipment of, 476

Wood and Barclay Company, 133

Worden, Jones, service of, as steamboat captain, 182, 445, 460, 461

Wyoming, 341, 471

Yager, Dick, 186

Yankee, operation of, 465

"Yellow Hills", 95

Yellow River, scenes around, 101

Yellowhead, The, 15 (see also Ozawindib)

Yellowstone, 217

Yellowstone River, steamboat bound for, 80; prophecy for, 83

Young, Captain, 240

Younger, Cole, 186

Zebulon M. Pike, arrival of, at St. Louis, 77; significance of, 77, 78; description of, 78

A CATALOG OF SELECTED DOVER
BOOKS IN ALL FIELDS OF INTEREST

CONCERNING THE SPIRITUAL IN ART, Wassily Kandinsky. Pioneering work by father of abstract art. Thoughts on color theory, nature of art. Analysis of earlier masters. 12 illustrations. 80pp. of text. 5⅜ × 8½.   23411-8 Pa. $3.95

ANIMALS: 1,419 Copyright-Free Illustrations of Mammals, Birds, Fish, Insects, etc., Jim Harter (ed.). Clear wood engravings present, in extremely lifelike poses, over 1,000 species of animals. One of the most extensive pictorial sourcebooks of its kind. Captions. Index. 284pp. 9 × 12.   23766-4 Pa. $11.95

CELTIC ART: The Methods of Construction, George Bain. Simple geometric techniques for making Celtic interlacements, spirals, Kells-type initials, animals, humans, etc. Over 500 illustrations. 160pp. 9 × 12. (USO)   22923-8 Pa. $9.95

AN ATLAS OF ANATOMY FOR ARTISTS, Fritz Schider. Most thorough reference work on art anatomy in the world. Hundreds of illustrations, including selections from works by Vesalius, Leonardo, Goya, Ingres, Michelangelo, others. 593 illustrations. 192pp. 7⅛ × 10¼.   20241-0 Pa. $8.95

CELTIC HAND STROKE-BY-STROKE (Irish Half-Uncial from "The Book of Kells"): An Arthur Baker Calligraphy Manual, Arthur Baker. Complete guide to creating each letter of the alphabet in distinctive Celtic manner. Covers hand position, strokes, pens, inks, paper, more. Illustrated. 48pp. 8¼ × 11.
24336-2 Pa. $3.95

EASY ORIGAMI, John Montroll. Charming collection of 32 projects (hat, cup, pelican, piano, swan, many more) specially designed for the novice origami hobbyist. Clearly illustrated easy-to-follow instructions insure that even beginning papercrafters will achieve successful results. 48pp. 8¼ × 11.   27298-2 Pa. $2.95

THE COMPLETE BOOK OF BIRDHOUSE CONSTRUCTION FOR WOOD-WORKERS, Scott D. Campbell. Detailed instructions, illustrations, tables. Also data on bird habitat and instinct patterns. Bibliography. 3 tables. 63 illustrations in 15 figures. 48pp. 5¼ × 8½.   24407-5 Pa. $1.95

BLOOMINGDALE'S ILLUSTRATED 1886 CATALOG: Fashions, Dry Goods and Housewares, Bloomingdale Brothers. Famed merchants' extremely rare catalog depicting about 1,700 products: clothing, housewares, firearms, dry goods, jewelry, more. Invaluable for dating, identifying vintage items. Also, copyright-free graphics for artists, designers. Co-published with Henry Ford Museum & Green-field Village. 160pp. 8¼ × 11.   25780-0 Pa. $9.95

HISTORIC COSTUME IN PICTURES, Braun & Schneider. Over 1,450 costumed figures in clearly detailed engravings—from dawn of civilization to end of 19th century. Captions. Many folk costumes. 256pp. 8⅜ × 11¾.   23150-X Pa. $11.95

STICKLEY CRAFTSMAN FURNITURE CATALOGS, Gustav Stickley and L. & J. G. Stickley. Beautiful, functional furniture in two authentic catalogs from 1910. 594 illustrations, including 277 photos, show settles, rockers, armchairs, reclining chairs, bookcases, desks, tables. 183pp. 6½ × 9¼. 23838-5 Pa. $8.95

AMERICAN LOCOMOTIVES IN HISTORIC PHOTOGRAPHS: 1858 to 1949, Ron Ziel (ed.). A rare collection of 126 meticulously detailed official photographs, called "builder portraits," of American locomotives that majestically chronicle the rise of steam locomotive power in America. Introduction. Detailed captions. xi + 129pp. 9 × 12. 27393-8 Pa. $12.95

AMERICA'S LIGHTHOUSES: An Illustrated History, Francis Ross Holland, Jr. Delightfully written, profusely illustrated fact-filled survey of over 200 American lighthouses since 1716. History, anecdotes, technological advances, more. 240pp. 8 × 10¾. 25576-X Pa. $11.95

TOWARDS A NEW ARCHITECTURE, Le Corbusier. Pioneering manifesto by founder of "International School." Technical and aesthetic theories, views of industry, economics, relation of form to function, "mass-production split" and much more. Profusely illustrated. 320pp. 6⅛ × 9¼. (USO) 25023-7 Pa. $8.95

HOW THE OTHER HALF LIVES, Jacob Riis. Famous journalistic record, exposing poverty and degradation of New York slums around 1900, by major social reformer. 100 striking and influential photographs. 233pp. 10 × 7⅞.
22012-5 Pa $10.95

FRUIT KEY AND TWIG KEY TO TREES AND SHRUBS, William M. Harlow. One of the handiest and most widely used identification aids. Fruit key covers 120 deciduous and evergreen species; twig key 160 deciduous species. Easily used. Over 300 photographs. 126pp. 5⅜ × 8½. 20511-8 Pa. $3.95

COMMON BIRD SONGS, Dr. Donald J. Borror. Songs of 60 most common U.S. birds: robins, sparrows, cardinals, bluejays, finches, more—arranged in order of increasing complexity. Up to 9 variations of songs of each species.
Cassette and manual 99911-4 $8.95

ORCHIDS AS HOUSE PLANTS, Rebecca Tyson Northen. Grow cattleyas and many other kinds of orchids—in a window, in a case, or under artificial light. 63 illustrations. 148pp. 5⅜ × 8½. 23261-1 Pa. $3.95

MONSTER MAZES, Dave Phillips. Masterful mazes at four levels of difficulty. Avoid deadly perils and evil creatures to find magical treasures. Solutions for all 32 exciting illustrated puzzles. 48pp. 8¼ × 11. 26005-4 Pa $2.95

MOZART'S DON GIOVANNI (DOVER OPERA LIBRETTO SERIES), Wolfgang Amadeus Mozart. Introduced and translated by Ellen H. Bleiler. Standard Italian libretto, with complete English translation. Convenient and thoroughly portable—an ideal companion for reading along with a recording or the performance itself. Introduction. List of characters. Plot summary. 121pp. 5¼ × 8½.
24944-1 Pa. $2.95

TECHNICAL MANUAL AND DICTIONARY OF CLASSICAL BALLET, Gail Grant. Defines, explains, comments on steps, movements, poses and concepts. 15-page pictorial section. Basic book for student, viewer. 127pp. 5⅜ × 8½.
21843-0 Pa. $3.95

BRASS INSTRUMENTS: Their History and Development, Anthony Baines. Authoritative, updated survey of the evolution of trumpets, trombones, bugles, cornets, French horns, tubas and other brass wind instruments. Over 140 illustrations and 48 music examples. Corrected and updated by author. New preface. Bibliography. 320pp. 5⅜ × 8½.							27574-4 Pa. $9.95

HOLLYWOOD GLAMOR PORTRAITS, John Kobal (ed.). 145 photos from 1926–49. Harlow, Gable, Bogart, Bacall; 94 stars in all. Full background on photographers, technical aspects. 160pp. 8⅜ × 11¼.						23352-9 Pa. $11.95

MAX AND MORITZ, Wilhelm Busch. Great humor classic in both German and English. Also 10 other works: "Cat and Mouse," "Plisch and Plumm," etc. 216pp. 5⅜ × 8½.							20181-3 Pa. $5.95

THE RAVEN AND OTHER FAVORITE POEMS, Edgar Allan Poe. Over 40 of the author's most memorable poems: "The Bells," "Ulalume," "Israfel," "To Helen," "The Conqueror Worm," "Eldorado," "Annabel Lee," many more. Alphabetic lists of titles and first lines. 64pp. 5³⁄₁₆ × 8¼.						26685-0 Pa. $1.00

SEVEN SCIENCE FICTION NOVELS, H. G. Wells. The standard collection of the great novels. Complete, unabridged. First Men in the Moon, Island of Dr. Moreau, War of the Worlds, Food of the Gods, Invisible Man, Time Machine, In the Days of the Comet. Total of 1,015pp. 5⅜ × 8½. (USO)		20264-X Clothbd. $29.95

AMULETS AND SUPERSTITIONS, E. A. Wallis Budge. Comprehensive discourse on origin, powers of amulets in many ancient cultures: Arab, Persian, Babylonian, Assyrian, Egyptian, Gnostic, Hebrew, Phoenician, Syriac, etc. Covers cross, swastika, crucifix, seals, rings, stones, etc. 584pp. 5⅜ × 8½. 23573-4 Pa. $12.95

RUSSIAN STORIES/PYCCKNE PACCKA3bI: A Dual-Language Book, edited by Gleb Struve. Twelve tales by such masters as Chekhov, Tolstoy, Dostoevsky, Pushkin, others. Excellent word-for-word English translations on facing pages, plus teaching and study aids, Russian/English vocabulary, biographical/critical introductions, more. 416pp. 5⅜ × 8½.						26244-8 Pa. $8.95

PHILADELPHIA THEN AND NOW: 60 Sites Photographed in the Past and Present, Kenneth Finkel and Susan Oyama. Rare photographs of City Hall, Logan Square, Independence Hall, Betsy Ross House, other landmarks juxtaposed with contemporary views. Captures changing face of historic city. Introduction. Captions. 128pp. 8¼ × 11.							25790-8 Pa. $9.95

AIA ARCHITECTURAL GUIDE TO NASSAU AND SUFFOLK COUNTIES, LONG ISLAND, The American Institute of Architects, Long Island Chapter, and the Society for the Preservation of Long Island Antiquities. Comprehensive, well-researched and generously illustrated volume brings to life over three centuries of Long Island's great architectural heritage. More than 240 photographs with authoritative, extensively detailed captions. 176pp. 8¼ × 11.		26946-9 Pa. $14.95

NORTH AMERICAN INDIAN LIFE: Customs and Traditions of 23 Tribes, Elsie Clews Parsons (ed.). 27 fictionalized essays by noted anthropologists examine religion, customs, government, additional facets of life among the Winnebago, Crow, Zuni, Eskimo, other tribes. 480pp. 6⅛ × 9¼.					27377-6 Pa. $10.95

FRANK LLOYD WRIGHT'S HOLLYHOCK HOUSE, Donald Hoffmann. Lavishly illustrated, carefully documented study of one of Wright's most controversial residential designs. Over 120 photographs, floor plans, elevations, etc. Detailed perceptive text by noted Wright scholar. Index. 128pp. 9¼ × 10¾.
27133-1 Pa. $11.95

THE MALE AND FEMALE FIGURE IN MOTION: 60 Classic Photographic Sequences, Eadweard Muybridge. 60 true-action photographs of men and women walking, running, climbing, bending, turning, etc., reproduced from rare 19th-century masterpiece. vi + 121pp. 9 × 12. 24745-7 Pa. $10.95

1001 QUESTIONS ANSWERED ABOUT THE SEASHORE, N. J. Berrill and Jacquelyn Berrill. Queries answered about dolphins, sea snails, sponges, starfish, fishes, shore birds, many others. Covers appearance, breeding, growth, feeding, much more. 305pp. 5¼ × 8¼. 23366-9 Pa. $7.95

GUIDE TO OWL WATCHING IN NORTH AMERICA, Donald S. Heintzelman. Superb guide offers complete data and descriptions of 19 species: barn owl, screech owl, snowy owl, many more. Expert coverage of owl-watching equipment, conservation, migrations and invasions, etc. Guide to observing sites. 84 illustrations. xiii + 193pp. 5⅜ × 8½. 27344-X Pa. $7.95

MEDICINAL AND OTHER USES OF NORTH AMERICAN PLANTS: A Historical Survey with Special Reference to the Eastern Indian Tribes, Charlotte Erichsen-Brown. Chronological historical citations document 500 years of usage of plants, trees, shrubs native to eastern Canada, northeastern U.S. Also complete identifying information. 343 illustrations. 544pp. 6½ × 9¼. 25951-X Pa. $12.95

STORYBOOK MAZES, Dave Phillips. 23 stories and mazes on two-page spreads: Wizard of Oz, Treasure Island, Robin Hood, etc. Solutions. 64pp. 8¼ × 11.
23628-5 Pa. $2.95

NEGRO FOLK MUSIC, U.S.A., Harold Courlander. Noted folklorist's scholarly yet readable analysis of rich and varied musical tradition. Includes authentic versions of over 40 folk songs. Valuable bibliography and discography. xi + 324pp. 5⅜ × 8½. 27350-4 Pa. $7.95

MOVIE-STAR PORTRAITS OF THE FORTIES, John Kobal (ed.). 163 glamor, studio photos of 106 stars of the 1940s. Rita Hayworth, Ava Gardner, Marlon Brando, Clark Gable, many more. 176pp. 8⅜ × 11¼. 23546-7 Pa. $10.95

BENCHLEY LOST AND FOUND, Robert Benchley. Finest humor from early 30s, about pet peeves, child psychologists, post office and others. Mostly unavailable elsewhere. 73 illustrations by Peter Arno and others. 183pp. 5⅜ × 8½.
22410-4 Pa. $5.95

YEKL and THE IMPORTED BRIDEGROOM AND OTHER STORIES OF YIDDISH NEW YORK, Abraham Cahan. Film Hester Street based on Yekl (1896). Novel, other stories among first about Jewish immigrants on N.Y.'s East Side. 240pp. 5⅜ × 8½. 22427-9 Pa. $6.95

SELECTED POEMS, Walt Whitman. Generous sampling from *Leaves of Grass*. Twenty-four poems include "I Hear America Singing," "Song of the Open Road," "I Sing the Body Electric," "When Lilacs Last in the Dooryard Bloom'd," "O Captain! My Captain!"—all reprinted from an authoritative edition. Lists of titles and first lines. 128pp. 5³⁄₁₆ × 8¼. 26878-0 Pa. $1.00

PERSPECTIVE FOR ARTISTS, Rex Vicat Cole. Depth, perspective of sky and sea, shadows, much more, not usually covered. 391 diagrams, 81 reproductions of drawings and paintings. 279pp. 5⅜ × 8½. 22487-2 Pa. $6.95

DRAWING THE LIVING FIGURE, Joseph Sheppard. Innovative approach to artistic anatomy focuses on specifics of surface anatomy, rather than muscles and bones. Over 170 drawings of live models in front, back and side views, and in widely varying poses. Accompanying diagrams. 177 illustrations. Introduction. Index. 144pp. 8⅜ × 11¼. 26723-7 Pa. $7.95

GOTHIC AND OLD ENGLISH ALPHABETS: 100 Complete Fonts, Dan X. Solo. Add power, elegance to posters, signs, other graphics with 100 stunning copyright-free alphabets: Blackstone, Dolbey, Germania, 97 more—including many lower-case, numerals, punctuation marks. 104pp. 8⅛ × 11. 24695-7 Pa. $7.95

HOW TO DO BEADWORK, Mary White. Fundamental book on craft from simple projects to five-bead chains and woven works. 106 illustrations. 142pp. 5⅜ × 8. 20697-1 Pa. $4.95

THE BOOK OF WOOD CARVING, Charles Marshall Sayers. Finest book for beginners discusses fundamentals and offers 34 designs. "Absolutely first rate . . . well thought out and well executed."—E. J. Tangerman. 118pp. 7¾ × 10⅝. 23654-4 Pa. $5.95

ILLUSTRATED CATALOG OF CIVIL WAR MILITARY GOODS: Union Army Weapons, Insignia, Uniform Accessories, and Other Equipment, Schuyler, Hartley, and Graham. Rare, profusely illustrated 1846 catalog includes Union Army uniform and dress regulations, arms and ammunition, coats, insignia, flags, swords, rifles, etc. 226 illustrations. 160pp. 9 × 12. 24939-5 Pa. $10.95

WOMEN'S FASHIONS OF THE EARLY 1900s: An Unabridged Republication of "New York Fashions, 1909," National Cloak & Suit Co. Rare catalog of mail-order fashions documents women's and children's clothing styles shortly after the turn of the century. Captions offer full descriptions, prices. Invaluable resource for fashion, costume historians. Approximately 725 illustrations. 128pp. 8⅜ × 11¼. 27276-1 Pa. $11.95

THE 1912 AND 1915 GUSTAV STICKLEY FURNITURE CATALOGS, Gustav Stickley. With over 200 detailed illustrations and descriptions, these two catalogs are essential reading and reference materials and identification guides for Stickley furniture. Captions cite materials, dimensions and prices. 112pp. 6½ × 9¼. 26676-1 Pa. $9.95

EARLY AMERICAN LOCOMOTIVES, John H. White, Jr. Finest locomotive engravings from early 19th century: historical (1804–74), main-line (after 1870), special, foreign, etc. 147 plates. 142pp. 11⅜ × 8¼. 22772-3 Pa. $8.95

THE TALL SHIPS OF TODAY IN PHOTOGRAPHS, Frank O. Braynard. Lavishly illustrated tribute to nearly 100 majestic contemporary sailing vessels: Amerigo Vespucci, Clearwater, Constitution, Eagle, Mayflower, Sea Cloud, Victory, many more. Authoritative captions provide statistics, background on each ship. 190 black-and-white photographs and illustrations. Introduction. 128pp. 8⅞ × 11¾. 27163-3 Pa. $13.95

EARLY NINETEENTH-CENTURY CRAFTS AND TRADES, Peter Stockham (ed.). Extremely rare 1807 volume describes to youngsters the crafts and trades of the day: brickmaker, weaver, dressmaker, bookbinder, ropemaker, saddler, many more. Quaint prose, charming illustrations for each craft. 20 black-and-white line illustrations. 192pp. 4⅝ × 6. 27293-1 Pa. $4.95

VICTORIAN FASHIONS AND COSTUMES FROM HARPER'S BAZAR, 1867–1898, Stella Blum (ed.). Day costumes, evening wear, sports clothes, shoes, hats, other accessories in over 1,000 detailed engravings. 320pp. 9⅜ × 12¼. 22990-4 Pa. $13.95

GUSTAV STICKLEY, THE CRAFTSMAN, Mary Ann Smith. Superb study surveys broad scope of Stickley's achievement, especially in architecture. Design philosophy, rise and fall of the Craftsman empire, descriptions and floor plans for many Craftsman houses, more. 86 black-and-white halftones. 31 line illustrations. Introduction. 208pp. 6½ × 9¼. 27210-9 Pa. $9.95

THE LONG ISLAND RAIL ROAD IN EARLY PHOTOGRAPHS, Ron Ziel. Over 220 rare photos, informative text document origin (1844) and development of rail service on Long Island. Vintage views of early trains, locomotives, stations, passengers, crews, much more. Captions. 8⅞ × 11¾. 26301-0 Pa. $13.95

THE BOOK OF OLD SHIPS: From Egyptian Galleys to Clipper Ships, Henry B. Culver. Superb, authoritative history of sailing vessels, with 80 magnificent line illustrations. Galley, bark, caravel, longship, whaler, many more. Detailed, informative text on each vessel by noted naval historian. Introduction. 256pp. 5⅜ × 8½. 27332-6 Pa. $6.95

TEN BOOKS ON ARCHITECTURE, Vitruvius. The most important book ever written on architecture. Early Roman aesthetics, technology, classical orders, site selection, all other aspects. Morgan translation. 331pp. 5⅜ × 8½. 20645-9 Pa. $8.95

THE HUMAN FIGURE IN MOTION, Eadweard Muybridge. More than 4,500 stopped-action photos, in action series, showing undraped men, women, children jumping, lying down, throwing, sitting, wrestling, carrying, etc. 390pp. 7⅞ × 10⅝. 20204-6 Clothbd. $24.95

TREES OF THE EASTERN AND CENTRAL UNITED STATES AND CANADA, William M. Harlow. Best one-volume guide to 140 trees. Full descriptions, woodlore, range, etc. Over 600 illustrations. Handy size. 288pp. 4½ × 6⅜. 20395-6 Pa. $5.95

SONGS OF WESTERN BIRDS, Dr. Donald J. Borror. Complete song and call repertoire of 60 western species, including flycatchers, juncoes, cactus wrens, many more—includes fully illustrated booklet. Cassette and manual 99913-0 $8.95

GROWING AND USING HERBS AND SPICES, Milo Miloradovich. Versatile handbook provides all the information needed for cultivation and use of all the herbs and spices available in North America. 4 illustrations. Index. Glossary. 236pp. 5⅜ × 8½. 25058-X Pa. $5.95

BIG BOOK OF MAZES AND LABYRINTHS, Walter Shepherd. 50 mazes and labyrinths in all—classical, solid, ripple, and more—in one great volume. Perfect inexpensive puzzler for clever youngsters. Full solutions. 112pp. 8⅛ × 11. 22951-3 Pa. $3.95

PIANO TUNING, J. Cree Fischer. Clearest, best book for beginner, amateur. Simple repairs, raising dropped notes, tuning by easy method of flattened fifths. No previous skills needed. 4 illustrations. 201pp. 5⅜ × 8½.   23267-0 Pa. $5.95

A SOURCE BOOK IN THEATRICAL HISTORY, A. M. Nagler. Contemporary observers on acting, directing, make-up, costuming, stage props, machinery, scene design, from Ancient Greece to Chekhov. 611pp. 5⅜ × 8½.   20515-0 Pa. $11.95

THE COMPLETE NONSENSE OF EDWARD LEAR, Edward Lear. All nonsense limericks, zany alphabets, Owl and Pussycat, songs, nonsense botany, etc., illustrated by Lear. Total of 320pp. 5⅜ × 8½. (USO)   20167-8 Pa. $6.95

VICTORIAN PARLOUR POETRY: An Annotated Anthology, Michael R. Turner. 117 gems by Longfellow, Tennyson, Browning, many lesser-known poets. "The Village Blacksmith," "Curfew Must Not Ring Tonight," "Only a Baby Small," dozens more, often difficult to find elsewhere. Index of poets, titles, first lines. xxiii + 325pp. 5⅜ × 8¼.   27044-0 Pa. $8.95

DUBLINERS, James Joyce. Fifteen stories offer vivid, tightly focused observations of the lives of Dublin's poorer classes. At least one, "The Dead," is considered a masterpiece. Reprinted complete and unabridged from standard edition. 160pp. 5³⁄₁₆ × 8¼.   26870-5 Pa. $1.00

THE HAUNTED MONASTERY and THE CHINESE MAZE MURDERS, Robert van Gulik. Two full novels by van Gulik, set in 7th-century China, continue adventures of Judge Dee and his companions. An evil Taoist monastery, seemingly supernatural events; overgrown topiary maze hides strange crimes. 27 illustrations. 328pp. 5⅜ × 8½.   23502-5 Pa. $7.95

THE BOOK OF THE SACRED MAGIC OF ABRAMELIN THE MAGE, translated by S. MacGregor Mathers. Medieval manuscript of ceremonial magic. Basic document in Aleister Crowley, Golden Dawn groups. 268pp. 5⅜ × 8½.
                23211-5 Pa. $8.95

NEW RUSSIAN-ENGLISH AND ENGLISH-RUSSIAN DICTIONARY, M. A. O'Brien. This is a remarkably handy Russian dictionary, containing a surprising amount of information, including over 70,000 entries. 366pp. 4½ × 6⅛.
                20208-9 Pa. $9.95

HISTORIC HOMES OF THE AMERICAN PRESIDENTS, Second, Revised Edition, Irvin Haas. A traveler's guide to American Presidential homes, most open to the public, depicting and describing homes occupied by every American President from George Washington to George Bush. With visiting hours, admission charges, travel routes. 175 photographs. Index. 160pp. 8¼ × 11. 26751-2 Pa. $10.95

NEW YORK IN THE FORTIES, Andreas Feininger. 162 brilliant photographs by the well-known photographer, formerly with *Life* magazine. Commuters, shoppers, Times Square at night, much else from city at its peak. Captions by John von Hartz. 181pp. 9¼ × 10¾.   23585-8 Pa. $12.95

INDIAN SIGN LANGUAGE, William Tomkins. Over 525 signs developed by Sioux and other tribes. Written instructions and diagrams. Also 290 pictographs. 111pp. 6⅛ × 9¼.   22029-X Pa. $3.50

CATALOG OF DOVER BOOKS

ANATOMY: A Complete Guide for Artists, Joseph Sheppard. A master of figure drawing shows artists how to render human anatomy convincingly. Over 460 illustrations. 224pp. 8⅜ × 11¼. 27279-6 Pa. $9.95

MEDIEVAL CALLIGRAPHY: Its History and Technique, Marc Drogin. Spirited history, comprehensive instruction manual covers 13 styles (ca. 4th century thru 15th). Excellent photographs; directions for duplicating medieval techniques with modern tools. 224pp. 8⅜ × 11¼. 26142-5 Pa. $11.95

DRIED FLOWERS: How to Prepare Them, Sarah Whitlock and Martha Rankin. Complete instructions on how to use silica gel, meal and borax, perlite aggregate, sand and borax, glycerine and water to create attractive permanent flower arrangements. 12 illustrations. 32pp. 5⅜ × 8½. 21802-3 Pa. $1.00

EASY-TO-MAKE BIRD FEEDERS FOR WOODWORKERS, Scott D. Campbell. Detailed, simple-to-use guide for designing, constructing, caring for and using feeders. Text, illustrations for 12 classic and contemporary designs. 96pp. 5⅜ × 8½. 25847-5 Pa. $2.95

OLD-TIME CRAFTS AND TRADES, Peter Stockham. An 1807 book created to teach children about crafts and trades open to them as future careers. It describes in detailed, nontechnical terms 24 different occupations, among them coachmaker, gardener, hairdresser, lacemaker, shoemaker, wheelwright, copper-plate printer, milliner, trunkmaker, merchant and brewer. Finely detailed engravings illustrate each occupation. 192pp. 4⅝ × 6. 27398-9 Pa. $4.95

THE HISTORY OF UNDERCLOTHES, C. Willett Cunnington and Phyllis Cunnington. Fascinating, well-documented survey covering six centuries of English undergarments, enhanced with over 100 illustrations: 12th-century laced-up bodice, footed long drawers (1795), 19th-century bustles, 19th-century corsets for men, Victorian "bust improvers," much more. 272pp. 5⅜ × 8¼. 27124-2 Pa. $9.95

ARTS AND CRAFTS FURNITURE: The Complete Brooks Catalog of 1912, Brooks Manufacturing Co. Photos and detailed descriptions of more than 150 now very collectible furniture designs from the Arts and Crafts movement depict davenports, settees, buffets, desks, tables, chairs, bedsteads, dressers and more, all built of solid, quarter-sawed oak. Invaluable for students and enthusiasts of antiques, Americana and the decorative arts. 80pp. 6½ × 9¼. 27471-3 Pa. $7.95

HOW WE INVENTED THE AIRPLANE: An Illustrated History, Orville Wright. Fascinating firsthand account covers early experiments, construction of planes and motors, first flights, much more. Introduction and commentary by Fred C. Kelly. 76 photographs. 96pp. 8¼ × 11. 25662-6 Pa. $8.95

THE ARTS OF THE SAILOR: Knotting, Splicing and Ropework, Hervey Garrett Smith. Indispensable shipboard reference covers tools, basic knots and useful hitches; handsewing and canvas work, more. Over 100 illustrations. Delightful reading for sea lovers. 256pp. 5⅜ × 8½. 26440-8 Pa. $7.95

FRANK LLOYD WRIGHT'S FALLINGWATER: The House and Its History, Second, Revised Edition, Donald Hoffmann. A total revision—both in text and illustrations—of the standard document on Fallingwater, the boldest, most personal architectural statement of Wright's mature years, updated with valuable new material from the recently opened Frank Lloyd Wright Archives. "Fascinating"—The New York Times. 116 illustrations. 128pp. 9¼ × 10¾. 27430-6 Pa. $10.95

PHOTOGRAPHIC SKETCHBOOK OF THE CIVIL WAR, Alexander Gardner. 100 photos taken on field during the Civil War. Famous shots of Manassas, Harper's Ferry, Lincoln, Richmond, slave pens, etc. 244pp. 10⅝ × 8¼.
22731-6 Pa. $9.95

FIVE ACRES AND INDEPENDENCE, Maurice G. Kains. Great back-to-the-land classic explains basics of self-sufficient farming. The one book to get. 95 illustrations. 397pp. 5⅜ × 8½. 20974-1 Pa. $7.95

SONGS OF EASTERN BIRDS, Dr. Donald J. Borror. Songs and calls of 60 species most common to eastern U.S.: warblers, woodpeckers, flycatchers, thrushes, larks, many more in high-quality recording. Cassette and manual 99912-2 $8.95

A MODERN HERBAL, Margaret Grieve. Much the fullest, most exact, most useful compilation of herbal material. Gigantic alphabetical encyclopedia, from aconite to zedoary, gives botanical information, medical properties, folklore, economic uses, much else. Indispensable to serious reader. 161 illustrations. 888pp. 6½ × 9¼. 2-vol. set. (USO) Vol. I: 22798-7 Pa. $9.95
Vol. II: 22799-5 Pa. $9.95

HIDDEN TREASURE MAZE BOOK, Dave Phillips. Solve 34 challenging mazes accompanied by heroic tales of adventure. Evil dragons, people-eating plants, bloodthirsty giants, many more dangerous adversaries lurk at every twist and turn. 34 mazes, stories, solutions. 48pp. 8¼ × 11. 24566-7 Pa. $2.95

LETTERS OF W. A. MOZART, Wolfgang A. Mozart. Remarkable letters show bawdy wit, humor, imagination, musical insights, contemporary musical world; includes some letters from Leopold Mozart. 276pp. 5⅜ × 8½. 22859-2 Pa. $6.95

BASIC PRINCIPLES OF CLASSICAL BALLET, Agrippina Vaganova. Great Russian theoretician, teacher explains methods for teaching classical ballet. 118 illustrations. 175pp. 5⅜ × 8½. 22036-2 Pa. $4.95

THE JUMPING FROG, Mark Twain. Revenge edition. The original story of The Celebrated Jumping Frog of Calaveras County, a hapless French translation, and Twain's hilarious "retranslation" from the French. 12 illustrations. 66pp. 5⅜ × 8½. 22686-7 Pa. $3.95

BEST REMEMBERED POEMS, Martin Gardner (ed.). The 126 poems in this superb collection of 19th- and 20th-century British and American verse range from Shelley's "To a Skylark" to the impassioned "Renascence" of Edna St. Vincent Millay and to Edward Lear's whimsical "The Owl and the Pussycat." 224pp. 5⅜ × 8½. 27165-X Pa. $4.95

COMPLETE SONNETS, William Shakespeare. Over 150 exquisite poems deal with love, friendship, the tyranny of time, beauty's evanescence, death and other themes in language of remarkable power, precision and beauty. Glossary of archaic terms. 80pp. 5³⁄₁₆ × 8¼. 26686-9 Pa. $1.00

BODIES IN A BOOKSHOP, R. T. Campbell. Challenging mystery of blackmail and murder with ingenious plot and superbly drawn characters. In the best tradition of British suspense fiction. 192pp. 5⅜ × 8½. 24720-1 Pa. $5.95

CATALOG OF DOVER BOOKS

THE WIT AND HUMOR OF OSCAR WILDE, Alvin Redman (ed.). More than 1,000 ripostes, paradoxes, wisecracks: Work is the curse of the drinking classes; I can resist everything except temptation; etc. 258pp. 5⅜ × 8½. 20602-5 Pa. $5.95

SHAKESPEARE LEXICON AND QUOTATION DICTIONARY, Alexander Schmidt. Full definitions, locations, shades of meaning in every word in plays and poems. More than 50,000 exact quotations. 1,485pp. 6½ × 9¼. 2-vol. set.

Vol. 1: 22726-X Pa. $15.95
Vol. 2: 22727-8 Pa. $15.95

SELECTED POEMS, Emily Dickinson. Over 100 best-known, best-loved poems by one of America's foremost poets, reprinted from authoritative early editions. No comparable edition at this price. Index of first lines. 64pp. 5³/₁₆ × 8¼.
26466-1 Pa. $1.00

CELEBRATED CASES OF JUDGE DEE (DEE GOONG AN), translated by Robert van Gulik. Authentic 18th-century Chinese detective novel; Dee and associates solve three interlocked cases. Led to van Gulik's own stories with same characters. Extensive introduction. 9 illustrations. 237pp. 5⅜ × 8½.
23337-5 Pa. $6.95

THE MALLEUS MALEFICARUM OF KRAMER AND SPRENGER, translated by Montague Summers. Full text of most important witchhunter's "bible," used by both Catholics and Protestants. 278pp. 6⅝ × 10. 22802-9 Pa. $10.95

SPANISH STORIES/CUENTOS ESPAÑOLES: A Dual-Language Book, Angel Flores (ed.). Unique format offers 13 great stories in Spanish by Cervantes, Borges, others. Faithful English translations on facing pages. 352pp. 5⅜ × 8½.
25399-6 Pa. $8.95

THE CHICAGO WORLD'S FAIR OF 1893: A Photographic Record, Stanley Appelbaum (ed.). 128 rare photos show 200 buildings, Beaux-Arts architecture, Midway, original Ferris Wheel, Edison's kinetoscope, more. Architectural emphasis; full text. 116pp. 8¼ × 11. 23990-X Pa. $9.95

OLD QUEENS, N.Y., IN EARLY PHOTOGRAPHS, Vincent F. Seyfried and William Asadorian. Over 160 rare photographs of Maspeth, Jamaica, Jackson Heights, and other areas. Vintage views of DeWitt Clinton mansion, 1939 World's Fair and more. Captions. 192pp. 8⅞ × 11. 26358-4 Pa. $12.95

CAPTURED BY THE INDIANS: 15 Firsthand Accounts, 1750–1870, Frederick Drimmer. Astounding true historical accounts of grisly torture, bloody conflicts, relentless pursuits, miraculous escapes and more, by people who lived to tell the tale. 384pp. 5⅜ × 8½. 24901-8 Pa. $8.95

THE WORLD'S GREAT SPEECHES, Lewis Copeland and Lawrence W. Lamm (eds.). Vast collection of 278 speeches of Greeks to 1970. Powerful and effective models; unique look at history. 842pp. 5⅜ × 8½. 20468-5 Pa. $13.95

THE BOOK OF THE SWORD, Sir Richard F. Burton. Great Victorian scholar/adventurer's eloquent, erudite history of the "queen of weapons"—from prehistory to early Roman Empire. Evolution and development of early swords, variations (sabre, broadsword, cutlass, scimitar, etc.), much more. 336pp. 6⅛ × 9¼. 25434-8 Pa. $8.95

CATALOG OF DOVER BOOKS

AUTOBIOGRAPHY: The Story of My Experiments with Truth, Mohandas K. Gandhi. Boyhood, legal studies, purification, the growth of the Satyagraha (nonviolent protest) movement. Critical, inspiring work of the man responsible for the freedom of India. 480pp. 5⅜ × 8½. (USO) 24593-4 Pa. **$7.95**

CELTIC MYTHS AND LEGENDS, T. W. Rolleston. Masterful retelling of Irish and Welsh stories and tales. Cuchulain, King Arthur, Deirdre, the Grail, many more. First paperback edition. 58 full-page illustrations. 512pp. 5⅜ × 8½. 26507-2 Pa. **$9.95**

THE PRINCIPLES OF PSYCHOLOGY, William James. Famous long course complete, unabridged. Stream of thought, time perception, memory, experimental methods; great work decades ahead of its time. 94 figures. 1,391pp. 5⅜ × 8½. 2-vol. set.
Vol. I: 20381-6 Pa. **$12.95**
Vol. II: 20382-4 Pa. **$12.95**

THE WORLD AS WILL AND REPRESENTATION, Arthur Schopenhauer. Definitive English translation of Schopenhauer's life work, correcting more than 1,000 errors, omissions in earlier translations. Translated by E. F. J. Payne. Total of 1,269pp. 5⅜ × 8½. 2-vol. set.
Vol. 1: 21761-2 Pa. **$11.95**
Vol. 2: 21762-0 Pa. **$11.95**

MAGIC AND MYSTERY IN TIBET, Madame Alexandra David-Neel. Experiences among lamas, magicians, sages, sorcerers, Bonpa wizards. A true psychic discovery. 32 illustrations. 321pp. 5⅜ × 8½. (USO) 22682-4 Pa. **$8.95**

THE EGYPTIAN BOOK OF THE DEAD, E. A. Wallis Budge. Complete reproduction of Ani's papyrus, finest ever found. Full hieroglyphic text, interlinear transliteration, word-for-word translation, smooth translation. 533pp. 6½ × 9¼. 21866-X Pa. **$9.95**

MATHEMATICS FOR THE NONMATHEMATICIAN, Morris Kline. Detailed, college-level treatment of mathematics in cultural and historical context, with numerous exercises. Recommended Reading Lists. Tables. Numerous figures. 641pp. 5⅜ × 8½. 24823-2 Pa. **$11.95**

THEORY OF WING SECTIONS: Including a Summary of Airfoil Data, Ira H. Abbott and A. E. von Doenhoff. Concise compilation of subsonic aerodynamic characteristics of NACA wing sections, plus description of theory. 350pp. of tables. 693pp. 5⅜ × 8½. 60586-8 Pa. **$13.95**

THE RIME OF THE ANCIENT MARINER, Gustave Doré, S. T. Coleridge. Doré's finest work; 34 plates capture moods, subtleties of poem. Flawless full-size reproductions printed on facing pages with authoritative text of poem. "Beautiful. Simply beautiful."—*Publisher's Weekly*. 77pp. 9¼ × 12. 22305-1 Pa. **$5.95**

NORTH AMERICAN INDIAN DESIGNS FOR ARTISTS AND CRAFTSPEOPLE, Eva Wilson. Over 360 authentic copyright-free designs adapted from Navajo blankets, Hopi pottery, Sioux buffalo hides, more. Geometrics, symbolic figures, plant and animal motifs, etc. 128pp. 8⅜ × 11. (EUK) 25341-4 Pa. **$7.95**

SCULPTURE: Principles and Practice, Louis Slobodkin. Step-by-step approach to clay, plaster, metals, stone; classical and modern. 253 drawings, photos. 255pp. 8⅛ × 11. 22960-2 Pa. **$10.95**

THE INFLUENCE OF SEA POWER UPON HISTORY, 1660–1783, A. T. Mahan. Influential classic of naval history and tactics still used as text in war colleges. First paperback edition. 4 maps. 24 battle plans. 640pp. 5⅜ × 8½.
25509-3 Pa. $12.95

THE STORY OF THE TITANIC AS TOLD BY ITS SURVIVORS, Jack Winocour (ed.). What it was really like. Panic, despair, shocking inefficiency, and a little heroism. More thrilling than any fictional account. 26 illustrations. 320pp. 5⅜ × 8½.
20610-6 Pa. $7.95

FAIRY AND FOLK TALES OF THE IRISH PEASANTRY, William Butler Yeats (ed.). Treasury of 64 tales from the twilight world of Celtic myth and legend: "The Soul Cages," "The Kildare Pooka," "King O'Toole and his Goose," many more. Introduction and Notes by W. B. Yeats. 352pp. 5⅜ × 8½.
26941-8 Pa. $8.95

BUDDHIST MAHAYANA TEXTS, E. B. Cowell and Others (eds.). Superb, accurate translations of basic documents in Mahayana Buddhism, highly important in history of religions. The Buddha-karita of Asvaghosha, Larger Sukhavativyuha, more. 448pp. 5⅜ × 8½.
25552-2 Pa. $9.95

ONE TWO THREE . . . INFINITY: Facts and Speculations of Science, George Gamow. Great physicist's fascinating, readable overview of contemporary science: number theory, relativity, fourth dimension, entropy, genes, atomic structure, much more. 128 illustrations. Index. 352pp. 5⅜ × 8½.
25664-2 Pa. $8.95

ENGINEERING IN HISTORY, Richard Shelton Kirby, et al. Broad, nontechnical survey of history's major technological advances: birth of Greek science, industrial revolution, electricity and applied science, 20th-century automation, much more. 181 illustrations. ". . . excellent . . ."—Isis. Bibliography. vii + 530pp. 5⅜ × 8½.
26412-2 Pa. $14.95